Mac OS X Hints
Jaguar Edition

Mac OS X Hints
Jaguar Edition

Rob Griffiths

POGUE PRESS™

O'REILLY®

Beijing • Cambridge • Farnham • Köln • Paris • Sebastopol • Taipei • Tokyo

Mac OS X Hints: Jaguar Edition

by Rob Griffiths

Published by Pogue Press/O'Reilly & Associates, Inc.,
1005 Gravenstein Highway North, Sebastopol, CA 95472.

May 2003:   First Edition.

Missing Manual, the Missing Manual logo, and "The book that should have been in the box" are registered trademarks of Pogue Press, LLC.

Many of the designations used by manufacturers and sellers to distinguish their products are claimed as trademarks. Where those designations appear in this book, and Pogue Press was aware of a trademark claim, the designations have been capitalized.

While every precaution has been taken in the preparation of this book, the publisher assumes no responsibility for errors or omissions, or for damages resulting from the use of the information contained herein.

ISBN: 0-596-00451-6   [5/03] M

Table of Contents

The Missing Credits

About the Author

 **Rob Griffiths** dove into Mac OS X with the public beta version in 2000, despite an innate fear of Unix and no understanding of the command line. Shortly thereafter, tired of searching the Net for the same answers to the same questions and looking for a way to force his Unix learning skills forward, he launched MacOSXhints.com, a site dedicated to tips and tricks on all things Mac OS X–related. Since then, MacOSXhints.com has amassed a searchable database of over 3,500 hints— and 15,000 followup comments on those hints from enthusiastic readers.

When he's not maintaining the site, finding new hints, working at his actual full-time job, or writing this book, Rob enjoys spending time with his family and friends, playing (bad) golf, and traveling. Email: *rgriffiths@macosxhints.com*.

About the Creative Team

David Pogue (editor) is the weekly computer columnist for the *New York Times* and the creator of the Missing Manual series. He's the author or co-author of 25 books, including eight in the Missing Manual series and six in the "For Dummies" line (including *Magic, Opera, Classical Music,* and *The Flat-Screen iMac*). In his other life, David is a former Broadway theatre conductor, a magician, and a pianist *(www.davidpogue.com)*. Email: *david@pogueman.com*.

Sarah Milstein (editor) is a writer and editor in New York. A frequent contributor to the *New York Times,* among other publications, she also mantains a Web site where she posts quirky movie reviews *(www.dogsandshoes.com)*. She follows baseball avidly, plays poker badly, and has an unusually cute dog.

Nan Barber (copy editor) co-authored *Office X for the Macintosh: The Missing Manual* and *Office 2001 for Macintosh: The Missing Manual.* As the principal copy editor for this series, she has edited the titles on iPhoto, Mac OS 9, AppleWorks 6, iMovie, Dreamweaver 4, and Windows XP. Email: *nanbarber@mac.com*.

Rose Cassano (cover illustration) has worked as an independent designer and illustrator for 20 years. Assignments have spanned everything from the nonprofit sector to corporate clientele. She lives in beautiful southern Oregon, grateful for the miracles of modern technology that make living and working there a reality. Email: *cassano@cdsnet.net*. Web: *www.rosecassano.com*.

Dennis Cohen (technical reviewer) has served as the technical reviewer for many bestselling Mac books, including several editions of *Macworld Mac Secrets* and most

Missing Manual titles. He is the author or co-author of *iLife Bible*, *Mac OS X Bible*, *AppleWorks 6 Bible*, and numerous other books. Email: *drcohen@mac.com*.

Phil Simpson (design and layout) works out of his office in Stamford, Connecticut, where he has had his graphic design business since 1982. He is experienced in many facets of graphic design, including corporate identity, publication design, and corporate and medical communications. Email: *pmsimpson@earthlink.net*.

Acknowledgments

This book would not have been possible without the wonderful MacOSXhints.com community, which has helped create one of the greatest Mac OS X resources on the Web. Every day, I'm amazed at the caliber not only of the hints (which are moderated prior to posting), but of the comments as well (which are not moderated). I feel thankful each day knowing that I'm involved in something this interesting and useful.

Very little of the Web site's material is repeated verbatim in the book (and where site members' original wording appears, they're credited). Still, the knowledge provided by the hints on the site made this book possible in the first place.

Craig Arko, John Hancock, and Phil St. Romain (along with Brian Duart) make possible the Macosxhints.com forum. Their daily attention to this important troubleshooting resource freed me to work on the main site and this project. In addition, their candid feedback on the sites and the book have made both much stronger over time. Thanks, guys, for making our forum a great place to find answers to Mac OS X questions!

Three people helped me with the Unix chapters—the most difficult part of the book (for me, anyway): Neal Parikh, head of technical operations for the Macintosh News Network and forum moderator of MacNN's Mac OS X and Unix forums; Brian Duart, a technology consultant and systems administrator at-large in the Bay Area of northern California; and O'Reilly's Chris Stone, author of the command reference in *Mac OS X in a Nutshell*. Their expertise and modifications helped make the Unix hints clearer, more accurate, and easier to implement.

A heartfelt thank you to editors David Pogue and Sarah Milstein, copy editor Nan Barber, and proofreaders Jennifer Barber, John Cacciatore, and Danny Marcus, who took my ramblings and somehow worked their magic to turn them into the elegant, flowing prose that you're now holding in your hands.

To James and Simon and Jacco and Jason and all the others who have enhanced my understanding of Mac OS X, Unix, the Web, and life in general: Your contributions have been invaluable in helping me gain the knowledge necessary to tackle this project.

Finally, thanks to my loving wife Marian, whose support was far more important than that of anyone else on this project. Little did we know when we started that this book would consume every moment of my free time for nearly five months. Through it all, her encouragement kept me going.

So thank you, Marian, for supporting me throughout the project. You are the love of my life, and I thank you for being there for me when I needed you the most.

—*Rob Griffiths*

About Pogue Press

Pogue Press is a joint venture of the dream team introduced on these pages and O'Reilly & Associates: Tim O'Reilly, Mark Brokering, and company.

Pogue Press books are designed to be superbly written guides to computer products that don't come with printed manuals (which is just about all of them). Each book features a handcrafted index, cross-references to specific page numbers (not just "see Chapter 14"), and a promise never to use an apostrophe in the possessive word *its*. Current and upcoming titles include:

- *iPhoto 2: The Missing Manual* by David Pogue, Joseph Schorr, & Derrick Story

- *iMovie 3 and iDVD: The Missing Manual* by David Pogue

- *Switching to the Mac: The Missing Manual* by David Pogue

- *Mac OS X: The Missing Manual, Second Edition* by David Pogue

- *Dreamweaver MX: The Missing Manual* by David Sawyer McFarland

- *Office X for Macintosh: The Missing Manual* by Nan Barber, Tonya Engst, & David Reynolds

- *AppleWorks 6: The Missing Manual* by Jim Elferdink & David Reynolds

- *Mac OS 9: The Missing Manual* by David Pogue

- *Windows XP Home Edition: The Missing Manual* by David Pogue

- *Windows XP Pro: The Missing Manual* by David Pogue, Craig Zacker, & L.J. Zacker

THE MISSING CREDITS

Introduction

You're about to gain insight into Mac OS X, an elegant operating system with Formula One power under the hood. This book is like your pit crew, helping you find easier, faster, and better ways of using the Finder, the Dock, the assortment of programs that come with Mac OS X, and a bunch of programs that don't. And if you want to become your own master mechanic, this book also includes two massive chapters of assorted hints on Unix, the engine under Mac OS X's hood.

The 500-plus hints in this book are based on tips published on the Mac os x hints: jaguar edition Web site *(www.macosxhints.com)*. But it's not just a rehash of what's there—that would be far too easy. Every hint has been rewritten, expanded, organized, indexed, tested for compatibility with the latest version of Mac OS X 10.2, and in many cases illustrated.

This book assumes that you are running version 10.2 or later. If you use any of these hints with previous versions of the system, you should expect that, as they say in the car business, your mileage may vary.

How This Book Works

Typically, computer books make the most sense when you read them from start to finish—but not this one. Most hints in these pages describe a single problem or solution that doesn't depend on any other hints. Think of the book as a vast table of appetizers for your brain.

Some Experience Required

This book assumes that you already know the basics of Mac OS X. It doesn't explain how to log in, open System Preferences, create an account, or other basics. (You might think of this book as a sort of intermediate sequel to *Mac OS X: The Missing Manual.*)

Once you have some experience with the system, this book can help you progress from anybody-can-do-this user to power user.

About→These→Arrows

Throughout this book, you'll find sentences like this one: "Open the System→Libraries→Fonts folder." That's shorthand for a much longer instruction that directs you to open three nested folders in sequence, like this: "On your hard drive, you'll find a folder called System. Open that. Inside the System folder window is a folder called Libraries; double-click it to open it. Inside *that* folder is yet another one called Fonts. Double-click to open it, too."

Similarly, this kind of arrow shorthand helps to simplify the business of choosing commands in menus, such as →Dock→Position on Left, as shown in Figure I-1. You'll also see arrow notation used to indicate which tab or pane of a dialog box you're supposed to click: "Open the System Preferences→Sound panel," for example.

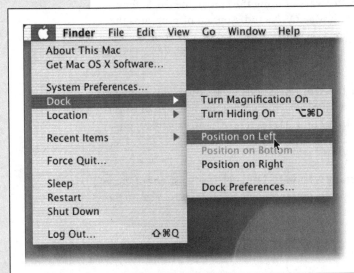

Figure I-1:
In this book, arrow notations help to simplify folder and menu instructions. For example, "Choose →Dock→ Position on Left" is a more compact way of saying, "From the menu, choose Dock; from the submenu that than appears, choose Position on Left," as shown here.

Gaffes and Goofs

On the MissingManuals.com Web site, you'll find corrections and updates to the book (to see them, click the book's title, then click Errata). In fact, you're invited and encouraged to submit such corrections and updates yourself. In an effort to keep the book as up-to-date and accurate as possible, we'll make any confirmed corrections you've suggested, each time we print more copies. We'll also note such changes on the Web site, so that you can mark important corrections in your own copy of the book, if you like.

Some Groundwork

Throughout the book, a handful of ideas and processes come up again and again. They're explained here so that you don't have to read them 639 more times.

Digging Around in Programs

You may have noticed that Mac OS X programs don't seem to have 50,000 support files strewn across your hard drive. For example, to open Internet Explorer, you don't need to first open any Internet Explorer *folder*. There's just one Internet Explorer icon, and that's all you have to double-click. That's a much better arrangement than in Mac OS 9 or Windows, where many programs must remain in special folders, surrounded by libraries, dictionaries, foreign language components, and other support files and folders.

Which raises the question: Where did all those support files go?

Most Mac OS X programs come in the form of *packages* or *bundles,* which are *folders that behave like single files.* A Mac OS X program may look like a single, double-clickable application icon. Yet to the Mac, it's actually a folder that contains both the application *and* all of its support files, which are hidden for your convenience. (In fact, even documents can be packages, including iDVD project files and TextEdit documents.)

Over and over in this book, you'll be directed to peek inside this cleverly disguised folder. And no, you can't do that by double-clicking it. Instead, follow the routine shown in Figure I-2.

Figure I-2:
Left: In the Finder, highlight a program, Control-click it, and then chose Show Package Contents from the contextual menu.

Right: A new window appears with a Contents folder. Open it to reach the Resources folder, which holds icons, images, and lists of options for the program.

Once you're inside, look around as much as you like, but don't move or remove any of the files you find there. Doing so may cause the program to quit working more suddenly than a McDonald's cashier at the end of a shift.

Dragging a Text File into TextEdit

TextEdit is a basic text processor included in Mac OS X. Among other things, it's the perfect freebie tool to help you create or modify Mac OS X's system and program preference files. Many of the hints in this book refer to TextEdit.

To open a file with TextEdit, drag its icon (the document) from the Finder or desktop onto the TextEdit icon on the Dock or in your Applications folder. (Because so many of the hints in this book direct you to do that, you'll find it worthwhile to install TextEdit's icon on your Dock right now. Simply drag it there from your Applications folder.)

TextEdit can create two kinds of files: unformatted *plain text* files, and *Rich Text* documents that contain formatting like bold and italic. Rich Text documents give you more artistic freedom, but they're baffling to Mac OS X. It's very important that when you edit Mac OS X system files, you save the results *exclusively* as plain text files.

Figure I-3 shows you how to make sure that's what you're getting.

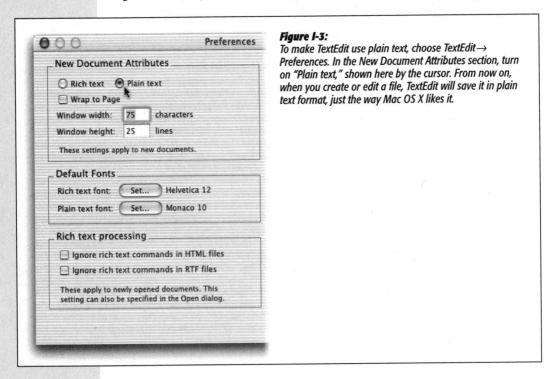

Figure I-3:
To make TextEdit use plain text, choose TextEdit→ Preferences. In the New Document Attributes section, turn on "Plain text," shown here by the cursor. From now on, when you create or edit a file, TextEdit will save it in plain text format, just the way Mac OS X likes it.

Finally, it's worth noting that TextEdit isn't the only program you can use to edit Mac OS X files. If you're an old hand at Mac OS X, you may have run across programs like BBEdit, BBEdit Lite, PropertyList Editor (which comes with the Developer Tools, described below), or any of the Unix editors like *vi* or *emacs* (which you reach through Terminal). In any of the hints in this book that direct you to open some file with TextEdit, feel free to substitute any of these other programs.

Terminal Basics

This book refers often to *Terminal*. Terminal is a program in your Applications→ Utilities folder that serves as the door to Mac OS X's Unix underbelly. Unfortunately, that underbelly has no graphics, icons, or menus. Terminal is all text, all the time.

Still, the *command line* (this "type a command to control the Mac" mode) opens up a world of possibilities. It lets you reach corners of Mac OS X that you can't get to from the regular desktop. It lets you perform certain tasks with much greater speed and efficiency than you'd get by dragging around icons. And it gives you a glimpse into the minds and moods of people who live and breathe computers.

When you double-click Terminal's icon, you're greeted with something like this:

```
Last login: Thu Sep 6 13:23:02 on ttyp0
Welcome to Darwin!
[PowerBook] chris%
```

The % sign is the *command prompt*—the Mac's way of saying, "I'm all yours. What's your pleasure?" The insertion point blinks just to its right, waiting for you to type a Unix command like the ones suggested in this book. After you type each specified command, press Return or Enter to seal the deal.

When you're done using Terminal, type *logout* or *exit,* press Enter, and then choose File→Quit.

Tip: All of the commands and scripts in this book are also available in a convenient text file that spares you from having to type anything at all. You can download it from *www.macosxhints.com/book/scripts.html.*

The Defaults Command

Many of the hints in this book direct you to change a program's settings by issuing a command, in Terminal, known as the *defaults* command. It's nothing more than the Unix way of changing some setting that doesn't have a corresponding button in the program's Preferences dialog box.

For example, hint 2-19 tells you how to turn off the Finder's zooming rectangles—those animated growing outlines you see when you double-click an icon. You're directed to open Terminal and type the following command next to the % prompt:

```
defaults write com.apple.finder ZoomRects -bool no
```

Note: Whenever you read instructions to type something into Terminal, note that capitalization counts. If you type a single letter lowercase that should be capped, or vice versa, the command won't work.

The full command breaks down like this:

- **defaults write.** This instruction tells Terminal that you'd like to modify (write) a new value for a preference setting.

- **com.apple.finder** refers to the Finder's preference file. That's the file you're going to change.

- **ZoomRects** refers to "zooming rectangles," the name of the setting you're going to change.

- **-bool** refers to the type of value you're going to write. In this case, *-bool* is short for Boolean. A Boolean variable has only two possible values, like true and false, or yes and no.

- **no** means no, just like your parents always told you. But in this case, it's also the value for the ZoomRects Boolean preference that you're writing to the file.

Put it all together, and you've got a command telling your system to modify the Finder's rectangle preference setting by turning it off. (You can reverse this command by repeating the command but changing *no* to *yes*.)

Tip: For more information on *defaults,* open Terminal and type *man defaults*. This command opens the manual pages for the command, so that you can learn in greater detail how it works.

Installing the Developer Tools

If you bought Mac OS X in the store, in a box, it came with a special CD called Developer. If Mac OS X came with your Mac, the Developer CD may be a *disk image* on one of your Software Restore discs. (Use Disk Copy to burn this image onto a real CD.)

The Developer Tools are essential for anyone who writes software for Mac OS X. The programs that come with them help you create, debug, and compile programs. But the Developer Tools can be useful even if you're not a programmer. They include some useful utilities, including PropertyList Editor (which makes it easy to edit a program's preference files), and they give you a bunch of extra Unix commands. In fact, some of the hints in this book require that you have Developer Tools installed (you'll see which ones).

If a Developer CD or disk image didn't come with your Mac or your copy of Mac OS X, you can download it from the Web for free, although doing so requires you to sign up for Apple's developer program—also free. A high-speed Internet connection is recommended: the files are more than 300 MB.

In your Web browser, visit *http://connect.apple.com*, scroll down to the middle of the page, and click Join ADC Now. Follow the instructions to create your free account. Next, log in at *http://connect.apple.com,* and then click Download Software to reveal a submenu. When you choose Mac OS X, you jump to a screen containing recent Developer Tools releases.

Find the latest version, click Download, and then wait. The download is long, even over a fast connection.

Once you've downloaded them, you install the Developer Tools the same way as many other Mac OS X programs. Just expand the archive, double-click the package installer, and then provide your administrative password when requested. Once the installation is done, you end up with a Developer folder on your hard drive containing all the goodies.

Designing Your World

Mac OS X may look "so good, you just want to lick it," as Steve Jobs famously put it. The truth is, though, that the best stuff is under the hood. The Unix core is incredibly stable, multitasks like a pro, and opens up a world of software that was not previously available to Mac users.

This OS is unlike anything that came before, which has tripped up more than one veteran computer fan. But if you invest the time necessary to learn Mac OS X, you'll be greatly rewarded. Most importantly, keep an open mind—think "Zen and the Art of Computing."

Startup and Shutdown

You won't get far with your Mac—or this book—until your Mac is turned on. But even that simple act, as it turns out, has a few nuances worth learning.

1-1   Keyboard Login

The dialog box shown in Figure 1-1 greets millions of Mac fans every morning. It's the *login* dialog box, which you use to identify yourself and make the Mac display your files, desktop picture, and settings—and hide everyone else's. (More on this *accounts* system in Chapter 5.)

You can save a bit of mousing around by navigating this box with the keyboard. For example, you can select your name from the list by typing your first initial (or the first couple of letters, if the list is long). As you do so, the highlight bar moves down the list, matching what you type. When the name you want is highlighted, hit the Return or Enter key, type the password, and hit Return again.

1-2   Automatic Login

Of course, the accounts system described in the previous paragraphs is primarily designed for families, schools, or businesses, where different people use the same Mac at different times. If you're the only one who uses your machine, and you're not worried about security, all of this business about choosing your name from a list and entering a password is so much red tape. "It's *me*," you feel like saying, "Who the heck else would it be?"

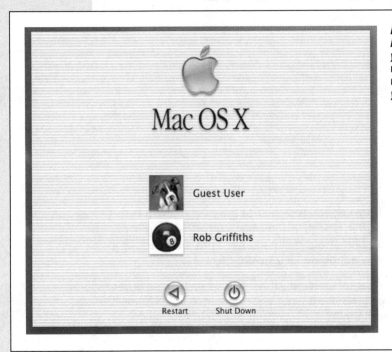

Figure 1-1:
Before you can start using your machine, your Mac wants to make sure you know who you are... or at least who you want to be today.

If that's your situation, you can set the system to log you in automatically at startup, bypassing the login dialog box altogether. To set this up, open System Preferences. Click the Accounts icon. On the Users tab, turn on Set Auto Login, and then fill in your password.

Note: This trick assumes that you have an *Administrator* account, which is pretty likely if you're the only one who uses your Mac.

1-3   The Listless Login Screen

There are two ways of displaying the login panel. The user-friendly way is the list of names shown in Figure 1-1.

But for greater security (though less convenience), you may prefer to require would-be Mac users to type *both* their names *and* their passwords into text boxes (Figure 1-2). This way, would-be evildoers have to know both the correct spelling of a legitimate account holder's name and the password.

UP TO SPEED

Administrator Accounts

Since the day you started using your Mac, you may have made a number of changes to your desktop—adjusted the Dock settings, set up your folders and desktop the way you like them, added some favorites to your Web browser, and so on—without realizing that you were actually making these changes only to *your account.*

Your account lives in your Home folder, which is named after you and stashed in the Users folder on your hard drive. It stores not only your own work, but also your preference settings for all the programs you use, special fonts that you've installed, programs you've installed for your own use, and so on. (To get there, choose Go→Home in the Finder.)

Now then: If you create an account for a second person, when she turns on the computer and signs in, she'll find the desktop exactly the way it was factory-installed by Apple—blue swirling desktop picture, Dock positioned at the bottom, and so on. She can make the same kinds of changes to the Mac that you've made, but nothing she does will affect your environment the next time *you* log in.

In other words, the accounts feature has two components: first, a convenience element that hides everyone else's junk; and second, a security element that protects both the Mac's system software and other people's work.

To see the list of accounts on your Mac, open System Preferences, and then click Accounts.

It's important to understand the phrase you see in the Kind column shown here. On your own personal Mac, it prob-

ably says *Admin* next to your name. This, as you could probably guess, stands for Administrator. The Mac assumes that you are its administrator—the person in charge. Only an administrator is allowed to install new programs into the Applications folder, add fonts that everybody can use, change certain System Preferences panels (including Network, Date & Time, Energy Saver, Login, and Startup Disk), create new folders outside of your Home folder, decide who gets to have accounts on the Mac, and so on.

Only Administrator account holders, moreover, can make many of the kinds of changes described in this book.

Anyone who *isn't* an administrator will probably just be an ordinary, everyday Normal account holder. That's anyone whose account *isn't* an Admin account. These people will have everyday access to their own Home folders and to some of the System Preferences, but most other areas of the Mac will be off-limits.

If you're only a Normal account holder, you can't make certain changes described by the hints in this book. Fortunately, you aren't required to log out so that an administrator can log in and make changes. You can just call the administrator over, click the padlock icon, and let him type in his name and password—if, indeed, he feels comfortable with you making the changes you're about to make.

How does the Mac know who's an administrator? Because they're all listed in the Accounts pane of System Preferences. An administrator can click your name in this panel, click Edit User, and turn on "Allow user to administer this computer." This is the master switch that turns an ordi-

Most people think that getting to this text box login screen entails opening System Preferences, clicking Users, clicking Login Options, and turning on "Name and password." Truth is, though, there's a much quicker way to switch, without even involving System Preferences—a trick you might use when, for example, you want to log in as *console* or *root* (advanced techies, you know who you are), which requires you to type the user name in.

From the list-of-names view, hold down the Option and Enter keys, and then click any name. The login panel switches to displaying the text entry boxes, where you can now log in as root or console.

Note: The last thing you want to do is hit Tab twice. Doing so will clear out an invisible character in the Name box, which will prevent your user name from being recognized by the system.

Figure 1-2:
Concerned that someone might guess your password? Switch the Mac to this "secure" login mode by pressing Option and Enter, then clicking your account name. To switch back to the list view, click the Back button at the lower left of the login panel.

(This shortcut changes the login panel only for the moment; at the next login, the dialog box will be back to its previous state.)

1-4   The Silence of the Startup Items

What Apple calls a *login item* is a program, file, folder, or other icon that you've designated to open automatically as soon as you log in. If the first thing you do is check your email or a favorite Web page, by all means, designate your email program or Web browser as a startup item, so it will be open and ready when you've finished your morning coffee. (You build your list of auto-opening items by dragging their icons into the Login Items panel of System Preferences.)

But sometimes you don't want your regularly scheduled programs to fire at startup. Maybe you're dying to see if your spouse, boss, or senator responded to your email and you just want to get to the desktop as quickly as possible, without waiting for your login items to open. Or maybe you've recently installed a program that you think might be causing problems when it autostarts.

In these cases, you'll want to prevent login items from opening. To do that, hold down the Shift key just after entering your user name and password on the login screen.

1-5   The Login Screen "Billboard"

In case you've been lying awake wondering how to add a line of customized text to your login window, as shown in Figure 1-3, help is at hand. Maybe you work somewhere that requires a disclaimer on the usage of computing resources. Or maybe you want to add a touch of personalization to your login window—a daily reminder to back up your hard drive or floss, for example.

Adding this line of text entails editing a special preference file—a running theme in the Mac OS X hacking community, as well as in this book.

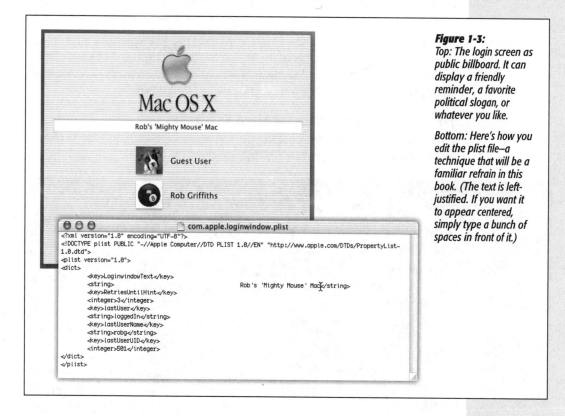

Figure 1-3:
Top: The login screen as public billboard. It can display a friendly reminder, a favorite political slogan, or whatever you like.

Bottom: Here's how you edit the plist file—a technique that will be a familiar refrain in this book. (The text is left-justified. If you want it to appear centered, simply type a bunch of spaces in front of it.)

In the Finder, open the Library→Preferences folder. Inside you'll find a file called com.apple.loginwindow.plist. To edit it, open it using TextEdit (read the details of this ritual on page 4).

The file contains a long list of bracketed words known to programmers as *tags* (Figure 1-3, bottom). Just below the first <dict> tag, insert these two lines:

```
<key>LoginwindowText</key>
<string>Your text goes here</string>
```

Replace *Your text goes here* with whatever you'd like displayed on the login window screen.

Choose File→Save. When TextEdit tells you, "Couldn't save document because the file is read-only. Attempt to overwrite?", click Overwrite.

The next time you log in, you'll savor the results of your modification.

1-6   Quick Restart, Shut Down, and Log Out

As confirmation boxes go, the one that appears when you choose Restart, Log Out, or Shut Down from the menu is especially pointless. If you're like most people, your reaction is: "Well, *duh*—I chose that command, didn't I? Of course I'm sure."

In that case, you're a perfect candidate for this trick: Hold down Option before selecting any of these three items in the menu. The instant you do so, the ellipsis (…) after each menu choice disappears. This is your clue that Mac OS X won't ask for any further comment as you restart, log out, or shut down.

1-7   Restart, Shut Down, or Sleep Keystrokes

If, like many an efficiency freak before you, you prefer keyboard shortcuts to choosing commands from menus, here's your cheat sheet:

UP TO SPEED

Feed the Hunger

Mac OS X *loves* memory (RAM). RAM is a relatively cheap upgrade that can pay large dividends in increased productivity and reduced frustration levels.

How much RAM is right for you? More is always better, so buy as much as you can afford. According to Apple, Mac OS X requires 128 megabytes. But 256 MB is a more realistic minimum, and Mac OS X gets really sweet with 512 MB or more depending on how many programs you like to keep open. Yes, yes, if you're someone who remembers the day when only rich snobs could afford a 2 MB Mac, that seems like a disgraceful amount. But times have

changed. RAM is relatively cheap, and it delivers a lot of boost for the buck. Buy as much as you can afford.

The primary advantage of more RAM is that you can open more programs at one time without enduring a moment of disk-swapping when you switch between them.

Mac OS X also loves hard drive space—not just the 3 GB that you need to install Mac OS X, but you should also keep at least 1 GB free on the drive that contains OS X at all times. The system will need that room to hold its *swap files,* which it uses when it can't keep everything in actual memory.

- **Shut down** by pressing Control-Option-⌘-Eject. (It's not as complex as it looks—the first three keys are all in a tidy row to the left of the Space bar.)

- **Restart** with Control-⌘-Eject.

- **Log out** by pressing Shift-⌘-Q.

And if your older Mac lacks an Eject key, substitute the F12 key in each of these keystrokes.

1-8   Restart/Sleep/Shut Down Dialog Box

Want to put your machine to sleep without mousing up to the ⌘ menu? Press Control-Eject (or Control-F12 if you don't have an Eject key, or, on a laptop, the power button by itself). You get the dialog box shown in Figure 1-4, where you tap a single letter to trigger the option you want.

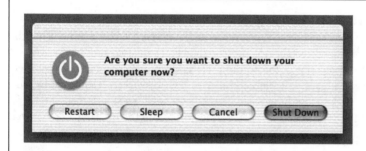

Figure 1-4:
Once the Shut Down dialog box appears, you can press the S key instead of clicking Sleep, R for Restart, Esc for Cancel, or Enter for Shut Down.

Display and Sound

Sight and sound are the primary senses you use to experience the glory of a Mac. (Smell cartridges are, mercifully, still years away.) Mastering the screen and speaker controls, therefore, offers big payoffs.

1-9   Opening Sound and Displays Panels

Ordinarily, you're supposed to adjust your screen or speaker settings by opening System Preferences and clicking the Displays or Sound icon. But if you're just seeking a quick brightness or volume adjustment, life's too short for that slow-lane method. Instead use the dedicated keys for adjusting brightness and volume that come on every modern Mac keyboard.

Sometimes, though, you need access to more sophisticated controls—you might want to adjust the screen resolution to see how your Web page might look on different screens, for example, or you might want to change the built-in alert beep sound. For these tasks, only the System Preferences panes will do.

So here's the tip: On a PowerBook or iBook, you can jump directly to the Displays preference panel by pressing Option-F1 or -F2 (the brightness function keys). To jump to the Sound panel, press Option-F3, -F4, or -F5 (the sound function keys).

If you have a desktop Mac instead, you can press Option plus any of the volume keys to open the Sound preferences panel. (There's no way to jump to the Displays panel from the keyboard on desktop Macs.)

1-10   Changing the Alert Volume

There are two sound volumes that you can adjust independently: the volume of alert beeps (noises you hear when your system has something to announce, like receiving an email or crashing a program) and the overall volume (the sound level for playing CDs, MP3s, and Doom).

Dragging the menu bar volume slider changes the overall system volume. But if you drag the slider while pressing the Option key, you'll change *only* the alert volume, not the total system volume. (If you don't see the little speaker icon on your menu bar, visit the Sound panel of System Preferences and turn on "Show volume in menu bar.")

1-11   The Volume-Changing Click

When you increase or decrease the volume on your Mac OS X machine using the keyboard, you hear a muted clicking noise to help you gauge the new level as you set it (unless you've disabled it in the Sound preferences panel). (You also see a super-imposed speaker icon.) If you want a louder or less co-worker–friendly noise, you can change this click to anything you'd like. All you need is a standard sound file in AIFF format—a Bart Simpson snippet, a rude noise from the Internet, or whatever.

Then proceed like this:

1. Open your System→Library→LoginPlugins→BezelServices.loginPlugin→ Contents folder.

   Your job is to replace the standard sound file within the Contents→Resources folder—but you'll be thwarted by the highly skeptical attitude that Mac OS X takes toward people who try to mess with its innermost settings. In short, you're not allowed to change anything in the System folder.

   But you, intrepid hacker, don't care about that. As long as you have an Administrator account (page 11), you can change whatever you like, just by telling the system software that the owner of the Resources folder is *you*, not it.

2. Highlight the Resources folder, and then choose File→Get Info.

   The Get Info window appears.

3. Expand the Ownership & Permissions triangle.

   If you see a locked padlock icon, click it. Mac OS X asks you to prove your administrator status by entering your account name and password and then clicking OK.

4. From the Owner pop-up menu, choose your account name (which is designated by the cute suffix "Me").

You've just told Mac OS X that *you* are the rightful owner of the Resources folder, and that therefore you're allowed to make any changes you like—such as replacing the volume-click sound.

Leave the Get Info window open for now.

5. Within the Resources window, highlight the file called **volume.aiff**. Choose File→Duplicate.

You've just created a backup, just in case you decide to restore the original clicking sound.

6. Delete the volume.aiff file. Drag your replacement sound into the window, and then rename it so that *it* is now called volume.aiff.

Finally, you need to return the ownership of the Resources folder to Mac OS X.

7. In the Get Info window, choose System from the Owner pop-up menu. Close the Get Info window.

The next time you log in and tap the volume keys to adjust your speakers, you'll hear your new volume-changing sound—for better or worse.

If anything went wrong—say you inadvertently chose a full-length sound file of the Wagner *Ring* cycle as the volume-key click—repeat these steps, but remove your "bad" new sound and rename the backed-up original to return the folder to its pre-modification state.

1-12   Resolutions You Never Knew You Had

Veteran public speakers will be only too eager to tell you about their migraine moments: They arrive with the PowerBook, hook it up to the projector provided by their hosts, and find that they're limited to an 800 x 600-pixel projected image (and, if Mirroring is turned on, a black-margined PowerBook screen to match). Not only is that too small for a decent demo, it's too small to run iMovie at all.

Virtually all modern projectors offer much greater resolution than 800 x 600, so it's usually not the projector's fault. Open System Preferences (page 125), click Displays, and turn off "Show modes recommended by display." You'll see a list of screen resolutions that your PowerBook was hiding from you. Just click the one that best suits the talk that, by now, you're more than ready to make.

Window Tricks

What would the Mac be without its glorious, overlapping, drop-shadowed windows?

Unix, that's what.

In any case, mastering the many wonders of the Mac OS X window is a key survival skill.

1-13   Maximizing Windows

The small, green, round button in the upper-left corner of each window is the *zoom button*, and its purpose is to make a window just large enough to show you all of its contents. (If your monitor isn't big enough to show all the icons in a window, the window just grows to show as many as possible.) In any case, a second click on the zoom button restores the window to its previous size. The Window→Zoom Window command does the same thing as clicking the zoom button.

But everyone knows that much. The trick here is that in some programs, clicking, Option-clicking, or Shift-clicking the zoom button makes it override its own intelligence and forces the window to grow as large as possible. In the Finder, it's Option-click; in OmniWeb, it's Shift-click; in general, it's just too bad this trick isn't consistent.

1-14   Insta-Closing Multiple Windows

When you find yourself with several open windows in one program, especially in the Finder, don't waste time trying to close them individually. Instead, Option-click the red close button at the top left of any open window. Presto: All windows close at once. (Except in Word X; Microsoft marches to a different drummer.)

1-15   Moving Background Windows

Suppose you're writing a training manual about a piece of software. As you write up your witty little descriptions of the elements of some dialog box, you may find it frustrating that your word processor's own window is covering up what you're trying to describe.

That's precisely when you should remember the ⌘-key trick. By pressing ⌘ as you drag their title bars, you can move background windows *without* bringing them to the foreground. (Don't click in the area that displays the window' name; anywhere else along the window top is where you want to click.)

1-16   Bringing Program Windows Forward

For efficiency's sake, sometimes you want to bring up *all* the open windows of one program. Unfortunately, as many Mac OS 9 veterans quickly discover, clicking in the window of a Mac OS X program brings only *that window* forward, leaving the program's other windows in the background (see Figure 1-5).

Figure 1-5:
Here's a delicious Safari/ System Preferences sandwich; notice how the System Preferences window is trapped between two Safari windows.

If you use ⌘-Tab to switch programs, however, or if you switch by clicking a program's Dock icon, all of the program's windows come forward.

Alternatively, you can also install a shareware program like DragThing, which includes a setting that brings "all windows forward" as the preferred behavior when you click on an individual window.

1-17   Three Scroll Bar Stunts

You may have noticed an intriguing option on the General panel of System Preferences, something called "Scroll to here."

Ordinarily, when you click in the scroll bar track above or below the gelatinous handle, the window scrolls by one screenful. But if you turn on "Scroll to here" mode, when you click in the scroll bar track, the Mac considers the entire scroll bar a proportional map of the document and scrolls precisely to the spot you clicked. That is, if you click at the very bottom of the scroll bar track, you see the very last page. (In general, this feature works only in *Cocoa* programs [page 99].)

But there's a tip within this tip: No matter which scrolling option you choose in the General panel, you can always override your decision on a case-by-case basis by *Option*-clicking in the scroll bar track. In other words, if you've selected the "Scroll to here" option, you can produce a "jump to next page" scroll by Option-clicking in the scroll bar track.

Even that's not the end of the Option-key magic:

- If you're trying to read something carefully and slowly, you can *slow down* the scrolling. If you press Option while dragging the scroll bar handle, the window shifts smoothly as you drag rather than turbo-scrolling a screen at a time. (This, too, works only in Cocoa programs.)

- Conversely, Option-clicking the up or down scroll arrow *speeds up* scrolling, shifting by a page at a time instead of a line at a time. (Yes, yes, that's what the Page Up and Page Down keys are for—but when you're already manipulating these scroll buttons with the mouse, it's nice to be able to switch between line scrolling and page scrolling.) And this trick works in *all* Mac OS X programs, Cocoa or not.

1-18   Double Arrows on Both Ends

In System Preferences, the General pane offers to "Place scroll arrows" either together at the bottom (or left) of the scroll bar, or apart, appearing at opposite ends of the scroll bar. Both settings can lead to a lot of excess mousing around.

The ideal arrangement, of course, would be to have *both* scroll arrows at *both* ends of the bar, as shown in Figure 1-6.

To create this effect, open Terminal (page 5). At the % prompt, type this, all on one line:

```
defaults write "Apple Global Domain" AppleScrollBarVariant
DoubleBoth
```

Now press Enter. (See page 5 for more on the *defaults* command.)

The next time you open any program, you'll find that its scroll-bar buttons are nestled, in duplicate, at both ends of the scroll bars.

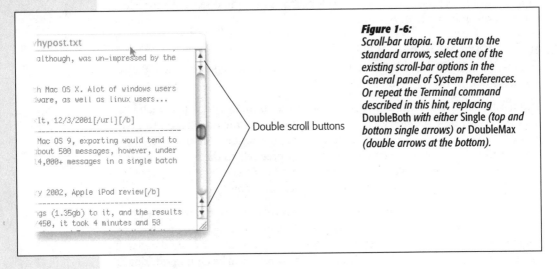

Figure 1-6:
Scroll-bar utopia. To return to the standard arrows, select one of the existing scroll-bar options in the General panel of System Preferences. Or repeat the Terminal command described in this hint, replacing DoubleBoth *with either* Single *(top and bottom single arrows) or* DoubleMax *(double arrows at the bottom).*

Double scroll buttons

Menulets

Apple calls them Menu Extras, but Mac fans on the Internet have named the little menu bar icons shown in Figure 1-7 *menulets*. A menulet is both an indicator and a menu that gives you direct access to some settings in System Preferences. But there's more to them than you may suspect.

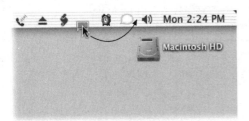

Figure 1-7:
You can rearrange the icons by holding down the ⌘ key and then dragging the icons (including the menu bar clock) around the screen. You may wish to put your most-used icon in the top-right corner.

1-19   Menulet Basics

In general, you install a menulet by turning on the representative checkbox in System Preferences. You'll find such checkboxes in the Date & Time, Displays, Sound, and other panels.

You can remove a menulet by ⌘-dragging it off of your menu bar (or by turning off the corresponding checkbox in System Preferences), and you move them around on the menu bar the same way—by ⌘-dragging them horizontally. Some judicious rearranging of menulets can make frequently used ones easier to hit with a hasty mouse.

1-20   The Secret Eject Icon

The prescribed way to eject a CD or DVD is to press the Eject (or F12) key on your keyboard. That's not much help if you have a non-Apple keyboard, though, or if, thanks to a rash of bad luck, you find yourself without a keyboard altogether.

Fortunately, there's a secret way to do the same thing: install the Eject *menulet*.

To find the installer, open your hard drive→System→Library→CoreServices→Menu Extras folder. Inside that window, double-click the icon called Eject.menu.

Now look at your menu bar: there's the new Eject icon (second from left in Figure 1-7). Use it like a menu to choose the drive you'd like to eject.

1-21   Changing the Time and Date Menulet

The menu bar clock in Mac OS X is useful, but less so than you might think the world's premier elegance-driven software company would create.

For example, you can't see the current date until you click the time, and Date and Time preferences panel doesn't offer much formatting flexibility. But if you're willing to dabble in the Terminal program (page 5), you can take this humble clock much further.

Open Terminal (in your Applications→Utilities folder). At the % prompt, type the following text (capitals count):

```
cd ~/Library/Preferences
```

(Note the space after cd.)

Press Enter. At the next % prompt, type this, followed by Enter:

```
pico .GlobalPreferences.plist
```

You've just used *pico*, one of Mac OS X's built-in Unix word processors, to open the Mac OS X file that stores the menu-bar time formatting.

Press Control-W to search, type *NSTime*, and then hit Enter. The display jumps to a line that looks like this:

```
<key>NSTimeFormatString</key>
```

Immediately below that is a line that specifies the menu bar clock format. It might look something like this (its appearance depends on your date and time preference settings):

```
<string>%1I:%M:%S</string>
```

This string of gibberish actually has meaning to Unix, and hence, to the Date and Time menulet. Taken one piece at a time, it breaks down like this:

- %1I means "show the hour in 12-hour format without the leading zero"

- %M means "show the minutes using two decimal places"

- %S means "show the seconds using two decimal places"

The colons are colons, so the format code above makes the time appear like this: 8:33:22 PM.

You can see a list of nearly all the date and time codes in the Terminal, assuming you have the BSD subsystem installed (see the note on page 345). Just type *man strftime* and press Enter; you'll see a long list of "%" abbreviations that you can use in your enhanced menulet.

If you'd like to experiment with some possible formats before committing them to the preferences file, type *date +"some_format"*, where the portion inside the quotes is replaced with a format as shown in *strftime*. For example:

```
date +"Today is: %D"
Today is: 09/19/02
```

Once you've picked a format you like, return to the *pico* editing window and enter your code, replacing what's between the "string" tags. For example, the following format string:

```
<string>[%a %b %e] %1I:%M:%S</string>
```

produces a menu bar clock that looks like this:

```
[Thu Oct 24] 8:52 PM
```

Some other possibilities:

%1I:%M %a, %b %e creates this clock: "9:17 Tue Mar 4"

%A %B %e [%H:%M] creates this one: "Tuesday March 4 [21:17]"

Tip: To prevent seeing the day of the week twice, turn off the "Show day of the week" checkbox in the Menu Bar Clock tab of the Date & Time panel in System Preferences. Similarly, don't include "%p" for AM and PM if you already have the "Show AM/PM" preference turned on.

One difference between the preferences file and the *strftime* formatting commands is the "%1I" in the above commands. While not listed in *strftime*, the "1" forces the hourly clock to drop the leading "0" when there are fewer than two digits in the number.

Once you have the edits done, tell *pico* to save the file by pressing Control-W and then hitting Enter to replace the original file. To check your handiwork, open the Date and Time panel of System Preferences, click the Menu Bar Clock tab, and then turn the "Show the date and time in the menu bar" checkbox off and on again.

Note: Be aware that you're modifying a global display command here, which may affect the date display in other programs. In iTunes, for example, the small window may not accommodate the width of a full date format.

Setting Up

Whether you've just started using Mac OS X or switched a long time ago, you should take some time to individualize your new computing world. After all, the odds that Apple came up with an operating system that perfectly suited you, NASA scientists, and the eight-year-old down the street are pretty slim.

1-22   Saving Memory

Mac OS X comes with a number of built-in features that you may not need—and in the meantime, they're drinking up memory and horsepower that could be used for stuff you *do* care about. These *services* include Personal File Sharing, Windows File Sharing, Web Sharing, Remote Login, File Transfer Protocol (FTP), Remote Apple Events, Printer Sharing, and so on.

You should turn off the ones you don't need. If you're not on a network, you don't need *any* of them. If you share files with a Mac or a Windows PC on the network, turn on the first and second items, respectively.

To turn these features on and off, choose →System Preferences. Click the Sharing icon, click the Services tab, and turn off the corresponding checkboxes.

1-23   Printer Sharing

It's a classic problem. You're sitting in a large office, with printers scattered all over the premises. You print an important document—and have no clue where to go to pick it up. (That's an especially worrisome situation if what you're printing is your résumé and cover letter to a headhunter.)

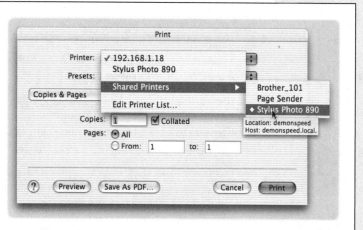

Figure 1-8:
From within an application, select a printer from the pop-up list in the Print dialog box, and then point to it with the mouse. A yellow tag appears showing the name of the machine that's hosting the printer. Of course, this trick won't actually help much if the machines aren't logically named after either users or locations—but it'll make you feel like an insider.

Fortunately, Figure 1-8 shows you a sneaky trick that lets you find out the name of the Mac that's attached to a certain printer, the better to stalk it down.

1-24 System Maintenance

Every night, without complaint or fuss, Mac OS X performs a series of system-maintenance tasks: exciting things like cleaning up temporary files left by your programs, updating databases that keep track of files, and deleting system logs. Without these regular operations, you'll wind up with wasted hard drive space, and some searches won't work.

But Mac OS X only does its janitorial duties if you leave your machine on at all times, wasting energy and filling the room with the hum of your fan.

That leaves you two options for running the maintenance programs. You can either get your hands dirty and run them yourself in the Terminal (see Chapter 15), or you can use a program like MacJanitor (available at *http://personalpages.tds.net/ ~brian_hill/macjanitor.html*) to run them from the Finder.

To use MacJanitor, double-click its icon, click the padlock icon next to "Click to allow tasks," and enter your administrator's password when prompted (page 11). The Daily, Weekly, Monthly, and All Tasks buttons in the toolbar spring to life.

Choose Help→MacJanitor Help for a detailed explanation of what each cleanup routine does, and then run the ones that sound good to you. If you haven't left your machine on for a long time (so that the normal tasks never had a chance to run), select All Tasks the first time you run the program. After that, you can follow the suggested schedule and run the appropriate tasks daily, weekly, or monthly.

1-25 Apple Help

You might not expect to need help with Help. After all, this built-in, online help system is supposed to be self-explanatory.

It's not.

For proof, go to the Finder and choose Help→Mac Help (or hit ⌘-?) to open the Help Viewer (Figure 1-9). The first aspect of the Help program that throws many a Mac fan is the right-hand drawer. This is meant to be an index that lists every program that has online help. As you use Mac OS X and install additional programs, the list of available help topics increases.

The theory of bunching up all of your programs' help in one master program is that you can cross-search. If you're in iPhoto, for example, and you're having trouble printing, you might not guess that the Printing topics are in the standard Mac OS X help, not iPhoto help.

You can resize this topics "drawer" by dragging its far right edge horizontally. If you reduce the size of the drawer too much, though, it disappears altogether. To bring it back, click the Help Center icon on the toolbar.

Your main interaction with the Help Viewer will probably be through the "Ask a Question" input box on the toolbar. Type your question in plain English ("How do I print?" for example), and then press Return or Enter.

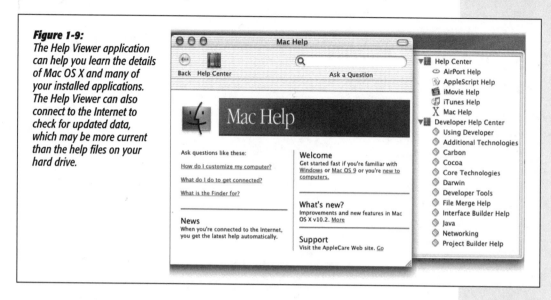

Figure 1-9:
The Help Viewer application can help you learn the details of Mac OS X and many of your installed applications. The Help Viewer can also connect to the Internet to check for updated data, which may be more current than the help files on your hard drive.

The results page contains columns with the topic name, Help Center's estimate of its relevance to your query, and a Location column showing which section of the Help Center contains the topic. You can sort by column by clicking on the column headings; click twice to reverse the sort order for the selected column.

If you use the Help Center a lot, spend a couple of minutes customizing its toolbar by adding buttons for commonly used tasks. See Figure 1-10 for instructions.

Figure 1-10:
From the menu, choose View→Customize Toolbar, and click the buttons you'd like to add. The Smaller and Bigger buttons can be very useful for tiny type. Forward and Print are often valuable, too. Add separators as you wish to help group the relevant buttons together.

The Finder and Desktop

T he Finder, also known as the desktop, represents what most people think of when they picture a Macintosh. It's user-friendly and efficient—but you can make it even more so, as you'll find out in this chapter.

Finder Basics

Although it appears simple on the surface, the Finder is actually a complex program, powerful enough to manage all of your disk and network interaction. To make the most of your time in the Finder, you'll want to get acquainted with some of its more subtle features.

2-1   The Status Bar

The Finder's status bar, as seen in Figure 2-1, lets you quickly check the quantity and size of items in hard drives, partitions, and folders. The only trouble is, most people

Figure 2-1:
The status bar displays the number of items in the selected folder and the space remaining on the disk.

don't even know that it's available. To make it appear, choose View→Show Status Bar (Figure 2-1).

Note, by the way, that the status bar always counts up the *visible* icons. For example, when you expand a folder in a list view (by clicking its flippy triangle), the status bar tallies only the icons in the *currently visible* inner folders.

2-2 The Status Bar in Narrow Windows

As any neat freak can tell you, tall, skinny windows have their advantages. They take up less space on the desktop (good for drag-and-drop operations), and you can see more of them at once. (Drag the lower-right corner of a window to shrink it.)

But in a narrow window, there's not enough width for the status bar to display both the number of files and the remaining disk space. As shown in Figure 2-2, however, there's a quick trick to solve this problem.

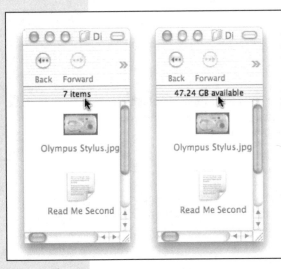

Figure 2-2:
Left: The status bar in narrow Finder windows shows only the number of items in the folder.

Right: If you click the number of items, you see the available disk space instead. Click on the disk space display to toggle back to the number of items.

2-3 Insta-Sort

When a Finder window is in list view, you can re-sort the list by clicking any column heading, like Date Modified or Kind, as shown in Figure 2-3.

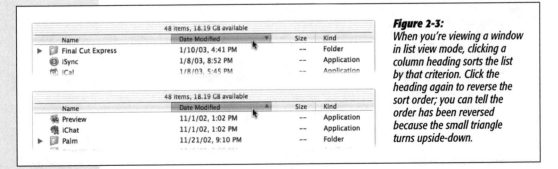

Figure 2-3:
When you're viewing a window in list view mode, clicking a column heading sorts the list by that criterion. Click the heading again to reverse the sort order; you can tell the order has been reversed because the small triangle turns upside-down.

But that's baby stuff. The power user, of course, can change the sort column *without* assistance from the mouse—just by pressing Control-Tab to "click" the column to the right, or Shift-Control-Tab to "click" the one to the left. (You can't, however, reverse the sort order this way.)

2-4   Search Results

When you use the Find command (⌘-F) to round up a missing file or folder, the results window is split in two. The top half shows all files matching your search criteria. When you click one of these icons, the bottom half shows where that icon is on your hard drive (see Figure 2-4 at top).

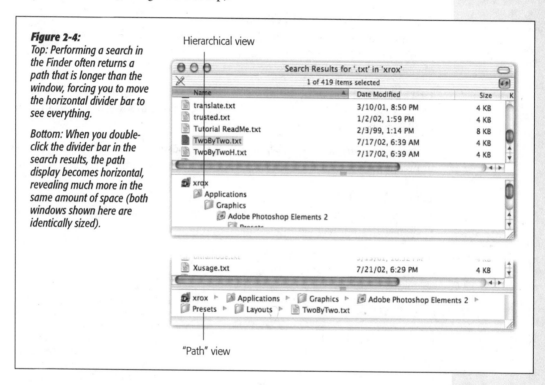

Figure 2-4:
Top: Performing a search in the Finder often returns a path that is longer than the window, forcing you to move the horizontal divider bar to see everything.

Bottom: When you double-click the divider bar in the search results, the path display becomes horizontal, revealing much more in the same amount of space (both windows shown here are identically sized).

Hierarchical view

"Path" view

Unfortunately, this path notation is often chopped off. For example, in Figure 2-4, you can see that the file called TwoByTwo.txt is in the xrox→Applications→ Graphics→Adobe Photoshop Elements 2 folder—but that's as much of the path as you can see.

The solution: If you double-click anywhere on the horizontal divider bar, the lower pane switches from the indented outline display to a "path notation" display, as shown at bottom in Figure 2-4. (Unfortunately, the Finder doesn't remember this setting, so you have to double-click the divider bar each time you want to see full search results.)

2-5 Erasing Disks

Mac OS X no longer comes with an Erase Disk command—at least not in the Finder. Instead, when you want to erase one of your disks, you must use Disk Utility, a program in your Applications→Utilities folder.

Once you're in the program, click Erase, and then select the disk you wish to erase from the list in the left-side window. Make sure that the proper name is reflected in the Name box on the right-hand side before you proceed! Click Erase and let the utility go to work—an especially useful tactic when you have CD-RW discs to erase and rewrite.

2-6 Window Size and Location

You can set the size of new Finder windows and where on the screen they open. This procedure is Apple's version of a secret handshake: It's easy to carry out, but it's not obvious how to do it.

First close all open Finder windows, and then open one new window (File→New Finder Window or ⌘-N). Set up the size and location of this window manually, and then close the window without selecting anything in it.

From now on, any new window you create (by choosing File→New Finder Window or pressing ⌘-N) will appear at the location you set and at the size you specified.

2-7 List View

In list view, the flippy triangle to the left of each folder's name (Figure 2-5) lets you peek inside each folder without double-clicking.

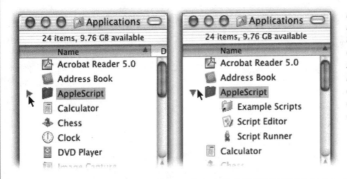

Figure 2-5:
In a list view (left), clicking the small triangle reveals the selected folder's contents in the same window, as shown at right. If you prefer the keyboard, you can also use the right arrow to open the expanded view, and the left arrow to collapse the expanded folder.

If you Option-click the triangle, all folders *within* the selected folder also open, giving you a one-click view of every nested folder's contents.

But the real power comes from combining the Option key with the arrow keys. Start by selecting all the folders you'd like to see expanded (⌘-click one at a time). Now release the ⌘ key, hold down Option, and then hit the right arrow key. You've just expanded all selected folders *and* all folders inside them. (Warning: If you select a folder with multiple buried subfolders and lots and lots of icons inside each, this can take a while!)

To return to the normal collapsed view, make sure each folder is selected again, and then hit the left arrow key.

2-8 Column View

The idea behind *column* view is simple: To create a means of burrowing down through nested folders without leaving a trail of messy, overlapping windows in your wake. As shown in Figure 2-6, the solution is a list view that's divided into several vertical panes. The leftmost pane always shows all the icons of your disks, including your main hard drive.

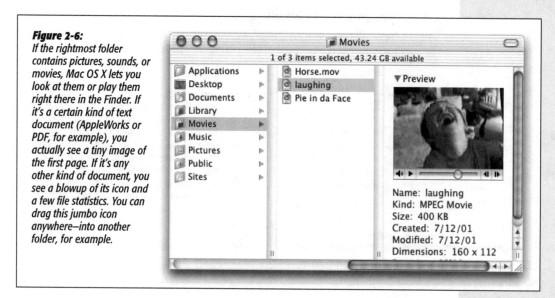

Figure 2-6:
If the rightmost folder contains pictures, sounds, or movies, Mac OS X lets you look at them or play them right there in the Finder. If it's a certain kind of text document (AppleWorks or PDF, for example), you actually see a tiny image of the first page. If it's any other kind of document, you see a blowup of its icon and a few file statistics. You can drag this jumbo icon anywhere—into another folder, for example.

When you click a disk (once), the second pane shows a list of all folders in it. Each time you click a folder in one pane, the pane to its right shows what's inside.

The beauty of column view is, first of all, that it keeps your screen tidy. It effectively shows you several simultaneous folder levels, but contains them within a single window. With a quick ⌘-W, you can close the entire window, panes and all. Second, column view provides an excellent sense of where you are. Because your trail is visible at all times, it's much harder to get lost, wondering what folder you're in and how you got there.

You can control this entire process by keyboard alone, a great timesaver for keyboard fans. For example:

• You can jump from one pane to the next by pressing the right or left arrow keys. Each press highlights the closest icon in the next or previous pane.

- The Back command (clicking the Back button on the toolbar, pressing ⌘-[, or choosing Go→Back) works just as it would in a Web browser: it lets you retrace your steps backward. You can use this command over and over again until you return to the setup that first appeared when you switched to column view. Similarly, pressing ⌘-] moves you forward through the panes you've recently visited.

- Within a pane, press the up or down arrow keys to highlight successive icons in the list. Or type the first couple letters of an icon's name to jump directly to it.

- When you finally highlight the icon you've been looking for, press ⌘-O or ⌘-down arrow to open it. You're free to open anything in any column; you don't have to wait until you've pinpointed a file in the rightmost column.

2-9   Resizing the Columns

You can make all the columns wider or narrower simultaneously by dragging any of the small handles at the bottom of the columns (circled in Figure 2-7).

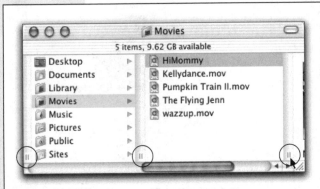

Figure 2-7:
In the Finder's column view, you can save space—and allow more columns to appear in one window—by tightening columns that have relatively short file names, while leaving other columns alone. If you press Option as you drag the column-divider widget (the small double vertical bar at the bottom of each column), you resize only that column.

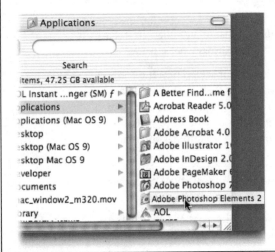

Figure 2-8:
If you press the Option key while mousing over a list of file names (or just point the cursor and wait, motionless), you force the Finder to show a pop-up balloon that reveals the full text of any files that have been truncated to fit the window.

Often, though, that isn't really what you want. Usually, you're more interested in expanding only a single column, not all of them at once.

To make a *single* column wider or narrower, Option-drag the column handle at the bottom of its right edge, as shown in Figure 2-7.

2-10   Viewing Full File Names

Mac OS X is generous: It allows file names of up to 255 characters long. But if you use views with restricted space, like narrow columns, the Finder shortens the names, chopping text out of the *middle* of the file names.

In other words, your magnificently titled photo *Vacation - Hotel Photo.jpg* becomes *Vacatio...hoto.jpg*. This contraction wouldn't be a problem, except that the same window also contains a file called *Vacation - Airport Photo.jpg*, which now appears to have the same name. The solution is revealed in Figure 2-8.

2-11   More Icons in a Column

If you've ever played around with the Finder's font size options (choose View→Show View Options) in icon or list view, you may have been disappointed to discover that shrinking the font size doesn't actually make room for more icons in a given window's height (see Figure 2-9, top). Fortunately, it's a different story in column view (at bottom in the figure).

Figure 2-9:
Top: Setting the font size in list view isn't particularly useful. As you can see here, dropping the font size from, say, 12 point to 10 point (left and right, respectively) doesn't fit any more icons in the list. It's the size of the icons that's controlling how much you get to see.

Bottom: Setting a font size in column view, however, can be quite useful. You can see many more icons by dropping the font size from 12 point to 10 point, because the icons themselves also shrink.

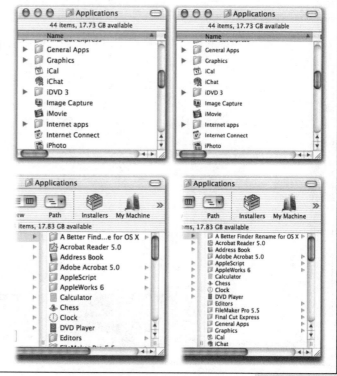

Find a font size that strikes a balance: large enough to read easily yet small enough to maximize the amount of data you can see without mousing for the scroll bars.

2-12   A Second Line of File Info

Start by opening any icon-view window, and then choose View→Show View Options (Figure 2-10).

While you've got the View Options palette open, try turning on "Show item info." Suddenly you get a new line of information, in tiny blue type, about any disk or folder icon in the window. For example:

- **Folders.** The info line lets you know how many icons are inside each folder without your having to open it.

Note: You may wish to leave this setting off for hard drives that are connected to a network. They contain a large number of folders, and you'll wind up analyzing the chemical makeup of the stains on your keyboard while you wait for the system to count all of their contents.

- **Graphics files.** Certain other kinds of files may show a helpful info line, too. For example, graphics files in TIFF, PDF, and certain other formats display their dimensions in pixels.

- **Sounds and QuickTime movies.** The light-blue bonus line tells you how long the sound or movie takes to play. For example, "02' 49"" means two minutes, 49 seconds.

You can see these effects illustrated in Figure 2-10.

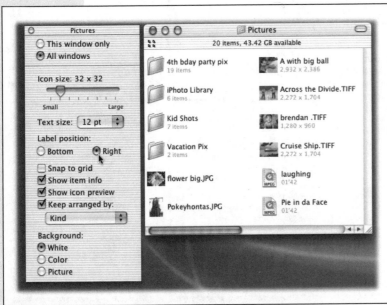

Figure 2-10:
Choose View→Show View Options, and then turn on "Show item info." A line of blue text appears below each icon, showing supplementary information depending on icon type. This works only in icon view.

2-13   Window Backgrounds

In icon view, you can use images or colors as the backgrounds for Finder windows. It may sound like nothing more than eye candy, but this option actually has a very practical *raison d'être*. If you color code your windows, you can tell which folders are open on your desktop without even looking for their title bars. And nothing makes it easier to tell windows apart when they're minimized to the Dock (see Figure 2-11).

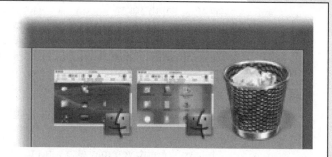

Figure 2-11:
Even in gray, it's obvious how different colors help you distinguish between minimized Finder windows in the Dock.

For more dramatic effect, for example, give your "Hot Projects" folder a light red background. Give less important stuff—lists of all the airline silverware you've ever stolen and your screenplay-in-progress for Disney about a team of dachshund puppies who break an international weapons-smuggling ring—a light blue background. Light green could signify your personal finances folder. An image of your favorite lawn ornament could serve as the background for your pictures folder.

To change the background color of a Finder window, follow these steps:

1. **Make sure the window is in icon view, and then choose View→Show View Options.**

   If you want to apply a color or picture to only one folder, turn on "This window only" at the top of the dialog box.

2. **At the bottom of the box, choose either Color or Picture.**

   Color brings up a little frame; when you click it, the Colors dialog box appears. Click anywhere in the Color Wheel to select a pleasing tint, or play with the color display options at the top of the box (Color Sliders, Color Palettes, Image Palettes, and Crayons).

   If you choose Picture, press Select to open a dialog box you can navigate through to pick an image.

As you work, remember that light background colors and low-contrast photos work best for legibility. What's more, if you decide to choose a photographic background, keep in mind that Mac OS X has no idea what sizes and shapes your window may assume in its lifetime and makes no attempt to scale down a selected photo to fit neatly into the window. If you have a high-resolution digital camera, your window background may show only the upper-left corner of a photo. Use a graphics program to scale the picture down to something smaller than your screen resolution for better results.

2-14   Making Column View Speedier

In column view, the rightmost panel shows a preview of whatever document or folder is selected in the previous column, as shown in Figure 2-6. Although this feature is handy for taking a sneak peak at a graphic or even a QuickTime movie, it can dramatically slow down your column view browsing, especially with folders containing lots of images. (It's even worse if you've highlighted a graphic or Quick-Time movie file that turns out to be damaged. You'll sit there, watching the "spinning beachball of death" cursor forever, or until you force-quit the Finder—whichever comes first.)

If you'd prefer to do without this final column in the name of speeding things up, choose View→Show View, and then turn off "Show preview column."

While you're at it, you may also want to turn off "Show icons," an option that refers to the tiny icons next to each file and folder name. They look nice, but on a slower machine, you could watch the entire *Godfather* trilogy while you wait for the window to fill in.

In any case, turning off these two options makes column view much more responsive. (And if you ever find yourself missing the information or the preview that would have appeared in the rightmost column, see the next hint.)

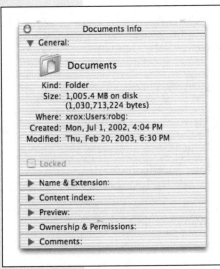

Figure 2-12:
Inspector sheets give you the full scoop on files and folders. If you leave the Inspector open, the information in it changes each time you select a new file in the Finder.

2-15 Previewing Multimedia Files

As noted earlier, the rightmost column in column view lets you check out your multimedia goodies without opening any additional programs—a time and memory saver. It not only shows you a thumbnail of any selected graphics file, it can even play QuickTime movies or MP3 music files.

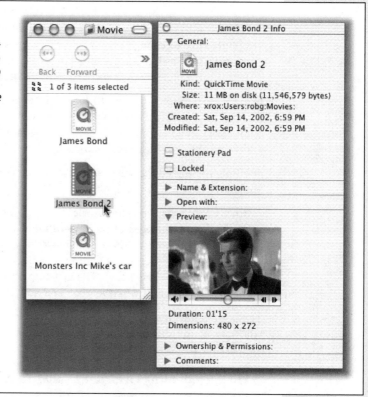

Figure 2-13:
When you want to preview a graphics or multimedia file in a list or icon view, just highlight the icon (left) and then press Option-⌘-I to bring up the Inspector dialog box (right). Click to expand the triangle next to Preview; you can now play the movie or sound. From now on, each time you click a file in the Finder, a preview appears in the Inspector, as shown at right

But what about list and icon views? Are you to be left, stranded and preview-less?

Of course not. Figure 2-13 shows how you can enjoy multimedia previews even when you're not in column view.

2-16 Get Info vs. the Inspector

It's been a proud and noble tradition since the earliest days of Macintosh: When you highlight any icon and then press ⌘-I, the Get Info window appears. It's a collapsible, multipanel screen that provides a wealth of information about a highlighted icon. For example:

- For a disk icon, you get statistics about its capacity and how much of it is full.

- For a document icon, you see when it was created and modified, and what programs it "belongs" to.

- For an alias, you learn the location of the actual icon it refers to.

- If you open the Get Info window when nothing is selected, you get information about the desktop itself, including the amount of disk space consumed by everything sitting on it.

- If you highlight a gaggle of icons all at once, the Get Info window shows you precisely how many you highlighted, breaks it down by type ("23 documents, 3 folders," for example), and adds up the total of their file sizes. This is a great opportunity to change certain file characteristics on numerous files simultaneously, such as locking or unlocking them, hiding or showing their file name extensions, changing their ownership or permissions, and so on.

In Mac OS X versions 10.0 and 10.1, a single Info window remained on the screen all the time as you clicked one icon after another. That was great for reducing clutter, but it didn't let you compare the statistics for the Get Info windows of two or three folders side by side. Macintosh purists howled.

So Apple responded the way a software company should: It put the old way back, but left the new way in as an option.

In other words, when you choose File→Get Info, you get a new dialog box each time you get info on an icon. But the one-window approach is still available for those occasions when you don't need side-by-side Get Info windows—if you know the secret. Highlight the icon and then press Option-⌘-I (or hold down Option and choose File→Show Inspector). The Get Info window that appears looks normal, but it changes to reflect whatever icon you now click.

The bottom line: If your intention is to compare a number of files, use Get Info. If you want to add the same comment to or adjust the same characteristic of many files, use the Inspector.

2-17   Temporarily Overriding "Snap to grid"

Finder windows let you turn on a setting that keeps everything neatly ordered. It's called "Snap to grid," and you can find it in View→Show View Options.

But if you want to place an icon within a window but outside the grid—perhaps to make it stand out—you can temporarily override this setting. The trick is to ⌘-drag the icon to free it from the magnetic pole of the invisible grid.

The opposite is true, too: If you haven't turned on "Snap to grid", ⌘-dragging makes an icon line up like a good soldier.

2-18   Custom Icons

There's no need to look at a boring blue folder image for your "Hot Projects" folder when you could instead be looking at an actual hot projects folder, as shown in Figure 2-14. Fortunately, Mac OS X is perfectly happy to accept new icons that you draw or paste yourself.

The first step in customizing a file or folder icon is to locate a set of icons that you'd like to use. If you're truly talented, you can create your own using your favorite graphics program or a specialized icon-making program like Iconographer, *www.mscape.com/products/iconographer.html.*

Figure 2-14:
Top: The basic blue Aqua folder is probably fine for most things, but when you really want a folder to stand out, give it a custom icon.

Bottom: To paste a custom icon, open a Get Info box for both the original item and the icon you'd like it to adopt. Click the custom icon, copy it, and then paste it onto the boring one.

If, on the other hand, you have as much artistic talent as a block of cement, just head out to the Internet to scour for icons to add to your collection. You'll find thousands of ready-made icons at, for example, *www.xicons.com* and *www.iconfactory.com.*

Start by clicking the icon you wish to customize in the Finder. Choose File→Get Info to open the Get Info window. Then click the icon whose picture you'd like to swipe (one that you downloaded, for example) and again choose File→Get Info. Position the two Get Info windows so that you can see both of them, as shown in Figure 2-14 at bottom.

To replace the standard icon with your selected custom icon, click once on the small icon in the Get Info window for the custom icon (bottom right in Figure 2-14). The icon sprouts a small blue glow to show that it's selected. Now choose Edit→Copy. Click into the *original* icon's Get Info window, click the small icon image, and choose Edit→Paste. You should see the new custom icon replace the standard icon. Close both Get Info windows. Your new custom icon appears in all its glory in the Finder.

If you ever change your mind, open the Get Info window for the customized folder, click the icon, and press the Delete key.

2-19   Nixing Zoom Effects

In the Finder, when you double-click a document or program, you see, just for a fraction of a second, a little animation—an expanding square shows you that the file is opening.

Somewhere deep inside the extremely busy Mac fan, however, a little birdie is saying: "I'm waiting for half a second about 20 times a day. Over the course of my lifetime, I'll have spent an entire afternoon just waiting for opening window animations!"

If that's your reaction, you can give it the axe in either of these two ways:

• Use Terminal, the Unix access program described on page 5.

• Download the free program called TinkerTool (available at *www.bresink.de/osx/TinkerTool2.html*) and click a couple of buttons.

The latter method, of course, is more user-friendly, but doesn't give you nearly the same rush of power as the Terminal method.

Note: These two alternative methods also apply to the following two hints, too.

In any case, if you decide to proceed with Terminal, start by opening the program (it's in Applications→Utilities). At the % symbol, type this:

```
defaults write com.apple.finder ZoomRects -bool no
```

Press Enter at the end of the line.

For more information on the "defaults" command, see page 5—or, in Terminal (page 5), type *man defaults* and then press Enter. This command opens the "manual" (man) pages for the command, so that you can learn in greater detail how it works. In any case, back to the task at hand: Quit Terminal (File→Quit).

All you have to do now is restart the Finder. You can do that either by logging out and logging in again, or by choosing →Force Quit, clicking Finder, and clicking Relaunch. Now, sure enough, whenever you open an icon, the animated zoom effect is gone.

If, upon reaching retirement age, you decide that you have time for the animation again, repeat the Terminal command, but replace *no* with *yes*.

2-20   A Quit Menu in the Finder

The Finder may start up automatically each time you log in, but behind the scenes, it's nothing more than a standard Mac OS X program. It may not appear to have a Quit command, but you can indeed quit the Finder when you need just a little bit more memory or computer horsepower for, say, some 3-D graphical battle simulator.

There are a number of different ways to quit the Finder—force quitting it, for example. But if you find yourself wanting to quit the Finder with any regularity, the simplest way is to add a Quit menu item at the bottom of the Finder's Finder menu (Figure 2-15). Here's how to go about it:

Open Terminal (which is in your Applications→Utilities folder), and type:

```
defaults write com.apple.finder QuitMenuItem -bool yes
```

Press Enter and restart the Finder, exactly as described in Figure 2-15.

Now, low and behold, you can press ⌘-Q (or choose Finder→Quit Finder) whenever you want to quit the Finder. When you need the Finder back, a simple click on its Dock icon revives it.

Figure 2-15:
You can quit the Finder just like any other program. And by the way: To remove the Quit menu item, repeat the Terminal command described in this hint, but replace yes with no.

2-21 Showing Hidden Files

Mac OS X is a massive operating system composed of thousands of little files scattered all over your hard drive. So why haven't you ever seen them? Because Apple sets Mac OS X to hide them in the folders that contain them (such as the Unix folders *bin, etc,* and *usr*). If you believe in corporate transparency—or if you have some advanced troubleshooting to do—you can make these files and folders visible in the Finder at all times.

To make them all appear, open the Terminal program (in Applications→Utilities) and type this, followed by Enter:

```
defaults write com.apple.finder AppleShowAllFiles -bool yes
```

The next time you log in, you'll see an amazing number of formerly hidden files and folders.

If these objects are clogging up your screen, you can hide them by repeating the Terminal command, this time replacing *yes* with *no*.

2-22 Printing Finder Windows I

Annoyingly enough, Mac OS X doesn't include a feature to easily print the contents of a Finder window. That's a crushing disappointment to people who like to print little table of contents pages for their CD cases, for example. But you can work around that omission with any of three methods.

The first method is simple. Just open the folder whose contents you wish to print. Highlight everything inside the window (press ⌘-A for the Select All command), copy the selection (⌘-C), and then switch to a word processor and paste (⌘-V). A tidy little list of the original window's contents appears, ready for you to edit, format, and print out. (You might want to add the name of the folder at the very top.)

2-23   Printing Finder Windows II

The copy-and-paste method described in the previous hint creates only a list of icon names—not sizes, dates, and so on. If you want to print out more information about a Finder window, you can use Terminal (page 5).

Open it up, and at the % prompt, type *cd* and then a space. Now drag the folder whose contents you would like to print straight *off the desktop* and into the Terminal window—a great shortcut for telling Terminal, "I'm talking about *this*"—and press Enter.

At the next prompt, type *ls | lpr* (create the vertical bar by pressing Shift-backslash), and then press Enter. Presto: A list of the window's contents starts spewing out of your printer.

2-24   Printing Finder Windows III

The Terminal method described in the previous hint is reliable, but not exactly effortless.

Fortunately, there's a method of printing window contents that's as complete as the Terminal method but as easy as the copy-and-paste method. Just download PrintWindow from *www.swssoftware.com.*

Once you've installed the program, you can drag-and-drop a folder onto PrintWindow's Dock icon and let it rip. The program lets you print full information (name, type, size, modified date) *or* names only, and you can specify how many columns print out. If you print lots of folder windows, PrintWindow is worth every penny of the $10 suggested donation.

2-25   Undo

Red alert: You just deleted the novel you've been working on since 1982. Panic-elimination move: Just choose Edit –> Undo, or press ⌘-Z; the Finder undoes your last operation.

This feature applies to most activities (renaming folders, moving a file or folder, duplicating an object), but not all. You can't undo a change from icon view to list view, for example. Most importantly, while you *can* undo moving an object into the Trash, you *cannot* undo emptying the Trash! Once it's emptied, everything is gone for good. Caveat emptier.

2-26   Open Files from the Trash

Once you've moved a file to the Trash, Mac OS X won't let you open it. If you double-click such a file, you're instructed to drag it out of the Trash first—a real hassle if the *reason* you're double-clicking it is to find out what the thing *is,* and therefore whether or not it should be trashed.

Fortunately, you can trick Mac OS X into letting you open a document while it's still in the Trash: Just drag it onto the Dock icon of a program that can open it. (Alternatively, Control-click the file's icon and choose "Open with," and then a program's name, from the contextual menu.)

Navigating the Finder

The Finder offers a variety of ways to navigate the various windows and menus on your screen. Some, like clicking, are obvious. Others, such as the hints in this section, are less obvious.

2-27 Keyboard Shortcuts

When you're typing up a storm, the six inches from your keyboard to your mouse can feel like six miles. To help keep your hands in one place, Apple has provided some keyboard shortcuts for the Finder:

- In the Finder, ⌘-1, -2, and -3 switch the window to icon view, list view, and column view, respectively.

- If you press ⌘-' (next to 1 on the keyboard), the Finder cycles among its open windows. The Finder treats the desktop itself as a window, so if you've got three open windows, you actually have to repeat the keystroke four times to return to the first one.

Tip: Better yet, this trick works in *any* program, not just the Finder.

- In list view, if you press the right arrow key, the Finder expands a selected folder's flippy triangle, revealing the files and folders inside it. If you press the left arrow key, the Finder collapses it again (Figure 2-5).

- If you press ⌘-delete, the Finder throws your selected item(s) in the Trash.

- If you press Shift-⌘-delete, the Finder empties the Trash.

- If you press ⌘-K, the Finder brings up the Connect to Server dialog box.

- If you press Shift-⌘ and the first letter of certain important Mac OS X folders, you jump directly to that folder: C for the Computer window, H for your Home folder, A for the Applications folder, F for the Favorites folder, and so on. (Inspect the Go menu if you need reminders.)

2-28 The Multibutton Mouse

Apple has long held that only one mouse button is required with a Macintosh. But once you've used a mouse with more than one button and a scroll wheel, you'll wonder what kind of Kool-Aid the company has been drinking all these years.

Happily, Mac OS X allows you to use two-button mice with scroll wheels. You don't even need to install software drivers; almost any USB mouse works right off the bat, although the scroll wheel probably won't work in your Classic programs.

Most of the time, right-clicking something on the screen is the same as Control-clicking it—that is, it makes a contextual menu appear.

Note: If you want to use *more* than two buttons, you can buy a multibutton mouse from Macally, Logitech, or Microsoft, all of which make drivers for Mac OS X. Or you can try a generic mouse from some random PC-mouse company in combination with a shareware driver like USB Overdrive (*www.usboverdrive.com*).

2-29   Secrets of the Scrolling Mouse

If you've invested in a non-Apple mouse that has a little scroll wheel on the top, a world of shortcuts and conveniences awaits you. For example:

- You can highlight commands in an open menu just by spinning the scroll wheel to move up or down the commands. (Then *select* a command by clicking or pressing Return or Enter.)

- In the Finder, pressing Option while you scroll turbocharges the scrolling—now you can jump half a page at a time, instead of a few lines at a time.

- If you press Shift, you can often make the scroll wheel scroll a window horizontally instead. This surprising trick works in, for example, the Finder, Microsoft Excel, the Desktop panel of System Preferences, and the Open or Save dialog boxes for certain programs.

2-30   Scrolling Diagonally

You probably know already that you can scroll a Finder window either vertically or horizontally, using the corresponding scroll bars. What you may not know is that in list or icon views, there's an invisible, third scroll bar—a diagonal one—that can be handy when you want to find a folder or file in one corner of the window and you don't want to use two scroll bars to do it.

The trick: Option-⌘-drag inside the window, as shown in Figure 2-16.

Figure 2-16:
How to scroll without the scroll bars? Press Option-⌘ and drag. The cursor changes into a hand, and the window scrolls—in any direction—as you move the mouse.

2-31   Canceling a Drag-and-Drop

Suppose you're dragging some icon across the screen—and halfway through the operation, you decide you don't want to drop it? You could, of course, mouse back and drop where you started.

But life's too short. It's much easier to press the Esc key (in the upper-left corner of your keyboard) while dragging, *then* release the mouse button. A collapsing rectangle shows you the icon returning to its original location—no harm done.

2-32   Opening the Home Folder

Need to get to your Home folder in a hurry? Sure, you can press Shift-⌘-H, but that's for sissies. The power way: Click the desktop, and then press ⌘-up arrow. (⌘-up arrow always means, "Take me to the folder that *contains* this one." Remember that in Mac OS X, the Desktop is nothing more than a folder inside your Home folder. So pressing ⌘-up arrow, as it turns out, is perfectly consistent.)

This trick is even more useful when you're not already in the Finder. From within some program, for example, you can almost always see some piece of the desktop, so you're just one mouse click and a keystroke away from Home.

2-33   Jumping Directly to Folders

Like a dog digging for a bone, you may find yourself sometimes rifling through a lot of dirt to reach buried folders. If you need to access some of them frequently, you'll be growling unhappily from dawn to dusk. Shed some hassle by using the following hint.

Choose Go→Go to Folder (or press Shift-⌘-G). In the sheet that rolls down from the Finder window's title bar, start typing the *path* to the folder. (The path is the sequence of folder icons you would have to double-click to get to a certain file, separated by slashes. Here's an example: *Macintosh HD/Users/chris/Pictures/Mount Rushmore.jpg.*)

Of course, you'd have to be crazy to type all of that every time you wanted to find a folder—and you'd have to have a photographic memory, too, to remember the precise spelling of each folder name. Fortunately, Mac OS X lets you use electronic shorthand. All you have to do is type a couple of letters and then press Tab—or just wait a moment—to make Mac OS X autocomplete that segment of the path.

If, for example, you want to reach Hard Drive→Library→WebServer→Documents, type */Lib* followed by a Tab to make the Finder autocomplete *rary/* for you. Type *Web* (and then hit Tab), and *Server/* appears. Finally, type *Do* (and then Tab, and the full path to the folder now appears. When you press Enter, the Finder opens the specified folder for you, waiting in its own window.

Aliases

Highlighting an icon and then choosing File→Make Alias (or pressing ⌘-L), generates an *alias,* a specially branded duplicate of the original icon (see Figure 2-17 at top). It's not a duplicate of the *file*—just of the *icon;* therefore it requires negligible storage space. When you double-click the alias, the original file opens. Even if you rename the alias, rename the original file, move the alias (even to a different drive), and move the original (on the same drive only), double-clicking the alias still opens the original icon.

Because you can create as many aliases as you want of a single file, aliases let you, in effect, stash that file in many different folder locations simultaneously.

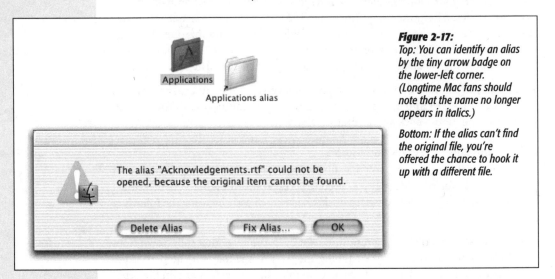

Figure 2-17:
Top: You can identify an alias by the tiny arrow badge on the lower-left corner. (Longtime Mac fans should note that the name no longer appears in italics.)

Bottom: If the alias can't find the original file, you're offered the chance to hook it up with a different file.

2-34   Aliases by Dragging

The only problem with creating an alias by using the Make Alias command is that you wind up with the word *alias* on the end of the file name. If you want the thing to look halfway decent, you're now committed to the tedious task of backspacing over that little suffix. You can also create an alias by Control-clicking a normal icon and choosing Make Alias from the contextual menu that appears, but once again, you get the word *alias* on the resulting alias.

Fortunately, you can avoid the whole issue by getting into the habit of creating an alias by Option-⌘-dragging the original icon out of its window. Aliases you create this way lack the word *alias* on the file name.

2-35   Finding the Original

Mac OS X makes it easy to find the file to which an alias "points" without actually having to open it. Just highlight the alias and then choose File→Show Original (⌘-R). Mac OS X immediately displays the original file, sitting patiently in its folder, wherever that may be.

2-36   An Alias of Your Home Folder

For quick access, you might want to add an alias of your Home folder to another folder—or lots of other folders. Alas, when your Home folder is highlighted, the File→Make Alias option is grayed out.

The solution: ⌘-Option-drag your Home folder out of its window. Presto: An alias is born.

Note: This workaround lets you create aliases of *any* folder that doesn't allow alias creation via the menu.

The Finder Toolbar

At the top of every Finder window is a row of navigation and function icons. One click on any of these icons takes you directly to the corresponding disk or folder or triggers the corresponding command.

The first time you run Mac OS X, for example, you'll find these icons on the toolbar:

- **Back, Forward.** As you've probably noticed, the Mac OS X Finder works something like a Web browser. Only a single window remains open as you navigate the various folders on your hard drive.

  The Back button returns you to whichever folder you were just looking at. (Instead of clicking Back, you can also press ⌘-[, or choose Go→Back—particularly handy if the toolbar is hidden.)

  The Forward button springs to life only after you've used the Back button. Clicking it (or pressing ⌘-]) returns you to the window you just backed out of.

Tip: The Back button is also how you return to the window you were in *before* you used the Finder's Search bar.

- **View controls.** The three tiny buttons next to the Forward button switch the current window into icon, list, or column view, respectively.
- **Computer, Home, Favorites, Applications.** Click these buttons to open the corresponding folders.
- **Search.** This is your Find command. It lets you pinpoint a certain icon within this window (or within any of its folders).

(If you don't see the toolbar at all, choose View→Show Toolbar.)

2-37 Removing or Shrinking the Toolbar

If you're desperate for screen space, you can eliminate the toolbar with one click—on the white, oval toolbar button in the upper-right corner. You can also hide the toolbar by choosing View→Hide Toolbar or pressing ⌘-B. (The same keystroke, or choosing View→Show Toolbar, brings it back.)

But you don't have to do without the toolbar altogether. If its consumption of screen space is your main concern, you may prefer to simply collapse it, which deletes the pictures but preserves the text buttons.

To make it so, choose View→Customize Toolbar. The dialog box that appears offers a Show pop-up menu at the bottom. It lets you choose picture-buttons, with Icon Only, or, for the greatest space conservation, Text Only. You can see the results without even closing the dialog box. (Figure 2-18 illustrates the three possible arrangements.)

Click Done or press Enter to make your changes stick.

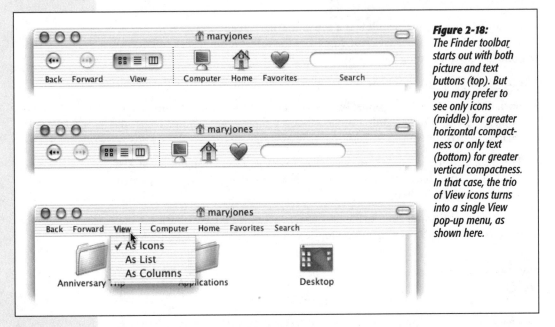

Figure 2-18:
The Finder toolbar starts out with both picture and text buttons (top). But you may prefer to see only icons (middle) for greater horizontal compactness or only text (bottom) for greater vertical compactness. In that case, the trio of View icons turns into a single View pop-up menu, as shown here.

2-38   Customizing the Toolbar

If you want to improve your workflow, or if you just like to put your personal stamp on everything in sight, you can customize the Finder's toolbar.

To customize your toolbar, open a Finder window and choose View→Customize Toolbar. Alternatively, Control-click the toolbar itself and choose Customize Toolbar from the contextual menu, or just Shift-click the toolbar button in the upper-right corner of the window.

In any case, the Customize Toolbar window now appears (Figure 2-19). It offers some commonly used tools, including the Path pop-up menu (which displays the path to a selected item), Delete (which tosses a selected item in the Trash), and Get Info (which opens the Get Info window for a selected item). Drag the icons you want to the toolbar, and add separators if you want them, too. Click Done when you're finished setting things up.

You can also add the icons of your own files, folders, programs, and disks to the toolbar, making it something like a miniature, secondary Dock. (The one key difference: the toolbar shows all icons at all times.) All you have to do is drag any icon onto the toolbar to put it there. (This feature is especially useful for programs like StuffIt Expander, because once you've installed a program's icon, you can drag-and-drop files onto it, right there in the toolbar.)

To rearrange the icons on your toolbar, ⌘-drag them horizontally; the others scoot around to make room.

Finally, you can remove icons from the toolbar by ⌘-dragging them away from it. If, for instance, you never use the Favorites menu, just drag it to the Trash (the wastebasket icon becomes a pair of scissors while you're dragging).

Note: Technically, you have to press the ⌘ key only while you're dragging *Apple's* toolbar icons—the ones that *you* put on the toolbar don't require you to press any key. Still, it's probably worth learning to press the ⌘ key *every* time you move or remove the toolbar icon, to spare yourself that moment of confusion: "Which method should I use? Is this my icon or Apple's?"

Figure 2-19:
While this window is open, you can add additional icons to the toolbar by dragging them into place from the gallery before you. You can also remove icons by dragging them up or down off the toolbar, or rearrange them by dragging them horizontally.

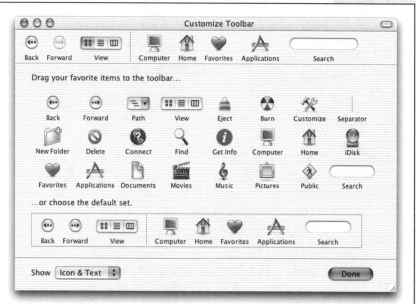

2-39   Folders on the Toolbar

When you click a folder on your toolbar, the Finder opens that folder in the *current* window. That's kind of a bummer if you really wanted to open the folder in a new, second Finder window.

For example, if want to remember whether you copied an item from your Kitchen Renovation folder into your Stalled Projects folder—which you use so often, you keep it on the toolbar—it'd be nice to leave Kitchen Renovation open *while* you check Stalled Projects.

The trick is to press ⌘ as you click Stalled Projects. Doing so makes the Finder open it in a new window.

In fact, there's a third possibility, too: If you press Option instead of ⌘, the folder opens in a new window while *closing* the old window. (It's a lot like holding down no keys at all, except that you aren't just summoning the contents of folder B into the existing window of folder A. You'll notice the difference in the new window's size, shape, and choice of view.)

2-40   Heavily Used Toolbar Icons

Often, you'll find that a certain window isn't wide enough to display all of the icons you've stashed up on the toolbar. That's a good argument for keeping tools that you use most often, like Delete or Path, on the left end of your toolbar (Figure 2-20).

Fortunately, keep in mind that the little >> at the right end of the toolbar is your friend. It's a pop-up menu that reveals whatever icons are hidden because the window is too narrow.

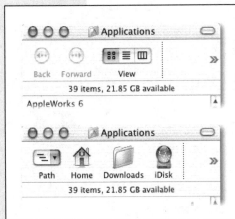

Figure 2-20:
The toolbar on top isn't very useful when you open a new window that cuts off your favorite tools—Path, Home, Downloads, and iDisk. The toolbar below, however, has the most frequently used icons on the left, making them accessible even in narrow Finder windows.

2-41   The Permanence of Server Icons

If you, a network maven, regularly connect to a couple of servers, consider dragging their icons onto the toolbar for easy access. In fact, you can set the icons to automatically log you in, so that a single click connects you. Here's how to go about it:

1. In the Finder, press ⌘-K.

   The Connect to Server dialog box appears. If your network is working properly, you'll see a list of the other computers on it at the left side of the window.

2. Select the server you want, and then click Connect.

   A new window opens.

3. **Enter your user name and password.**

   This is the name and password that were set up for your account on the *other* machine—the one you're connecting to.

4. **Click Options.**

   This is the most important move.

5. **In the Options box, turn on Add Password to Keychain, and then click OK.**

   You return to the Connect to Server dialog box, having just told Mac OS X to memorize your password so that you'll never have to type it again.

6. **Click Connect.**

   The icon of the other computer's shared disk or folder—the server—now shows up on your desktop. (See Chapter 6 for more on networking.)

7. **Drag the server's icon from the desktop to the toolbar.**

   From now on, when you want to connect to another machine, just click that icon. One click does the trick—Mac OS X remembers your name and password.

Note: When the server isn't online at the moment, the icon appears as a question mark. (The same ? icon appears for removable disks like CDs and external hard drives that aren't connected at the moment.)

Working with Files and Folders

When you're not actually working on a document, you're probably manipulating one or more files or folders in the Finder. The following hints will help you get the most out of your file and folder manipulation time.

2-42 Copying by Dragging

You can drag icons from one folder to another, from one drive to another, from a drive to a folder on another drive, and so on. Unfortunately, understanding when the Mac *copies* a dragged icon and when it just *moves* the icon bewilders many a beginner. Here's the scheme:

- Dragging from one folder to another (on the same disk) *moves* the icon.

- Dragging from one disk (or disk partition) to another *copies* the folder or file.

- Option-dragging *copies* the icon instead of moving it. Doing so within a single folder produces a duplicate of the file called "[Whatever its name was] copy."

- Dragging an icon from one disk to another while pressing ⌘ *moves* the file or folder, in the process deleting it from the original disk. (Press ⌘ just *after* you start to drag.)

Note: This method is not recommended for moving batches of files. The system deletes the originals after the move is completed. If the power goes out during the operation, you have no way of knowing when that deleting will occur, and you could lose files as a result. For moving large selections, it's better to copy the files and manually delete the originals, so that they remain intact until it's safe to remove them.

2-43   Copying by Pasting

Instead of copying files by dragging and dropping, as described in the previous hint, you can copy them from one folder to another using the everyday Copy and Paste commands. (This feature has been available in Windows for years—but hey, it's not as though Microsoft has never borrowed anything from the Mac.)

To make it work, highlight one or more icons. Choose Edit→Copy, or press ⌘-C, or Control-click any one of the selected icons and choose Copy from the contextual menu. Either way, you'll note that the command itself changes to reflect what you've selected—"Copy 5 items," for example.

Now open the folder or disk where you want the copies to appear, and then choose Edit→Paste or press ⌘-V. Ta da! You have copied the selection to the new location. (You can't *cut* and paste icons—you can only copy them.)

2-44   Copying System Folders

If you've tweaked your machine to the moon and back, you may find yourself wishing that you could back up your System folder to preserve all of your ingenious changes. But if you want to recreate your tweaked world on another machine or drive, Apple thwarts you: Mac OS X won't let you drag a System folder to another drive to create a copy.

CarbonCopyCloner, however, will. (You can download it from *www.bombich.com/software/ccc.html*.) This program takes advantage of a number of built-in Unix programs to create an exact clone of one drive on another drive.

2-45   Spring-Loaded Folders

Here's a common dilemma: You want to drag an icon not just into a folder, but into a folder nested *inside* that folder. This awkward challenge would ordinarily require you to open the folder, open the inner folder, drag the icon in, and then close both of the windows you had opened. As you can imagine, the process is even messier if you want to drag an icon into a sub-subfolder or even a *sub*-sub-subfolder.

Fortunately, Mac OS X's spring-loaded folders feature saves you all of that hassle. As shown in Figure 2-21, it lets you drag an icon into a deeply nested folder with a single mouse movement. When you finally release the mouse, all the windows except the last one close automatically. You've neatly placed the icon into the core of the nested folders.

All of this means that you can navigate around without a lot of clicking; just drag an icon over a folder, wait, drag to the next subfolder, wait, and so on. It also means you don't need to know where you want to file something *before* you head to the Finder.

2-49 Weird Sorts

You have a report cunningly named "The Boss Will Fire Me If I Don't Finish This Report." If you file it in your Documents folder, and you sort the contents of that folder alphabetically (by clicking the Name column heading), the report could get lost in the fray.

You can force it to the top of the list by adding punctuation in front of the file name. (Heads up if you're a Mac OS 9 convert: In that system, if you added punctuation in front of a folder or file name, the item would move to the *bottom* of a Finder window sorted alphabetically.)

Most punctuation marks (and spaces) force an icon to the *top* of a file list. If you do want to force something to the bottom, precede its name with one of these characters: μ (Option-M); π (Option-P); Ω (Option-Z),   (Shift-Option-K). This list of symbols, as shown here, indicates the proper sorting order—that is, something named Ω Fish Heads appears higher in the list then something called   Fish Heads.

2-50 Editing Multiple File Names

If your job is to rename a whole bunch of files, here are a few thoughts that can make your life easier:

- Put the window into list or column view. Click the first icon. Press Enter to open the renaming box, edit the file's name (use the arrow keys to move around within the name), press Enter, press the down arrow to highlight the next icon, press Enter to open its renaming box, and so on. Lather, rinse, repeat.

- The trouble with that method is that each time you press Enter after editing a name, the icon might jump around in the list to maintain its new alphabetical position, which can drive you crazy.

  The solution, of course, is to put the list view into a sorting order that isn't alphabetical. Click Date Modified, for example, to sort the list by date. Now the file names you edit won't have any effect on the sorting order.

- If you work on, for example, computer books—or any other endeavor in which you must frequently rename or renumber batches of graphics, chapters, and so on, invest in A Better Finder Rename. This amazing shareware program can slice and dice file names in any conceivable way, en masse: adding or removing sequence numbers, searching and replacing text in a batch of file names, adding or truncated in prefixes or suffixes, and so on. (You can download it from *www.publicspace.net/ABetterFinderRename*, among other places.)

2-51 Folder Action Scripts

Folder action scripts are a fascinating and rarely explored feature of AppleScript, the Mac's built-in programming language. These special scripts let you monitor certain folders—and trigger automatic events accordingly.

For example, Mac OS X comes with a script that can play a certain sound whenever somebody adds new icons to a watched folder—a handy feature when, say, you've shared a folder on a network and you want to be alerted whenever some other network citizen deposits something in your Repaid IOUs folder.

Before you can run a folder action script, you must place the Script Menu icon on the system toolbar. To do that, open your Applications→AppleScript folder; inside, double-click the icon called Script Menu.Menu. As if by magic, a new icon called Script Menu appears in your toolbar; it resembles a piece of paper rolled at either end (see hint 4-13 for more information about the Script menu). You're ready to begin.

1. **From the Script menu, choose Folder Actions→Enable Folder Actions.**

   You've just flipped the master switch.

2. **From the Script menu, choose Folder Actions→Attach Script to Folder.**

   A box appears with a list of three predefined scripts. *Add* notifies you when any icon is put into this folder and offers you the chance to inspect it. If you attach the folder action to a shared folder in a network, you'll be notified whenever a co-worker drops anything into it.

   Close closes all windows that come from folders you may have opened from the special one (the one with the attached script)—a nice way to keep your desktop tidy. (For example, if you opened the Ohio, Connecticut, and New York folders, they all close when you close the America folder.)

   And *Open* makes a dialog box spring onto the screen whenever you try to open a selected folder, revealing whatever comments you've added in that folder's Get Info dialog box (see hint 2-53)—"Waiting for customer response," "In final bid," "Leftover from 3/03 hard drive cleanup," or whatever. It's a really great way to leave notes for yourself regarding the purpose of each folder you create.

3. **Click the script you want, and then click OK.**

   The Choose a Folder dialog box appears. The Mac wants to know which folder you want the script to apply to.

4. **Navigate to the folder in question, click it, and then click Choose.**

   That's all there is to it. From now on, when you open the folder or when somebody drops an icon into it, a sound will play, folders will be collapsed, or a dialog box will appear to reveal its comments (depending on the script you chose).

   To remove a folder action, go to the Script menu and choose Folder Actions→Remove Folder Actions. You'll be guided through the process of specifying which folder you want the action attached to.

You can write your own scripts, too. For more information on Folder Action scripts, see Apple's help page at: *www.apple.com/applescript/folder_actions.*

2-52   Renaming System Folders

Mac OS X gives you lots of freedom in lots of areas, but it's fairly stern about one: You're not allowed to rename any of the key system folders—Applications, Library, and so on, nor the preinstalled folders inside your Home folder (like Movies, Pictures, Documents, and Music). You can try renaming them using the Terminal program, but bad digital things may happen when your programs go looking for folder names that no longer exist.

But in fact, you can safely rename any folder (Figure 2-24)—if you know the secret.

The following technique gives you custom names in the Finder only (other programs and their features, like Open or Save dialog boxes, don't show the new names). If you're still game, the ritual goes like this:

Figure 2-24:
"Flix" instead of "Movies"? "Messy Desktop" instead of "Desktop"? "Snaps" instead of "Pictures"? What kind of evil is afoot here? Just you and your handy-dandy folder-name hacking.

1. In the Finder, open The System→Library→CoreServices→SystemFolderLocalizations folder. Inside, click the en.lproj folder once.

   This folder contains the file that stores System folders' names. Of course, if English is not your native language, open the folder that matches your language.

2. Choose File→Get Info. In the Get Info dialog box, click the triangle next to Ownership & Permissions.

   The dialog box expands.

3. Click the small lock icon (so that it appears unlocked). Using the Owner pop-up menu, choose your account name.

If a password dialog box appears to confirm that you are indeed an Administrator account holder (page 11), enter your password and then click OK. In any case, the point is that you have just seized control of a folder that Mac OS X normally keeps to itself.

4. **Open the en.lproj folder. Inside, you'll find a file called SystemFolderLocalizations.strings. Drag this icon onto the icon of TextEdit.**

   You'll find TextEdit inside your Applications folder; see page 5 for an important primer on the procedure you're about to follow.

   In any case, you just opened what appears to be a document filled with computer code, starting with this:

   ```
   /* Top-level folders */
   "System" = "System";
   "Applications" = "Applications";
   "Library" = "Library";
   ```

   What you're actually seeing is a little table. Behind the scenes, Mac OS X maintains a list of the original names of certain folders (on the left side of this table), along with the names you actually see in the Finder (on the right side).

   Again, the name on the left side of each pairing is the actual name of the folder; do not change the left side! You can change the name on the right side to anything you like.

   So much for the main system folders. What about the folders inside your Home folder?

   Look for a section heading called "Folders in user homes." If you don't see it, you need to add a file named .localized in each folder that you wish to rename (Desktop, Movies, Pictures, and so on).

   You can create these files in Terminal. Open Applications→Utilities→Terminal. Type this—*touch ~/Desktop/.localized*—and then press Enter to add the file to the Desktop folder. Repeat the command with each remaining folder. Log out and log back in. When you reopen the SystemFolderLocalizations.strings file, you now have the "Folders in user homes" section, which you can edit as described above.

5. **Once you've made all your edits, save the file.**

   When TextEdit warns you about permissions on the file, click Overwrite to save your changes.

6. **Log out and log back in, open a Finder window, and discover your folders' new vanity plates.**

Note: Your custom names won't show up if you have the Finder preferences set to "Always show file extensions."

2-53   The Return of Labels

Icon labels were among the most beloved Mac OS 9 features. You could easily attach customized text (and colors) to files and folders, flagging them as "Unfinished," "Back me up," "Done," or whatever. Labels are gone in Mac OS X, but you can achieve much the same effect using *comments*.

Comments—notes you can append to a folder or files—show up in the Finder's list view (Figure 2-25), and in Get Info and Inspector dialog boxes. They can help you identify a group of files by client ("Duct Tape Marketing Council"), or by importance ("Defcon 1"), or by any other category ("Siberia Vacation Photos," "Hawaiian Klezmer songs, rare").

Once you've added comments, you can sort them alphabetically, allowing you to see a whole batch of "Duct Tape Marketing Council" MP3s together. Figure 2-25 tells you how to append comments.

Figure 2-25:
Open a list view window showing the files you wish to label. Choose View→Show View Options and make sure the Comments box is turned on. Now you can add comments to one file at a time by highlighting it, choosing File→Get Info, expanding the Comments triangle, and typing your remarks into the box.

This trick works reasonably well for a small number of files, but it's quite tedious if you wish to put the same label on 3,500 files. Fortunately, Mac fan David Stewart has written a brief AppleScript he calls Commen'Tater, which adds comments to a bunch of files in one shot.

Open Script Editor (it's in Applications→AppleScript), and in the lower box, type up the following code (indents are not important):

```
on open (itemList)
  display dialog "Set this comment for all selected files:"
```

```
default answer ""
  set the comment_string to the text returned of the result
  repeat with eachOne in itemList
  tell application "Finder"
  set the comment of eachOne to comment_string
  end tell
  end repeat
end open
```

Choose File→Save, choose Application from the Format pop-up menu, type a name like *Commen'Tater,* and save the file onto your desktop.

Next time you want to label a bunch of icons, drag them onto the new application icon. After a few seconds, a dialog box asks for the comment you'd like to attach to all of the files. Enter your text, press Enter or Return, and marvel as the "labels" appear in the Comments column.

Save the script to your desktop as a compiled program.

Note: If you don't think this trick quite matches the utility of Mac OS 9's labels, which allowed you to readily attach identifying text and color to files and folders, see hint 14-2 about Labels X.

2-54 Unused Languages: Your Free Megabytes

Many Mac OS X programs let you work in a number of languages. iPhoto, for example, comes with more than ten languages, which is part of the reason it takes up a whopping 60 or more megabytes of your hard drive.

You can recover some of that real estate by deleting the languages you don't need. You can slim down iPhoto, for example, to just under 13 MB by deleting everything but English. Not bad for two minutes' worth of work.

Before you proceed, note that this operation involves removing files from inside a software package. If you're worried about damaging the program you're going to alter, first create a backup copy of it by Option-dragging the application to another spot on your hard drive).

1. **Control-click a program's icon. From the contextual menu, choose Show Package Contents.**

   Many Mac OS X program icons are, in fact, thinly disguised *folders*—and this is how you get into them.

2. **Open the Contents→Resources folder.**

   Inside this folder, you'll probably see a lot of files. You're only interested in folders that end in ".lproj," such as "da.lproj" and "Dutch.lproj." These are the OS X language files.

---

3. Throw away the files for the languages you don't speak. Close all the open windows.

To make sure you've left the application in a healthy state, double-click it once before emptying the Trash. If, for some reason, the application won't run (indicating that you may have dragged out something more than just .lproj files), open the Trash and drag all the files you've removed *back* into the Contents→Resources folder to restore the program (or just reinstate the backup you made).

Desktop Interior Design

One of the great things about the Mac has always been the degree of customization that you can apply to your environment. Icons, sounds, graphics, and color can make your computer truly *your* computer. The following hints will let you go beyond the standard tricks and create a unique operating environment.

2-55   Changing the Screen Behind the Login Window

Behind the initial login screen, the background image is blue with some white arcs running through it in a semicircular pattern. It's very pretty—the first *four thousand times* you look at it.

If you'd like to express your creativity by replacing this background with something groovy and personal, try this technique:

Note: Because you're changing the screen everyone sees before login, this change affects all account holders on the Mac, not just your own account.

---

1. Choose an image you'd like to use.

   Any JPEG or PDF file is fine.

2. In the Finder, open the Library→Desktop Pictures folder.

   A list of the standard Apple desktop images appears. "Aqua Blue.jpg" is the file you want to replace. Drag it out of the folder to a safe place as a backup (or just rename it).

3. Drag your own graphic into the Desktop Pictures folder. Rename your file "Aqua Blue.jpg."

   This sleight-of-hand allows the system to find it during the startup process.

4. Restart the machine.

   Presto: Your new image appears behind your login screen.

2-56   Screen Saver as a Desktop Background

Apple supplies some great photos in its screen savers, especially those in the Beach and Cosmos packs. Problem is, the only obvious way to see the pics is to turn on the screen saver. You can, however, also use any of those images as a desktop background—if you know the secret.

1. **Preview the images to find one that you like.**

   To do that, choose System Preferences→Screen Effects→Screen Effects. Highlight the screen saver that contains the photos you want, and click Test. Moving the mouse ends the test.

2. **In the Finder, open the System→Library→Screen Savers folder.**

   Inside are the actual screen saver modules, beginning with Abstract.slideSaver and Beach.slideSaver.

3. **Control-click the screen saver whose images you want; from the contextual menu, choose Show Package Contents (Figure 2-26).**

   A secret window opens, containing the components of the screen saver (see page 3 for details).

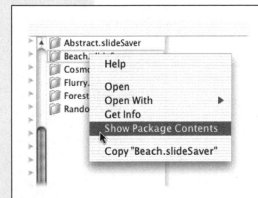

Figure 2-26:
Here's how you raid the Mac OS X screen savers to swipe its photos.

4. **Open the Contents→Resources folder.**

   Inside are the actual JPEG files used by the screen saver. To preview them, use the Finder's column view preview pane (hint 2-8).

5. **Drag any (or all) of the images to your Home→Pictures folder.**

   Because the System folder is always locked, Mac OS X automatically copies them instead of moving them.

6. **Choose →System Preferences. Click the Desktop icon. In the Collection pop-up, choose Pictures folder.**

   You've just recycled the screen saver photos for use as your desktop wallpaper.

2-57 Extra-Large Desktop Icons

There's no good reason to use enormous desktop icons, as shown in Figure 2-27. But there's no good reason to bungee jump, either, and tons of people do it.

Figure 2-27:
Mac OS X won't make desktop icons larger than 128 pixels square (that is, about 20 percent the height of an 800 x 600-pixel screen). But you can override that maximum by editing the com.apple.finder.plist file. As long as your monitor is large enough, you can make icons that are visible from outer space.

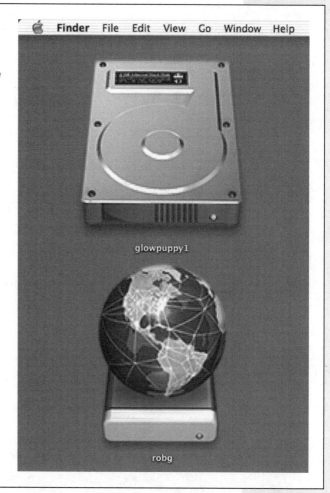

If you, too, hear the siren call of the hacker, here's how to proceed:

1. **Open TextEdit.**

   TextEdit is a stripped-down word processor in your Applications folder.

2. **Choose File→Open.**

   The Open File dialog box appears.

3. **From the From pop-up menu at the top of the dialog box, choose Home. Then open the Library→Preferences→com.apple.finder.plist file.**

One of Mac OS X's secret preference files opens before you, looking like gibberish.

4. **Choose Edit→Find→Find Panel. Type *desktopview* and click Next.**

TextEdit highlights part of a line that reads:

```
<key>DesktopViewOptions</key>
```

A few lines below that, two lines read something like:

```
<key>IconSize</key>
<integer>64</integer>
```

The second line might have a different number than 64.

5. **No matter what the number is, change it to the icon pixel size you'd like to use.**

Numbers in even increments of 16 (144, 160, 176…) give the best results. Although there's no theoretical limit, you probably don't want to be the first person to find out what happens if you set the icon size to something greater than the width of your screen.

6. **Save the file and quit TextEdit. Quit and restart the Finder by choosing ⌘→Force Quit→Finder→Relaunch.**

Gape at your new icons.

Note: These babies will disappear if you open the Finder, select the desktop, choose View→Show View Options, and even slightly move the "Icon size" slider.

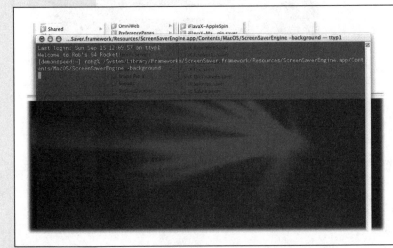

Figure 2-28:
In this picture, the Flurry screen saver is running behind the open Terminal and Finder windows. You can continue to use your machine as you normally would—sort of. The Mac may seem a tad drugged as it tries to divide its time between running the screen saver and performing other tasks.

2-58 Screen Saver as the Finder Background

If you're *really* bored, you can display your screen saver as the Finder background—yes, an animated desktop. It's hours of fun for the whole family!

Start by finding a screen saver you like (using the Screen Effects pane of System Preferences). Then open Terminal (in your Applications→Utilities folder). At the % prompt, type the following on one line, with no added spaces at any point:

```
/System/Library/Frameworks/Screen saver.framework/Resources/
Screen saverEngine.app/Contents/MacOS/Screen saverEngine -
background
```

When you press Enter, the screen saver appears in your Finder, as shown in Figure 2-28.

To end the fun, make the Terminal window active and then press Control-C.

The Dock

The Dock, a central and critical component of Mac OS X, combines several important operating-system functions into a single row of icons across one edge of your screen. It's a program launcher, a program switcher, a document-storage site, an information hub, a floor wax, and a dessert topping!

Seriously, though, the Dock can help simplify your workflow, and you can personalize it to within an inch of its life. The hints in this chapter are designed to make your time with the Dock more productive. And if you can't stand the thing, the last hint explains how to get rid of the Dock completely.

The Dock Makeover

You already know, of course, the basics of the Dock. Any icon you drag onto it is installed there as a large, square button (Figure 3-1). A single click, not a double-

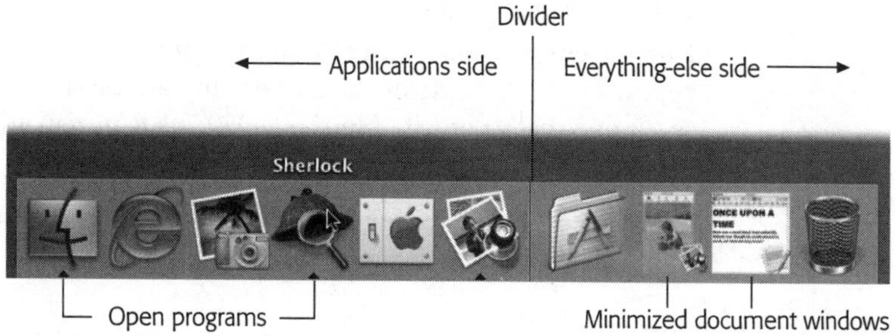

Figure 3-1:
Everything on the left side is an application—a program, in other words. Everything else goes on the right side—files, documents, folders, and disks.

Divider

←— Applications side   Everything-else side —→

Open programs

Minimized document windows

click, opens the corresponding icon. In other words, the Dock is an ideal parking lot for the icons of disks, folders, documents, and programs you frequently access.

The other basic Dock information morsel is that folders and disks are hierarchical. That is, if you click a folder or disk icon on the right side of the Dock and *hold down* the mouse button, a list of the icon's contents sprouts out. This is a hierarchical list, meaning that you can burrow into folders within folders this way. See Figure 3-2 for an illustration.

Tip: To make the pop-up menu appear instantly, just Control-click the Dock icon, or (if you have a two-button mouse) right-click it.

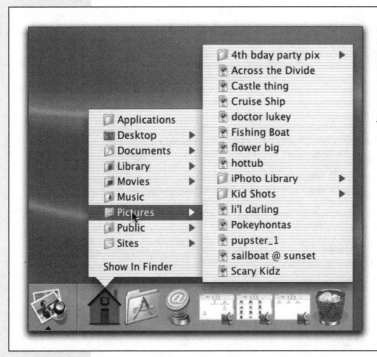

Figure 3-2:
As long as you keep the mouse button pressed, you can burrow into folders within folders—either with the intention of opening a file or folder (by releasing the mouse button as you point), or just to see what's inside.

3-1   Adding Icons

Nobody but you can put icons on the *right* side of the Dock. But program icons appear on the left side of the Dock automatically whenever you open a program (even one that's not listed in the Dock). Its icon remains there for as long as the program is running.

This presents an interesting secondary way to add a program's icon onto your Dock for good, as shown in Figure 3-3.

This also presents a third way to add a program's icon—one that strikes many people by accident. If you drag an open program's Dock icon, even by the tiniest bit, it may become a permanent addition to the Dock. That's because you've just dragged the icon off of the Dock and then back onto it, and as you know, dragging any icon onto the Dock installs it there as a permanent fixture.

Figure 3-3:
Once a program is running, Control-click its Dock icon. If you choose Keep in Dock from the contextual menu, the program's icon stays in the Dock forever…or at least until you drag it out.

3-2   Removing Icons

To remove a program's icon from the Dock, just drag it away from the Dock. (You're not erasing the program—only its Dock representation.) If the program isn't running, the program's icon vanishes in an exciting puff of smoke.

If the program *is* running when you remove its icon, the picture bounces back into the Dock. Ah, but your gesture hasn't been in vain; when you quit the program, the icon vanishes.

3-3   Resizing the Dock

If the Dock takes up too much room on your screen, or if you wish it were larger, Mac OS X offers two ways to change its size.

One way is to choose menu→Dock→Dock Preferences. In the Dock dialog box that appears, drag the slider on the Dock Size bar and the Dock changes size.

The other, much more secret way, is to move your mouse over the Dock's divider bar. The cursor magically becomes a resize bar (Figure 3-4), so that you can drag either up or down to make the Dock grow or shrink. (Its expansion is limited by the edges of your screen, though. If you already have 436 icons installed, they may not have much room to grow.)

Figure 3-4:
To prevent fuzziness of resized Dock icons, Option-drag the divider Dock's divider bar. You've just forced the program to restrict icons to sizes that the programmers have explicitly drawn.

3-4 Hiding the Dock

To retain maximum monitor acreage, you can keep the Dock hidden. This trick is particularly useful if you use the Dock primarily to switch programs and otherwise don't need to see it. It's also a good option to remember when the Dock intrudes upon the windows of Classic programs, which, because they predate Mac OS X, generally aren't smart enough to get out of the way of the Dock.

Choose menu→Dock→Turn Hiding On (or, if time is of the essence, press Option-⌘-D). Choose Turn Hiding Off, or press the same keystroke again, to make it reappear.

Of course, you may not ever need to. Even after it's been hidden, the Dock springs temporarily back into view whenever you move the mouse to its edge of the screen, or whenever you press ⌘-Tab to switch programs.

3-5 Moving the Dock to the Side

The bottom of the screen isn't necessarily the ideal location for the Dock. Because most screens are wider than they are tall, the Dock eats into your limited vertical screen space.

Fortunately, you can rotate it in either of two ways:

- **The indirect way.** From the →Dock submenu, choose "Position on Left," "Position on Right," or "Position on Bottom."

- **The direct way.** While pressing Shift, drag the Dock's divider line, as though it's a handle, directly to the side of the screen you want.

You'll probably find that the right side of your screen works better than the left. Most Mac OS X programs position their document windows against the left edge of the screen, where the Dock and its labels might get in the way.

3-6 The Top-Mounted Dock

Apple provides three standard screen positions for the Dock: left, right, and bottom (see hint 3-5). But that leaves one possible spot unexplored: the top. If you're a Macintosh iconoclast—you know, the kind who uses Curlz MT as your everyday font—you might want to do something wacky like move the Dock to the north edge of your monitor. Here's how:

Tip: Instead of trudging through the following steps, you should know that you can also put that Dock at the top by clicking a single button in TinkerTool, a free program that's available at *www.bresink.de/osx/ TinkerTool2.html.*

The same alternative applies to hints 3-7 through 3-10.

---

1. **Open Terminal.**

   This program is in your Applications→Utilities folder.

2. **At the % prompt, type this:** *defaults write com.apple.Dock orientation top* (and then press Enter).

   See page 5 for an explanation. In this case, you've just issued the magic command that puts the Dock at the top of the screen.

3. **Quit Terminal. Then, to make your change take effect, quit the Dock.**

   One way is simply to log out and then log in again. If you don't have that kind of patience, open Process Viewer (a program in your Applications→Utilities folder). Now sort the list by name (click the Name column) so you can easily find Dock.

   Highlight Dock, and then choose Processes→Quit Process. The Dock quits and restarts—and the Dock is now at the top of your screen. If you ever tire of the effect, you can always move the Dock back to a standard location by Control-clicking its divider bar in choosing, for example, "Position at Right" from the contextual menu.

Note: If you prefer keeping the Dock hidden, move the mouse just to the bottom of the menu bar to make it slide back into view—*not* the very top of the screen

---

3-7 Changing the Minimize Animation

When you minimize a window (hint 3-14), it flies to the Dock using a cute little animated effect. In fact, you have a choice of at least two animated effects: Genie, which looks like Barbara Eden funneling into a bottle; and Scale, which fades smaller and smaller boxes into the corner. (You can find these choices in menu→Dock→ Dock Preferences, or by Control-clicking the Dock's divider bar and choosing Dock Preferences.)

But because you are now an official Mac OS X power user, you're entitled to learn about the secret third animation, entitled Suck In. It makes the window appear to get sucked into the Dock by one corner. It's not hugely different from Genie, but it's a tad faster.

To try it out, open the Terminal program (page 5) and type this:

```
defaults write com.apple.Dock mineffect suck
```

Press Enter, and then quit Terminal. To make your change stick, quit the Dock using Process Viewer, as described in hint 3-6.

Note: To return to one of the original animation styles, choose →Dock→Dock Preferences and click the one you prefer.

3-8   Pinning the Dock to a Corner

You can place the Dock on any edge of the screen, but it's always centered on that edge. If you'd find it less intrusive in a corner, however, or if you like the Trash nestled in a corner, you can "corner" the Dock. Figure 3-5 shows the three possible placements for a Dock and tells you how to move it.

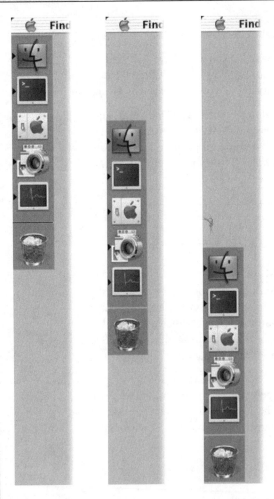

Figure 3-5:
Three placements for a vertical Dock. Yes, some of these look a little bizarre, but hey–it's a free country.

To move the Dock back to the middle, repeat the command described in this hint, but replace the word location with the word middle. Quit and restart the Dock.

Open Terminal (page 5). At the % prompt, type this:

```
defaults write com.apple.Dock pinning location
```

Instead of the word *location*, however, type either *start* or *end* (to push the Dock against the left or right side of the screen, respectively). Press Enter, quit Terminal, and then quit the Dock using Process Viewer, as described in hint 3-6. Presto: Your Dock is left- or right-justified.

3-9   Differentiating Hidden Programs

Pressing ⌘-H (or choosing the Hide command from the menu that bears the front-most program's name) is all well and good—it makes all the windows of the program invisible to get them out of your way. Even when you do that, however, its Dock icon remains fully visible, oblivious to the fact that the program has now been hidden. The result for you is confusion, since it's now harder to remember which programs you've hidden.

With a small settings tweak, however, you can have the Dock display hidden programs with a semi-transparent icon and triangle, as shown in Figure 3-6.

Figure 3-6:
Hidden windows, transparent Dock icon. All is well with the world.

Transparent icons of hidden programs

Open Terminal. At the % prompt, type this:

```
defaults write com.apple.Dock showhidden -bool yes
```

Now press Enter. (See page 5 to find out what you've just done.)

To trigger your change, quit the Dock using Process Viewer, as described in hint 3-6.

To return to the normal look for all icons, repeat the above command but replace *yes* with *no*. Quit and restart the Dock.

3-10   Adding Quit to the Dock's Finder Icon

Hint 2-20 explains how to add a Quit menu command to the Finder. But why stop there? You can also add Quit to the Finder's *Dock* icon, as shown in Figure 3-7, providing yet another way to quit or relaunch the Finder in a jiffy.

Figure 3-7:
When you're absolutely, positively desperate for every last kilobyte of memory, you can quit the Finder just by using this hidden command.

Open Terminal. At the familiar % prompt, type this:

```
defaults write com.apple.Dock QuitFinder -bool yes
```

Press Enter, quit Terminal, and then quit the Dock itself as described in hint 3-6. (See page 5 for details on the *defaults* command that you just used.)

From now on, whenever you want to quit the Dock, Control-click the Finder icon. From the contextual menu, choose Quit. (In times of troubleshooting, at this point you can also press Option to make the command say Relaunch instead of Quit.)

Note: To remove this menu item, repeat the above command but replace *yes* with *no*. Quit and restart the Dock.

3-11 Hide Commands on the Dock

Control-clicking an icon on the Dock brings up a handy contextual menu, but it isn't quite as handy as you might have hoped: It lacks the obvious choices of Hide and Hide Others. These commands are, of course, available in each program's application menu, but they would make more sense in the Dock.

Fortunately, as Figure 3-8 shows, a bit of Terminal editing can make it so.

Figure 3-8:
Usually, the menu that appears when you Control-click a program's Dock icon lists commands like Quit and Show In Finder. But if you want commands like Hide and Hide Others, a trudge to the menus at the top left of your screen is in order.

At least, it is until you add Hide and Hide Others to the contextual menu like this.

This hint requires editing in Terminal (page 5), as follows:

1. **Open Terminal; at the prompt, type the following commands (press Enter after each):**

```
cd /system/Library/CoreServices/Dock.app/Contents/Resources/
English.lproj

sudo cp DockMenus.plist DockMenus.bak
sudo pico DockMenus.plist
```

(Note that the first blob of text should all be on one line, from *cd* all the way to *lproj*.)

The first line switches to the folder that holds the file containing the Dock's contextual menus. The second line backs up that file (after you enter your administrative password). The third line opens the file in a Unix text processor called *pico*.

2. **Once *pico* is open, press Control-W to enter search mode. Then type *process* and press Enter.**

You've just searched for the word *process*. A line appears that looks like this:

```
<key>process</key>
```

3. **By pressing the down-arrow key repeatedly, scroll down about 25 lines until you get to this section of the file:**

```
<dict>
  <key>command</key>
  <integer>1005</integer>
  <key>name</key>
  <string>Show In Finder</string>
</dict>
```

4. **Click after </dict>, press Enter to create a new line, and then insert the following lines. (Remember that you can just copy all of this from the document at *www.macosxhints.com/book/scripts.html*.)**

```
        <dict>
    <key>command</key>
    <integer>1006</integer>
    <key>dynamic</key>
    <integer>0</integer>
    <key>name</key>
    <string>Hide</string>
    </dict>
        <dict>
    <key>command</key>
    <integer>1007</integer>
    <key>dynamic</key>
    <integer>1</integer>
    <key>name</key>
    <string>Hide Others</string>
    </dict>
  <dict>
   <key>command</key>
   <integer>2000</integer>
   <key>separator</key>
   <true/>
  </dict>
```

5. Press Control-O to save the file; press Enter to accept the proposed file name. Press Control-X to quit the *pico* editor.

It was a lot of grisly typing, but the worst is over.

6. To make your change take effect, quit the Dock using Process Viewer, as described in hint 3-6.

You now have Hide and Hide Others items in the contextual menus on your program's Dock icons.

If you Control-click a Dock icon, you can pick Hide to both hide the active program *and* switch to the program whose icon you're clicking.

To choose Hide Others, Control-click an icon; when the contextual menu pops up, press Option, which changes Hide to Hide Others. Everything but the program you're clicking will disappear.

Note: If the Dock isn't working as you'd expect, or if you just want to return to the original contextual menus, proceed like this: Open Terminal, make sure you're in the folder specified in the first line of this hint, and type *sudo cpDockMenus.bak DockMenus.plist*. Then press Enter.

This command replaces the modified file with your backup file. After restarting the Dock again, you're back to Ye Olde Docke.

Working with the Dock

Sure, anyone can work with the Dock by dragging stuff to and fro, Control-clicking various icons to use contextual menus, and so on. But much more power lurks in the heart of the Dock. (Use it only for the forces of goodness.)

3-12   Keyboard Combos

Most of the fun of the Dock comes from pressing modifier keys (Shift, Option, and so on) as you click. Here are the major things you can do with modifier keys and the Dock:

- If you Option-click a program's Dock icon, that program opens, but the Dock instantly hides one you *were* using, along with all of its windows.

- If you Option-⌘-click a program's Dock icon, that program opens, and the Dock hides the windows of *all* the other running applications. This trick is a fantastic way to leap into one program—the Finder is a frequent candidate—and instantly get everything else out of your hair.

    When you use this trick, already-minimized windows vanish from the Dock altogether. (When you unhide a program, its minimized window icons reappear.) This is ideal when, say, you're surfing the Web, and you've minimized 20 windows to the Dock; now if you hide the browser, you don't have to look at all that screen clutter until you want it.

- If you ⌘-click any icon on the Dock, you jump to the Finder, where a folder window opens, highlighting whatever you clicked on the Dock. You might use this technique when you want to back up a document or folder whose icon is on the Dock, and you don't want to sift through the whole hard drive.

- If you Control-click the divider bar that separates the two sides of the Dock, a menu appears (Figure 3-9).

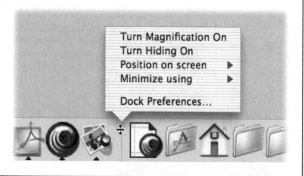

Figure 3-9:
The Dock's very own contextual menu. It allows fast Dock setting changes for things like position, magnification, and minimization effect.

- If you ⌘-drag an icon onto the Dock, the existing Dock icons freeze in place. This simple modifier makes it much easier to drag and file things into existing Dock folders or program icons. Without the ⌘ modifier, the existing folders scoot aside in an attempt to make room for the new icon, as seen in Figure 3-10.

Figure 3-10:
Oops—you missed the folder! The Dock folders tried to move aside to avoid accepting the new icon.

If you Option-⌘-drag a document's icon from the Finder or Dock onto a program's Dock icon, you force that program to open the document. This trick can be very useful when you want to open a file with a program that "thinks" it doesn't know how.

Consider a text file that you created in Terminal. If you drag such a document onto the Dock icon of BBEdit (a favorite text editor of programmers and Web designers), you ordinarily have no luck. The BBEdit icon doesn't darken, because BBEdit believes that it can't open Terminal text files. But if you hold down ⌘-Option and *then* drag the file onto the icon, BBEdit will accept and open the dropped file.

You can use this method to force any application to try to open any type of document. Of course, the results can be unpredictable, so don't be surprised if, say,

Terminal can't open a QuickTime movie! But if you've saved a JPEG image from a Web site, and you want to edit it in Photoshop, this is a handy move.

- If you Control-click any program's or folder's Dock icon—or click an icon without any keys pressed and wait a moment—you get a list of all of that program's open windows or the folder's contents. Choose a window's name from the list to jump directly to it. (See Figure 3-11.)

Figure 3-11:
When you open a window by Control-clicking a program's Dock icon, the other open windows in the program don't come forward. That's very different from bringing the entire program forward by clicking its Dock icon or switching to the program by pressing ⌘-Tab.

- If you bring up a program's contextual menu as described above, and then press Option, the menu's Quit item changes to say Force Quit. (While the contextual menu is open, you can press and release Option freely, changing Force Quit to Quit and back again until you get bored.)

Force Quit, of course, is a command of last resort when you can't get a frozen program to respond. (You lose any unsaved changes in that program, but at least you force it to close.)

- You can switch programs without touching the mouse by pressing ⌘-Tab—a glorious keystroke well worth committing to memory. (See hints 4-4 and 4-5 for details.)

- In combination with the ⌘-Tab trick, you can also hide or quit any open program from the keyboard alone. Use ⌘-Tab to flip to the program you want out of your face. While still holding ⌘, press H to hide the program and all of its windows, or Q to quit it. (Weirdly, if you hide a program whose windows you've minimized to the Dock, those window icons also become hidden in the Dock!)

- You can hide the Dock completely whenever it suits you, either by choosing →Dock→Turn Hiding On or, more conveniently, just by pressing Option-⌘-D.

The second way is for you control-freak Dock purists who don't put *anything* onto the left side of the Dock by hand, so that that area never shows anything except currently open programs. For these people, dragging ScreenSaverEngine onto the Dock would represent a devastating loss of purity.

In that case, create an alias of the aforementioned ScreenSaverEngine by ⌘-Option dragging it to your desktop. Once you've placed this alias onto the Dock, you can activate the screen saver by Control-clicking it and selecting ScreenSaverEngine from the pop-up menu. Although this solution requires an additional click to start the screen saver, it's a small price to pay to keep those shifty, non-running programs on the right side of the tracks.

3-18 Recovering from a MicroDock

What is a MicroDock? It's what you get when you try to store 355 JPEG files by dragging them onto a folder in the Dock, but you just miss the folder (thanks to its tendency to scoot aside). As a result, you drop all of the graphics directly onto the Dock. You can see a partial result of such a mistake in Figure 3-13.

Figure 3-13:
A MicroDock. Actual size. Not pretty.

Once this has happened, you're faced with a serious problem: how to get the Dock back to normal. Sure, you could drag the icons off the Dock one at a time—but you'd spend two presidential administrations doing it. Quitting the Dock won't help, either; because these are documents, not programs, they'll still be on the Dock when you restart it. If you're a true power user, you might even consider editing the com.apple.Dock.plist file to delete the inadvertent documents by hand. But that's tedious and time-consuming, too.

In the end, you may be better off just wiping the Dock clean, restoring it to its original, virginal, Apple-installed condition—and then recustomizing it.

The easiest way to return to a normal Dock is to delete the Dock preferences file from your Home→Library→Preferences folder. The file is named com.apple.Dock .plist, and you can just drag it into the Trash.

To restart the Dock, use the Process Viewer, as described in hint 3-6. When it restarts, you have the standard Apple Dock.

Tip: Incidentally, if the fear of MicroDock keeps you awake at night, it might be worth backing up your current Dock configuration—especially if you've spent a lot of time customizing it with folders and applications. Backing it up is easy enough: Just copy that com.apple.disk.plist file to another folder. Then, if you're struck by MicroDock in the future, it's a simple matter to replace the contaminated preferences file with your clean backup.

3-19   An AppleScript to Restart the Dock

If you tweak your Dock settings often, or if you just have occasional garden-variety Dock problems (stuck icons, unresponsiveness, and so on), you might find it worthwhile to create a simple AppleScript that restarts the Dock. (Yes, *restarts*—the Dock is actually a regular old Mac OS X program.)

To create such a script, open the Script Editor program (which is in your Applications→AppleScript folder). Type this:

```
tell application "Dock"
 quit
end tell
```

Choose File→Save, change the Format pop-up menu to Application, type a name for the script, and then save it somewhere where you'll have easy access to it. (The Script Menu folder described in hint 4-13 is a great location for it.) Now whenever you want to restart the Dock, just run your AppleScript!

Random Acts of Coolness

Sure, the Dock is useful, boosts your productivity, and so on—but if productivity were the only point of using a computer, we'd all be using DOS. Using these tricks, you can express your inner coolness.

3-20   The Colored Poof

Each time you drag an icon off the Dock, you're treated to a little animated puff of white smoke. (Never say Apple didn't benefit from its $500 million investment in the Newton.)

But if that's all you want out of life, you're no better than the other downtrodden masses using Mac OS X. Why not use a colored puff of smoke instead?

This modification requires a graphics program that can edit PNG files—Photoshop, Photoshop Elements, or Graphic Converter, for example. It also requires some Terminal editing (page 5).

The first order of business is to create the new graphics that will serve as the replacements for the existing white poof. In a graphics program, create a file that's 128 pixels wide, 640 pixels high, 72 dpi, and has a transparent background. You are going to use this image template to create five images, each in a 128 x 128 pixel square.

If you're using Photoshop Elements, for example, create a grid with 128-pixel spacing (Preferences→Grid) and then make sure it's visible (View→Grid). Create each individual image such that it's centered within its own square; this step ensures a smooth animation in your custom poof. You can see a very simple example of a finished image in Figure 3-14.

Once you've completed your masterpiece, choose File→Save As, and change the file format to PNG (no interlacing). Save the file somewhere that's easy to find, like your desktop, and name it something obvious like "newpoof.png."

Figure 3-14:
This disappearing mechanical-looking button is about to become the Dock's new poof animation. You can work with layers, transparency, and so on, as you normally would; just make sure that each of the five images is located in exactly the same portion of its 128 x 128 cell as the others.

At last you're ready to begin the operating-system surgery:

1. **Open Terminal. At the % prompt, type the following commands, pressing Enter after each:**

   ```
   cd /System/Library/CoreServices/Dock.app/Contents/Resources
   sudo cp poof.png poof_original.png
   ```
   Along the way, you'll be asked for your administrator's password.

   Once you've provided it, Terminal backs up the original file, just in case. (The *cp* command means *copy;* the text that follows it specifies which file to copy, and what name to give the duplicate.)

2. **Type *sudo cp* and then a space. Drag the icon of your new poof off the desktop and directly into the Terminal window.**

   That's a shortcut that saves you the trouble of typing out its specific "address" on your hard drive.

3. **Type a space, type *poof.png,* and then press Enter.**

   You've just given your custom poof the correct name and then copied it over the old poof. You're nearly done.

4. **To activate your change, quit the Dock using Process Viewer, as described in hint 3-6.**

Test your poof by dragging an item out of the Dock.

If the Dock isn't working as you'd expect, or if you just want to return to the original poof, open Terminal, type out the first line shown in step 1, press Enter, and then type *sudo cp poof_original.png poof.png*. When you press Enter, Terminal replaces your modified file with your backup file. After restarting the Dock again, you get the familiar Dock and poof.

3-21   The Customized Trash Can

But why stop at changing the animated puff of smoke? If your graphic instincts are running rampant, you can replace your Dock Trash can, too (Figure 3-15).

Figure 3-15:
If you don't like Apple's rendition of the Trash cans, replacing two PNG files in the Dock's resource folder solves the problem.

To do so, follow the same steps in hint 3-20. In this case, however, the Dock Trash cans are 128 x 128 pixel images instead of 128 x 640. Also, you should use two images—one that shows a full Trash, another that shows an empty Trash—called trashfull.png and trashempty.png, both located in the same folder as in the previous hint).

You don't need to quit the Dock to see the new Trash cans; just emptying the trash should do the trick. If, after rebooting, you find the old Trash cans have returned, look in your hard drive's Library→Caches folder for com.apple.dock.icon-cache.*username*, and throw it away. This file contains a cached version of the old image, and it can cause the Dock to ignore your new versions.

3-22   Supersizing Magnified Dock Icons

This hint is wildly impractical but visually interesting nonetheless. By making a simple modification, you create gigantic magnified Dock icons—something you've probably wanted since you were a teenager (Figure 3-16).

1. **In the Dock panel of System Preferences, turn on Magnification and crank it up.**

   Behind the scenes, you've just inserted a *largesize* command into the Dock's preferences file—more on this in a moment.

Ordinarily, of course, this magnification process affects only the Dock icons that are directly beneath the cursor as it passes over them.

2. **Open your Home→Library→Preferences folder. Drag the com.apple.dock.plist document onto the icon of TextEdit, the text processor in your Applications folder.**

   See page 4 for more on opening *plist* files in TextEdit.

3. **Near the top of the file, look for the word "largesize."**

   In fact, you should see a couple of lines that look like this:

   ```
   <key>largesize</key>
   <real>92.26524233</real>
   ```

   (The number in the second row may not match what you see here.)

   If you *don't* see a "largesize" line, click at the end of the first <dict> line in the text file (about four lines into the file), press Return, and then type the two lines exactly as shown above, beginning with *<key> largesize</key>* and pressing Return after each line.

4. **To supersize the magnification size, change the number after <real> to something larger. Try 256 as a starting point.**

   Fun though it might be to try, don't go over 512. The Dock won't run, and you might burst open the edges of your monitor.

5. **Choose File→Save. Quit TextEdit.**

   Return to the Finder.

6. **To make your change take effect, quit the Dock as described in hint 3-6.**

Note: If you use the Dock's preference pane to adjust the magnification value, you lose your supersize icons. This move is the easiest way to return to a normal Dock.

Figure 3-16:
Because the system only "knows about" icons up to 128 pixels, it has to take an educated guess regarding what they should look like at larger sizes. Therefore, so the icons may appear a bit fuzzy.

3-23   Minimizing and Maximizing in Slow Motion

This hint does nothing whatsoever for your productivity—in fact, it detracts from it. But isn't that the real secret to happiness?

In any case, making windows shrink down to Dock icons—minimizing them—in super-slow motion is one of the favorite onstage demonstrations of Apple CEO Steve Jobs. And how does he do it? He presses Shift before clicking the yellow Minimize button in any window.

The same holds true for expanding a minimized window: Hold Shift before you click the window icon in the Dock, and it comes back to life slower than a replay of Barry Bonds jacking a baseball into McCovey Cove.

For maximum "wow" factor, try this trick with a QuickTime movie while it's playing. Note with amazement that it keeps on rolling during slo-mo minimization. It also continues playing *while* minimized in the Dock, which is good for impressing your friends and influencing PC fans.

3-24   Killing the Dock

So you're a Mac OS X fan who loves the system but hates the Dock. How can you rectify this situation? Easy—kill the Dock!

To perform this little software assassination, open Terminal (in your Applications→Utilities folder), and at the % prompt, type the following (press Enter after each line):

```
cd /System/Library/CoreServices
sudo mv Dock.app ~/Documents/Dock.app
```

The first command switches Terminal's attention to the folder that contains the Dock, and the second moves it into your Documents folder as a backup.

The next time you log in, you'll find that the Dock is gone. (For best results, of course, you'll want to use some other Dock-like program—maybe a shareware program like DragThing or LaunchBar—to help you open your favorite files and programs. After all, you'll no longer have the Dock to kick around.)

If you ever want the Dock back, open a Terminal and type *sudo mv ~/Documents/ Dock.app /System/Library/CoreServices/Dock.app*—followed by the Enter key. Log out and log in again. The Dock will be back in its usual spot.

Programs

For the longest time, the success of Mac OS X was up in the air. It all boiled down to one thing: programs. Without applications, no operating system can survive. And for most people, switching to Mac OS X once meant having to buy all new, Mac OS X–compatible programs.

Fortunately, the tide has turned at last. All of the big-name programs have finally been (or soon will be) made over in the Mac OS X mold, and hundreds or thousands of smaller, lesser-known programs are sprouting up to make this operating system more interesting, useful, and fun.

All you have to do now is figure out how to use them.

Managing Programs

As you start using all your marvelous Mac OS X programs, you could find yourself spending more time sifting through open windows than breathing. The following hints can help you manage the window glut.

4-1:   Hide Others I

If you have a lot of open windows cluttering your screen, you can minimize them individually to the Dock as a housekeeping measure. But hiding them one by one would take a lot of time that would be better spent playing Bugdom.

It's easier to use the Hide Others command, which appears in each program's application menu (the boldfaced menu that bears its name). Choosing Hide Others instantly hides all windows of all programs *except* the one you're currently using—an especially likeable trick if your program offers the semi-standard Option-⌘-H keyboard equivalent.

Hiding them isn't the same thing as quitting the other programs (which takes time) or even minimizing the other windows (which entails a good deal of clicking to bring them back later). It's an invisibility mode unto itself.

4-2:   Hide Others II

Alas, not every program offers the Option-⌘-H keyboard shortcut, and in those situations, mousing up to the Hide Others command is a lot of trouble.

Fortunately, this shortcut has a shortcut of its own: Rather than using the Hide Others command, you may find it faster simply to Option-⌘-click the *Dock icon* of the program you want to keep around. (Option-⌘-clicking the Finder icon is an especially useful tactic.) All other programs make themselves scarce.

Tip: Shareware launcher programs like DragThing *(www.dragthing.com)* can also perform this "other program hiding" service automatically every time you switch programs.

4-3:   Leave Your Programs Open

Most open programs in Mac OS X don't occupy much memory or use up much of your processor's attention, especially when they're in the background. This may sound like heresy, but here it is: Get into the habit of opening your most used programs and *leaving them open forever.* Some applications eat processor cycles just by being open (Word X is particularly hungry), but most sit nicely in the background, awaiting your next command (see Figure 4-1).

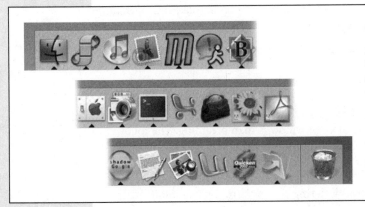

Figure 4-1:
This Dock (shown here split to fit) shows a workload of open applications, including some major programs like Photoshop Elements, Microsoft Word, FileMaker Pro, and Quicken. In a lesser operating system, this scenario would be a recipe for crash soufflé; in Mac OS X, it just means you've learned to stop fearing system instability and you're focused on getting your work done.

Learning to leave programs running is part of the adjustment that OS 9 users must make in adapting to Mac OS X. In the bad old days, many users' OS 9 workflow involved opening a program, doing what needed to be done, saving the file, and quitting the application.

No longer. In Mac OS X, individual programs do crash (rarely), but they don't take down your entire computer in the process. In fact, Apple's engineers are so proud of this improvement, they actually point it out when an application does crash (see Figure 4-2).

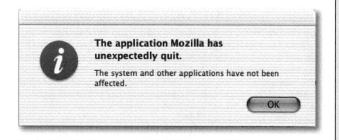

Figure 4-2:
In Mac OS X, the system goes out of its way to tell you that, even though an application just crashed, your system is fine and there's no need to restart or worry about lost data in other applications.

The application Mozilla has unexpectedly quit.

The system and other applications have not been affected.

OK

4-4: Switching Programs

Although the Dock apparently provides an easy way to switch between open programs (by clicking their icons), there are two reasons why you might use the keyboard combination ⌘-Tab instead. First, the true efficiency expert grows to detest the time it takes to remove his hands from the keyboard to grab the mouse and click a Dock icon. Second, if you leave a large number of programs running, it can be hard to find the Dock icon you want.

The trick is to keep the ⌘ key pressed. Now, with each press of the Tab key, you highlight the Dock icon of another program, in left-to-right order (or top-to-bottom, if you've reoriented your Dock). Release both keys when you reach the one you want. Mac OS X brings the corresponding program to the front. (To move *backward* through the open programs, press *Shift*-⌘-Tab.)

4-5: Bouncing between Two Programs

The best part of the ⌘-Tab trick is that a *single* press of ⌘-Tab takes you to the program you used *most recently,* and another single press returns you to the program you started in. Imagine that, for example, you're doing a lot of switching between two programs—your Web browser and your word processor, for example. If you have five other programs open, you don't waste your time ⌘-Tabbing your way through *all* open programs just to "get back" to your Web browser.

General Productivity

Now that you've tweaked your machine to suit your style, use these hints to greatly increase your productive use of the system.

4-6: Open and Save Dialog Boxes

The Open and Save dialog boxes offer an ingenious, column-view look at your entire hard drive, making it easy for you to choose a folder (for saving a new document) or document (to open). The trouble is, the dialog box appears with all the majesty of a peanut floating in the middle of your screen. It's just too small—and there's no reason it should be that way.

Fortunately, Mac OS X lets you expand them—and once you do so, the Open or Save dialog box in a certain program will remember the way you like it. It will still be that way the next time you open or save something.

Follow the directions in Figure 4-3.

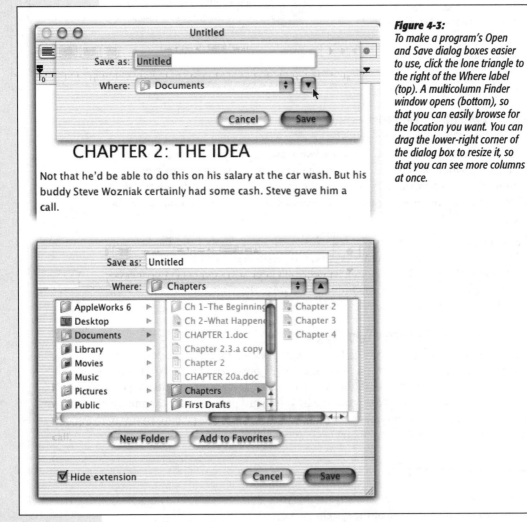

Figure 4-3:
To make a program's Open and Save dialog boxes easier to use, click the lone triangle to the right of the Where label (top). A multicolumn Finder window opens (bottom), so that you can easily browse for the location you want. You can drag the lower-right corner of the dialog box to resize it, so that you can see more columns at once.

4-7: Shortcuts in Open and Save Dialog Boxes

When you bring up an Open or Save dialog box in Mac OS X, you can, if you like, click various columns, folders, and pop-up menus to navigate your system.

It's often far faster, though, if you tell the dialog box, "Look here!" and shove its nose into the disk or folder you want by dragging a file or folder off the desktop and directly into the dialog box, as shown in Figure 4-4.

Figure 4-4:
If you're looking for a buried folder, it's often easier to find it in the Finder than to navigate using the dialog box. Once you've found the file or folder you want, drag it directly off the desktop and into the main portion of the dialog box, thus making it the highlighted selection.

What makes this trick especially handy is that you can move, resize, or even switch out of the dialog box to navigate directly in the Finder, making it easy to find the icon you want to drag into the dialog box.

4-8: Keystrokes for Save Sheets

In Mac OS X, the Save dialog box is actually a save *sheet*—a panel that slides down from a file's title bar so that you can name and choose a location for the file you're saving (Figure 4-3). Unlike the dialog box, a sheet remains attached to its document, even if you switch into other programs or other windows within the same program, so you never get confused about which document you're trying to save.

If you're like most people, much of your work on the Mac entails the creation of documents, so you'll encounter these sheets over and over again. That's why it's worth getting used to the secret keystrokes that operate within them:

- **Return** or **Enter** "clicks" the blue, pulsing button (usually Save or Open).

- **The Esc key** (or ⌘-period) "clicks" Cancel to close the dialog box.

- **⌘-D** selects the *D*esktop as the location for the file you're about to save or open. This way, when you're finished working, your newly saved documents will be waiting as icons on the desktop, ready for filing manually.

- **Shift-⌘-H** shifts the dialog box's view to your *H*ome folder. Similarly, the other keystrokes for the primary folders listed in the Go menu also work: Shift-⌘-I brings your iDisk to the screen, Shift-⌘-A jumps to your Applications folder, and so on.

4-9: Is That Document Saved?

The Close button (the red upper-left button of every window) is more than a button—it's also an indicator. When you save the document you're working on, it's solid red, as shown in Figure 4-5 (left). If you make changes but haven't yet chosen the File→Save command, the button sprouts a small dot at its center (right). That's a handy reminder that your document needs saving.

Figure 4-5:
Right: The document has unsaved changes.
Left: No dot in the Close button; all changes are saved.

4-10: Creating PDF Files

No doubt you've had the unnerving experience of receiving an email from a friend with a note saying, "You're the one person on the planet who would really appreciate the attached." And then the file opens—to 43 pages of gibberish.

This sort of annoyance could have been avoided if the document was sent to you as a Portable Document Format (PDF) file, of the sort that you read using the free Acrobat Reader program (or Mac OS X's Preview program). PDFs are often required by print shops like Kinko's, which may not have all 263 fonts you used on your band's latest flyer.

PDF files have a number of advantages over standard document files. For example, when you distribute PDF files to other people, they see precisely the same fonts, colors, page design, and other elements that you included in your original document, even if they don't have the fonts or the software you used to create the document.

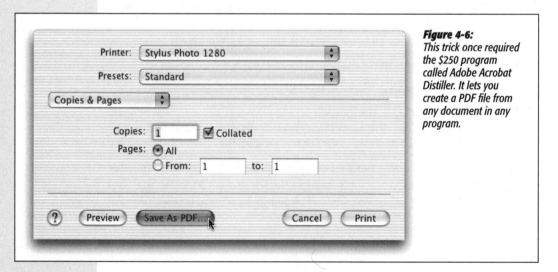

Figure 4-6:
This trick once required the $250 program called Adobe Acrobat Distiller. It lets you create a PDF file from any document in any program.

Many a software manual, Read Me file, and downloadable "white paper" comes in this format. But PDF files are also one of Mac OS X's common forms of currency. In fact, you can turn *any document* (in any program with a Print command) into a PDF file. From within a program with an open file, choose File→Print, and then click Save As PDF (Figure 4-6).

PDF files are also very useful for saving information on Web sites. If you find a Web page you'd like to keep, simply save it as a PDF file. You'll have a permanent record of the text and images on the page, making this a great way to preserve online shopping receipts and travel confirmations. (The links on the page won't work, of course, but you'll otherwise have a snapshot of all the graphics, text, and formatting that were on that page at the moment you captured it.)

4-11: Creating a Software Library

If you download and use lots of demos, freeware, and shareware from the Web, consider creating a software installation library: a collection of folders that makes it easier to reinstall things you've downloaded, without having to download them again. If you get a new computer, install a new hard drive, or need to reinstall the system, you'll have an easy way of finding the programs.

Create a folder on a hard drive or partition with lots of space. Then create alphabetic subfolders within the main folder, as in Figure 4-7. When you download an update or installer, drag it into the proper alphabetic folder.

Tip: You may wish to create a special Apple folder to hold system updates and Apple-supplied applications.

Figure 4-7:
By setting up a folder of alphabetic subfolders, you can keep downloaded installers ready for easy access at any time. If you've ever redownloaded a 100 MB demo more than once, you'll quickly appreciate having a library of installers readily available.

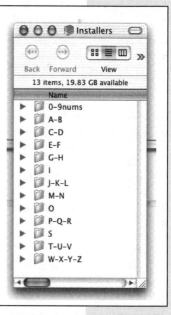

4-12: Dragging and Dropping Text

The ability to drag and drop text has been around in the Mac OS for years—and it's a terrific way to rearrange words, sentences, or paragraphs without having to copy and paste. But many Mac fans panic when they discover that in Mac OS X, it no longer seems to work.

The truth is, text drag-and-drop is still available in Mac OS X—but in many programs, there's a trick to it. Truth is, how you drag and drop text depends on which kind of program you're using at the time: Carbon or Cocoa (page 99).

- **Carbon programs.** In Carbon applications, drag-and-drop works as it always has: After selecting some text, position your cursor within the highlighted area and then drag to a new spot in the word processing document (or even another word processing document).

- **Cocoa programs.** You have to keep the mouse pressed within the highlighted text for nearly a full second before you can drag it. If you don't wait long enough, the drag won't work.

4-13: The Script Menu

AppleScript is a simple programming language that lets you devise mini programs to perform certain tasks. For instance, you could you AppleScript to tell iTunes to play "I Love Rock 'n' Roll" at 8:03 every morning. Or you could use an AppleScript to send an email every three hours to your co-workers telling them how many shopping days are left until Christmas. (There are plenty of frivolous uses for AppleScript, too.)

Mac OS X comes with a handful of ready-made AppleScripts, including one that checks the current temperature in your area code and one that lets you count messages in all your mailboxes.

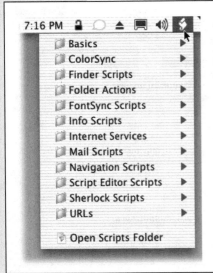

Figure 4-8:
The Script Menu.Menu image appears to be a normal folder, but when you double-click it, a new icon appears in your toolbar. You've just created the Script menu, which lists dozens of useful AppleScript mini programs.

Most Mac fans never even know they exist, because they're buried in the Application→AppleScript→ExampleScripts folder. Fortunately, they're also listed in something called the ScriptMenu, an icon on your menu bar that puts the scripts at your fingertips. To make it appear, open your Applications→AppleScript folder, and double-click the folder icon called Script Menu.Menu (see Figure 4-8).

Some of the scripts in the Script menu operate on familiar components of the Mac OS, like the Finder; others show off applications or features that are new in Mac OS X. Here's a listing of some of the most useful:

Finder Scripts

All of these scripts have to do with working in the Finder: manipulating files and windows, for example. Several are designed to change file or folder names en masse, which can be a huge timesaver.

- **Add to File Names, Add to Folder Names.** These scripts tack on a prefix or suffix to the name of every file or folder in the frontmost Finder window (or, if no windows are open, on the desktop). You could use this script to add the word *draft* or *final* or *old* to all of the files in a certain folder.

- **Change Case of Item Names** offers to capitalize, or uncapitalize, all the letters of the file names in the window before you.

- **Finder Windows - Hide All** minimizes all open Finder windows to the Dock. **Finder Windows - Show All,** of course, brings them back from the Dock.

- **Replace Text in Item Names** lets you do a search-and-replace of text bits inside file names, folder names, or both. When one publisher rejects your 45-chapter book proposal, you can use this script to change all 45 chapter files from, for example, "A History of Mouse Pads—A Proposal for Random House, Chapter 1" to "A History of Mouse Pads—A Proposal for Simon & Schuster, Chapter 1."

- **Switch to Finder** is a great one. It brings the Finder to the front *and* hides all of the other running applications.

Folder Actions

You can read about folder actions in hint 2-47.

Info Scripts

- **Current Date & Time** displays the current date and time in a dialog box, complete with a Clipboard button that copies the information, ready for pasting.

- **Font Sampler** is designed to show you what all your fonts look like (see Figure 4-9).

Internet Services

- **Stock Quote** and **Current Temperature by Zipcode** fetch those respective bits of information, popping them into a dialog box without your having to use a Web browser.

Mail Scripts

This collection of script communicates with Mail (see Chapter 7).

- **Count Messages in All Mailboxes** counts all messages and unread messages in all of your mailboxes and displays the result.

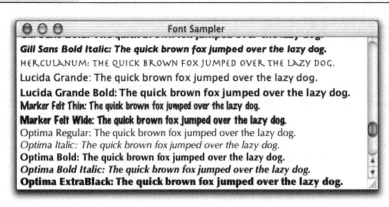

Figure 4-9:
The Font Sampler script launches TextEdit, opens a new document, and fills it with dozens of copies of the classic "What does this font look like?" test sentence: The quick brown fox jumped over the lazy dog. Then, as you watch, it formats each line with a different font, creating a good page to print out and keep as a reference.

- **Crazy Message Text** is Apple at its wackiest. When you run it, a dialog box asks you what message you want to send ("Happy Birthday," for example). Mail then creates a colorful, zany, outgoing message in which each letter has a random typeface, style, color, and size. It's ideal for making people think you spent a long time with your Format menu for their entertainment.

- **Create New Message** walks you through the creation of a new message including the recipient, sender, attachments, subject, and so on, saving you a step if the Mail program isn't already open and active.

- **Import Addresses** grabs names from the address book in Entourage, Eudora, Outlook Express, or Palm Desktop. It's not actually a Mail script—it brings the addresses into Mac OS X's Address Book program—but it's still handy if you've decided to switch from one of those programs to Apple's Mail program.

- **Quick Mail** prompts you for an address and a subject line, launches the Mail application, and sets up a new message for you with those attributes. With a little analysis of this script, you should be able to see how it could save you time in generating canned, regularly scheduled outgoing mail messages.

Sherlock Scripts

The sole script here, Search Internet, prompts you for a *search string* (the words you want to search the Web for). When you click Search, the script opens Sherlock and proceeds to execute your search. It may save you a few mouse clicks, but this script was likely designed to serve primarily as a model for study by scripting hopefuls.

It's worth noting that the Script menu is nothing more than a reflection of what's in two special folders:

- **Library→Scripts.** This is where you'll find all of Apple's starter scripts as described above. If you feel inspired to rename any of the commands or subcommands in the Script menu, these are the files whose names you want to edit.

- **Home→Library→Scripts.** (If you don't have this folder, open your Home→ Library folder and create it yourself.) If you become an AppleScript fan and write little programs of your own, you can drop them into this folder to make them appear in the Script menu.

Three Kinds of Programs: Cocoa, Carbon, Classic

Mac OS X was supposed to make life simpler. It was supposed to eliminate the confusion and complexity that the old Mac OS had accumulated over the years—and replace it with a smooth, simple, solid system.

Five years from now, that's exactly what Mac OS X will be. For the moment, however, you're stuck with running three different kinds of programs, each with different characteristics: *Cocoa, Carbon,* and *Classic.*

The explanation involves a little bit of history and a little bit of logic. To take full advantage of Mac OS X's considerable technical benefits, software companies must write new programs for it from scratch. So what should Apple do—send out an email to the authors of the 18,000 existing Mac programs, suggesting that they throw out their programs and rewrite them from the bottom up?

At big companies like Microsoft and Adobe, such a suggestion would wind up on the Joke of the Week bulletin board.

Instead, Apple gave software companies a break. It wrote Mac OS X to let software companies choose precisely how much work they wanted to put into compatibility with the new system. The various levels include:

Write new programs from scratch (Cocoa). As Mac OS X becomes a bigger and bigger hit, more and more programmers and software companies create new programs exclusively for it. The geeks call such programs *Cocoa* applications. Many of the programs that come with Mac OS X are true Cocoa applications, including iChat, iPhoto, iMovie 3, iDVD 3, TextEdit, Stickies, Mail, Address Book, and so on.

Update the existing programs (Carbon). If software companies and programmers are willing to put *some* effort into getting with the Mac OS X program, they can simply adapt, or update, their existing software so that it works with Mac OS X. The resulting software looks and feels almost every bit like a true Mac OS X program. You get the crash protection, the good looks, the cool-looking graphics, the Save sheets, and so on, but behind the scenes, the bulk of the computer programming is the same as it was in Mac OS 9. These are what Apple calls *Carbonized* programs, named for the technology (Carbon) that permits them to run on Mac OS X.

Carbonized programs include Microsoft Office, AppleWorks, iTunes, Photoshop, FileMaker, Internet Explorer, and, believe it or not, the Finder itself. Many can run both in Mac OS X and Mac OS 9.

Do nothing (Classic). Software companies go out of business, unprofitable product lines are dropped, and shareware authors go off to law school. All of them leave behind orphaned programs that run only on the old Mac OS.

Your Mac OS X machine can still run this entire library of older, Mac OS 9–compatible software. When you try to open one of these older programs, Mac OS X launches a Mac OS 9 *simulator* called the Classic environment (which comes with hints of its own, described at the end of this chapter). Suddenly your screen is taken over by the ghost of Mac OS 9. Sure, you leave behind all the trappings and benefits of Mac OS X—its new look, the Dock, crash protection, and so on—but at least you're still running your favorite programs.

In fact, if you create a folder *within* the Scripts folder, you get a submenu in the Script menu, just like the ones Apple put there. (Scripts and folders in the Library→Scripts folder appear at the top of the menu; scripts in your Home→Library→Scripts folder appear beneath them.)

Either way, though, newly added folders and scripts don't appear in the Script menu until you "restart" it. To do so, ⌘-drag the AppleScript icon away from the menu bar to make it disappear. To make it reappear, do just what you did the first time you summoned it: Open your Applications→AppleScript folder, then double-click the folder icon called Script Menu.Menu.

4-14: Capturing Screenshots

Screenshots are "snapshots" of a frozen moment in Macintosh time, a graphic image of the screen. Screenshots are very useful for showing somebody else an error message you've received, showing off a neat desktop you've created, or illustrating books of Macintosh hints.

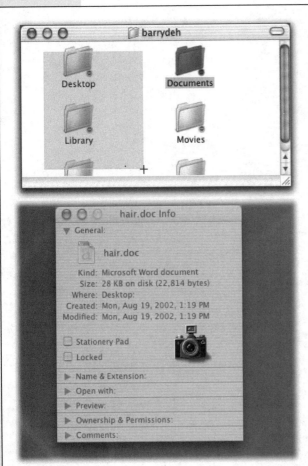

Figure 4-10:
Top: If you're interested in capturing only part of the screen, press Shift-⌘-4 to turn your cursor into a tiny + symbol. Now drag diagonally across the screen to capture only a rectangular chunk of it, as illustrated here.

Bottom: Once you've got your menu or window open onscreen, or the icon visible (even if it's on the Dock), press Shift-⌘-4. But instead of dragging diagonally, press the Space bar. Now your cursor turns into a tiny camera. Move it so that the misty highlighting fills the window or menu you want to capture—and then click. The resulting Picture file snips the window or menu neatly from its background. (Press the Space bar a second time to exit "snip one screen element" mode and return to "drag across an area" mode.)

Here's how to capture:

- **The whole screen.** Press Shift-⌘-3 to create a picture file on your desktop, in PDF (Acrobat) format, that depicts the entire screen image. A satisfying camera-shutter sound tells you that you were successful. You'll find the resulting file, called Picture 1, on your desktop.

  Each time you press Shift-⌘-3, you get an additional file, called Picture 2, Picture 3, and so on.

- **One section of the screen.** You can capture only a rectangular *region* of the screen by pressing Shift-⌘-4. When you drag and release the mouse, you hear the camera-click sound, and the Picture 1 file appears on your desktop as usual.

- **One menu, window, icon (with its name), or dialog box.** See Figure 4-10, bottom, for the sneaky feature that lets you neatly crop a single window or icon without having to edit out the background in Photoshop afterward.

  But beware: If a portion of the window you want is hiding behind another window, the bizarre situation shown in Figure 4-11 may result.

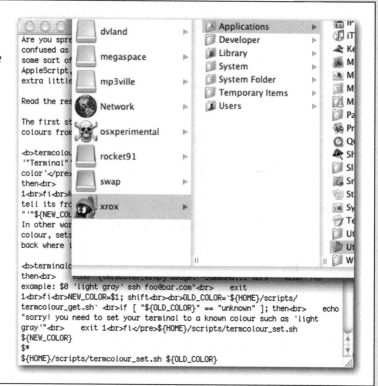

Figure 4-11:
If the screen you try to capture is hidden behind another screen, the size and shape of the screenshot match the window you are trying to capture, but you get a portion of the foreground window, too. Use the camera tool on a fully revealed window.

• **The Dock.** That business of pressing Shift-⌘-4 and then the Space bar also lets you capture the Dock in one quick snip. Once you've got the camera cursor, just click any *blank* spot on the Dock (between icons).

Tip: If you hold down the Control key as you click or drag (using any of the techniques described above), you copy the screenshot to your *clipboard,* ready for pasting (in JPEG format) rather than saving it as a new graphics file on your desktop.

Mac OS X also offers another way to create screenshots: The utility program Grab (found in Applications→Utilities), which offers a timer option that lets you set up the screen before it takes the shot.

But if snapping pictures of the screen is part of your job, you should probably opt for the $30 shareware program Snapz Pro X *(www.ambrosiasw.com)* instead. Simple to install and easy to use, Snapz Pro has enough options to satisfy even the most advanced screenshot professional (Figure 4-12).

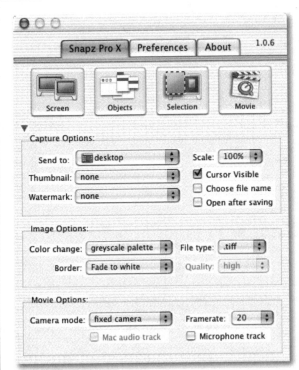

Figure 4-12:
In Snapz Pro, you can easily control the format, file name, destination, scaling, thumbnail creation, color changes, and border of each screenshot you make.

You can also use the $50 version to capture movies, which is a critical feature for anyone in a training or support role.

4-15: Reassigning Documents to New Parents

Every operating system needs a mechanism to associate documents with the applications that created them. When you double-click a Microsoft Word document icon, for example, it's clear that you want Microsoft Word to launch and open the document.

Mac OS X recognizes two different systems for making these associations:

- **The Mac OS 9 way.** A Macintosh document's invisible, behind-the-scenes, four-letter *creator* code identifies the program that will open it: MSWD for Microsoft Word, MSIE for Internet Explorer, and so on.

  Each Mac OS 9 document also bears a *second* four-letter code: the *type code*. This code specifies the document's file format. Photoshop, for example, can create graphics in a multitude of different formats: GIF, JPEG, TIFF, and so on. If you inspect your Photoshop documents, you'll discover that they all share the same creator code, but have a wide variety of type codes.

- **The Windows way.** In Windows, every document bears a three-letter file name suffix. If you double-click something called *memo.doc,* it opens in Microsoft Word. If you double-click *memo.wri,* it opens in Microsoft Write, and so on.

The bottom line is that Mac OS X offers *two different* mechanisms that associate documents with the programs that created them. Mac OS X looks for type/creator codes first. Where they're absent, the file name suffixes kick in.

Reassigning a certain document—once

Double-clicking a graphics file generally opens it in Preview, the graphics viewer included with Mac OS X. But Preview can only *display* graphics. What if you decide to edit a graphics file? You'd want it to open, just this once, into a different program—GraphicConverter, for example.

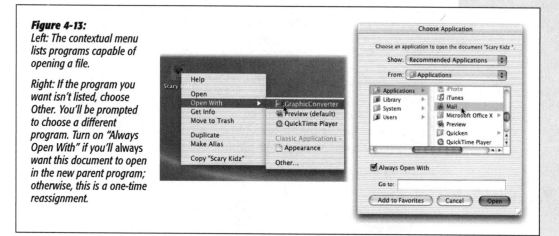

Figure 4-13:
Left: The contextual menu lists programs capable of opening a file.

Right: If the program you want isn't listed, choose Other. You'll be prompted to choose a different program. Turn on "Always Open With" if you'll always want this document to open in the new parent program; otherwise, this is a one-time reassignment.

To do so, you must access the Open With command. You can find it in two places:

- Highlight the icon, and then choose File→Open With.

- Control-click the file's icon. From the contextual menu, choose Open With.

In any case, study the submenu for a moment (Figure 4-13, left). The program whose name says "(default)" indicates which program *usually* opens this kind of document. From this pop-up menu, choose the name of the program you'd *rather* open this particular file, right now, just this once.

Reassigning a certain document—permanently

After opening a TIFF file in, say, GraphicConverter for editing, you haven't really made any changes in the fabric of your Mac universe. The very next time you double-click that file, it will open once again in Preview.

If you wish this particular file would *always* open in GraphicConverter, the steps are slightly different. In fact, there are three different ways:

- Extend the one-shot reassignment method illustrated in Figure 4-13: In the Choose an Application dialog box, turn on "Always Open With" (shown at right in Figure 4-13).

- Start out with one of the techniques described above (highlight the icon, and then choose File→Open With, or Control-click the file's icon and choose Open With). Sfter you see the menu, press the Option key, too. Before your very eyes, the Open With command changes to say *Always* Open With.

- Highlight the icon, and then choose File→Get Info. Open the "Open with" panel. Choose a new "parent" program's name from the pop-up menu. You'll see that the word "(default)" changes position, now tacking itself onto the name of the new program you've chosen.

Tip: You can use the Get Info method to reassign the parenthood of a whole bunch of selected icons at once.

Reassigning all documents of this type

If you want *all* documents of a certain type to open in a certain program—all PDFs in Acrobat Reader, all graphics in Photoshop, all HTML documents in BBEdit, or whatever—use the Get Info method described above. (You can't do it using the File→Open With command, nor by Control-clicking the icon.)

Start by highlighting *any* TIFF file. Choose File→Get Info. Open the "Open with" panel.

From its pop-up menu, choose the program you want to open this kind of document from now on. (If the one you prefer isn't listed, use the Other option, which opens the Choose Application dialog box so that you can navigate to the one you want. Find, and double-click, the program.)

This time, however, follow up by clicking Change All beneath the pop-up menu. Mac OS X asks you to confirm by clicking Continue or pressing Enter.

From now on, double-clicking any similar kind of document opens it in the newly selected program.

4-16: Text-Box Selection Tricks

Want to select all the text in a field, like the address bar in Safari or the search box in TextEdit, as quickly as possible? You'd never guess this one:

Click the mouse with the cursor tip just below the top border of the box. One click selects all the text in the box.

When does this work? The best answer is, "Most of the time." It seems to work in most Cocoa applications and some Carbon applications. For example, it works in Mail *unless* you're trying to select the "To:" field.

Printing, Fonts, and Text

For a company whose core audience includes graphic designers and printers, the printing features of Mac OS X got off to a shaky start. With each new version of Mac OS X, the situation (especially regarding printer drivers) improves—and in the meantime, you've got these tips.

4-17: Custom Print Settings

It could happen to you: Over and over again, you're supposed to print out something in draft mode on your printer—in triplicate. Your hand is growing weary from changing the settings in the Print dialog box over and over again every time you need to make such a printout.

Fortunately, although few Mac fans realize it, the Print dialog box lets you save certain combinations of settings. To create custom print settings and save them for easy future use, follow the directions in Figure 4-14.

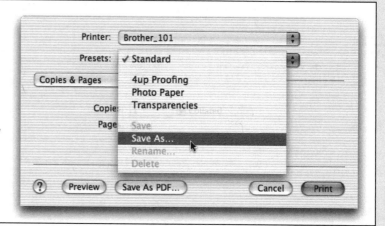

Figure 4-14:
To preserve some printing settings, choose File→Print to summon the Print dialog box. Make the settings you'd like to preserve. Then choose Save As from the Presets pop-up menu. Name your setting. You can recall the settings in the future by simply selecting your canned name from the pop-up menu.

Tip: To delete a custom setting from the Presets pop-up menu, choose it in the menu, and then choose Delete from the same menu.

4-18: Previewing Fonts

If you're used to Windows or Mac OS 9, you may have mourned the loss of one delicious feature: the ability to double-click a font file to see what its typeface looks like. As far as most Mac OS X fans know, there's no longer any way to get a sneak preview of what all the characters of a certain font look like.

But there is—you just have to know where to look for it.

Begin by opening up a Cocoa program—TextEdit, Mail, or Stickies, for example. Now open the Font dialog box (usually ⌘-T, but always in the program's Format menu). From the Extras pop-up menu at the bottom of the dialog box (shown in Figure 4-15), choose Show Preview.

The top part of the box changes to preview the selected font. Make the window bigger, if you like, to see more font choices.

Tip: There's another method of taking a look at your fonts: using one of the prepared AppleScripts as described in hint 4-13.

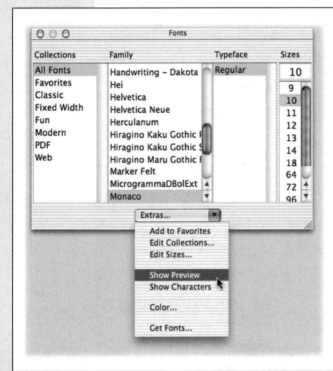

Figure 4-15:
Mac OS X does indeed let you see a preview of your fonts—within the Fonts panel. And here's a tip within a tip: By clicking the name of the font in the preview area, you can see how an actual piece of your writing will look in the chosen font.

4-19:   Install Windows Fonts Without Conversion

If you've been emailed a document that requires a Windows TrueType font, you're in luck. It turns out that Mac OS X and Windows can both use precisely the same kind of font, without any conversion whatsoever. Just drag the font file in question from the Windows source (which could be a network folder, a CD-ROM, or an email attachment) into your Home→Library→Fonts folder, and you're good to go.

4-20:   Unicode Characters

Maybe you've heard of Unicode, maybe you haven't, but the odds are pretty good that you don't have any idea how to use it. That's too bad, because it's a really cool Mac OS X feature.

The trouble with the traditional computer system of representing text (known as ASCII text) is that it has room for only 256 letters, numbers, and characters. That's fine for typing letters to your mom. But what if you're writing a treatise on the potential popularity of Formula One racing in Asia, and you need to insert the Korean symbol for car?

Enlightened modern operating systems, therefore, recognize something called the Unicode alphabet—a computer representation of over 32,000 characters, covering a large number of languages, symbols, and drawing characters. Characters are each identified by a four-digit number, like 2318 (which happens to be the code for the Command-key symbol ⌘), and you can insert them into any Cocoa program.

To find out the four-digit code for certain international characters, the Mac's Key Caps utility won't quite cut it. You'll have to go online to consult one of the master charts, like the one at *www.unicode.org/charts*. Then open System Preferences, click the International icon, click the Input Menu tab, and turn on Unicode Hex Input. Proceed as shown in Figure 4-16.

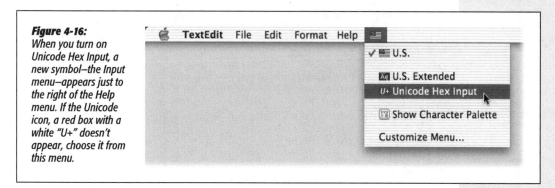

Figure 4-16:
When you turn on Unicode Hex Input, a new symbol—the Input menu—appears just to the right of the Help menu. If the Unicode icon, a red box with a white "U+" doesn't appear, choose it from this menu.

You can now input Unicode into any Cocoa program by holding down Option and typing the character's four-digit code number. For instance, to create the Command-key symbol (⌘) in TextEdit, select the Unicode Input menu item. Then, while pressing Option, type 2318.

4-21: The Character Palette

There are a slew of characters—arrows, math symbols, dingbats, stars and asterisks, and accented letters—that you can easily add to Cocoa files without looking up their Unicode symbols (see the previous hint). And no, you don't have to open the Key Caps program to find them, either.

The trick is to use the little-known Character Palette dialog box. To make it appear, open System Preferences, click the International icon, click the Input Menu tab, and then turn on the Character Palette checkbox. Now inspect your menu bar: You've just added the Input menu, if it wasn't there already, and it now includes a command called Show Character Palette.

From within any Cocoa program, choose this command. The dialog box shown in Figure 4-17 appears, filled with useful symbols. To find a particular symbol, click the "by Category" tab, and then click the various category headings: Arrows, Stars/Asterisks, Math, and so on. When you find the symbol you want, double-click it to make it appear in your document.

Figure 4-17:
The Character Palette is your key to hundreds of useful hidden symbols. If you really want to know what font one of them came from, click the black, down-pointing triangle button; you'll see the font name in parentheses.

Note: You can use the Character Palette in Carbon programs like Word and AppleWorks, too—sort of. You'll get the right *character* in your document, but usually not in the right *font.* You have to change the font manually.

If that's not enough choices for you, you can see hundreds more by choosing the View pop-up menu and then selecting All. The tabs change, and the one labeled Unicode Blocks displays a *huge* collection of icons.

4-22: New Spelling Words

The nightmare: A word processor, spreadsheet, presentation program, and email program, each with its own spelling checker—and its own spelling dictionary. Over and over again, you find yourself having to teach your Mac that your last name is correctly spelled, darn it.

The fantasy: A computer with a single, centralized spelling dictionary that works with every program you use.

Clearly, that's what Apple had in mind when it created the master Mac OS X spell checker. So far, Cocoa programs (Mail, TextEdit, iPhoto and so on) are generally the only ones to capitalize on it, but the list is sure to grow.

In any case, here's how it works. As you type, a red dotted underline appears beneath any words the Mac considers incorrectly spelled. Instead of editing the word when you see the red underline, Control-click it. A menu containing recommended substitutions appears (Figure 4-18)—and so does an option to teach the word to the Mac so that it won't flag it the next time around. If you use a lot of nonstandard words (or even non-words), use the Learn function to prevent the spell checker from flagging them.

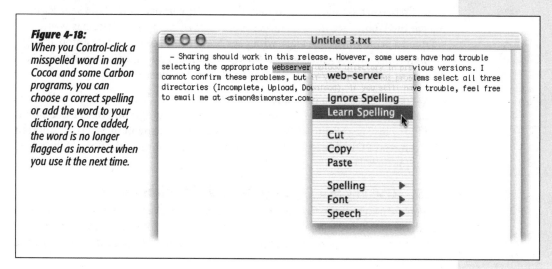

Figure 4-18:
When you Control-click a misspelled word in any Cocoa and some Carbon programs, you can choose a correct spelling or add the word to your dictionary. Once added, the word is no longer flagged as incorrect when you use it the next time.

4-23:   Changing the Spell Check Language

In Cocoa programs, you can control which language the spell checker uses. Control-click any blank section of a document. From the contextual menu, choose Spelling→Spelling. Inside the Dictionary area of the resulting dialog box is a pop-up menu that lets you specify the dictionary's language, such as Español, Italiano, or British English. (This is your opportunity, Brits, to make the Mac quit flagging *colour* as a spelling error.)

Tip: If you choose Multilingual, the Mac tolerates words from all languages it knows in the same document.

Classic

As described on page 99, Mac OS X is like the renaissance operating system: It's a polyglot, capable of running three different kinds of software: Cocoa (written from scratch for Mac OS X), Carbon (an older program that has been updated for Mac OS X), and Classic (Mac OS 9 programs that are still Mac OS 9 programs).

For the next several years at least, Classic programs (older, Mac OS 9–compatible ones) are likely to be part of most Mac fans' lives. So it's well worth getting to know Classic, the Mac OS 9 simulator that opens up automatically whenever you try to launch a Mac OS 9 program.

4-24:   Printing on Unsupported Mac OS X Printers

Do you have an aging printer that works great in Classic programs but doesn't work in Mac OS X programs?

Your first resort should be to contact the printer company or, at the very least, to search the Web to see if, by chance, some enterprising programmer has written or adapted a printer driver to work with your Mac. That should include a stop at *http://gimp-print.sourceforge.net,* where you'll find something called Gimp-Print: a collection of hundreds of Mac OS X printer drivers for older printers.

If you're still having no luck, and you need to print on that old printer only occasionally, here's a method of last resort. In a Mac OS X program, save the document as a PDF file (File→Print→Save as PDF). Open the document in a Classic program that can read PDF files, like Adobe Acrobat (look in your Applications [Mac OS 9] folder for the Classic version), and print away.

4-25:   Opening Mac OS 9's Menu and Control Panels

If, when working in the Classic mode, you frequently change the system settings or use the menu programs, you've probably spent a lifetime switching to a Mac OS 9 program, opening Control Panels or the menu, and then hunting down the panel or program you want.

But there's a much quicker way. Open the System Folder, which is the folder that contains your copy of Mac OS 9. (Don't confuse this with the folder called simply System—the one that bears an X—which is the Mac OS X operating system.)

Once this window is open, drag the Control Panels folder and the Apple Menu Items folder onto the right side of your Dock. From now on, you can access these settings directly from these Dock-installed folders, just as you would use any Dock folder (Figure 4-19).

Figure 4-19:
Once you've installed the Mac OS 9 Control Panels and Apple Menu Items folders on your Dock, Control-click them (or click and hold on them) for direct access to any of their contents. To make the folders stand out, paste custom icons on them (see hint 2-18).

4-26:   Web Sites That Work Better in Classic

Mac OS X browsers have a history of animosity towards Web sites that rely heavily on the Java programming language. But Web browsers that were written in the Classic era have had more time to mature and develop some compatibility.

If you hit a site that isn't working as you'd expect it to (a pop-up window won't pop, or a gaming feature plays dead, for instance), try opening it in a Classic browser. For example, although you may not have realized it, you have a second copy of Internet Explorer on your hard drive—the Mac OS 9 version. It's inside the Applications (Mac OS 9)→Internet Explorer 5 folder, ready for you to put to use.

4-27:   Sharing Settings between Classic and Mac OS X Programs

If you regularly use both the Classic and Mac OS X versions of Internet Explorer, you've probably encountered—and despised—the efficiency-defying task of synchronizing the browsers' bookmarks by hand. Fortunately, it's possible to trick your system into updating both sets of bookmarks automatically, along with your browsers' history files and whatever Web sites you've captured on the Scrapbook panel of Internet Explorer.

1. **Rescue your Favorites from Mac OS 9.**

   Before you create one set of files for both operating systems, save anything important from your Mac OS 9 Internet Explorer setup, because you're going to replace these files.

   Here's how. In the Mac OS X version of Internet Explorer, choose File→Open File. Navigate to the System Folder→Preferences→Explorer folder.

   Open the document inside called Favorites.html (see Figure 4-20).

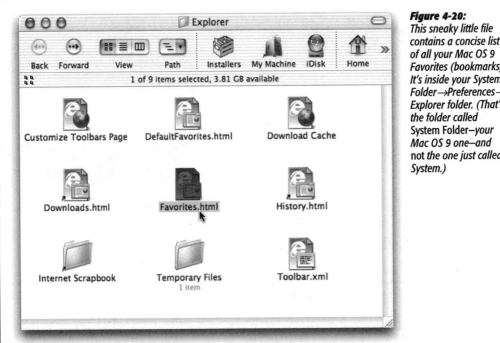

Figure 4-20:
This sneaky little file contains a concise list of all your Mac OS 9 Favorites (bookmarks). It's inside your System Folder→Preferences→ Explorer folder. (That's the folder called System Folder—your Mac OS 9 one—and not the one just called System.)

Once you've opened this list, ⌘-click one of your links inside it to open the corresponding Web page in a new window. Press ⌘-D to add it to your Mac OS X bookmarks file, and then press ⌘-W to close that Web site window. Repeat with the next link in the old Favorites file. Continue until you're certain you've saved all your critical bookmarks in the Mac OS X version of Internet Explorer. (Behind the scenes, they're being saved in Mac OS X's own Explorer folder.)

2. **Rescue your Scrapbooked Web sites from Mac OS 9.**

   If you've never captured a snapshot of a Web page by using the Scrapbook tab at the left side of the Internet Explorer window, you can skip this step.

   Otherwise, here's what you do. Switch to the Finder and open two side-by-side windows. In the first, open System Folder→Preferences→Explorer→Internet

Scrapbook. In the second, open your Home→Library→Preferences→Explorer→ Internet Scrapbook folder. You should now see a list of everything you've added to Internet Explorer's Scrapbook panel in both Mac OS 9 (the first window) and Mac OS X (the second window). Copy any Web pages that you want to save from the Mac OS 9 folder to the Mac OS X folder. (Leave the windows open.)

3. **Now that you've saved your critical bookmarks and Internet Scrapbook items, it's time to make sure you'll never have to go through this again.**

   In the two Finder windows you've already opened, move up one level in both the Mac OS 9 and Mac OS X folders (that is, click inside each window and press ⌘-up arrow) so that you're in the Explorer folder in each window.

4. **In the Mac OS 9 Explorer folder, move Downloads.html, Favorites.html, and the Internet Scrapbook folder to your desktop (or somewhere else) for temporary safekeeping. Leave the window open.**

   Technically, you could delete these files now. But putting them on the desktop insures that if anything goes wrong, you'll be able to move them back and return the Classic version of Internet Explorer to square one, no questions asked.

5. **In the Mac OS X Explorer folder, select Favorites.html, History.html, and Downloads.html. (The best way to select them all at once is to ⌘-click each.)**

   While pressing ⌘-Option, drag any one of the highlighted icons into the Mac OS 9 Explorer folder, as shown in Figure 4-21.

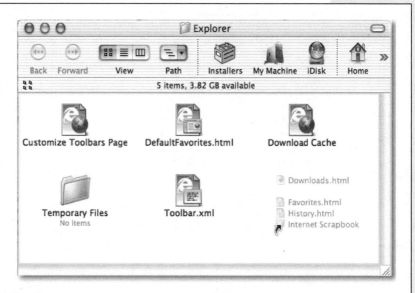

Figure 4-21:
⌘-Option-dragging the icons creates aliases of them, in this case in the Explorer folder (in the Mac OS 9 System Folder). When you drag, the cursor becomes a shortcut arrow, as seen here, indicating that you're creating aliases, not copies.

That's all there is to it. If you open the Classic version of Internet Explorer, you'll find that your bookmarks, history, and scrapbook now match their Mac OS X counterparts.

Even better, any changes you make in the Classic version of Internet Explorer also appear in the Mac OS X version. (Once you're confident that everything works, you can delete the Classic files you moved in step 4.)

Tip: Best of all, this technique works with other programs that have both Classic and Mac OS X incarnations (Eudora, Graphic Converter, and so on). You may have to figure out which files they can share and look for settings like window size and position, default fonts, and save locations.

4-28: Speeding the Opening of Classic

Mac OS X duplicates many of the functions of the Classic System Folder—and in a much superior way. Turning off as many Mac OS 9 extensions as possible, therefore, makes using your Classic environment a much smoother and more stable experience and dramatically accelerates its startup process.

The key to controlling which extensions load is to press and hold the Space bar *just* after the progress bar begins filling up, as shown in Figure 4-22. Release the Space bar only after you see the appearance of the Extensions Manager window.

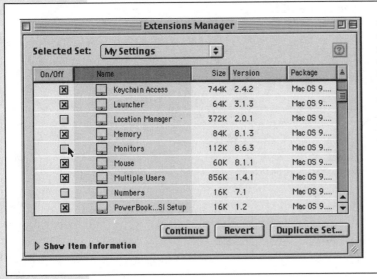

Figure 4-22:
Pressing the Space bar while Classic is starting up opens Extensions Manager, just as when you press Space while starting up a Mac OS 9 computer. (If you've bought Conflict Catcher 9—a commercial replacement for Extensions Manager with many more features—you'll see its screen appear here instead.)

To set up your winnowed-down extension set, click Duplicate Set in the lower-right corner of the window. In the dialog box that appears, type a name for the set you're about to create (such as *Classic Speedy Startup*), and then click OK.

Now you're ready to start paring down the extensions and control panels that delay Classic's startup process and make it so prone to crashes. Depending on what functions you need to use in Classic, you might consider turning off the extensions and control panels in these function categories (by clicking their checkboxes so that the X no longer appears):

- **Control Panels.** Many of Mac OS 9's control panel functions are superseded by new panels in the Mac OS X System Preferences. Changing your mouse speed using Mac OS 9's Mouse control panel, for example, doesn't have much meaning if you've already set your mouse speed in Mac OS X.

  Therefore, you should turn off the following control panels immediately, since they don't work in Classic and gain you nothing: Control Strip, Energy Saver, File Sharing, Infrared, Location Manager, Modem, Monitors, Mouse, Multiple Users, Password Security, PowerBook SCSI Disk Mode, Remote Access, Software Update, TCP/IP, Trackpad, and Web Sharing.

Note: The following Mac OS 9 control panels work, albeit with limited functions, within Classic: Appearance, AppleTalk, Date & Time (for menu-bar clock control only), General Controls (some commands, like Show Desktop, are dimmed), Keyboard (duplicated functions are dimmed), Memory (Disk Cache only), Monitors, and Sound (for alert sounds only).

- **Internet.** If you do all your Internet dialing from within Mac OS X, you may have little need for the equivalent functions in the Classic environment. If that's the case, you can safely turn off DialAssist, Internet, Location Manager Extension, Apple Modem Tool, Internet V.90 Modem (and other modem names, such as PowerBook Modem), the LDAP extensions, NBP Plugin, NetSprocketLib, Remote Only, and ShareWay IP Personal Bgnd, in addition to the control panels listed above. You may as well turn off the Software Update extensions, too, since they rely on Internet access.

- **Networking, Multiuser features.** If you won't be connecting to other computers on your office network from within Classic, turn off AppleTalk, any AirPort extensions, Keychain Access, IrDA Tool and IrDALib, Apple Enet, Apple Enet DLPI Support, AppleShare, EnetShimLib, File Sharing Extension, File Sharing Library, Multi-User Startup, OpenTpt Remote Access, Network Setup Extension, and SLPPlugin.

- **Printing.** If you don't plan to print from within Classic programs, you can turn off anything containing the words Print, Printer, Printing, or ColorSync, as well as the extensions bearing specific printer names (Color SW 1500, Color SW 2500, LaserWriter, and so on).

- **DVD.** The old, Mac OS 9–style DVD Player program doesn't even work in Classic. Turn off everything containing "DVD" in its name.

• **CD burning.** Here again, Mac OS X does a far better job of burning CDs than Mac OS 9 does. For example, Mac OS X can even burn data *DVDs,* which hold a delightful 4.7 GB per disc. By all means, turn off the Disc Burner Extension.

• **Video games.** A few video games require the OpenGL, QuickDraw 3D, NVIDIA, and ATI extensions. If you're a gamer, you'll experience the best game play by *restarting* your Mac in Mac OS 9, rather than trying to play Mac OS 9 games in the Classic mode. If you agree, turn off all extensions that contain the words QuickDraw 3D, OpenGL, NVIDIA, and ATI.

• **FireWire.** Even if you have a digital camcorder for use with iMovie, you may as well turn off the FireWire extensions, as the Mac OS X version of iMovie is better than the Mac OS 9 version. Leave the FireWire extensions on only if you have FireWire gadgets like external hard drives that you want to access from within Mac OS 9.

Once your pruning session is complete, click Continue. You should find that the Classic mode now starts up dramatically faster than before.

Note: These are only suggestions. If, after turning off some of these extensions and control panels, you find that certain familiar Mac OS 9 functions are no longer available, exit Classic, restart it with the Space bar pressed again, and experiment with restoring some of the things you turned off. And if you don't have the time to fiddle with individual extension settings, you can always turn on the entire Apple-authorized original set by choosing Mac OS 9 All (or Mac OS 9.2.2 All, or whatever) from the Selected Set pop-up menu.

Similarly, note that the commercial program Conflict Catcher can switch extension sets *automatically,* depending on whether the System Folder is being used for Classic mode or an actual restart.

Extensions to leave on

You can't go totally hog-wild turning off System Folder elements. Classic expects to find certain System Folder items when it launches. If you turn them off, an error message will explain that "Some Classic-specific resources need to be added to or updated in your System Folder on [Disk Name]." If you click OK, Mac OS X copies them into the Mac OS 9 System Folder. Here's a list, current as of Mac OS 9.2.2:

• *Control Panels:* General, Startup Disk

• *Extensions:* Apple Guide, CarbonLib, Classic RAVE, Open Transport, Open Transport ASLM Modules

• *Loose in the System Folder:* Classic Support, Classic Support UI, ProxyApp

4-29: Speeding Your System with Two Mac OS 9 Folders

The Classic simulation mode is a perfectly satisfactory substitute for a true Mac OS 9 computer—most of the time. Occasionally, though, some people run up against tasks that don't work except on a true-blue, Mac OS 9–booted computer, not some sissified Mac OS 9 simulator. Certain older scanners, for example, work only on a machine that is actually running Mac OS 9; ditto with certain Mac games.

If this is your situation, consider creating two copies of Mac OS 9:

- **A Classic copy.** You'll use this System Folder only as the basis for running the Classic simulator. In this one, turn off a huge number of the extensions, control panels, and drivers that typically clog the arteries of the System Folder. This will result in a much faster Classic startup and a much more stable Classic emulator.

- **A full copy.** You'll use the second System Folder for starting up the machine when necessary.

This trick, alas, comes with two very specific hardware requirements:

- A pre-2003 Macintosh that *can* be restarted in Mac OS 9. (Mac models introduced in 2003 and later can start up only in Mac OS X.)

- A second hard drive (an iPod, for example) or hard drive partition.

You can create a Classic-only version of Mac OS 9 by copying your hard drive's System Folder to the new drive or partition. When you need to use your "real" version of Mac OS 9, just choose it in the Classic panel of System Preferences, and then restart the Mac.

Here are some general guidelines to streamline a Classic-only System Folder:

- To create a Classic-only version that will load quickly and run solidly, trash items like shareware and freeware extensions, and control panels that provide features you don't absolutely need. You can toss, for example, things that modify sounds, create themes, and install items in your menu bar.

- Turn off all of the extensions and control panels for features that Mac OS X already handles, as described in the previous hint.

- To conserve disk space, empty out the Preferences folder in the System Folder that you'll use for Classic purposes.

  Then, open the System Folder you'll use for restarting the computer. Open its Preferences folder, press ⌘-A to highlight all the files inside, and then ⌘-Option-drag any one of them to the Classic-only System Folder→Preferences folder.

  In short, you've just eliminated the necessity to maintain duplicate sets of preferences. You really only have one set of preference files—but thanks to the aliases, they're mirrored automatically in the second System Folder.

Once you have two Mac OS 9 folders, tell the Mac what to do with them like this:

- **Choose the System Folder for Classic use.** To do so, open System Preferences→Classic. On the Start/Stop tab, click the icon for the System Folder that will represent your Classic copy (Figure 4-23). (This is a one-time step.)

- **Designate the System Folder for startup purposes.** You'll perform this step only when you want to restart the Mac in Mac OS 9.

This time, open System Preferences→Startup Disk. Click the icon for the System Folder that you want to be the "start me up" operating system. Then restart the Mac.

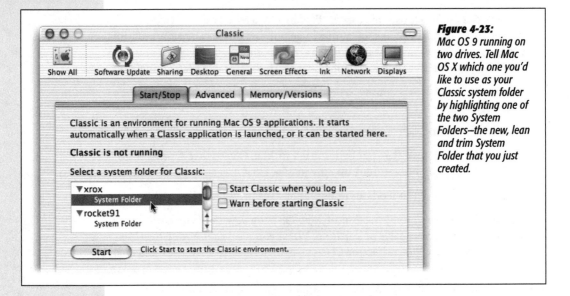

Figure 4-23:
Mac OS 9 running on two drives. Tell Mac OS X which one you'd like to use as your Classic system folder by highlighting one of the two System Folders—the new, lean and trim System Folder that you just created.

4-30: Running Classic from a Disk Image

As companies write more programs for Mac OS X, and Mac OS 9 fades in utility, you may wonder if you need the older system lingering around, taking up desktop space. You don't. Instead, you can run Classic from a simulated drive known as a disk image, much like the .dmg files that often serve as "digital wrappers" for software you download from the Web.

Why encapsulate your Classic System Folder in a disk image? Let us count the ways:

• It's hidden from view until you need it.

• It's preserved in its virginal, perfectly operational condition. You can't accidentally delete something from, or save something into, your System Folder.

• You can compress it to save disk space.

• You can copy it from Mac to Mac, confident that it will be identical in each copy.

If you want to forge ahead, bear in mind that you need at least 500 MB of drive space to hold the disk image. You also need a tolerance for Terminal (page 5).

1. **Make sure that Classic is not running. Then open Disk Copy (in Applications→Utilities). Choose File→New→Blank.**

   Disk Copy asks you to name the disk image you're about to create.

2. **Set up the name, size, and characteristics of the disk image.**

   Name it whatever you like, just so long as you use the same name for both Save As and Volume Name.

   Set the size to around 500 MB. If you have an existing Mac OS 9 folder that you intend to drag to the new disk image, you can use Get Info to find its size (highlight its icon and then press ⌘-I); then set the size slider in Disk Copy to something slightly larger than that.

   Make sure the format is Mac OS Extended, and don't encrypt the image.

3. **Click OK.**

   Disk Copy makes the new image, which is basically a file on your hard drive of the size you specified. This process takes a few minutes.

4. **Once the disk image appears on your desktop, double-click its icon to mount it.**

   Mounting a disk means bringing its icon onto the desktop, as shown in Figure 4-24.

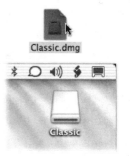

Figure 4-24:
When you double-click a .dmg file (top), the system eventually spits out an icon that looks like a regular disk (bottom). You can treat these disk images as you would a recordable CD.

5. **Put Mac OS 9 onto the new disk image.**

   You can either install Mac OS 9 from your original CDs onto the simulated disk, or drag your existing Mac OS 9 System Folder onto the image.

   If you drag, you create a copy of Mac OS 9 as you've customized it. If you install from the CDs, you create a factory-fresh copy.

   The customized version will probably be more useful to you, but the factory version will be much smaller and cleaner—free from the various bits that accumulate in the System Folder over the years.

6. **Open Terminal.**

   It's in your Applications→Utilities folder. Position its window so that you can see its window *and* the Finder window that contains the new Mac OS 9 folder you just created.

7. At the % prompt in Terminal, type *sudo bless -folder* and then press the Space bar to leave a space at the end of the line.

The "bless" command tells the Mac that the folder you're about to specify is a legitimate, working Mac OS 9 System Folder. (Type *man bless* and then press Enter if you'd like more information on the command.)

8. In the Finder, drag the newly created System Folder from the disk image directly into the Terminal window.

That's a shortcut for telling Terminal which file you intend to operate on. You see something like this:

```
sudo bless -folder /Volumes/Classic/System\ Folder
```

9. Type a space, followed by *-folder9* and another space. Drag the exact same System Folder icon from the Finder into Terminal again.

You've just built a command that looks like this:

```
sudo bless -folder /Volumes/Classic/System\ Folder -folder9 /
Volumes/Classic/System\ Folder
```

10. Type another space and then *-bootBlocks.*

Make sure you use the uppercase B.

The entire command looks like this (with just one space instead of the line break shown here):

```
sudo bless -folder /Volumes/Classic/System\ Folder -folder9
 /Volumes/Classic/System\ Folder -bootBlocks
```

The name of the disk image you created takes the place of "Classic" in the example above, but the remainder of the command should look the same. If everything looks right, press Enter.

If you did everything right, Terminal executes your command without complaint. Quit Terminal.

11. Back in the Finder, open System Preferences→Startup Disk.

You're going to use this application to trick the Classic preference panel into searching for working Mac OS 9 System Folders again.

12. Select the Classic folder you just created.

Figure 4-25 shows the effect.

13. Quit System Preferences.

When it asks if you want to change your startup disk, agree by clicking Change. (You have to quit and reopen System Preferences to make it recognize the new Startup Disk.)

14. **Open System Preferences again. Click Classic, then the Start/Stop tab.**

    The search indicator spins as Mac OS X looks for new disks containing Mac OS 9 System Folders.

Figure 4-25:
Use Startup Disk to select the new Classic folder. Select the Mac OS 9 system that's on the Classic disk image you just created. You won't actually restart your computer by booting from the disk image (it wouldn't work, anyway). By selecting it as the startup disk, however, you force the Classic preference panel to search for new Classic disks the next time you launch it.

15. **Find your new Classic folder (the one on the disk image) in the list, and select it as Classic for Mac OS X.**

16. **Still in System Preferences, click Startup Disk. Click the icon of the System Folder that you want to start up the Mac the next time it starts.**

    That would probably be Mac OS X.

17. **Return to the Classic preference panel and click Start.**

    If you installed Mac OS 9 using the original CDs, a dialog box opens asking if you wish to add the necessary resources for Classic to run; click Yes. (If you made a copy by dragging your existing folder, there's no warning.)

18. **Use your old Mac OS 9 programs in Classic as usual.**

    When you're done, stop Classic from its System Preferences panel first, and then click the Show All icon (or switch to any other preference panel) to avoid a warning about your disk selection.

    Once Classic has stopped, you can drag the Classic disk-image icon to the trash to remove it from sight, or just press the Eject key on your keyboard.

The next time you need to run a Classic program—SimpleText, say—just double-click the SimpleText icon as usual. The Finder will mount your disk image (that is, turn it into a virtual disk on the screen) and then start Classic from it, all without your intervention.

Classic takes a bit longer to open this way than it does when launched directly from your hard drive. But look on the bright side: You have a Classic that is completely gone when you're not using it. Meanwhile, you can boast to your friends that you "run Classic off a disk image, just like VirtualPC." They'll either be awed or disturbed by your geek prowess.

Troubleshooting

Although Mac OS X is nice and stable, you may still experience problems from time to time. When you do, here are some simple things you can try to resolve the issue.

4-31: Memory Leaks

If you notice that your Mac seems to get slower the longer you use it each day, and you hear your hard drive thrashing for no apparent reason, you may have a *memory leak.* This problem occurs—very rarely, thank goodness—when a program wildly bloats your *virtual memory swap files* (invisible files that hold portions of one open program while you're using another).

Investigate by opening Mac OS X's virtual memory folder. Although this folder is normally invisible, you can get there in the Finder by choosing Go→Go to Folder, typing */var/vm* in the box, and then pressing Enter. When you press Enter, the Finder opens the vm (for Virtual Memory) folder.

If your system is running normally, you probably see at between one and three files named "swapfile0," "swapfile1," and "swapfile2." If you see more than about three swap files, there are two possible causes. The first is that you've just been running many more programs than your machine has room for in its memory. (If you suspect this is the case, consider installing more RAM.) But if you've only been running a handful of programs, and yet you see a whole bunch of files here (as in Figure 4-26), then you may have a program with a memory leak.

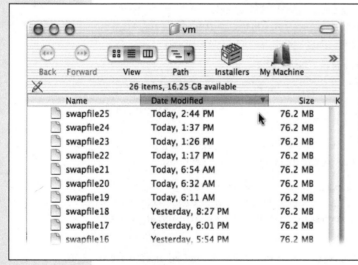

Figure 4-26:
Under normal circumstances, you'd only see three files in the Virtual Memory folder. In this case, the folder has 26 swap files, consuming nearly 2 GB of drive space. Whether it's the result of a memory leak or pushing Mac OS X too hard, this overpopulation of your Virtual Memory folder leads to nothing but trouble.

Note: You don't *necessarily* have a memory leak, though. If you've been working for a long time in Photoshop, for example, you may have numerous perfectly harmless swap files. Memory-intensive programs like this often create swap files.

Unfortunately, troubleshooting a memory leak is relatively complicated. Start by rebooting your machine to clear the existing swap files. Then try running only one or two programs at a time, keeping an eye on the Virtual Memory folder. If the swap files start piling up when you open a certain program, then you may have found the culprit.

Memory leaks are most common in prerelease or beta-test software versions, non-Apple utility programs (\U{F8FF} menu replacements, screen-capture programs, and so on), or programs from small, one-person software companies.

Maintaining at least 3 GB of free hard drive space is one way to hedge against memory leaks. That way, there's enough room for the swap files even in the case of a bad memory leak.

4-32:   Trashing Preferences

Corrupted preference files can cause all kinds of strange behavior in certain programs: A program that used to work perfectly suddenly starts quitting at random, Mail stops working altogether, and so on. Wiping out the preference file for a balky program can often restore it to working order. Although you lose your preference settings when you do this, it's occasionally a necessary evil of troubleshooting.

Mac OS X maintains a separate preference file for each person who has an account (page 11). You can find your personal collection in the Home→Library→Preferences folder. Look for a file with the name of your misbehaving program, and drag it to the trash. (If you don't see a file associated with the program you're looking for, check the ByHost folder.) If this action fixes the problem, you're done troubleshooting! (If not, gnash your teeth and try the next hint.)

Note: In the case of the above-mentioned Mail malfunction, a bad Address Book entry could be at fault because Mail reads the Address Book each time it opens. If that's at the root of your woes, you'll be able to get Mail working again only by trashing Address Book's database.

4-33:   A Separate Account for Troubleshooting

One of Mac OS X's most useful troubleshooting features is its multiuser capacity. If you're having trouble with some element of the system, and the previous hint didn't resolve it, the next step is to create a new "troubleshooting only" account.

Open System Preferences, click Accounts, and on the Users tab, click New User. Fill in the dialog box that opens, and give the account a useful name like "Test Account" or "Save My Bacon." At the bottom of the dialog box, turn on "Allow user to administer this computer" to make sure your test account has full system-management powers. Click OK to create the account.

Now log out of your Normal account, and log in as the test user. Try to recreate the problem you were experiencing before. If you can't make it happen again, then you've narrowed the problem down to something within your Normal account. If, on the other hand, the problem persists, you know you've got some sort of system-level problem, and it may be time to call in the experts (Apple Support, your favorite troubleshooting Web site, or an ultrageeky friend).

Note: Don't use your test account for normal computing, and don't install any hacks or nonstandard system modifications on that account. You want to keep it as close as possible to the original, from-the-factory setup.

4-34:   The System Build and Serial Numbers

Every release of Mac OS X has an associated *build number*—a special number that represents what Apple called this version of the software internally before it was released publicly. You may need to know it if you call Apple's tech support line, to make sure you get the appropriate version of certain knowledge base articles on Apple's support Web site, or when discussing your Mac online with other geeks. To find out your Mac OS X build number and serial number, follow the directions in Figure 4-27.

Figure 4-27:
Choose —About This Mac. In the resulting dialog box, click Version. The first click reveals the build number; a second click reveals your system's serial number. (And a click on More Info opens Apple System Profiler for you.)

System Preferences

System Preferences is like your brain's cortex: it coordinates fine-motor skills. It's the program to use if you want to change characteristics of your machine (like the speed of your mouse) or system-wide functions (like the color used for highlighting text). If you're an old Mac or Windows hand, note that System Preferences has replaced the Control Panels of yore.

And while you won't find hidden secrets in every one of the preference panels, you'll find enough for at least a chapter or so...

System Preferences

This section provides hints on using the System Preferences program itself.

50 Ways to System Preferences

There's more than one way to skin a cat, and there's certainly more than one way to open System Preferences.

Most people get there by clicking the little light-switch icon on the Dock. If you don't see it there, somebody you love may have dragged it off the Dock, accidentally or not. Fortunately, there's a backdoor: You can also choose →System Preferences.

These are only shortcuts to the third method: Open your Applications folder and double-click the icon for System Preferences itself.

Of course, the true Mac aficionado bypasses all of these sophomoric efforts and dives directly into the specific panel they want, simply by adding a pop-up list of System Preferences to the Dock. Hint 5-2 has the details.

5-1   Alphabetizing Preference Panels

The trouble with System Preferences is that Apple has sorted them into categories that *it* may find logical, but strikes most Mac fans as more or less arbitrary (see Figure 5-1).

Figure 5-1:
Quick—without looking, which category contains Date & Time? Is it the Personal, Hardware, Internet & Network, or System row? Hint: It's highlighted.

There's a much better way: Change System Preferences to eliminate the category rows, and instead display all of the preference icons in alphabetical order. Now you know *exactly* where to find Date & Time.

To bring about this arrangement, choose View→Show All Alphabetically. If you decide you prefer the grouped view, just press ⌘-L (or select View→Show All In Categories).

Although this secret isn't especially buried—it's right there in the View menu—hardly anyone knows about it.

UP TO SPEED

Why Some System Preferences Are Dimmed

Only a system administrator (see page 11) can change settings that affect everyone who shares a certain machine: its Internet settings, Energy Saver settings, and so on.

The tiny padlock in the lower-left corner of a panel is the telltale sign. If you, a nonadministrator, would like to edit some settings, call an administrator over to your Mac and ask him to click the lock, input his password, and supervise your tweaks.

5-2   System Preferences from the Dock I

Leave the ranks of the downtrodden masses, who make system adjustments by opening the System Preferences program, looking for the control-panel icon they want, and then clicking it. Instead, you, Speed Racer, can choose any panel directly from a Dock pop-up menu.

Here's how to set it up:

In your main hard drive window, open the System→Library folder. In the window folder, you'll find a folder called PreferencePanes. If you drag it onto the right side of the Dock, you'll have yourself a handy pop-up folder that provides direct access to any System Preference panel (something like what you see in Figure 5-2).

5-3   System Preferences from the Dock II

Unfortunately, the listing that results from the previous hint bears such user-hostile names as LoginItems.prefPane and DigiHubDiscs.prefPane. And because Mac OS X stores these in a sacred place (the innards of your System folder), you're not allowed to rename them.

There's a second problem, too: You won't have access to any additional preference panes that you can see in your Home→Library→PrefPanes folder. (These would be little shareware and freeware things you've installed, like FruitMenu, LabelsX, Xounds, WindowShadeX, or ASM.)

You can solve both problems in one of two ways.

The short way

Download Prefling (available at *homepage.mac.com/asagoo*), shown in Figure 5-2.

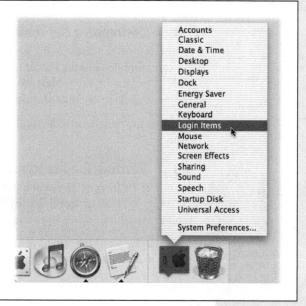

Figure 5-2:
Prefling is a free little program that, when you double-click it, instantly places a pop-up System Preferences folder onto your Dock. This method not only displays all the preference panes in one long list, but it actually uses plain-English names for them. If you decide you don't need or want Prefling, just drag it off the Dock.

The long way

1. In your main hard drive window, open the System→Library→PreferencePanes folder.

So far, of course, this sounds a lot like the technique described above.

2. Click your desktop. Choose File→New Folder. When the new folder appears, name it something like *Control Panels* or *System Panels.*

Instead of putting the actual preference panes on your Dock, you're about to place *aliases* of them—because you're allowed to rename aliases.

3. In the open Preference Panes window, press ⌘-A to select all of the panes. Drag them onto your new Control Panels folder, taking care to press Option-⌘ as you release the mouse.

If you press those keys when you complete the drag, you create aliases of whatever you dragged.

4. Open your Control Panels folder. Rename or delete the various panels as you see fit.

Not only can you rename these aliases, but you can also get rid of the ones you rarely or never use.

5. Drag the Control Panels folder onto your Dock, where it's ready for action as a pop-up menu.

What to do with the original Control Panels folder? Answer: Stick it anywhere you like—in your Home folder, in your Applications folder, just about anywhere but the Trash. You'll never open it directly, since it only uses its Dock representation.

5-4   Customizing the Toolbar

At the top of the System Preferences window is a toolbar. Turns out that it's customizable, just like the Finder toolbar or the Mail toolbar. If you load this toolbar with the icons for the preference panels you use most often, you save yourself a couple of clicks every time you change a setting.

Just drag the panels onto the toolbar; you can drag them horizontally to rearrange them.

5-5   Resizing Toolbar Icons

It's not as exciting as 31 flavors, but System Preferences lets you choose from six different icon sizes in the toolbar, as shown in Figure 5-3. The more you ⌘-click this toolbar button, the more you condense the display of toolbars.

At the largest icon size, you have room for about seven or eight icons in the toolbar. In the smallest icon-only view, you can fit at least twelve to fifteen icons in the same horizontal space. (It defeats the purpose of putting them in the toolbar in the first place, but it looks really neat.)

Note: This "⌘-click the toolbar button to resize the toolbar icons" feature is common to all Cocoa programs. You can use the same technique in Mail, Safari, or any other Cocoa program with a toolbar.

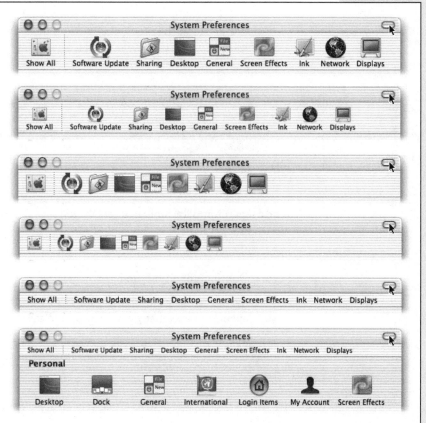

Figure 5-3:
The incredible shrinking toolbar. ⌘-click the oblong widget at the top right of the window to cycle between the six styles of toolbar. With each click, the icons get smaller, the text labels get smaller, and finally the icons disappear altogether, leaving only a row of tiny text labels.

5-6   Adding Separators and Spaces to the Toolbar

Seeing as Apple lets you drag icons onto your System Preferences toolbar, you'd think they'd give you an easy way to add separators and spaces to create logical groupings, too. No such luck. But no matter: Here's a workaround that looks pretty decent (Figure 5-4).

1. **Add all the icons you want onto the System Preferences toolbar, and then quit the program.**

   It's very important that you quit before the next step, as the program remembers any additions to the toolbar only after you quit.

2. In the Finder, open your Home→Library→Preferences folder. Drag and drop the file called *com.apple.systempreferences.plist* onto the icon of TextEdit.

See page 4 for details on using TextEdit to tweak preference files.

When the document opens, look for two lines that read:

```
<key>TB Item Identifiers</key>
<array>
```

This area lists the icons shown on the toolbar. Immediately below these lines is the code for the Show All icon (com.apple.prefpane.showall), followed by everything else you've placed on the toolbar.

Figure 5-4:
You can add divider bars and white space to help organize your System Preferences toolbar.

3. To add a separator to the toolbar, insert the following line between the two items you wish to separate:

```
<string>NSToolbarSeparatorItem</string>
```

Of course, you should put this on its own line.

Alternatively, you can type the following line, which creates a space between icons (the size depends on how many items you add to the toolbar):

```
<string>NSToolbarFlexibleSpaceItem</string>
```

Place it between two items you want to separate. Add as many spaces as you like.

4. Once you've added your desired separators and spaces, save and close the preferences file.

Open the System Preferences program and admire your fancy new toolbar. (If the changes don't appear, quit System Preferences and reopen it.)

Note: You can rearrange the separators and spaces you added by ⌘-dragging them horizontally.

5-7   Eliminating the Toolbar

These Mac OS X toolbars are cute, but they do not, shall we say, maximize your screen real estate. They add another inch to every window.

If you'd rather reclaim that space in System Preferences, click the upper-right, white toolbar button to hide the toolbar entirely. At that point, you can still switch from one System Preferences panel to another in any of these ways:

- *Fast:* Press ⌘-L, the keyboard shortcut for the Show All In Categories command. Then click the icon of the new panel you want.

- *Faster:* Choose any panel's name from the View menu. (You never even noticed that menu up there, did you?)

- *Equally fast:* Choose the name of the exact panel you want from the Dock, after first having checked out hint 5-2.

5-8   Removing Preference Panels

The System Preferences that you see the day you first turn on your Mac aren't necessarily the only ones you'll ever see in System Preferences. It's perfectly possible to install additional icons into System Preferences in the form of shareware or commercial installers. Some of the most popular shareware add-ons, for example, are LabelsX, Xounds, TinkerTool, and WindowShadeX.

The problem arises when you get tired of one of these things. How are you supposed to get rid of it? Some of these non-Apple preference panels don't know when the party is over, and their icons hang around at System Preferences even after you've deleted them. This glitch happens when the system has *cached* (memorized) the preference pane information.

Clear the cache this way: In the Finder, open your Home→Library→Caches folder. Delete the file called com.apple.preferencepanes.cache.

When you quit and restart System Preferences, you'll find that the troublesome pane is gone. Use this procedure to trigger any preference pane modifications.

5-9   Renaming Long Preference Pane Names

The names of System Preferences icons can get out of hand. If, for example, you have a Microsoft mouse, you have a preference pane named Microsoft Mouse. This is a fine, utilitarian name. But it's long, and it won't stack on two lines. As a result, in the System Preferences window, the name tends to run into other names, making it hard to read (Figure 5-5).

Happily, you can shorten the displayed name of any preference pane or add a line break (Figure 5-5). This hint walks you through changing the Microsoft Mouse preference pane name, but you can use the same techniques to edit any non-Apple panes.

Note: Some panel icons get installed into the system-wide PreferencePanes folder, so that they show up in the accounts of everybody who uses your machine. Other panes get installed into only your Home folder, so that only you see them. This hint uses a system-wide example. To edit a file in your Home folder, change the path in step 1 to Home→Library→PreferencePanes; after that, the instructions are the same.

---

1. Quit System Preferences, and then open your hard drive's System→ Library→PreferencePanes folder.

   Inside are the icons that represent the various system preferences.

2. **Control-click Microsoft Mouse.prefPane. From the contextual menu, choose Show Package Contents (see page 3). In the new window that opens, open the Contents→Resources→English.lproj folder. Click once on the InfoPlist.strings icon.**

If this is a preference pane that appears only in your account, skip to the next step. Otherwise, you must now take an intermediate step: modifying the *permissions* of the InfoPlist.strings (the Mac OS X file-protection parameters).

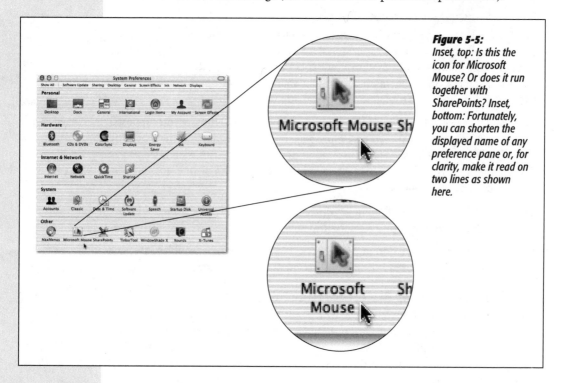

Figure 5-5:
Inset, top: Is this the icon for Microsoft Mouse? Or does it run together with SharePoints? Inset, bottom: Fortunately, you can shorten the displayed name of any preference pane or, for clarity, make it read on two lines as shown here.

Once the icon is highlighted, choose File→Get Info, click the triangle to expand Ownership & Permissions, and then click the lock icon to unlock it. Click the Owner pop-up menu, and change the owner to your account name. Enter your administrative password when asked.

Leave the Get Info window open, as you'll be returning here shortly to restore the ownership setting.

3. **Drag the InfoPlist.strings file onto the icon of TextEdit (which is in your Applications folder).**

The file opens, looking like so much computer code. You're looking for a line that reads:

```
CFBundleName = "Microsoft Mouse";
```

4. Shorten the name by rewriting "Microsoft Mouse" (Figure 5-6).

You might, for example, go for something clever like "MS Mouse."

To insert a line break (to produce a two-line, stacked name), simply type \n wherever you'd like the break to appear (between, say, "Microsoft" and "Mouse").

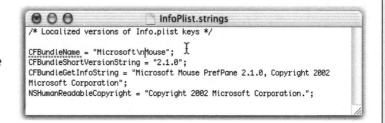

Figure 5-6:
In the footsteps of generations of hackers before you, editing the secret preferences file in TextEdit and a steady hand are all it takes.

```
/* Localized versions of Info.plist keys */

CFBundleName = "Microsoft\nMouse";
CFBundleShortVersionString = "2.1.0";
CFBundleGetInfoString = "Microsoft Mouse PrefPane 2.1.0, Copyright 2002
Microsoft Corporation";
NSHumanReadableCopyright = "Copyright 2002 Microsoft Corporation.";
```

5. Save and close the file. If you adjusted the permissions of the file in step 2, change them back again now.

To do so, use the Get Info box you left open. Click the Owner pop-up menu again, set the owner back to System, enter your password when prompted, click the lock icon, and close the Get Info window.

6. Make sure System Preferences is not running, and then, in the Finder, open your Home→Library→Caches folder. Locate the file called com.apple.preference-panes.cache and delete it.

You want Mac OS X to forget what the System Preferences icon used to look like.

7. Open System Preferences, and admire the new name.

Figure 5-5 at bottom (inset) shows the result.

5-10   Renaming the System Preference Categories

Why stop at renaming the icons in System Preferences? Once you're on a roll, you can rename the categories, too (Personal, Hardware, and so on). Although this modification has no effect on speed, productivity, or stability, you might prefer some special names—particularly if you've installed non-Apple preference panes, like TinkerTool or SharePoints, that get lumped into the Other category. Change Other to Custom Panels, as in Figure 5-7, and you're the master of all you survey.

1. Quit System Preferences, open Terminal (page 5), and type the following (pressing Enter after each line):

```
cd "/Applications/System Preferences.app/Contents/Resources/
English.lproj"
sudo cp NSPrefPaneGroups.strings NSPrefPaneGroups.bak
sudo cp NSPrefPaneGroups.strings ~/Desktop/MyPrefs.strings
```

The *cd* command opens the System Preferences software bundle and directs Terminal's attention to the folder that contains the file you want to modify.

When you enter the second command, Terminal asks you for your Administrator account password. The first *sudo* line creates a backup of the preference pane groups file, just in case something goes wrong. The second *sudo* line copies the file to your desktop, so that you can edit it in the Finder.

Figure 5-7:
If "Other" doesn't strike you as particularly informative, an easy edit will let you rename the bottom System Preferences category label (and others, too).

Why edit the file in the Finder? The NSPrefPaneGroups.strings file is in Unicode (hint 4-20), which you can't easily open using any of Mac OS X's Unix text editors (like *pico* or *emacs*). You can, however, open the file in programs like TextEdit, BBEdit, or Property List Editor.

2. **Claim ownership of the MyPrefs.strings file.**

This may seem like the recurring theme, but it's unavoidable: Whenever you hack one of Mac OS X's personal files, you must explicitly change its ownership setting so that you own it.

In any case, the ritual goes like this (leave Terminal running):

Click the MyPrefs.strings icon on your desktop once, and then press ⌘-I (Get Info). In the Get Info dialog box, click the triangle to expand the Ownership & Permissions panel. Click the little padlock icon to unlock it. Using the Owner pop-up menu, specify your own account name. Prove your worthiness by typing your account name and password when asked. You're now ready to proceed.

3. **Drag the MyPrefs.strings icon onto the icon of TextEdit (located in your Applications folder).**

   If you, a power user, have installed the Developer Tools CD that came with Mac OS X, you can also use the program called Property List Editor for this purpose. In this case, when the file opens, click the small triangle next to Root.

   In either editor, your goal is to change the words on the right side of the screen, not the left. So don't touch "addons," "DigitalHub," and so on.

4. **Edit the Other category to make it say something more pleasing.**

   The specific steps depend on which program you're using.

   Property List Editor: To rename the Other category, double-click the word "Other" next to "addons," and then type *Custom Panels* (or whatever you want to call it).

   TextEdit: Highlight the text next to "addons"—leave the quotation marks in place—then type the new name for this category.

   Change any of the other category names you think are stupid, save the file, and quit the program.

5. **Return to the Terminal window. Type this (and then press Enter):**

   ```
   sudo cp ~/Desktop/MyPrefs.strings NSPrefPaneGroups.strings
   ```

   This industrious command copies the file from your desktop back onto the System Preferences program bundle, renames it, and hands its ownership back to Mac OS X.

6. **Open System Preferences, and marvel at your new category names.**

If System Preferences is misbehaving, quit it and return to Terminal. Make sure Terminal is focused on the right folder by repeating the very first *cd* command in step 2, and then type this (followed by Enter):

```
sudo cp NSPrefPaneGroups.bak NSPrefPaneGroups.strings
```

This command overwrites the bad file with your good backup, and also leaves the backup in place in case you have any future editing problems.

Accounts

As described in the box on page 11, Mac OS X is a true *multiuser* system: If you set up accounts for each person who uses your machine, Mac OS X can separate and protect everyone's preferences, files, and email.

Although it may come as a surprise, this feature has its payoffs even if you're a solo operator; for one thing, you can create a new account that you use only for troubleshooting (hint 4-31).

5-11   Limiting Account Privileges

When you've got a machine with more than one account on it—for you, your spouse, your son, and your Turkish exchange student—you may wish to limit everyone else's ability to do things like remove stuff from the Dock, change the machine-wide System Preferences, burn CDs or DVDs, and run certain programs. Apply software handcuffs, if you will.

In System Preferences→Accounts, select any nonadministrative user, click the account on the Users tab, and then click Capabilities.

Take a break while your Mac scans its hard drive for information about all the programs you've got installed—it can take a minute or two. Eventually, a sheet slides out of the top of the Accounts window, as shown in Figure 5-8.

From here, you can restrict this person's access to the Mac in three different ways.

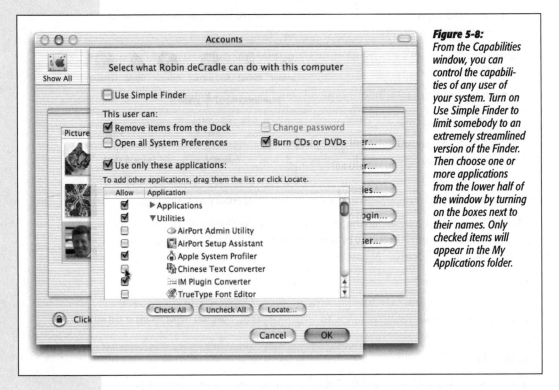

Figure 5-8:
From the Capabilities window, you can control the capabilities of any user of your system. Turn on Use Simple Finder to limit somebody to an extremely streamlined version of the Finder. Then choose one or more applications from the lower half of the window by turning on the boxes next to their names. Only checked items will appear in the My Applications folder.

Limit the programs

At the bottom of the dialog box shown in Figure 5-8, you see a list of all the programs in your Applications folder (an interesting read in its own right). If you turn on "Use only these applications," you can then turn the programs' checkboxes on or off. Only checked items will show up in the account holder's Applications folder.

If you're setting up an account for use in the classroom, say, you might well want to turn off access to programs like Disk Utility, iChat, and Tomb Raider.

Limit the features

When you first create a Normal account, all of the checkboxes above the master list of programs are turned *on*. That is, Normal account holders are free to burn CDs or DVDs, change the icons on the Dock, change their passwords, and view the settings of all System Preferences panels (although they can't *change* all of these settings).

Depending on your situation, you may find it useful to turn off some of these options. In a school lab, for example, you might want to turn off the ability to burn discs (to block software piracy). If you're setting up a Mac for a technophobe, you might want to turn off the ability to change the Dock (so your colleague won't accidentally lose access to her own programs and work).

Limit the interface (Simple Finder)

If you're *really* concerned about somebody's ability to survive the Mac—or the Mac's ability to survive them—then turn on the Use Simple Finder checkbox (shown at top in Figure 5-9). Also turn on the checkboxes of the programs that person is allowed to use.

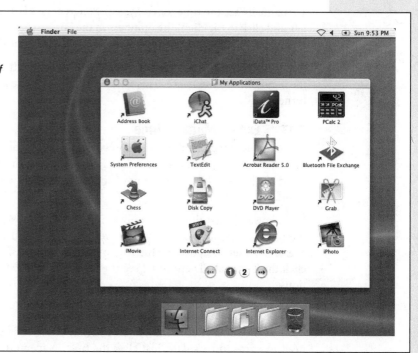

Figure 5-9:
The Simple Finder doesn't feel like home—unless you've got one of those Spartan, space-age, Dr. Evil–style pads. But it can be just the ticket for less-skilled Mac users with few options and a basic one-click interface. Every program in your My Applications folder is actually only an alias to the real program, which is safely ensconced in the off-limits Applications folder.

Suppose you're the lucky Mac fan who's been given a Simple Finder account. When you log in, you'll discover the barren world shown in Figure 5-9. There are only three menus (, Finder, and File), a single onscreen window, no hard drive icon, and a bare-bones Dock. The only folders you can see are in the Dock. They include My Applications (aliases of the applications the administrator approved, presented on strange, fixed, icon view "pages"); Documents (your Home→Documents folder); Shared (a folder provided so that you and other account holders can exchange documents); and the Trash.

The menu is *really* bare-bones: You can Log Out and go to Sleep. That's it.

Date & Time

Your Mac's conception of the current date and time is more important than you think—and much more customizable.

5-12   Setting the Time

Your Mac can set its own clock by checking in with an atomic clock on the Internet. If you're one of those people who likes all their clocks running five minutes fast in a thinly veiled attempt to prevent themselves from being late all the time, you can set the time manually. (To find out if your Mac is already set up to synchronize its clock with the Internet, choose System Preferences→Date & Time→Network Time tab. If "Use a network time server" is on, your Mac is set up to set its clock via the Internet.)

To manually set the time, open System Preferences→Date & Time→Date & Time tab, and click to highlight the numbers in the box below Current Time. Click the up or down arrows as needed for hours, minutes, and seconds.

A more entertaining but less precise method of setting the clock is to simply drag the hands on the clock face. This trick only works if "Use a network time server" is turned off.

5-13   Exiting Military Time

If you're frustrated that the Mac is showing you the 24-hour "military time" on your menu bar (that is, *17:30* instead of *5:30 PM*)—or it *isn't* showing military time when you'd like it to—click the Menu Bar Clock tab and turn "Use the 24-hour clock" on or off.

Note, however, that this affects only the Menu bar clock—not any other dates (like the ones that show when your files were modified in list views). To change that overarching setting, go to the International panel of System Preferences. Once there, click the Time tab. There you'll see the "24-Hour clock" and "12-Hour clock" options.

5-14   The Menu bar Calendar

Most of the time, your menu bar clock always shows the current *time.* When you need to know today's *date,* just click the time. A menu drops down revealing the complete date. (The menu also lets you switch between digital and analog clock types and provides a shortcut to the Date & Time preference panel.)

Desktop

The desktop is the canvas on which you paint the image that expresses your feelings of the moment. It's an emotional mural for your inner child. It's...

OK, enough of that. Basically, the desktop is a great place to slap a favorite photo.

5-15   The Desktop Picture

Here's a secret: In the Desktop panel, you can drag almost any graphics file—even a PDF or Photoshop file—directly onto the *well* (the preview square just below the words "Current Desktop Picture"; see Figure 5-10). When you release the image, it becomes the new desktop background.

Figure 5-10:
The Desktop preference panel lets you use almost any image type as your desktop background. So if you want a reminder as to why you're working so hard, go ahead and use a PDF of your 2002 tax return as your desktop picture.

5-16   Adding New Picture Folders

When it comes to specifying the source for your desktop background, Apple gives you a bushel of choices. In the Desktop preference panel, you can opt for your Pictures folder, one of the Apple-supplied image collections, or another folder of your choice.

But what if you want more of your own choices? This hint explains how you can go nuts adding as many folders as you'd like (Figure 5-11).

Before you begin, stash all of your desktop-only pictures in a special folder called, say, "Slideshow Folder." Put it into your Documents folder, for example. Within it, create folders for each picture collection that you want to add to the preference panel ("Cats," "Dogs," "Javelinas"). File your graphics files in these inner folders (but skip aliases—they don't work). Now proceed like this:

1. **Quit System Preferences. Open your System→Library→PreferencePanes folder. In the resulting window, Control-click the icon called DesktopPictures.prefPane. From the contextual menu, choose Show Package Contents.**

The DesktopPictures window opens, revealing its secret contents.

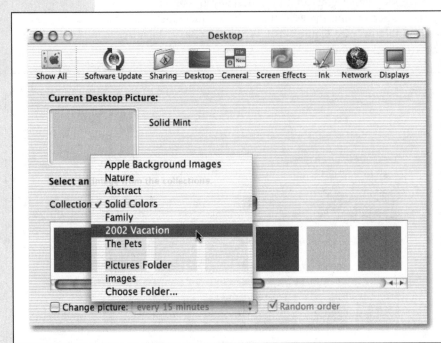

Figure 5-11:
You can add extra folders of your own stuff to the desktop picture options. Instead of being restricted to just one "other" folder, you can have as many as you may need. In the mood to view your 2002 vacation pictures today, and family images tomorrow? No problem.

2. **Open the Contents folder. Inside, click once on Resources, and then choose File→Get Info (⌘-I). Change the ownership of the Resources folder to make it your own.**

This may sound familiar if you've worked through, for example, hint 5-9, but here's a summary. In the Get Info window, click the triangle next to Ownership & Permissions, and then click the lock icon to unlock it. Click the Owner pop-up menu, and change the owner to your account name. Enter your administrative password when asked.

3. **Inside the Resources folder, click Collections.plist once, and repeat step 2 to make yourself its owner.**

You've now got temporary ownership of Collections.plist and the holy power to edit it. Leave the two Get Info windows open, as you'll use them again in a moment.

4. **Drag Collections.plist onto the icon of TextEdit (in your Applications folder).**

The document opens, looking like a bunch of computer programming, which it is. (Details on this TextEdit ritual on page 4.)

Scroll down to this section at the end of the file:

```
},
{
identifier = usersPictures;
path = "~/Pictures";
showScalingPopUp = YES;
}
```

5. **To make your folders appear in the list, add a new section before the bracket above "identifier= userPictures," like this (being sure to press Enter after each line):**

```
{
identifier = "Name to Use";
path = "/Path/To/Pictures/Folder";
showScalingPopUp = NO;
},
```

"Name to Use" is the folder name you'd like displayed in the Desktop preference panel. The path should reflect the full path to the folder where you stored the images. For example, if you wanted to use a folder named Kidshots in your Documents folder, and your name is Chris, the full path would be */Users/Chris/Documents/Kidshots*. Don't forget the trailing comma after the final bracket.

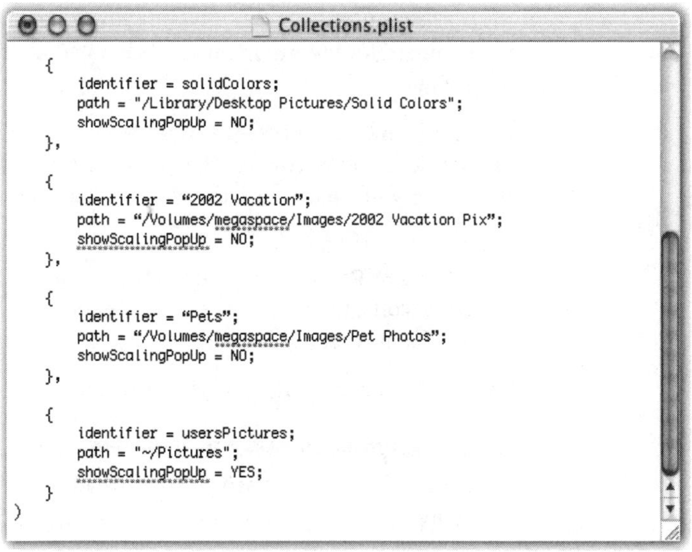

Figure 5-12:
To add your own collections to the pop-up list in the Desktop preference panel, you just need to add some funny-looking code to a property list (plist) file.

```
{
    identifier = solidColors;
    path = "/Library/Desktop Pictures/Solid Colors";
    showScalingPopUp = NO;
},

{
    identifier = "2002 Vacation";
    path = "/Volumes/megaspace/Images/2002 Vacation Pix";
    showScalingPopUp = NO;
},

{
    identifier = "Pets";
    path = "/Volumes/megaspace/Images/Pet Photos";
    showScalingPopUp = NO;
},

{
    identifier = usersPictures;
    path = "~/Pictures";
    showScalingPopUp = YES;
}
)
```

Add one new section for each folder you created (remember the trailing comma for each one), and then save the file when you're done. Figure 5-12 shows how the file might look after you've added a couple of your own image folders to the list.

6. Use the Get Info window to switch the ownership of Collections.plist and Resources back to System, undoing your work in steps 3 and 4 (click the lock icon when you're done). Finally, open System Preferences.

If the technology gods are smiling, you now see your custom folders in the list of possible desktop images.

If everything didn't work correctly—you get a blank preference pane, for example—then the Desktop preference panel must not have liked something you've added to Collections.plist. Regain ownership of the file, open it again, and remove the stuff you added.

If you're feeling patient, add the new folders back in one at a time until you find the one that's causing the problem.

Keyboard

Long-time Mac keyboard advocates have reason to rejoice—Mac OS X is by far the keyboard-friendliest Mac OS ever released. Not only do you have access to Terminal (page 5), which is about as keyboard-centric as you can get, but the graphic world of Mac OS X now sports a number of features designed to make it easier to manipulate from the keyboard.

5-17   Keyboard Navigation of Your Mac

The mouse is a great invention. But at heart, it's a rodent—and rodents are pests. In short, the mouse slows you down. If you'd like to exterminate your mouse and use the keyboard for tasks in menus, windows, toolbars, palettes, and the Dock, this hint is for you.

Open System Preferences→Keyboard→Full Keyboard Access tab, and turn on "Turn on Full Keyboard Access." In the "Press Control (ctrl) with" pop-up menu, choose a set of keys you'd like to use to reach the items listed below the pop-up.

For example, if you choose "Letter keys," then pressing Control-D highlights the first item on the Dock. From here, the left and right arrows highlight successive or previous icons; the up arrow opens the selection's contextual menu; the Enter key opens whatever icon is highlighted; Esc gets you out.

To turn off (or turn on) full keyboard access, press Control-F1.

5-18   KeyboardPower in Windows and Dialog Boxes

If the full keyboard access feature described in the previous hint displeases your fingertips, the Keyboard preference panel has a compromise setting.

Open System Preferences→Keyboard; at the bottom of the Full Keyboard Access tab, find the section labeled "For windows and dialogs, highlight." If you turn on "Any control," you can use the keyboard to reach everything in windows and dialog boxes.

For example, you can press Tab to move the "focus" (a subtle highlighting) through controls like pop-up menus, buttons, and dialog boxes. The up and down arrow keys navigate menus; the right and left arrows move you through submenus and subfolders; Enter is like clicking a chosen command; Esc gets you out.

Screen Effects

The rest of the world calls it a screen saver; Apple calls it Screen Effects, since these animated displays don't actually save your screen. Flat-panel screens, for one thing, never develop the "burn in" syndrome that screen savers were designed to protect. For another thing, even CRT (traditional bulky) monitors don't burn in unless you leave the exact same image, undisturbed, on the screen for two solid years.

In short, screen effects are just for fun—but what a lot of fun they are.

5-19   The Instant iPhoto Screen Saver

iPhoto 2 (in your Applications folder) lets you organize your photos into *albums* (subfolders). You can turn any album into a custom screen saver with just one click (on the Desktop icon at the bottom of the Share panel). In the resulting dialog box, use the pop-up menu to choose the name of the album you want to use for this screen saver, and then click OK.

5-20   Your Own Screen Saver Folders

If you like to stare at your monitor even when you're not working, Apple provides a handful of screen savers that play slide shows. The system also lets you create your own slide show by using your Pictures folder as the screen saver's source, or (if you click Configure in System Preferences) some other folder of photos.

Unfortunately, these methods—as well as the iPhoto trick in hint 5-19—make it inconvenient to *change* slide-show photo folders. What if sometimes you want to watch scenes from your daughter's first basketball championship game, and other times you want to watch a time-lapse sequence of your cat outgrowing its first litter box? Apple only lets you create one slide show at a time.

What the world really wants is a way to expand the list of photo modules listed on the Screen Effects tab of System Preferences, along with Forest and Cosmos.

Here's one quick way: Option-⌘-drag the folder that contains your photos into your Home→Library→Screen Savers folder. (If there's no Screen Savers folder in your Home→Library folder, create one.)

You've just created an alias of the photos folder. Add *.slideSaver* to the end of the folder's name (capitalization counts). Repeat with any other photo folders that you want to turn into screen savers.

Now check out System Preferences→Screen Effects: There are your new photo folders in all their glory (Figure 5-13)! Click Configure to see all the special effects that you can apply to your slide show (including random order).

The beauty of this approach is that as you add new images to the original folder, they'll automatically be included in your slide show, as you're using an alias to point to the original folder.

Figure 5-13:
By tricking the system, you can easily create your own slide-show screen savers, each of which appears at the bottom of the list of available screen savers.

5-21   From Screen Saver to Desktop Picture

The canned screen saver modules are stored in your System→Library→Screen Savers folder. If you Control-click one of the icons inside and choose Show Package Contents from the contextual menu, you'll find a Contents→Resources folder that contains the individual JPEG files for each module (the outer space photos for the Cosmos screen saver, for example).

Why bother? Because some of these spectacular photos make really good desktop pictures. You're free to copy them out of the Resources folder for that purpose, ready for dragging directly into the Desktop panel of System Preferences (hint 5-15).

Software Update

Software Update is Apple's way of cleaning up after itself. A window like the one shown in Figure 5-14 appears from time to time, offering to install patches and updates that Apple's just released.

5-22   Stifling Irrelevant Software Updates

Unfortunately, you may not be interested in installing every update that Software Update proposes, especially if you use a dial-up modem. Maybe you just don't care about a 23 MB DVD-burning enhancement or an update to the Dutch language profiles. Yet every time you run Software Update, it will keep nagging about the update you declined and, when you try to bypass the update screen, it'll keep asking if you're sure you don't want to install it.

The easy, but secret, solution to this problem is to highlight the update you aren't interested in, and then choose Update→Make Inactive. OS X promptly removes the update from your list.

If you ever change your mind—maybe you decide to learn Dutch after all—you can bring the declined item back into the list by choosing Update→Show Inactive Updates (or press Shift-⌘-minus).

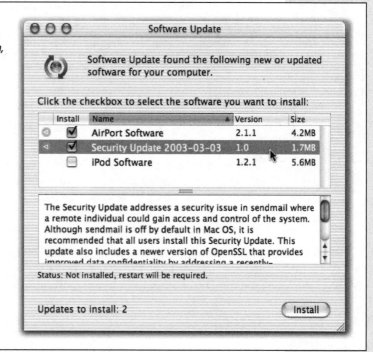

Figure 5-14:
Apple's Software Update, found in the System Preferences application, can help keep your machine's software up to date. This is especially important with OS X, whose software Apple regularly updates behind the scenes to fix bugs and close security holes.

5-23   Storing Apple Software Updates

Software Update has another drawback, too. If you ever reinstall Mac OS X from its original CD or DVD (when you install a new hard drive or move to a new computer, for example), you'll have to download and install all relevant updates again. You can't skip the reinstallation process, but you can skip the download step.

Preserving these updates on your hard drive is easy enough. Each time Software Update finds updates to install, turn on the ones you wish to install and then choose Update→Download Checked Items to Desktop, as shown in Figure 5-15.

Later, you can reinstall your downloaded updates at any time by just double-clicking each installer. (The downside: When there are multiple updates that require restarting your Mac, you have to restart after each one you install. On its own, Software Update would save up its one restart until all of the updates are installed.)

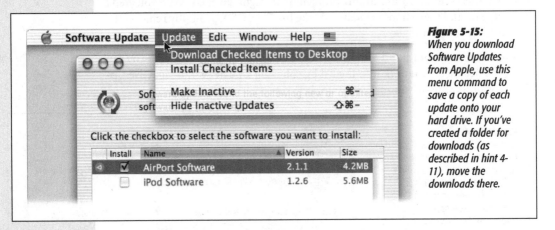

Figure 5-15:
When you download Software Updates from Apple, use this menu command to save a copy of each update onto your hard drive. If you've created a folder for downloads (as described in hint 4-11), move the downloads there.

5-24 Checking for Software Updates

It's a good idea to run Software Update from time to time, given that Apple provides critical security patches and other important upgrades. But updates occasionally include glitches, which leads some Mac fans to wish that they could check for, and install, updates manually—after they've had the chance to read about the success of these updates on, for example, Macintouch.com or Macfixit.com.

To run a check on command, open System Preferences, and then *Option*-click the Software Update icon. The system checks for updates as soon as the panel opens. (You must be online for this to work, of course.)

Speech

Ever get tired of typing? Sick of the mouse, too? Want to yell at your computer… and have it respond? If you answered yes to any of these questions, then Mac OS X's speech features are worth a look.

5-25 Minimizing the Speech Feedback Window

When you turn on speech recognition (in System Preferences→Speech), a small speech feedback window appears and floats over all your programs (Figure 5-16). Like a gnat, this window can get annoying.

Swat it away by double-clicking anywhere above the triangle on the bottom; you just minimized it to the Dock. Once minimized, the icon continues to display the volume level of sounds it hears.

Figure 5-16:
The speech bubble floats over all other windows.

5-26 Prefix-free Spoken Alerts

You can have your computer announce certain events out loud. It won't say stuff like, "The American Idol runners-up tour is coming to town!" But you can get it to tell you when your email program can't connect, or when it can't complete a copying operation.

This feature is useful if you like to set your system to do stuff while you're in another room. It's also good when you have more than one machine hooked up to one monitor, and you want to know what's going on with a machine that's running but isn't up on your screen. To turn on spoken alerts, see Figure 5-17.

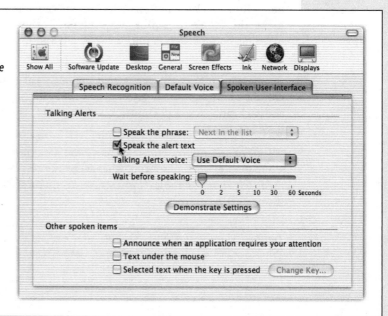

Figure 5-17:
To make your Mac try to get your attention when something's gone awry, choose System Preferences→Speech→Spoken User Interface, and turn on "Speak the alert text," as shown here.

A downside of spoken alerts, by the way, is that the computer clears its throat by saying something like, "Alert from Terminal" before it reads out the actual error message. (It does this even if you've turned off the "Speak the phrase" checkbox shown at top in Figure 5-17.)

If you'd rather just hear the alert without the prefix, you can outsmart the system. Turn on "Speak the phrase," and then click its pop-up menu and select Edit Phrase List. The Alert Phrases dialog box opens; click Add, and in the blank box that appears, type a single space. Click OK, and then select your new blank alert from the pop-up menu (it's the blank row just below "Excuse me!"). Your Mac's voice is now prefix-free.

Universal Access

The Universal Access panel of System Preferences is, in principle, designed to make the Mac easier to use for people with sight, sound, or motor-control challenges. Yet they harbor enough handiness for just about anyone.

5-27   Zooming in on the Screen

The Zoom feature (in the Universal Access preference panel) is helpful to the visually impaired, but its usefulness goes far beyond that application. Its ability to magnify the screen is ideal for graphic designers trying to see how a certain icon or font is built (pixel by pixel), or for anyone who encounters a Web page with tiny type, or for people who want to watch online movies. (Enlarged movies are nicely smoothed when you zoom in.)

Open the System Preferences→Universal Access→Seeing tab, and click the enormous Turn On Zoom button at the top. You can now zoom in and out of the screen using the ⌘-Option-plus (+) and ⌘-Option-minus (−) keystrokes. The magnification focuses on the cursor, and if you move the mouse, the zoom slides over.

But surely you knew all that. Here's the fancy part: You can make zooming more useful by creating a keyboard shortcut that zooms in to a specified magnification and back out to normal. This trick is also useful for magnifying Web pages with tiny, unchangeable fonts.

Click Zoom Options, and then move the Maximum Zoom slider to some point along the scale. From now on, whenever you press ⌘-Option-plus, the screen immediately zooms to the level you set; when you press ⌘-Option-minus, it returns to the normal view.

Tip: You can use zooms to take close-up screen captures. Just zoom in and then use the normal Shift-⌘-3 or Shift-⌘-4 commands to create a screenshot of the zoomed-in image. (See hint 4-14 for more on screenshots.)

5-28   Tappy-type Sounds

Miss the glorious days of the electric typewriter? Then turn on Mac OS X's Selectric simulator!

In System Preferences, click Sound and turn on "Play user interface sound effects." Click Show All, and then Universal Access.

On the Keyboard tab, turn on Slow Keys. Move its Acceptance delay slider all the way to the right. Confirm that "Use key click sounds" is turned on.

Now start typing—and enjoy this sonic blast from the past. (For awhile, that is. There's still enough of a delay to drive you crazy.)

5-29   Modifier-Key Ghost Reminders

Sticky Keys is designed to help people with small or stiff hands to press multiple-key shortcuts (involving keys like Shift, Option, Control, and ⌘) one at a time instead of all together.

But whenever you press one of these keys, it shows up as a symbol on the screen (see Figure 5-18), which can be a handy reminder to almost anyone that the Mac thinks you've pressed one of these keys. On some keyboards, for example, the ⌘ or Control key may have a habit of getting stuck down, resulting in all kinds of loopy behavior—but with this visual reminder, you'll know what's going on.

To make Sticky Keys work, proceed as shown in Figure 5-18.

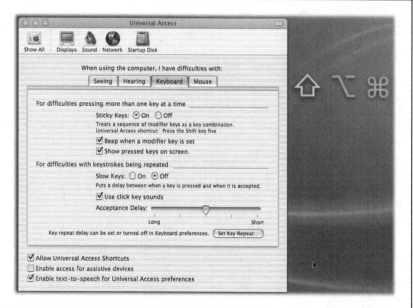

Figure 5-18:
Open System Preferences, click Universal Access, then click the Keyboard tab. Now turn on the master Sticky Keys switch at the top of the dialog box.

Then go to work on the Mac, triggering keyboard commands and enjoying the symbols that appear. (If they're in the way of something you're working on, you can even drag them around the screen!)

If you press a modifier key *twice,* you lock it down. (Its onscreen symbol gets brighter to let you know.) When a key is locked, you can use it for several commands in a row. For example, if a folder icon is highlighted, you could double-press ⌘ to lock it down—and then type O (to open the folder), followed by W (to close the window). Press the key a third time to "un-press" it.

Tip: If you turn on Allow Universal Access Shortcuts at the bottom of the dialog box, you give yourself an easier way to turn on Sticky Keys—one that gives you the flexibility of turning Sticky Keys on and off at will, without a trip to System Preferences. Whenever you want to turn on Sticky Keys, press the Shift key five times in succession. You'll hear a special clacking sound effect alerting you that you just turned on Sticky Keys. (Repeat the five presses to turn Sticky Keys off again.)

Networking

I n today's computing environment, no machine is an island. In many homes, having two or more computers is the norm, and it's virtually impossible to find a business of any size that doesn't rely on its network every day. Luckily for you, Mac OS X is the most connectable version of the operating system that Apple has ever produced. You can easily connect your Mac to a wide variety of networks, from a simple two-machine hookup to the largest Windows NT Server environment.

While networking can seldom be described as simple, OS X makes it about as painless as possible. These hints will show you how to be even more productive when networking your machine.

Making Connections

When it comes to making connections to other individual computers (as opposed to, say, Web sites), a humble little rectangle called the Connect to Server dialog box is your Grand Central Station. This is where you see the icons and names of all other available computers—Windows PCs, Macs, whatever. You double-click one to bring its icon to your screen, ready for opening, transferring files, and so on. But there's more to it than that, of course.

6-1   Deleting Orphaned Servers

You summon the Connect to Server dialog box in the Finder by choosing Go→Connect to Server (or pressing ⌘-K). Once the box appears, the pop-up menu at the top of the dialog box displays a list of servers you've recently used, as shown in Figure 6-1. Trouble is, if someone moves, renames, or breaks any of the computers you connect to, the list provides no way to remove the dead items.

The solution is shown in Figure 6-1. Just delete the icons for the servers you don't want to see on the list.

Note: You can also use the Recent Servers folder to create a Dock shortcut. Just drag the folder's icon onto the Dock, and now you've got pop-up access to your recently visited servers.

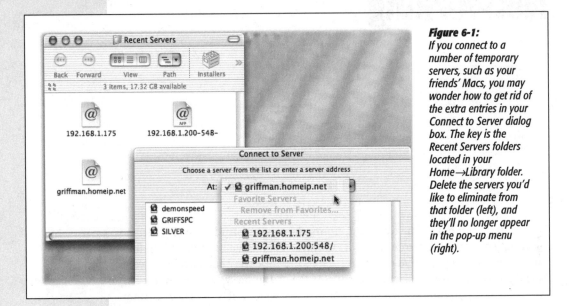

Figure 6-1:
If you connect to a number of temporary servers, such as your friends' Macs, you may wonder how to get rid of the extra entries in your Connect to Server dialog box. The key is the Recent Servers folders located in your Home→Library folder. Delete the servers you'd like to eliminate from that folder (left), and they'll no longer appear in the pop-up menu (right).

6-2   Adding New Neighborhoods

If your network includes Windows machines, chances are good that they don't start out having the same Neighborhood names as your Mac. (A Neighborhood, in Windows parlance, is a certain sector or cluster of the network.)

That's a problem if you hope to capitalize on Mac OS X's spectacular ability to share files with a PC, because your Mac and PC won't see each other on the network. Similarly, if you move a laptop back and forth from home to work, you may have problems finding the right network when you use ⌘-K (Connect to Server).

To avoid the problem, you can add Neighborhood names to the list of places that Mac OS X browses for servers. To do so, wait until the Connect to Server dialog box is before you on the screen, then press the secret keystroke ⌘-N. An Add Neighborhood dialog box appears, so that you can type in a new Neighborhood name.

Just be aware that once you've added a name, there's no easy way to remove it.

6-3   Location Files for Quick Remote Connections

If you frequently connect to the same machines on the network, you're probably sick of opening the Finder's Connect to Server dialog box, waiting for the list to build itself, clicking the name of the machine you want, and then entering your account name and password. Who needs that kind of hassle?

You can bypass all of these steps by using a *location file,* which is something like the network version of an alias. It's an icon that, when double-clicked, automatically connects to a particular network machine. Almost any Cocoa program can create location files, and a number of enlightened Carbon programs (like Internet Explorer, AppleWorks, BBEdit, Entourage) can, too.

Here's how to create one:

1. **Open a Cocoa program like TextEdit. Type the special connection address into a new document window.**

   The connection address is based on this formula:

   ```
   afp://name:password@hostname.or.address/volume_name
   ```

   That is, suppose that your account name is sallym and your password is cre8ive, and you want to connect to your iBook. You've determined the *IP address* of your iBook—that is, its unique network address—by consulting the "Other Macintosh users can access your computer at" line at the bottom of the System Preferences→Sharing panel. (It's everything *after* the "afp://" part.)

   Suppose that you discover that the IP address for the iBook is 192.168.1.140. In that case, the complete formula would be this:

   ```
   afp://sallym:cre8ive@192.168.1.140/
   ```

2. **After typing that network address, highlight the whole thing. Position your cursor within the highlighting, hold the mouse button down for a moment, and then drag the entire blob of text completely out of the window and onto the desktop.**

   The result should look something like Figure 6-2 at top—a location file.

Figure 6-2:
If your file doesn't look anything like the icon at top, and instead claims to be a "clipping file" or just raw text (bottom), then the program from which you dragged the text cannot create location files.

As you can see in the figure, the password is listed right in the name of the location file—not such a great security move. So the very first thing you should do is rename the file; "My iBook," for example, would be an ingenious name.

3. Store the location file somewhere convenient.

When double-clicked, this location file will automatically connect you to the shared disk or folder in question. So put it somewhere that's especially convenient: on your Dock or on your Finder toolbar, for example. In fact, if you connect to that other computer on a daily basis, you might want to drag it into the System Preferences→Login Items list, so that it will connect automatically when you log into your Mac.

The iDisk

In exchange for $100 per year, Apple's .Mac ("dot mac") provides a number of services, including a .mac email address, virus protection, backup software, and 100 MB of Internet-based storage space called the *iDisk*.

The iDisk is like a 100 MB hard drive that's accessible from almost any modern computer, anywhere. The iDisk is very well integrated with Mac OS X. You can see one example of this integration in the Internet System Preferences panel, whose iDisk tab provides information on how much of your 100 MB you've used up.

6-4   Quick Finder iDisk Access

If you have a .Mac account, you can open your iDisk in two easy ways:

The first way is in the Finder: Choose Go→iDisk (Shift-⌘-I).

The second way is also in the Finder: Add the iDisk icon to the Finder toolbar (choose View→Customize Toolbar, and then drag iDisk to the toolbar). Thereafter, simply click it whenever you want to connect to your iDisk.

6-5   Quicker iDisk Access

Opening your iDisk from the Finder is super-handy—indeed, it represents the long-promised integration of Internet and operating system—but it's slow, slow, slow. In fact, if you connect to the Internet with a dial-up modem, by the time the iDisk appears on your screen, you practically could have run to Apple headquarters in Cupertino to grab the darned files yourself.

You can speed up the connection with a program called Goliath. It's designed to permit quick connections to any *WebDAV* server. That's a special kind of Internet-based server (hard drive) that can remain on your screen practically forever, remaining idle when necessary. But all you need to know is that the iDisk *is* WebDAV, which makes Goliath by far the fastest way to open your iDisk.

Here's how to use it:

1. Download and install Goliath.

It lives at *www.webdav.org/goliath/*.

2. **Double-click the Goliath icon.**

   When the New WebDAV dialog box appears, just click Cancel.

3. **In Goliath, choose File→Open iDisk Connection.**

   A dialog box opens.

4. **Enter your .Mac user name and password, and then press Enter.**

   Goliath connects to your iDisk—fast. It displays the contents of your little Internet-based stash, as shown in Figure 6-3.

   You work with this list of files and folders exactly as though it's a Finder list-view window. View the contents of a folder, for example, by clicking to expand its flippy triangle. Drag files and folders into or out of the iDisk list, exactly as though it's just another hard drive connected to your Mac.

Tip: Before you wrap things up, choose File→Save Connection As. Name and save a location-file icon (hint 6-3) to make future access an easy double-click proposition.

5. **When you're finished working with the iDisk, just close its window or quit Goliath.**

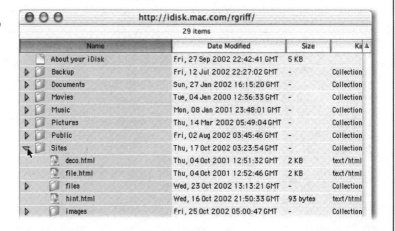

Figure 6-3:
In Goliath, click a triangle to see a list of documents within that folder; click it again to hide the contents.

6-6   Connecting to the iDisk from Windows

Relax; you haven't started reading a Windows book. But you may occasionally want to access your iDisk at your office or a friend's house, perhaps, from a computer running Windows or even Linux.

The procedure varies by operating system, but the general idea is the same: creating a new "network place" that uses the address *http://idisk.mac.com/yourname,* where *yourname* is your .Mac account name.

In Windows 2000, Me, or XP, there's a quick way to do that. Choose File→Open from within Internet Explorer. Turn on the "Open as Web Folder" checkbox, and then type your iDisk's address *(http://idisk.mac.com/yourname)*. Enter your name and password when you're asked for it. When it's all over, your iDisk window appears on the screen exactly as though it's a very slow hard drive.

Thereafter, you can summon your iDisk by double-clicking its icon in the Network Places folder.

- *Windows XP:* Choose Tools→Map Network Drive in any desktop window.

- *Windows 2000:* Choose Tools→Map Network Drive. Click "Web folder or FTP site."

- *Windows 98:* Open My Computer. Double-click the Web Folders icon, then double-click Add Web Folder.

In each case, you should now type in this address as the location to add: *http://idisk.mac.com/yourname* (where *yourname* is your .Mac member name), as shown in Figure 6-4. When you're asked for a name and password, type in your usual .Mac name and password.

After a minute or two, you'll find the icon for your iDisk in the My Computer window, sitting there as though it's a hard drive attached to the PC. (In Windows XP, for example, it's in the Network Drives category, called something like "Frank23 on 'idisk.mac.com.'")

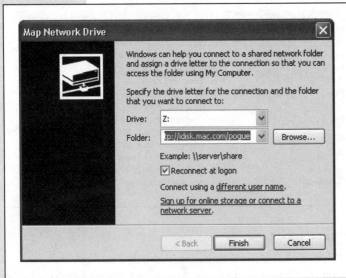

Figure 6-4:
The iDisk is an equal-opportunity file cabinet. You can get to it from any kind of computer in the world: Mac OS 9, Mac OS X, Windows (shown here), Linux, and so on.

6-7 Connecting to the iDisk from Terminal

Here's another tip for people who know their way around manipulating the Mac from the Terminal program (page 5):

From time to time, you may want to reach your iDisk from Terminal rather than from the Finder. For example, if you have a permanent Internet connection at home (cable modem or DSL), you could use Mac OS X's remote connection feature to reach your home Mac from afar during the workday. That means you could open Terminal to connect to your iDisk, and then begin downloading a large file from your iDisk's Software folder onto your home Mac's hard drive so that it will be ready for you when you arrive home.

Open Terminal and type this (pressing Enter after each line, and substituting your .Mac account name and password where you see *dotmac_name* and *password* here):

```
cd /Volumes
mkdir dotmac_name
mount_afp afp://dotmac_name:password@idisk.mac.com/dotmac_name
 /Volumes/dotmac_name
```

Notice there's a space before the */Volumes* portion of the last line. When your Mac connects to the iDisk, you may see some error messages like this:

```
kextload: extension /System/Library/Filesystems/AppleShare/
 asp_tcp.kext is already loaded
```

Don't worry about these; they won't affect your iDisk in any way. If all goes well, you can now use the command *cd /Volumes/dotmac_name* to switch into your iDisk's directory and browse your iDisk's contents remotely using *cd, ls, cp,* and the other Unix commands beloved by the power elite.

Remote Connections

If you've ever turned on file sharing within a small office network, you know the convenience of copying, distributing, and opening files that aren't actually on your machine—all without ever budging from your chair. Now just imagine the convenience of accessing those same files from thousands of miles away, via the Internet.

As long as both machines are connected to the Internet at the time, you can do exactly that. This is a great feature when, say, you've left an important quarterly report on your home computer 35 miles away, and you have to present it to your CEO in five minutes.

6-8 Long-Distance File Sharing

Here's how to tap into your home-base Mac from another Mac miles away. In this example, the home-base Mac (the one you'll be connecting *to*) is a Power Mac, and you're on the road with your PowerBook.

1. **Before you leave for your trip, on the Power Mac at home, open System Preferences and click the Sharing icon. On the Services tab, turn on File Sharing.**

   Also while you're on this machine, make note of its *IP address*—its unique Internet address, identified by a string of numbers separated by periods. (You can find your IP address by opening System Preferences→Sharing. The IP address appears below the list of checkboxes, where it says, "Other Macintosh users can access your computer at.")

   All this will work much better, of course, if the home-base Mac has a full-time Internet connection—to a cable modem or DSL box, for example. If it connects to the Internet via dial-up modem, you'll have to call somebody at home to put it online before you can connect from the road.

2. **Go on your trip. When you need to connect, press ⌘-K on the PowerBook.**

   The Connect to Server dialog box opens.

UP TO SPEED

IP Addresses and You

Every computer connected to the Internet, even temporarily, has its own exclusive *IP address* (IP stands for Internet Protocol). What's yours? Open the Sharing pane of System Preferences to find out. As you'll see, an IP address is always made up of four numbers separated by periods.

Some Macs with broadband Internet connections have a permanent, unchanging address called a *fixed* or *static* IP address. Clearly, connecting to your home-base Mac from the road is simpler if you have a fixed IP address, because you'll always know where to find it.

Other Macs get assigned a new address each time they connect (a *dynamic* IP address). That's virtually always the case, for example, when you connect using a dial-up modem. (If you can't figure out whether your Mac has a static or fixed address, ask your Internet service provider.)

You might suppose that Mac fans with dynamic addresses can't use any of the remote-connection technologies described in this chapter. After all, your Mac's Web address *changes* every so often, making it difficult to provide a single, permanent address to your friends and co-workers.

The answer is a *dynamic DNS service* that gives your Mac a name, not a number. Whenever you're online, these free services automatically update the IP address associated with the name you've chosen (such as *macmania.dyndns.org*), so that your friends and colleagues can memorize a single address for your machine.

To sign up for one of these services, just go to their Web site: *www.dyndns.org, www.dhs.org, www.dtdns.com, www.hn.org, www.no-ip.com,* and so on.

You'll also need to download and run a utility called an *update client,* which contacts your DNS service and keeps it up to date with your latest IP address, regularly and automatically. Check your DNS service's Web site for a list of compatible update clients.

Once you've got a fixed DNS name associated with your Mac, you'll be able to access it from elsewhere (provided it's online at the time) via File Sharing, the screen-sharing program called Timbuktu, or any of several other methods.

If you have a fixed address, you can also pay a few dollars a year to register your own *domain name,* a bona fide address like *www.yournamehere.com.* To register one (or to find out if the name you want is taken), visit a site like *www.networksolutions.com.*

---

3. In the Address line, type *afp://123.456.78.9/* and press Enter.

Of course, you'll want to substitute the Power Mac's actual IP address for the number shown here. In any case, the name and password dialog box opens.

4. Fill in your account name and password, and then press Enter.

A list appears, showing available disks and partitions.

5. Double-click the name of the disk whose icon you want to access.

After a moment, its icon appears on your screen, exactly as though it were sitting a few feet away from you in your home office. You can open this icon, copy files back and forth, and so on, with the understanding that you may have to be patient, especially if you've connected to your home machine using the laptop's dial-up modem.

6-9   Secure Shell for Remote Connections

The trouble with Finder-based file sharing, as described in the previous hint, is that the data you send and receive over the connection is not encrypted. In theory, at least, some hacker lurking on the Internet could see the data you're transferring. Finder-based file sharing also requires that you use another Mac to reach your home-base machine.

There is another way, however. A Unix utility called *secure shell* (*ssh*) encrypts your data while it's in transit. *Ssh* also allows you to connect to your Mac from any computer that has secure shell—it doesn't have to be another Mac. (For pre–Mac OS X Macs, for example, you can connect using programs like MacSSH, which you can download from *www.macssh.com*. To find *ssh* programs for Windows, visit *www.versiontracker.com*, click the Windows tab, and search for *ssh*.)

Once you're connected, you can take complete control of the distant Mac, copying files, running commands, rearranging folders, or even shutting it down, all by remote control.

Here's how it works. Before you leave on your trip, sit down at the home-base machine. Turn on *ssh* by opening System Preferences, clicking the Sharing icon, and on the Services tab, turning on Remote Login.

Then, once you're on the road, you can tap into the home-base Mac in either of two ways.

The Terminal way

Most people operate *ssh* from within a program like Terminal by typing Unix commands, as described in Chapter 15.

When you're ready to connect to the machine back home, open up Terminal (which is in Applications→Utilities). At the % prompt, type *ssh -l username hostname* and then press Enter. The program prompts you for your password and then (after you supply the password) connects you to your home machine's Home folder.

You can now do anything you would do while sitting ten inches away from the machine itself, using Unix commands. You can even download information from your iDisk (see hint 6-7).

A related, very useful program is *secure copy* (*scp*), which lets you copy files to and from remote machines using *ssh* encryption without first initiating an *ssh* session.

For instance, if you had a file on your home machine's desktop named hacker_honey.jpg, you could copy it to the Documents folder on your laptop machine with this command (type it all on one line, with a space after *honey.jpg*):

```
scp chris@home_mac:/Users/chris/Desktop/hacker_honey.jpg
~/Documents/
```

Replace *chris* with your account name on the home machine, and *home_mac* with the home machine's IP address (or name).

The Easy way

If typing cryptic Unix commands isn't your thing, the $30 shareware program Rbrowser *(www.rbrowser.com)* neatly obliterates that roadblock. It adds a tidy, Finder-like column view, so that copying files back and forth is as easy as dragging their icons.

6-10   Password-Free Secure Remote Connections

When you use the *ssh* and *scp* commands, as described in the previous hint, the system prompts you for a password each time you connect. This measure is good for security, but it's not so good for things like backup scripts that need to run unattended.

Ssh, however, works with a computer-to-computer recognition system known as *public key cryptography.* Using a pair of special codes known as *keys*—one on the local computer and another on the remote computer—you can connect the two machines without entering a password.

This method has two disadvantages, though. While the data transfer is every bit as secure as a connection that requires a password, the setup is less so, because a person with physical access to one of the machines can connect to the other. You'll have to decide if the potential risk is worth the convenience of connecting without passwords.

The second disadvantage is that the following procedure is somewhat technical, requiring a certain comfort level in Terminal.

This hint explains how to create a password-free *ssh* connection between a computer at work and one at home. (Of course, the two machines could be anywhere provided both are connected to the Internet.)

1. Open Terminal (page 5). At the % prompt, type *ssh-keygen -t rsa* and then press Enter. When prompted for a save location, simply press Enter.

The program asks you to supply a passphrase; if you do so, you will be asked to provide that passphrase each time you connect. Since that would defeat the purpose of this exercise, just press Enter twice (the second one confirms the blank passphrase).

The program generates some gunk like this:

```
Your identification has been saved in /Users/username/.ssh/
id_rsa.
Your public key has been saved in /Users/username/.ssh/
id_rsa.pub.
The key fingerprint is:
b4:3f:0a:52:d3:4f:52:ba:f2:d6:54:d6:32:b1:12:54 user@localhost.
```

You now need the public key that was saved in *.ssh/id_rsa.pub*.

2. **Type *cat ~/.ssh/id_rsa.pub* (and then press Enter) to make Terminal display the public key, and then use the mouse to select the text of the entire key as it's displayed on the screen. Press ⌘-C.**

You've just copied the key to the clipboard.

3. **Connect to your home Mac using the *ssh* command described in the previous hint, and then type *cd ~/.ssh* (followed by Enter) to switch to the *ssh* directory.**

That's the directory (folder) that holds the key files that *ssh* uses to authenticate when you connect remotely.

Before you proceed, make sure you're in the *.ssh* directory by typing *pwd* (it'll display the directory you are currently in).

4. **Type the following line, pressing ⌘-V between the single quote marks in order to paste in the public key you copied in the previous step:**

```
echo '[⌘-V]' > authorized_keys2
```

5. **Press Enter.**

Terminal creates a text file named *authorized_keys2*, which holds the public keys of the machine from which you will be connecting.

6. **Type *exit* to disconnect from your work Mac, and then try your *ssh* command again.**

This time the system doesn't prompt you for a password. Similarly, it allows you to use *scp* without a password.

Just remember that anyone with physical access to the local machine will also be able to gain access to the remote machine. (For some security, you can set up the Mac's screen saver to require a password so that intruders can't get into it when you're away from your desk.)

File Sharing

The Mac's *file sharing* feature revolutionized computer-to-computer networking. Mac fans could create folders that were visible to other people on the network with a few simple mouse clicks and without a computer science degree. Mac OS X continues the tradition of easy Mac-to-Mac networking.

6-11   Monitoring File-Sharing Activity

If you suspect a hacker is infiltrating your machine, or if you've set up an FTP server and you're just curious about who's using it, you might want to track file-sharing activity. This hint tells you how to turn on Mac OS X's secret activity monitor.

1. Open NetInfo Manager (a program in your Applications→Utilities folder). Click the padlock icon in the lower-left corner of the NetInfo Manager window. When prompted, enter your administrator's password and press Enter.

   The system asks for your password to make sure that you are an administrator— somebody with the necessary authorization and expertise to mess around with important system settings in NetInfo Manager.

Tip: Indeed, it's a good idea to back up your settings before modifying any NetInfo Manager data, using the program's built-in backup feature. Choose Management→Save Backup.

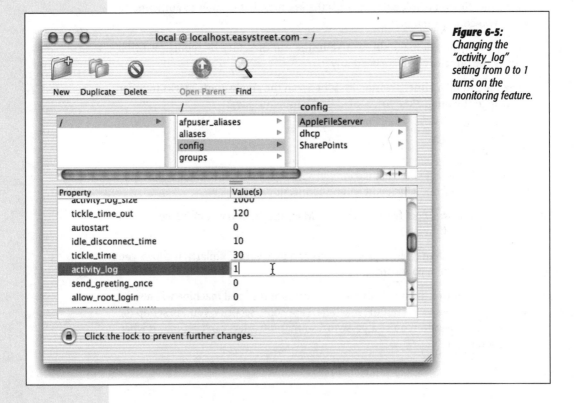

Figure 6-5:
Changing the "activity_log" setting from 0 to 1 turns on the monitoring feature.

2. In the upper NetInfo window, click Config; in the right column, click AppleFileServer.

As you can see, working with Mac OS X system settings in NetInfo Manager is something like working with nested folders in the Finder's column view. When you click the name of a feature in the rightmost column, you see a scrolling list of its parameters in the lower pane.

3. In the lower window, scroll down until you see "activity_log" on the left-hand side.

It should have a 0 next to it, meaning "this feature is turned off."

4. Click the 0 and change it to 1.

Figure 6-5 shows the effect.

5. Save your changes by choosing Domain→Save Changes, or by pressing ⌘-S. Then quit NetInfo Manager.

You've just flipped the master switch to turn the activity monitor on.

6. Open System Preferences, click the Sharing icon, and turn off File Sharing (if it was already running). Then turn it back on.

You now have a tool that tracks file-sharing activity as it occurs, by writing it out in little text files known as *logs*. You can find the logs by opening your Library→Logs→AppleFileService folder; inside is the text file called AppleFileService-Access.log (see Figure 6-6).

You can, of course, read these logs using a word processor. However, one of the most convenient ways to read them is through the program called Console (in Applications→Utilities). Once you've opened this program, choose File→Open Log,

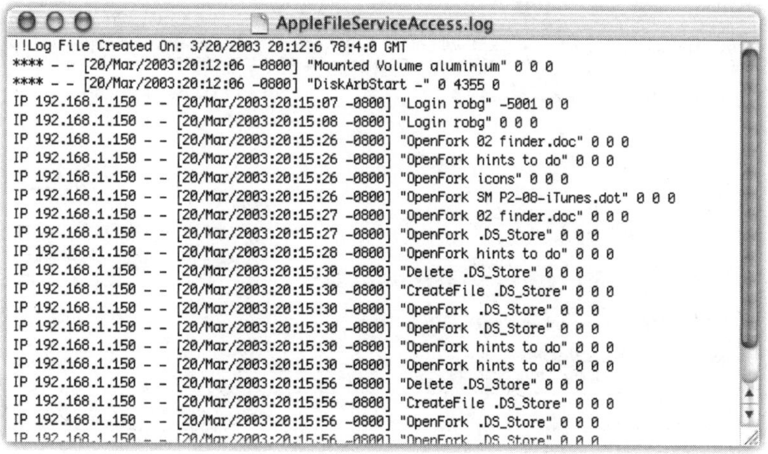

Figure 6-6:
Once you've enabled AppleShare logging in NetInfo Manager, it's easy to use the Console application to see exactly who is doing what to your machine while they're connected.

and then navigate to and open the log file. A window opens that lets you watch in real time as the system tracks activity on your file server.

Note: If you ever want to disable logging, just run NetInfo Manager, switch 1 back to 0, save your changes, and restart File Sharing.

6-12   Sharing Folders with Other Mac Users

File sharing in Mac OS X is notable for its reliability and security—but not for its flexibility. The File Sharing switch in Mac OS X is an all-or-nothing master switch that permits Administrator account holders access to your entire machine, and Normal account holders access only to the Public folders of each home folder. There's no simple way to designate, say, the Fourth-Quarter Results folder on your desktop as available to all account holders on the network.

The simplest solution is a little shareware program called SharePoints, available at *http://hornware.com/sharepoints*. It's a must-have networking application if you frequently share your Mac with other people on the network, because it lets you make any folder available on the network and gives you complete control over who is allowed to access it.

SharePoints can run either as a standalone program or a new panel added to System Preferences. Either way, once you've opened it, click the Normal Shares tab. Fill in Share Name (short for *shared folder* name), set permissions for the Owner, Group,

Figure 6-7:
This MP3 collection has been set up as "my_music" (the name that other Macs will be able to see), pointing to the /Volumes→ ripped_CDs→iTunes folder, with read and write permissions for the Owner and the Group, and read access for Everyone.

and Everyone, and choose a folder to share. (Permissions settings allow you to govern exactly what each person is allowed to do with this folder—whether or not they can delete things from it, for example. The settings apply only to the selected folder, not to any folders inside it.) Figure 6-7 illustrates a typical shared-folder setup.

Click Create New Share, and then click Restart AppleFileServer. If you want to make sure the sharing worked, go to another machine on your network, connect as a guest to the first machine, and look for the new shared folder.

SharePoints also allows you to create "file sharing only" accounts. These are special user accounts that don't actually have a Home folder and can't connect to your Mac remotely—but are great when you want to let somebody into a folder without going to the trouble of creating a full account. You can also use SharePoints to perform tasks like turning on file-sharing logs (see hint 6-11) and disallowing sharing in your Public folder.

6-13   Unsharing Your Public Folder

Every Mac OS X account comes with a Public folder—a folder that's available to anybody on the network, making it a great place to distribute files to your co-workers. Public folders don't really present much of a security risk, but if you like your machine sealed tight, you can prevent others from reaching your Public folder.

To do so, highlight the Public folder (in your Home folder), and then choose File→Get Info (⌘-I). When the Get Info box appears, click to expand the triangle next to Ownership & Permissions.

Figure 6-8:
Left: When you choose No Access, nobody on the network will be able to access your Public folder. While this isn't a very neighborly thing to do, you may be the private type who doesn't like to share. You disable sharing by changing the Group and Others settings to No Access via the Get Info box.

Right: To share your Public folder again, just change the Get Info settings for Group and Others back to "Read only."

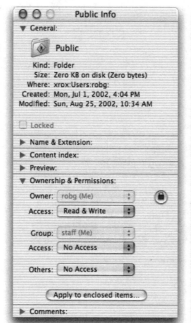
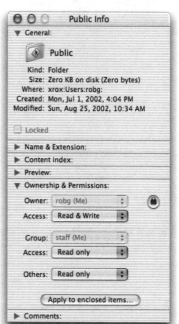

In the Group information row, change the Access menu to No Access. Do the same for the Others menu, as shown in Figure 6-9. Your Public folder is now private.

6-14   Finding Your Ethernet Address

Sometimes when you contact tech support or when you set up a network-connected gadget, you're supposed to reveal your Ethernet address. (It's also referred to as your MAC address—not to be confused with your *Mac's* address, which is probably where you sit all day.) And unlike your street address or your email address, it's probably not on the tip of your tongue.

Ethernet addresses consist of six two-character pairs, which aren't typically easy to find or memorize. But Apple, in its infinite wisdom, makes finding *and* copying them a snap.

Open System Preferences and click the Network panel. On the TCP/IP tab, choose Built-in Ethernet (from the Show pop-up menu). Your Ethernet address is at the bottom of the window. See Figure 6-9 for instructions on copying it.

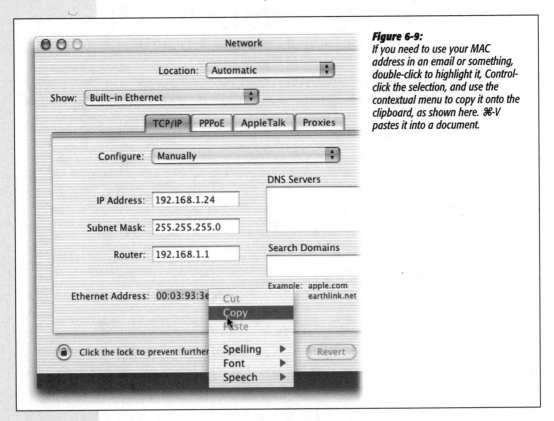

Figure 6-9:
If you need to use your MAC address in an email or something, double-click to highlight it, Control-click the selection, and use the contextual menu to copy it onto the clipboard, as shown here. ⌘-V pastes it into a document.

Mail

For your communications pleasure, Mac OS X comes with a free email program bearing the not-so-creative name Mail. It has a number of subtle behaviors and hidden features that will make you squirm with delight—once you know about them. Read this chapter to get better acquainted with the program.

The Mail Window

Unlike most email programs, Mail lets you keep open as many view windows as you like. While this seems odd at first, you'll soon grow to appreciate being able to have a "search" view, "just my important stuff" view, and "normal" view of your mailboxes. Read the rest of the hints for more inside info.

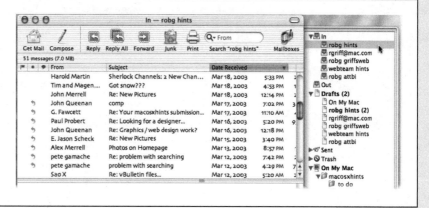

Figure 7-1:
If you can't see the Mail drawer (indicated at right by the cursor), make your window smaller, and make sure the drawer is not hidden; Shift-⌘-M hides and unhides it.

7-1   Moving the Mailbox Drawer

The Mail *drawer* is a sliding panel, usually on the right side of the Mail window, that holds the various folders into which you file your messages (see Figure 7-1).

On most Mac OS X machines, the drawer sits on the right side of the window—because that's where it starts out. But there's no reason to leave it there if you prefer it on the opposite side.

To make it swap sides, center the window on the screen (drag it by the title bar). Then—here comes the weird part—click any email message and drag it to the opposite side of the Mail window. The drawer switches sides as you near the opposite edge (if there's room on the screen for it). Release the mouse before you file the message in another mailbox.

7-2   Customizing the Columns

When you set up your Mail program, don't miss the View→Columns command. It lets you choose which columns the program displays—including some useful ones that start out hidden.

For instance, you might want to be able to glance at a message and see whether it has any attachments and how big it is. If you turn on the corresponding columns, as shown in Figure 7-2, you're all set.

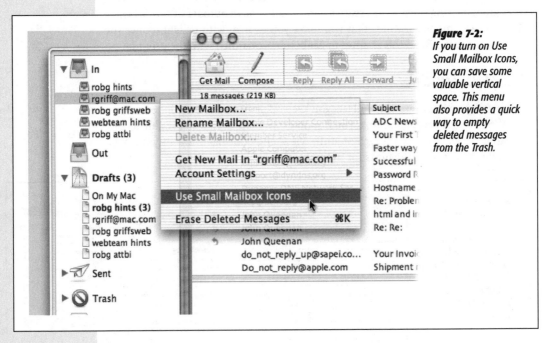

Figure 7-2:
If you turn on Use Small Mailbox Icons, you can save some valuable vertical space. This menu also provides a quick way to empty deleted messages from the Trash.

7-3   The Drawer's Contextual Menu

If you select a folder or mailbox and then Control-click the drawer, a menu appears with a bunch of useful options (Figure 7-2). All of these commands are duplicated in the main menus, but you can reach them much more directly through the drawer's contextual menu.

7-4   Mousing to the Activity Viewer

Want to watch the progress of a large download or upload? Mail has a little-known progress dialog box called Activity Viewer. The unwashed peons open it by choosing Window→Show Activity Viewer (⌘-0). But you, the power user, can also open it with one secret click. Figure 7-3 explains how.

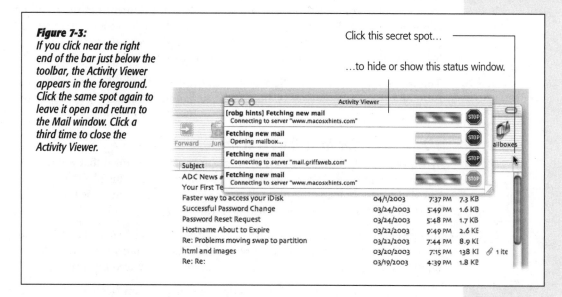

Figure 7-3:
If you click near the right end of the bar just below the toolbar, the Activity Viewer appears in the foreground. Click the same spot again to leave it open and return to the Mail window. Click a third time to close the Activity Viewer.

Click this secret spot...

...to hide or show this status window.

7-5   Intelligent Searches

Mail's Search function lets you track down a certain message in either the currently selected folder or in all of your folders. Searching is easy if you're looking for a one-word term like "anniversary" or "platypus." But what if you want to find a reference to "dog food"?

If you type that phrase in the search box without any quotation marks or other characters, Mail finds all messages that contain *either* "dog" *or* "food." You get back a slew of messages about appointments with the vet and restaurants you've tried, but you may not spot the one recommending a particularly nutritious kibble.

To force Mail to search the entire phrase, put quotes around it. If you type *"dog food,"* for example, the program will look only for messages that contain both words.

You can get even fancier and use *and, or,* and *not* to limit searches. If you search for *golf and (par or birdie),* for example, Mail looks for messages that contain the word "golf" *and* either "par" or "birdie." Similarly, if you search for *lunch not (free or cheap)*, Mail returns only messages that discuss expensive lunches.

Note: For more information on advanced searches, check out Mail's Help files.

7-6   Apple's Mail Development Team

If you spend 23 hours a day in front of Mail, you may be pleased to learn that your machine holds pictures of the members of Apple's Mail development team. Or you may consider this secret akin to a virus. It's your call, but here's how to find them.

In the Finder, open your Applications folder. Inside, Control-click the Mail program's icon. From the contextual menu, choose Show Package Contents; in the resulting window, open the Contents→Resources folder. Inside you'll see an extremely rare example of an Apple Easter egg: a collection of eight pictures—the individual cuties behind Mail—that opens up in Preview or your favorite graphics program.

This isn't just pure egocentric fluff, however: If you ever happen to receive an email from one of the team members, his or her photo will automatically appear in the message window.

7-7   Rewriting Mail, the Program

When you're feeling overwhelmed by work (or so underwhelmed that you're looking for something to do), you might enjoy hacking the underlying files that make up the Mail program. Using these simple techniques, you can change the text that appears on buttons and in dialog boxes and error messages.

As with any hint that modifies a program, you'd be well advised to make a backup of Mail (Option-drag it out of your Applications folder) before you crawl under the hood. Note, too, that these hacks require an Administrator account (page 11).

1. **In the Applications folder, Control-click the Mail program's icon. From the contextual menu, choose Show Package Contents. In the new window that opens, open the Contents→Resources→English.lproj folder.**

   You find yourself facing a list of technical-looking files that only a programmer could love. (See page 3 for details on this routine.)

2. **Use TextEdit to open the file called Compose.strings.**

   That is, drag the Compose.strings icon onto the icon of TextEdit (see page 4 for details on this technique).

   As you scroll through this file, you'll see each entry described in plain English by a phrase between these marks: /* */. These comments let you know what you're about to change ("/*Message of alert sheet shown when the user tries to close a compose window that hasn't been sent or saved */," for example).

3. **Edit the little blobs of text between the quotation marks to suit your sense of humor and evil.**

When making modifications, do *not* change the left side of any command (to the left of the = sign on each line); modify only the right (see Figure 7-4).

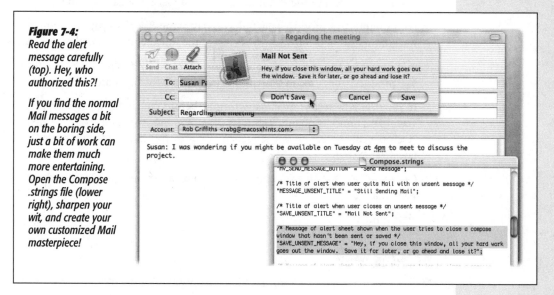

Figure 7-4:
Read the alert message carefully (top). Hey, who authorized this?!

If you find the normal Mail messages a bit on the boring side, just a bit of work can make them much more entertaining. Open the Compose .strings file (lower right), sharpen your wit, and create your own customized Mail masterpiece!

For example, to modify the message that appears when you change an email from rich text (that is, formatted text) to plain text, change this line:

```
"MAKE_TEXT_PLAIN" = "Make Plain Text";
```

to look like this line:

```
"MAKE_TEXT_PLAIN" = "Use Boring Text";
```

1. **Close the window and save your changes. Use TextEdit to open the file called Localizable.strings and edit it, also.**

The icon called Localizable.strings is in the same window as the Compose.strings file. This file, too, has handy comment lines, but it contains even more onscreen goodies you can modify, as well as various date formats.

You can change the date format that Mail uses (primarily in lists of messages), too. Use the Edit→Find→Find Panel command to search for *Date* to pull up the first instance, which should look something like this:

```
/* Date format with arguments full month, day, and year, to be
followed by time */
"FULL_DATE_AND_TIME_FORMAT" = "%B %e, %Y ";
```

The symbols on the right are Unix date-formatting symbols, which you can use to specify how dates and times appear in Mail. In the example above, "%B %e, %Y" translates to a display format of "August 1, 2003."

To learn what these symbols mean, visit *www.osxfaq.com/man/3/strftime.ws*. You'll discover that each of the % codes represents a piece of a date or time.

For example, %A produces the full weekday name, %a gives you the abbreviated weekday name, and %B and %b represent the full and abbreviated *month* name.

%D produces the month, day, and year separated by slashes (like "11/20/03"); %T produces the time, in hours:minutes:seconds format; and so on.

If you'd like to test your chosen format before committing the changes, use Terminal's *date* command. Typing *date* + "%B %e, %Y", for example, displays "October 30, 2003." Find a sequence of codes you like, and then paste it into Localizable.strings.

2. Once you've made all your edits, save the files, and then open Mail to check out your changes.

Sigh contentedly.

Reading Mail

Mail is…well, a mail program. You'll probably spend most of your time reading, filing, replying to, and deleting mail.

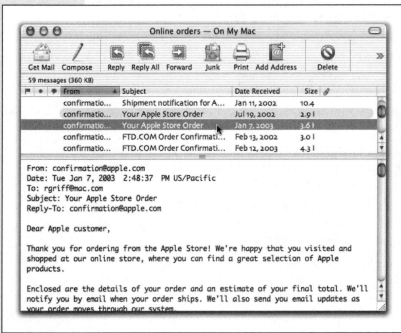

Figure 7-5:
The preview pane is the lower half of this screenshot. It lets you read your mail messages without opening a new window. However, it also has the side effect of marking any unread messages as read when you click on them in the upper half of the window. If you'd rather not have that happen, double-click the divider bar that separates the preview pane from the message list. The preview pane vanishes.

7-8   Leaving Messages Marked as Unread

Mail marks new, unread emails with a blue dot to make them stand out from others in your Inbox. But as soon as you click a marked message, its blue dot vanishes. If you accidentally click something without reading it, it can get lost in the Inbox underbrush.

Making a message return to its unread state is easy enough: Control-click it and, from the contextual menu, choose Mark as Unread.

But if you'd rather teach Mail to quit marking messages as read until you've really, truly read them, you must sacrifice the preview pane (the lower window area that displays the text of a selected message). To do that, drag the horizontal divider bar off the bottom of the main window until the preview pane disappears (see Figure 7-5).

Messages now retain their little blue dot until you double-click them to open them in a new window.

7-9   A Little Privacy, Please I

Whenever you click one of your Mail folders in the drawer (Figure 7-1), Mail, in an effort to be helpful, automatically highlights the first message and reveals its contents in the preview pane.

However, if you're concerned that your co-workers or cats are spying on you, and you'd rather the preview pane appear blank, ⌘-click the selected message. The Preview pane dutifully fades to white.

7-10   A Little Privacy, Please II

Here's a corollary to the previous hint: Whenever you delete a message, the highlight bar automatically moves to the next message, therefore revealing the message contents in the preview pane.

If that co-worker or cat is still spying on you, press Option-Delete instead of the Delete key alone. Doing so makes the current message head to the Trash, but the highlight line disappears, leaving you with a blank preview pane.

7-11   Messages in Other Formats

HTML messages are those that have been sent to you—most often by junk emailers, but occasionally by misguided ordinary individuals—with formatting (background colors, background graphics, funky fonts, and so on) rather than just plain text.

If you receive HTML-coded messages that you find unreadable as a result (see Figure 7-6), click its name once in the list. Then choose View→Show→Plain Text Alternative (⌘-Option-P).

Mail instantly strips out the HTML formatting, leaving only the text of the message (Figure 7-6, middle). At least it does this most of the time; the Plain Text Alternative command is dimmed and unavailable for certain messages.

If you're a sleuth, you may want to try the related View→Show→Raw Source command (⌘-Option-U); see Figure 7-6, bottom.

Note: You're not permanently scarring the message. The view you specify hangs around only as long as you leave the message selected. If you click out and back into the message, it reverts to its original HTML format.

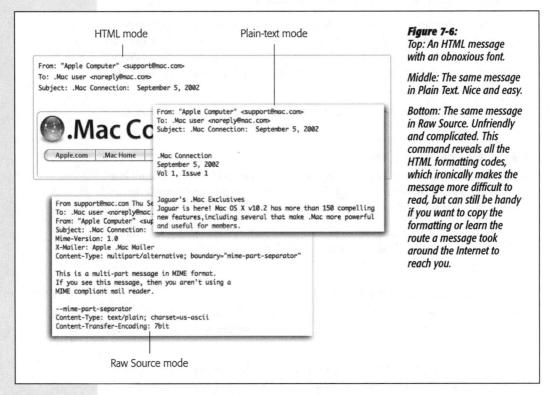

HTML mode   Plain-text mode

From: "Apple Computer" <support@mac.com>
To: .Mac user <noreply@mac.com>
Subject: .Mac Connection: September 5, 2002

.Mac Co

Apple.com   .Mac Home

From: "Apple Computer" <support@mac.com>
To: .Mac user <noreply@mac.com>
Subject: .Mac Connection: September 5, 2002

.Mac Connection
September 5, 2002
Vol 1, Issue 1

Jaguar's .Mac Exclusives
Jaguar is here! Mac OS X v10.2 has more than 150 compelling
new features, including several that make .Mac more powerful
and useful for members.

From support@mac.com Thu Se
To: .Mac user <noreply@mac.
From: "Apple Computer" <sup
Subject: .Mac Connection:
Mime-Version: 1.0
X-Mailer: Apple .Mac Mailer
Content-Type: multipart/alternative; boundary="mime-part-separator"

This is a multi-part message in MIME format.
If you see this message, then you aren't using a
MIME compliant mail reader.

--mime-part-separator
Content-Type: text/plain; charset=us-ascii
Content-Transfer-Encoding: 7bit

Raw Source mode

Figure 7-6:
Top: An HTML message with an obnoxious font.

Middle: The same message in Plain Text. Nice and easy.

Bottom: The same message in Raw Source. Unfriendly and complicated. This command reveals all the HTML formatting codes, which ironically makes the message more difficult to read, but can still be handy if you want to copy the formatting or learn the route a message took around the Internet to reach you.

7-12   Pop-Open Folders

If your Mail drawer houses many folders with inner folders left in their expanded state, your list of mailboxes can stretch out of the drawer, forcing you to scroll down when you want to file something at the bottom.

Forget the scrolling—leave the folders closed all the time. Instead, whenever you want to file a message, drag it directly onto one of your main folders without releasing the mouse. The inner folders suddenly appear, as shown in Figure 7-7. Then when you release the mouse, the subfolders clam back up.

7-13   Mail from Multiple Mailboxes

The little Mail folders designed for housing your messages are all well and good. The only trouble is that once your Mail is scattered to the four winds (or the 40 folders), hunting down a certain message takes much longer, since you have that many more places to look.

Fortunately, a little-known secret easily overcomes the challenge of viewing the contents of several folders simultaneously. The trick: ⌘-click the folders. The full contents of all the folders now appear in the main window in a glorious, unified list.

This technique is particularly useful when you can't remember where you filed a message. Once you've ⌘-clicked a few candidate folders, you can use the Search box on the toolbar to search only those folders.

Figure 7-7:
Subfolders can grow beyond the size of your Mail window, forcing you to scroll to use them all. But Mail offers a form of spring-loaded folders, so go ahead and leave your subfolders closed. When you need to file an email, just drag it over a closed folder to make the subfolders open, allowing you to file the message in the folder of your choice.

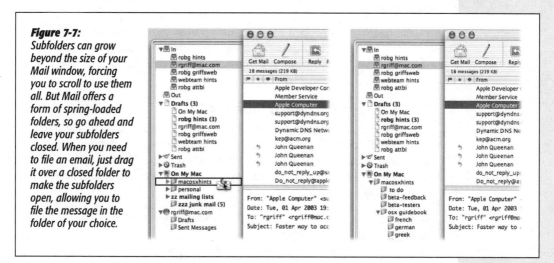

Figure 7-8:
The bolded folder names have unread mail in them. But how are you supposed to view all of the new messages at once—click one folder at a time? Life's too short. Instead, select all the folders simultaneously by ⌘-clicking them.

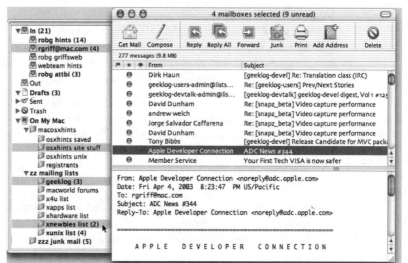

7-14   Preserving Your Junk Mail Brains

Over time, clicking the Junk or Not Junk buttons for the hundreds of messages that enliven your life teaches Mail quite a bit about what's spam and what's not, in your opinion. But what are you supposed to do when you upgrade to a new Mac, or add a laptop to your arsenal? Leave all of that manually input intelligence behind?

Never!

All you have to do is open your Home→Library→Mail folder and rescue the LSMMap file inside it. That single icon represents all of the training you've ever given Mail about spam.

On the new machine, open Mail, set up your accounts, and choose Mail→Junk Mail→Automatic. Then quit the program, copy your LSMMap file into your Home→Library→Mail folder, and make sure you've replaced the LSMMap file that's already there. Brain transplant complete!

7-15   "You've Got Mail, O Wise One"

Want to add a bit of interest and excitement to the arrival of new mail messages? How about listening to a British accented voice tell you, "O master of the universe, new mail has arrived that requires your attention." Thanks to the power of Mail's rules, and the AT&T Natural Voices Web site, you can create an infinite variety of customized voice alerts.

Start by visiting *www.naturalvoices.att.com/demos,* and proceed as shown at top in Figure 7-9.

When you've typed the text you'd like to use, click the Go button. After a slight pause, a new page opens showing the QuickTime controller; you'll hear your announcement read aloud.

If it sounds good, choose File→Save As from your browser's menu to save the sound file onto your hard drive (the desktop, for example). Create as many samples as you think you may wish to use. You might consider creating a different announcement for each of the people who regularly send you email.

Now, in Mail, choose Mail→Preferences; click Rules. Click Add Rule to open the rule definition dialog box, and enter a name for your new rule (like *Announce*) in the Description box. To create a rule that acts on every new message you receive, choose Every Message from the From pop-up menu. If you're creating a rule for a specific person, enter the email address (or name) in the box next to the Contains pop-up.

At the bottom of the dialog box, choose Play Sound from the Transfer Message pop-up menu, and then, from the pop-up menu to its right, choose Add/Remove. A new dialog box opens with Add, Remove, and Done buttons.

Click Add and navigate to the spot where you saved your samples (the desktop, for example). Double-click the sound you'd like to use for this rule, and then click Done.

Now your downloaded sound appears in the pop-up menu (next to the Play Sound pop-up menu). Choose it from the list. The dialog box should look something like Figure 7-9 at bottom.

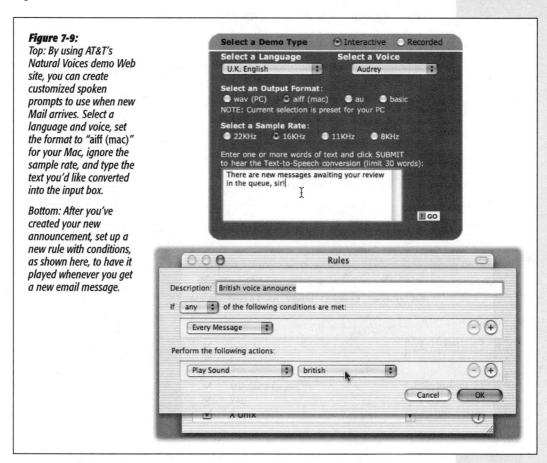

Figure 7-9:
Top: By using AT&T's Natural Voices demo Web site, you can create customized spoken prompts to use when new Mail arrives. Select a language and voice, set the format to "aiff (mac)" for your Mac, ignore the sample rate, and type the text you'd like converted into the input box.

Bottom: After you've created your new announcement, set up a new rule with conditions, as shown here, to have it played whenever you get a new email message.

Click OK. You return to the Rules dialog box. If you've created other rules, drag this new rule *below* any of them that handle junk mail. After all, with the amount of spam that probably floods your inbox each day, you'd probably get tired of hearing an announcement for each and every special offer direct from the Nigerian embassy.

In any case, your talking Mail program is ready to roll. Each time a new message rolls in, the Mac will speak your specified attention-getting phrase. Adjust the volume to taste, so you'll be sure to hear it when you're watching TV, making dinner, or sleeping.

Sending Mail

Here are some hints to make your time as an email composer much more efficient.

7-16 Quoting Portions of Emails in Replies

You may have noticed that when you reply to a piece of mail, Mail automatically quotes the original message in its entirety, as shown in Figure 7-10. It's better email etiquette, however, to quote back only the *relevant* portion of the message—especially when you're dealing with some long-winded gasbag.

To do that, highlight the relevant section of the message *before* you click Reply.

Note: If this tip doesn't seem to work for you, choose Mail→Preferences. Click the Composing icon and make sure that "Include the selected text, if any, otherwise include all" is selected at the bottom of the dialog box.

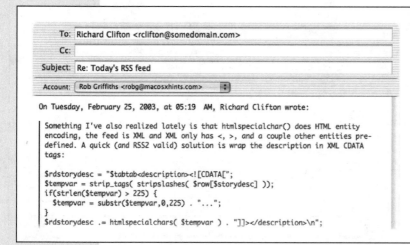

To: Richard Clifton <rclifton@somedomain.com>
Cc:
Subject: Re: Today's RSS feed
Account: Rob Griffiths <robg@macosxhints.com>

On Tuesday, February 25, 2003, at 05:19 AM, Richard Clifton wrote:

```
Something I've also realized lately is that htmlspecialchar() does HTML entity
encoding, the feed is XML and XML only has <, >, and a couple other entities pre-
defined. A quick (and RSS2 valid) solution is wrap the description in XML CDATA
tags:

$rdstorydesc = "$tabtab<description><![CDATA[";
$tempvar = strip_tags( stripslashes( $row[$storydesc] ));
if(strlen($tempvar) > 225) {
   $tempvar = substr($tempvar,0,225) . "...";
}
$rdstorydesc .= htmlspecialchars( $tempvar ) . "]]></description>\n";
```

Figure 7-10:
Your correspondents will be much happier if your replies don't include every single word they originally sent to you. The easiest way to do that is to just select the relevant portion of the original email, and then click Reply. Mail will helpfully include only your selected text in the reply window (indicated here by the vertical line at left).

7-17 Toggling Between Reply and Reply to All

You just typed a reply to a department-wide email, but you mistakenly responded only to the author and not to the whole team. *Doh!*

Fortunately, if you haven't sent the message yet, you can recover in an instant. Just click the Reply icon in the toolbar. Each time you click this button, it goes back and forth between Reply and Reply to All, inserting only one address or all recipients' addresses. No matter which mistake you made, recovering is only one click away.

7-18 Resending a Message

You're sailing along, zinging emails to the four corners of the Internet, when you suddenly realize you sent a message to the wrong recipient. While you can't retrieve the first message, you can easily resend it to the proper person—in either of two ways:

- In your Sent folder, click the message once, and then choose File→Open As New Message. The message opens with the original recipient, subject, and message. Fortunately, you can change any or all of that and resend it; when the message goes out, it will have a new date and time stamp.

- In the Sent folder, Control-click the message and choose Redirect from the contextual menu. Readdress the message that opens, and click Send.

7-19   Blind Carbon Copy and Reply-To Fields

The organization of the Mail menus isn't always screamingly self-evident. You'd think, for example, that anything related to a message would be located in the Message menu—but no.

The classic example is the Add Bcc Field command. You need this option whenever you want to send a certain message secretly to a third party. (For example, if you're writing your boss to praise a co-worker, and you want that co-worker to learn of your good deed, you might "Bcc" her by typing her address into the "Bcc:" line. The boss's copy of the message won't bear any indication that a copy went to said co-worker.)

If you want to add a Bcc field to a message, and you look in the Message menu, you'll search until the cows come home. Instead, open the Edit menu, where you'll find Add Bcc Field (Shift-⌘-B). You've just put a new line on the message in which you can type the secret recipient's address.

Incidentally, the Edit menu also offers a command called Add Reply-To Header (⌘-Option-R). Use this box to type in a different address—not your regularly scheduled one—for any replies to go to. (That's a handy feature when, for example, you're sending mail from your work Mac, but you want replies to go to your home account.)

7-20   Sending Messages Later

Mail likes to stay on the ball: If you click Send, it promptly tries to shoot your message out into the ether. But what if you want a message to hit the digital road later, perhaps after you leave the office—or, if you're answering email at 39,000 feet, after you land? Although Mail lacks the Send Later option of some other email programs, you can work around it.

After you've received new messages, choose Mailbox→Go Offline. Now proceed with your message-answering session. Each time you compose a message and click, Mail stores it in your Outbox without attempting to connect to the Internet.

When you're finally ready to connect, choose Mail→Go Online. When Mail connects as usual, all your stored-up replies go along for the ride.

7-21   Sending a File from the Finder

Most people know of only two methods to add an attachment to an outgoing message:

- Click the toolbar's Attach icon (which looks a paper clip), and then browse your hard drive for the desired file.

- Drag the attachment icon right off the desktop or a Finder window and into the outgoing message.

But if the Mail program isn't actually running, you can employ a much more enjoyable method: Just drag the file you want to send onto Mail's *Dock* icon (or its toolbar icon, if you've dragged the Mail icon there). In the blink of an eye, your Mac opens Mail, brings up a New Message window, attaches the dragged file, and deposits the insertion point in the To field. Now *that's* productivity.

7-22   Copying Entire Folders

Mail provides a "Save As" feature (File→Save As, or Shift-⌘-S), which lets you save a copy of an individual message elsewhere on your hard drive or iDisk. But what if, say, you want to move those 639 emails from your sweetie off your machine at work and onto your iDisk? Mail has no Export feature—at least not that most people know about.

You, however, are about to learn the secret: Just drag the folder you want from the Mail drawer clear out of the Mail window and onto your desktop. (You can drag only your own homemade filing folders—not the built-in ones like In, Out, or Drafts.) As you go, the cursor shows a plus sign, indicating that the Mac is making a copy; when you release the mouse, a *Mailbox's name*.mbox icon appears on your desktop. You've got yourself a convenient backup.

Like many Mac OS X programs, the *Mailbox's name*.mbox file is what's known as a bundle: It may look like a single file icon, but it's actually more like a folder. You can open it, if you like, by Control-clicking the icon and choosing Show Package Contents from the contextual menu.

To move this mail backup to another machine, you first have to burn it to a CD or find some other method to transport it there. Make sure Mail isn't running on the new Mac; drop the backup into your Home→Library→Mail→Mailboxes folder. (If there's already a mailbox there with the same name, rename your backup first.) When you relaunch Mail, you'll see your backup folder in the "On My Mac" section of your folder list.

Troubleshooting

Few people run into any problems using Mail. But if you do, the following hints may help you work through the issues you're having.

7-23   Preventing Mac.com Mailbox Overflow

If you have a Mac.com account—the $100-per-year suite of special Apple features described at *www.mac.com*—it's a good idea to learn about a fundamental difference between its email account and regular email accounts.

Most people with ordinary Internet service providers have a kind of email account called *POP* (Post Office Protocol). If you have this kind of account, whenever you check your email, it's transferred to your email program and removed from the Internet computer (the server) where it was waiting for you.

If you have a .Mac account, however, you have the more modern *IMAP* account (Internet Message Access Protocol). This kind of account is somewhat different: Even after you've downloaded your mail, copies of your messages remain on the IMAP server, freeing you from having to use the same Mac all the time to check your email. You can log onto the .Mac Web page using almost any computer on earth— and you'll find your entire email collection, neatly sorted and ready to go.

As you can imagine, you must therefore be more diligent about deleting messages when you're through with them. If you don't pay attention, IMAP servers (including those that hold your Mac.com mail) can max out their storage limit. When that happens, you won't get any more messages until you create some room on the server. Even worse, friends sending you emails will probably receive error messages explaining exactly how your lack of housekeeping skills has caused your mailbox to overflow.

To remove messages from an IMAP server, transfer them to any folder (in the Mail "drawer") that you've created for mail storage. The IMAP server will remove the messages from its own storage area the next time you check your mail.

7-24   Incomplete Message Error

From time to time, you may encounter an error message that shows the header for a previously received email message, but then states that the remainder of the message cannot be read until the account is taken online. More than likely, this is a problem with the *index file*—the behind-the-scenes email table of contents—that Mail uses to keep track of email messages. No worries, though; it's easily fixed.

Highlight the mailbox that contains the problem message. Then choose Mailbox→Rebuild Mailbox. The system zips through the box and recreates the index file, repairing any corruptions.

In fact, this is a handy practice for any kind of mailbox eccentricity. It never hurts anything, and frequently helps.

7-25   Diagnosing Opening-Sequence Crashes

If your Mail program crashes when you open it, your Address Book might be responsible.

To find out, open your Home→Library→Application Support folder. Drag the AddressBook folder onto the desktop. Open Mail now; if it starts without incident, then you have a corrupted entry in your Address Book (just the entry, not necessarily the person it represents).

The only solution is to delete the current Address Book (that is, throw away the folder that you dragged to the desktop in the previous paragraph). The next time you start up Address Book, it will be empty. You'll just have to add your entries from scratch, restoring them from a recent backup (see the tip below). (You're more fortunate if you have a .Mac account and you've used iSync to synchronize your Mac with it. In that case, just resynchronize your Address Book with the copy on your .Mac account.)

Tip: If you haven't created a backup of your AddressBook folder (in Home→Library→Application Support), this hint should provide incentive for you to do so. Take two seconds to drag the AddressBook folder to another drive, or Option-drag it to another folder on the same drive.

---

iTunes

iTunes, which sits at this moment in your Applications folder, is the ultimate software jukebox. It can play music CDs, tune in to Internet radio stations, load up your iPod music player, and play back *MP3 files* (sound files in a popular format capable of storing CD-quality music in remarkably small files) and other popular audio formats. It can also turn selected tracks from your music CDs *into* MP3 files, so that you can store favorite songs on your hard drive to play back anytime—without having to dig up the original CDs. In fact, iTunes can even load your MP3 files onto certain portable MP3 players. And if your Mac can burn CDs, iTunes even lets you burn your own custom audio CDs that contain only the good songs.

But you knew all that already. The good stuff is yet to come.

8-1   Mini Modes

iTunes can run in three size modes: large, medium, or small (Figure 8-1). Here's how you pull this off:

- **Large.** This is what you get the first time you open iTunes.

- **Medium.** You can switch back and forth between large and medium by clicking the green zoom button at the top- or middle-left corner (or by choosing Window→Zoom). Either way, this mode is handy for playing tunes in the background while you work, without your screen being overtaken.

- **Small.** If your desktop isn't big enough for even the narrow iTunes window in Figure 8-1, try taking it down a notch. To create the mini bar shown at lower right in Figure 8-1, start with the medium-size window. Then drag the Resize handle (the diagonal lines in the lower-right corner) leftward. To expand it, just reverse the process.

8-2   Quicker Resizing

If the visual updating of the iTunes window lags as you resize it, press ⌘ as you drag the lower-right corner. This way, the rectangle that shows the iTunes window shrinks or grows smoothly and quickly, showing only an outline (Figure 8-2) while you drag. Then it fills in when you release the mouse.

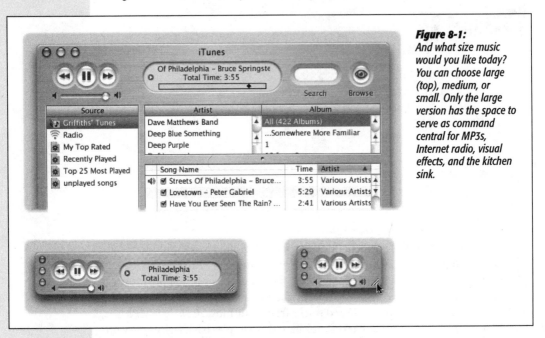

Figure 8-1:
And what size music would you like today? You can choose large (top), medium, or small. Only the large version has the space to serve as command central for MP3s, Internet radio, visual effects, and the kitchen sink.

Figure 8-2:
On slower machines, iTunes is very jerky when it comes to resizing the window while you drag the corner. The solution is to press ⌘ as you drag.

8-3 The Column Contextual Menu

When you get right down to it, iTunes is really a database. Its primary view shows columns of information about the songs in its little head.

As with any good database, you can specify which columns you want to see in its main song listing, as shown in Figure 8-3.

Tip: While the menu shown in Figure 8-3 is open, can also choose to autosize a selected column (widen or shrink to fit the column's text) or all columns using the secret pop-up menu. Be careful with Auto Size All Columns—it discards all of your carefully crafted, hand-adjusted column widths.

Figure 8-3:
When you Control-click any of the existing column headings, a menu appears. It lists all of the information columns available to you. Select a column's name to add or remove it. (You can't hide the song name or number.)

8-4 Changing the Displayed Play Time

If you click the Library (the top icon in the Source list at the left side), the bar at the bottom of the player displays the total duration and disk-space consumption of the songs in your collection. It might read something like "1253 songs, 3 days, 7.28 GB."

If you click this text, it changes to show the time in days, hours, *and* minutes: "1253 songs, 3:12:23:37 total time, 7.28 GB"—handy information for parties. In this example, the party will last for three days, twelve hours, 23 minutes, and 37 seconds before the music stops and everybody goes home.

8-5   Renaming the Library

You're not stuck with Library as the name of your music collection. A single click on the word "Library" (at the top of the Source list) opens up a renaming rectangle for your redubbing pleasure.

8-6   Splitting a Song

Think how convenient it'd be if you could chop up your songs. You could divide up audio books into easier-to-manage chunks for listing on your iPod. You could split apart those "hidden bonus track" songs on a CD—you know, the ones with five minutes of silence before the hidden song starts. You could even chop out the self-indulgent dialogue that certain artists tack onto the beginning of certain songs.

Start by Control-clicking a song in the iTunes list. Choose Get Info from the contextual menu, click the Options tab, type the timings you want into the Start Time and Stop Time boxes, and then click OK.

Next, choose Advanced→"Convert selection to MP3." iTunes makes a new song based on your chosen start and end times, leaving the old intact.

Navigating iTunes

A whole section on navigating iTunes? How hard can it be? It's got a couple buttons and a volume slider! But hiding behind that deceptively simple interface are a variety of hidden (and not-so-hidden) features that let you get the most out of iTunes.

8-7   Controlling iTunes Through the Dock

You're working away in Word when suddenly you realize that iTunes has played "The Long and Winding Road" 47 times in a row. You must change the song *immediately.* What do you do?

See Figure 8-4.

8-8   Marking or Unmarking All Songs

When you're browsing a library or playlist, you can ⌘-click the checkbox next to a song to turn off (or turn on) all the songs.

This trick can be a big timesaver when, for example, you want to import only a few songs from a CD. Insert the CD, ⌘-click a song to unmark the whole playlist, and then just turn on the songs you want to import.

8-9   Keyboard Navigation

You can fast-forward and rewind a song right from the keyboard, as long as you know the completely undocumented keyboard shortcut: Option-⌘-left or -right arrow key.

8-10 Hover Focus

If you own a mouse with a scroll wheel, you can take advantage of *hover focus* to scroll the various lists in iTunes—the list of songs, for example, or your list of playlists. You don't have to click the list you want to flip through; just move the cursor over it and then turn the scroll wheel. As soon as you move the cursor out of that area, the scrolling stops.

Figure 8-4:
When you need to shut up your Mac now, what are you supposed to do—switch out of Word, switch into iTunes, find the proper menu or click the right button, and then return to Word? That's a lot of work for a quick song change.

Instead, hit the Dock, as shown here. If you Control-click (or click and hold) iTunes' Dock icon, a handy menu pops up. Use this menu to control iTunes without switching out of the program you're already using—choose Pause, for example. When you make menu choices this way, iTunes doesn't come to the foreground.

8-11 Cranking It Up (or Down)

If you use iTunes in its minimized states (either small or tiny; see hints 8-1 and 8-2), you have a quick keyboard shortcut for setting the volume level all the way up or all the way down: Shift-up arrow (maximum volume) and Shift-down arrow (silence).

Tip: You can also press Option-⌘-up arrow to mute iTunes. For added convenience, this keyboard combo works even when the window is maximized.

8-12 Controlling Dialog Boxes with a Keystroke

When iTunes dialog boxes appear—as one does when, say, you remove an item from your library—they often give you choices of Yes, No, and Cancel. Instead of clicking the buttons or using a ⌘-key shortcut, just press Y, N, or C, respectively. (In fact, this trick works in many Mac OS X programs.)

Note: Be careful with this trick: If you were to select the library, press Delete, and then reflexively press Y, you'd wipe out your whole collection.

8-13 Clearing Searches

Although this hint is amazingly simple, it's also easy to overlook, especially if you're a long-time iTunes user. After you've just rounded up a certain subset of songs using the Search box at the top of the iTunes window, you can click the small X icon at the end of the search bar to clear the text from the search box, as shown in Figure 8-6. The list returns to showing you the complete playlist or music library. No more tedious backspacing to clear your typed text!

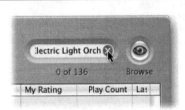

Figure 8-5:
How do you get rid of that search you just ran? X marks the spot. Click it, and the search field clears.

8-14 Keyboard Control

You can control iTunes' music playback using its menus, of course, but the keyboard can be far more efficient. Here are a few of the control keystrokes worth noting:

Function	Keystroke
Play, Pause	Space bar
next song/previous song	right arrow, left arrow
next source/previous source	down arrow, up arrow
louder	⌘-up arrow
quieter	⌘-down arrow
mute	⌘-M
fast-forward/rewind	Option-⌘-right arrow, -left arrow
eject	⌘-E
Turn Visuals on	⌘-T
Turn Visuals off	⌘-T or mouse click
Full-screen visuals	⌘-F
Exit full-screen visuals	⌘-T, ⌘-F, or mouse click

8-15 Extended Help Labels

Like many Mac OS X programs, iTunes displays yellow pop-up labels—*tooltips,* as Microsoft would call them—when your cursor pauses on a button, icon, or other screen element.

In iTunes, however, pressing ⌘ offers an extended, more complex form of the tooltip, as shown in Figure 8-6.

8-16 One Library for Mac OS X and Mac OS 9

If you live a double life, using Mac OS X and Mac OS 9 on different occasions, you may run into iTunes' irritating insistence on keeping two separate music libraries. Fortunately, you can prevent this separation of state and state.

In the Mac OS 9 version of iTunes, choose iTunes→Preferences, click the Advanced icon, and then click Change (next to iTunes Music Folder Location). In the window that opens, navigate to your Home folder (choose its name from the From pop-up menu or press Shift-⌘-H). Double-click your way into the Music→iTunes folder. Click the iTunes Music folder once, and then click Choose. From now on, your Mac OS 9 copy of iTunes will use your Mac OS X's collection of iTunes music. Update one, and you've updated them all.

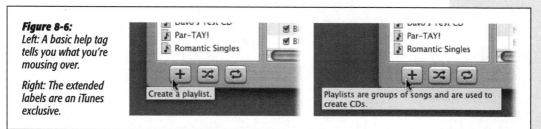

Figure 8-6:
Left: A basic help tag tells you what you're mousing over.

Right: The extended labels are an iTunes exclusive.

8-17 One Library for Multiple Family Members

The accounts feature described on page 11 is great for keeping each family member or co-worker's email and preferences separate. Trouble is, it also keeps each person's *music* separate. If Dad has a massive iTunes collection, his wife and kids don't have access to it.

Fortunately, the solution is easy enough.

Whoever is the administrator—probably the 8-year-old—should move the iTunes folder (currently in somebody's Music folder) to the Users→Shared folder. Next, remove the original iTunes folder from the original Home→Music folder. Finally, drag an alias of the iTunes folder in the Shared folder into the place formerly occupied by the original iTunes folder (make sure it's still called iTunes). Now it's available to everybody.

At this point, each account holder can log in, fire up iTunes, choose iTunes→Preferences→Advanced, and click the Change button to choose the relocated iTunes Music folder in the Shared folder. From now on, each person can see and access the entire library of iTunes tunes, while still enjoying the flexibility to build individual playlists.

8-18 Computer, Play This Song!

Too bad Apple doesn't make computers like the ones on *Star Trek,* where you can just say what you want done and marvel as the computer executes your wishes.

Still, the seed of this feature awaits inside Mac OS X. Using the speakable items technology and AppleScript, you can create a script that will let you *tell* iTunes what song you'd like to hear. Not point, not click, not type—*say*.

Start by opening Script Editor (in your Applications→AppleScript folder). In the main window, enter the following script.

Note: Don't type the ¬ symbols shown here. They're used here to tell you, "This is really all one line, but we've had to break it up at this point because the book page is too narrow." And remember that you can download all this from *www.macosxhints.com/book/scripts.html*.

```
tell application "iTunes"
 set myList to (get name of every track of playlist 1) as list
 set myFinishedList to myList & "Cancel"
end tell

tell application "SpeechRecognitionServer"
 set myTrack to (listen for myFinishedList ¬
 with prompt myFinishedList)
end tell

if myTrack is not "Cancel" then
 tell application "iTunes"
  set myTrackList to (get every track of playlist 1 where ¬
  name is myTrack)
  if number of items of myTrackList is 1 then
   play (get first item of myTrackList)
  else
   set myArtistNames to {"Cancel"} & (get artist of every ¬
   track of playlist 1 where name is myTrack)
   tell application "SpeechRecognitionServer"
    set myArtist to (listen for myArtistNames with prompt ¬
    myArtistNames)
   end tell
   if myArtist is not "Cancel" then
    set myFocusedTrackList to (get every track of ¬
    playlist 1 where name is myTrack and artist is myArtist)
    set randnum to (random number ((number of items of ¬
    myFocusedTrackList) - 1)) + 1
    play (get item randnum of myTrackList)
   end if
   set randnum to ((random number (numitems - 1)) + 1)
   play (get item randnum of myTrackList)
  end if
 end tell
end if
```

When you've entered the whole script, click the Check Syntax button to make sure you haven't made any mistakes. If you get an error message, compare what you've typed with what you see above.

When the program is error-free, choose File→Save, type *play* as the name for your script, choose Compile Script from the Format pop-up menu, and save your script in your Home→Library→Speech→Speakable Items folder.

To test your script, open System Preferences. Click Speech. On the Speech Recognition tab, click the "Apple Speakable Items is" On button. You may wish to turn on the "Speak confirmation" box, too; it will tell your computer to "read back" each command you give it.

The script works in two steps. You first activate it by saying the name of the script: "*play.*" Once the computer recognizes that (you'll hear a sound, and, if you turned on "Speak confirmation," the Mac will say, "Play," too). Then say the name of the song you wish to hear.

So if you want to listen to "Penny Lane" by the Beatles, you would say, "Play" (pause and wait for confirmation) "Penny Lane." To be most effective, iTunes should already be running; otherwise, you'll have to wait for it to open after saying "Play."

Tip: If you have two songs with the same name, you can speak the name of the artist after the song—after confirming that the Mac has heard you say the song name.

The Visualizer

Visuals is the iTunes term for an onscreen laser-light show that pulses, beats, and dances in sync to the music you're listening to. The effect is hypnotic and wild. (To turn on the visualizer, click the flower-power icon in the lower-right corner of the window, or choose Visuals→Turn Visuals On.)

The show begins immediately—although it's much more fun if you choose Visuals→Full Screen so that the movie takes over your whole monitor.

8-19   Add Your Own Visualizers

Visualizers are iTunes plug-ins. So when Apple's built-in collection starts wearing a little thin, you can download a variety of new ones from *www.versiontracker.com*.

Once you run a plug-in's installer, the software winds up in your Home→Library→iTunes→iTunes Plug-ins folder. The next time you run iTunes, you'll see a new command at the bottom of the Visualizer, so that you can choose your favorite with each song. (The one called Flower Power, for example, is kind of pretty—it makes different colored flowers appear in time to the music.)

8-20   Keyboard Controls for the Visualizer

Once the screen is alive with visuals, you can turn it into your personal biofeedback screen by experimenting with these keys:

Key	Function
?	Displays a cheat sheet of secret keystrokes. (Press it repeatedly to see the other shortcut keys.)
F	Displays, in the upper-left corner of your screen, how many frames per second iTunes' animation is managing—a quick, easy way to test the power of your graphics circuitry.
T	Turns *frame rate capping* on or off—a feature that limits the frame rate to 30 frames per second, to avoid sapping your Mac's horsepower when you're working in other programs (not really much of an issue in Mac OS X, of course).
I	Shows/hides info about the current song.
C	Shows/hides the current Visuals configuration (the name of the current waveform, style, and color scheme) in the upper-right corner of the screen.
M	Turns slideshow mode on or off. In slideshow mode, the visuals keep changing color and waveform as they play. (Otherwise, the visuals stick with one style and color.)
B	Turns on an Apple logo in the center of the Visuals screen.
R	Chooses a new waveform/style/color at random.
Q or W	Cycles through the various waveform styles stored in iTunes.
A or S	Cycles though *variations* on the currently selected waveform.
Z or X	Cycles through color schemes.
Number keys	Cycle through the ten different preset, preprogrammed waveform/color/style configurations.
D	Restores the default waveform settings.

When you download additional visuals from the Web, each comes with its own custom set of keyboard controls.

8-21   Capture a Visual

The only problem with iTunes's stunning visual special effects—the Visualizer—is that you can enjoy them only while you're actually in iTunes, actually playing music.

Or can you?

Once you've got visuals playing full-screen (choose Visuals→Full Screen), press the screen-capture keystroke ⌘-Shift-3 (see hint 4-14). You've just created a full-screen snapshot of the visuals, in PDF format, on your desktop.

You're free to use this graphic *as* your desktop (hint 2-56), or in a Web design program, in Photoshop, or wherever you need an interesting background or texture.

Songs and Playlists

A *playlist* is nothing more than a subset of your library, consisting of songs you've added. The following hints will help you create automated playlists to keep your favorite music handy, and will reveal some hidden features that will help you manage your music collection.

8-22   The Song List Contextual Menu

When browsing your song collection, don't overlook the usefulness of iTunes' contextual song menu, which you can summon by Control-clicking any song in the library or a playlist (Figure 8-7).

The contextual menu includes a number of useful choices, including an easy way to reset the rating (from one to five stars) for a given song.

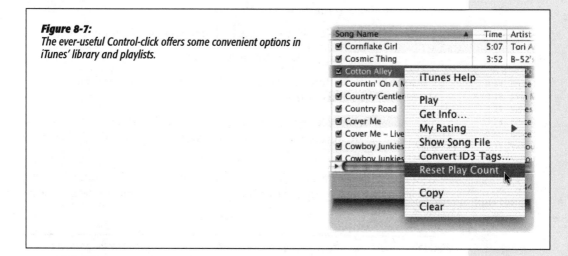

Figure 8-7:
The ever-useful Control-click offers some convenient options in iTunes' library and playlists.

8-23   Playing a Song Without Adding It to the Library

Whenever you drag a file into the iTunes window, the program's instinct is to make it a permanent part of your collection. But that isn't always what you want. Maybe you're just trying to play a 15-second song preview from an online service, or listen to an audio joke recorded by a buddy. Either way, you probably don't want to make that sound file a permanent part of your library.

To turn off this feature for good, choose iTunes→Preferences, click the Advanced button, and turn off "Copy files to iTunes Music folder when adding to library." Click OK.

If that seems a bit drastic, you can also prevent this gulping action on a one-shot basis. The trick: Press Option as you drag the file into the iTunes window. Now, instead of copying the file, iTunes creates an *alias* in the library. So although you see the file in your library list, it doesn't actually exist in your iTunes music folder.

Tip: Unfortunately, it's not easy to distinguish an alias from an actual song in the iTunes display. To identify an alias, highlight a song in the main window and then choose File→Get Info (⌘-I).

In the Info tab, "Where" shows the file's actual location. If this location matches that of your iTunes music folder, then the song exists in your real library. If the listed location is elsewhere, the song is an alias.

8-24 Seeing into the Future

If you enjoy iTunes random mode but still want to see what's coming up, you can set the program to give you a sneak preview. Here's how:

1. **Create a new playlist.**

   Do that by choosing File→New Playlist, or click the + button in the bottom left corner of the window. Name it whatever you like, and then drag in all the songs from your library (or just the ones you like to hear).

2. **In the main panel, click the top of the Playback Sequence column.**

   That's the column just to the left of the song names.

3. **Click the Shuffle button (second from left at the bottom of the iTunes window; the one with the crossed arrows).**

   You've now put your playlist into Shuffle (random) mode—and yet because you've sorted the list by song number, you can see exactly what the order of the songs will be.

   If you don't like what you see, click the Shuffle button again. Each time, you get a new random order, which is clearly revealed by the list of songs in the main window.

Note: You can, of course, use this trick on regular playlists; it's not reserved just for the entire library.

8-25 Reshuffling a Playlist

iTunes' Shuffle mode occasionally forgets that it's already played something, and treats you to a certain sequence of songs twice.

To slap iTunes into submission, force the program to recreate the shuffle order by clicking the Shuffle mode button twice—to turn it off and then on again.

8-26 Skipping Albums During Random Play

iTunes lets you play a random mix in two ways: by song (which shuffles your entire library and plays the songs randomly) or by album (which plays the *albums* in random order, but leaves the *songs* in order within them). You specify which method you want by choosing iTunes→Preferences, and then clicking the Advanced icon.

If you're listening to albums in random mode, you can skip an entire album by pressing Option and one of your arrow keys. Option-left arrow jumps to the previous album; Option-right arrow jumps to the next.

8-27 Radio Stations

iTunes has some nifty Internet radio features; in fact, the program lets you treat radio stations almost like songs. You can add them to a playlist or your library (Figure 8-9), and you can use File→Get Info to set their *tags*—associated information about the artist, album, year recorded, genre, and so on. Once that's done, you can sort your stations by genre, add an artist name of "Radio" for all of them, use smart playlists to make sub-selections based on your tags (see hint 8-33 for creating smart playlists), and so on.

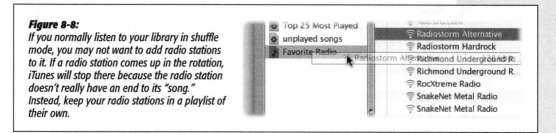

Figure 8-8:
If you normally listen to your library in shuffle mode, you may not want to add radio stations to it. If a radio station comes up in the rotation, iTunes will stop there because the radio station doesn't really have an end to its "song." Instead, keep your radio stations in a playlist of their own.

8-28 Moving Songs to the Top of a Playlist

You've just created the playlist for a weekend-long bash, but it's not yet in any order. As you prepare for the shindig, you realize that you'd like many of the songs near the bottom of the list to play first.

At first glance, you might suppose that the only way to move them up your gigantic music list is to drag them toward the top of the iTunes window, wait for the long list of songs to scroll by, and then drop the selections at the top.

Fortunately, there's a better way.

Note: The following trick works only within a playlist—not within your entire library.

Select all the songs you want to move (⌘-click to select individual, nonadjacent songs in the list). But instead of dragging them, drag the handle of the scroll bar toward the top of the window. Scan the list for a song near where you want the selected songs to wind up. Then ⌘-click this new "top song" to temporarily add it to your selection.

Now—this gets a little weird—click the song you just selected and keep the mouse button down. Now wiggle the mouse around. If you move it just enough, the horizontal insertion indicator appears without actually moving the file.

Move the insertion line back to the spot where you grabbed this top song, and then release the mouse button. Almost like magic, the top song drops into place along with all of your selections from the bottom of the list just beneath!

8-29　Burning MP3 CDs

You're probably aware that iTunes can burn customized CDs—containing only the music you like in the order that you want—that play in any CD player.

You may not be aware, though, that iTunes can also burn *MP3 CDs*, discs that work just like regular music CDs but hold many, many times more music. Whereas an audio CD holds just over an hour's worth of music (15 or 20 songs), an MP3 CD can hold well over 100 songs (MP3 CDs are also handy for transferring a lot of MP3 files from one machine to another.)

Before you get squirmy in your chair, however, there are two caveats. First, not all CD players can play MP3 CDs. Most recent models can, but you can't be sure until you try it. Second, purists complain that the quality of MP3 isn't as high as audio CDs. (It's plenty good enough for everyday jogging use or yard work, however.)

To make an MP3 CD, choose iTunes→Preferences; click the Burning icon. Here you can specify which kind of CD you intend to make *most* of the time—Audio CD or MP3 CD.

But if you mostly burn audio CDs, you can leave the preference panel set to Audio CD. Thereafter, when you need to make the occasional MP3 CD, use this method: Just insert a blank CD, and then drag a selection of songs directly out of the iTunes window and onto the CD's desktop icon. Eject the CD as usual, and indicate that yes, you want it burned before ejecting.

Note: A CD made this way may wind up with inaccurate track information, so it's best for transferring files or creating quick-and-dirty, casual CDs. For example, the songs will play in alphabetical order. (If you want a different order, name the songs with numerical prefixes. You can rename a song by control-clicking it and choosing Get Info from the contextual menu.)

8-30　The Browser

If you click the Browse eyeball icon in the upper right (or press ⌘-B), the iTunes window changes to show you three panes. At the upper left, you see a list of the singers or bands. Click one to see, in the upper-right panel, a list of the albums by that group. Either way, you see a list of the matching songs in the bottom half of the window. The point of all this is to give you a quick way to narrow down your database when you want to see only the songs on one album, or from one artist (see Figure 8-9).

Before iTunes 3, you could only view the browser when the library—your complete music collection—was selected. Now, however, it's also available when you're viewing playlists—and it's very useful. Once you've opened up the browser, you can view subsets of a playlist by artist, album, and so on, just by clicking names in the Browser list.

8-31 Creating a Playlist from the Browser

One thing that makes the browser so useful is its ability to instantly create a playlist whose songs contain only one artist or album. Just highlight the artist or album on the right, and then drag the selection into the playlist window on the left (Figure 8-10). iTunes instantly builds a new playlist containing the subset of songs you selected.

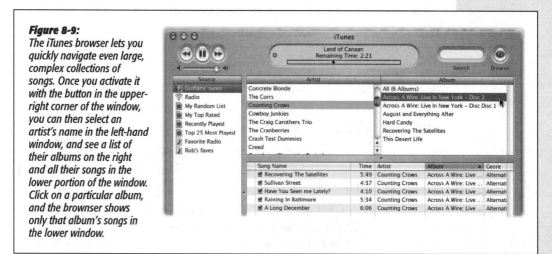

Figure 8-9:
The iTunes browser lets you quickly navigate even large, complex collections of songs. Once you activate it with the button in the upper-right corner of the window, you can then select an artist's name in the left-hand window, and see a list of their albums on the right and all their songs in the lower portion of the window. Click on a particular album, and the brownser shows only that album's songs in the lower window.

Tip: If you drop the selected artist or album on an existing playlist, iTunes adds all albums (or songs) to that playlist.

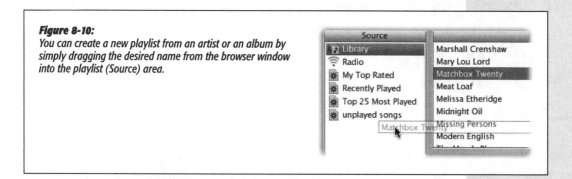

Figure 8-10:
You can create a new playlist from an artist or an album by simply dragging the desired name from the browser window into the playlist (Source) area.

8-32 Printing a Playlist

Print a playlist to make a jewel-case cover in a hurry.

1. Select a playlist, choose Edit→View Options, and then turn on the columns you want to appear on your cover.

   Click OK when you're finished.

2. Make sure the main iTunes window is active (click any column heading), and then choose Edit→Select All (⌘-A).

iTunes highlights all the songs in the playlist.

3. Press ⌘-C to copy the song names. Switch to your favorite word processor (or spreadsheet or paint program or whatever) and paste (⌘-V).

The listing of songs and song information appears, ready to format and print.

Tip: If you're working in Microsoft Word or AppleWorks, you can create a nicely formatted table from your playlist. After pasting, Select All (⌘-A), and then choose Table→Convert→Convert Text to Table (Word) or Table→Convert→Convert Text to Table (AppleWorks).

Smart Playlists

"Smart playlists" are self-creating lists of songs that update themselves according to rules you define—the number of times a song has been played, its rating, its genre, or other such details.

To create a new smart playlist, choose File→New Smart Playlist (Option-⌘-N), or see Figure 8-11. The Smart Playlist dialog box opens, allowing you to set the rules you'd like to use. When the dialog box closes, you can type a new name for your playlist.

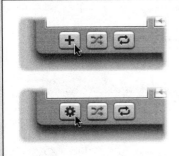

Figure 8-11:
Here's another way to open the Smart Playlist dialog box: Option-click the + (New Playlist) button. When you've done it right, the usual + icon (top) becomes a gear shape (bottom). Click it to open the dialog box.

8-33   Playlists That Play All Songs Once

One of the most useful smart playlists—a playlist that simply plays every song once—sounds as easy as pie, but there's a little more to it than you might suspect.

Open the Smart Playlist dialog box (Option-⌘-N), and then proceed as shown in Figure 8-12.

A song is not considered played until it ends, so if you skip ahead with the "next song" button (the >> button above the volume bar), the skipped songs remain in the unplayed category and will come up again. If, later, you decide that you want to hear the rest of them after all, click the << button.

Note: The smart playlist is a great way to give your song star ratings. Even while the playback continues, you can Control-click in the My Rating column–or, if you're working in some other program as you listen, the rating menu in the iTunes Dock icon (Control-click the icon)–to rate each song on a scale of one to five stars. Eventually, you'll have heard all of the music in your collection and rated every song.

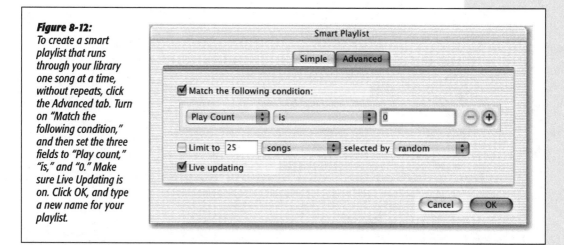

Figure 8-12:
To create a smart playlist that runs through your library one song at a time, without repeats, click the Advanced tab. Turn on "Match the following condition," and then set the three fields to "Play count," "is," and "0." Make sure Live Updating is on. Click OK, and type a new name for your playlist.

8-34   Modifying Random Playlists

When you set iTunes to randomly play the library or a normal playlist, you can't modify the order or contents of the list. But what if you see that the "Love Boat" theme song is in the list, and you suddenly remember it caused your dog to toss his cookies on the rug last week? Better to have a playlist you can modify.

Choose File→New Smart Playlist, and then set things up as shown in Figure 8-13.

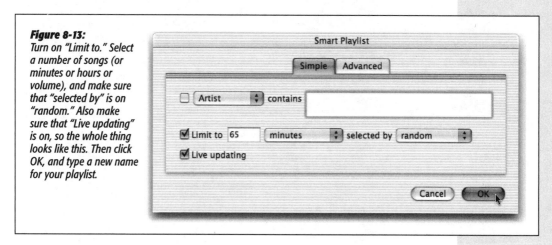

Figure 8-13:
Turn on "Limit to." Select a number of songs (or minutes or hours or volume), and make sure that "selected by" is on "random." Also make sure that "Live updating" is on, so the whole thing looks like this. Then click OK, and type a new name for your playlist.

The smart playlist you just created is not only random but completely controllable, too. You can drag songs around to set their play order, and you can delete songs (like the "Love Boat" theme) that you don't want to hear. When you delete a song, iTunes picks a new song from the library to replace it.

iPhoto 2

Digital cameras encourage lots of snaps. Once you've bought enough batteries and memory cards, there's no additional cost to taking tons of photos. But how to keep those pictures organized? Carefully labeled slide trays aren't going to do the trick.

iPhoto 2, one of the free "iApps" included with every Mac, allows you to create digital albums and assign searchable keywords to photos, making it a very good solution for all but the most prolific of picture takers.

The Basics

iPhoto is a masterpiece, a breakthrough, a revolution. It's also slowish, especially when your collection approaches 1,000 to 2,500 photos (depending on how much memory your Mac has). If you're like most iPhoto fans, then, you'll appreciate every efficiency tip you can get.

9-1   Speeding Up iPhoto

When you're viewing a library, film roll, or album, iPhoto comes set to display your photos with a subtle drop shadow in the main window. While this effect looks very cool, it slows down scrolling and resizing on all but the fastest machines. Boost your speed by turning off the shadow.

Choose iTunes→Preferences, and in the Appearance section, select either Border or No Border. (You can also change the background shade if you want.)

Return to Organize mode, and try enlarging the photos using the slider in the lower-right corner, or scroll through a collection. You'll gasp at the speed increase.

9-2   Rotating Clockwise

When you click the Rotate icon below the album list area (the button on the right in Figure 9-1), iPhoto rotates your images counter-clockwise—a handy action for photos you took after rotating the camera 90 degrees. Unfortunately, if you want to rotate a photo 90 degrees to the *right*, you have to click that button three times—right? Not necessarily...see Figure 9-1.

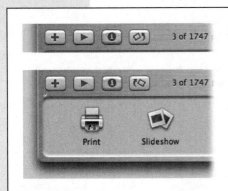

Figure 9-1:
Top: The Rotate button (at right) generally indicates that it will spin a selected photo counterclockwise.

Bottom: But if you hold down Option, the icon changes to display a clockwise rotation.

9-3   Zooming In

When, in Edit mode, you zoom in on a photo using the slider in the corner of iPhoto's main window, the program focuses on the center of the photo. To zoom in on a different portion, use your mouse to "drag out" a box over the area you'd like to work on, and *then* use the zoom slider. iPhoto not only zooms in on that selection, it centers it in the window, making it much easier to work with.

9-4   Sideways Zooming

If your mouse has a scroll wheel, you've probably already noticed that you can scroll images up and down while zoomed in on them. But if you press Shift, you can use that same wheel to scroll the zoomed area horizontally.

9-5   Long Comments

iPhoto includes a Comments box for storing notes about your photos (if you don't see it, click the small "i" below the album area—twice, if necessary). Unfortunately, the Comments box doesn't automatically widen if you have a long note—and it doesn't have a scroll bar.

If these annoyances are preventing you from savoring the genius of the extensive comments you've typed in, two solutions await.

• Click inside the Comments box once, and then use the up and down arrows on the keyboard to scroll through the box.

- Resize the Comments box by dragging the small dot that separates the bottom of the album list from the information area (Figure 9-2).

- Resize the entire album pane by dragging the bar that separates it from the photos.

Figure 9-2:
When you resize the Comments box, the cursor changes from an arrow to a two-headed creature.

9-6   Commenting Rolls, Albums, or the Library

You've just decided to create separate albums for each year of your annual Civil War reenactment party. Problem is, you don't want to name the albums "Civil War 2000," "Civil War 2001," and so on. And it's a hassle to add a date comment to every photo.

Figure 9-3:
Select the item you want to add a comment to. Next, make sure that no individual image is selected. (Click anywhere in the right-hand panel except on a photo; you've done this right if, in the information area below the album list, the first line is the name of your album.) To add a comment, just type it in the Comments box.

Instead of renaming them, the better way might be to add a *comment* to each album, listing the date, the participants, and the dips you served. Most people use the Comments box only for individual photos, but you can also attach text to an album, a film roll, or even an entire library, which could be handy if you have multiple libraries. See Figure 9-3.

9-7   Editing Windows I

Using the options in iPhoto→Preferences, you can tell iPhoto what to do when you double-click a photo: Either open the picture in the main window (in Edit view), or in a separate editing window.

But every now and then, you may prefer whichever arrangement *isn't* selected— instead of switching to Edit mode in the main window, for example, one day you may want to open a photo into its own window.

Fortunately, no matter which mode you've chosen, you can temporarily override the setting by *Option*-double-clicking a picture. So if you had selected "Edit view," Option-double-clicking opens a picture in a separate window, and vice versa.

9-8   Editing Windows II

Unfortunately, the Option-double-clicking trick (hint 9-7) doesn't work if you've selected the third option in the Preferences window, "Open in other." Which means that you now have a *lot* of variables to keep in your head. Option-click? Current Preferences setting? External Editor? Ack!

You may be better off forgetting hint 9-7 altogether—and whenever you want to edit a photo, just Control-click it. The resulting contextual menu offers all three choices: "Edit" (that is, switch iPhoto into Edit mode), "Edit in separate window," and "Edit in external editor." Click your choice.

9-9   Before and After Pictures

Want to see your photo edits before you commit to them? While you're working in Edit mode, hold down the Control key for a quick trip back in time to see a pre-edited view of your picture (not counting rotation). When you release Control, the image reverts to its edited state.

9-10   Crop Photos with the Keyboard

When you've dragged across part of a photo in preparation for cropping it, you can avoid one unnecessary trip to the mouse by pressing Shift-⌘-C, which means "Crop now."

This keyboard shortcut isn't documented in Help or the menus. So where is it written, you may well ask? In the contextual menu that appears when you Control-click a graphic in Edit mode. In addition to Crop, the contextual menu contains options for Retouch, Enhance, and so on—each a timesaver in its own right, especially if you're editing in a window where the complete collection of toolbar icons isn't visible.

9-11 Backing Up the Preferences File

iPhoto's preferences file doesn't just store your program settings. It also stores any keywords you've created, as well as the association of those keywords with various photos. If that file gets wiped out, you lose your ability to sort photos by keyword. And if your library is large, you could spend one very tedious Christmas vacation reassigning all the keywords.

To back up iPhoto's preferences, switch to the Finder and open the Home→ Library→Preferences folder. Copy the file called com.apple.iPhoto.plist to a safe location. Store the backup in a fire-proof, flood-proof, hail-and-sleet-proof place.

If you ever need to reinstall your system, drop the iPhoto preferences-file backup into your Home→Library→Preferences folder. Your full collection of keywords and image associations survives intact.

Libraries

Behind the scenes, all of your photos sit in an extremely important folder called the *iPhoto Library* folder. Knowing that is the first step to mastering a useful bunch of hints.

9-12 The Library Location

iPhoto wants to store its iPhoto Library folder in your Home→Pictures folder. But what if you want to keep your photos somewhere else, such as on an external drive (so that you can easily move your photos from one Mac to another), or on a larger second hard drive?

iTunes lets you choose any folder you like for storing your music, but iPhoto doesn't have a similar preference setting. Still, you can do the deed using either iPhoto Library Manager (described in the next hint) or Terminal.

Open Terminal (page 5). At the % sign, type this all on one line:

```
defaults write com.apple.iPhoto RootDirectory "/path/to/new/
home"
```

The only part of the command you need to change is the */path/to/new/home* part, which specifies the new iPhoto Library location.

For example, if you wanted to park the library on a hard drive named Room to Grow in a folder named My Images, then */path/to/new/home* would become *"/Volumes/Room to Grow/My Images"*. (Quotes are required in Unix if the folder or file names contain spaces.) And you have to add "Volumes" whenever you specify any location that isn't on your main, startup hard drive.

(See page 5 for details on the *defaults write* command.)

Once you press Enter and then exit Terminal, iPhoto creates and manages your photo library at the location you specified. If you ever wish to return to the original location, just open Terminal again and type:

```
defaults remove com.apple.iPhoto RootDirectory
```

Note: This command doesn't affect any albums and photos—that is, it doesn't copy them into the newly specified folder. (You can do that manually, if you like.) Instead, this command teaches iPhoto to look in the newly specified location the next time it runs.

9-13   Multiple Libraries

iPhoto bogs down when you have thousands of pictures in the library. So if you're going nuts taking photos of your seahorses' development...*and* you photo-document every item in your *Star Wars* action-figure collection...*and* you tend to snap every airport, hotel lobby, and toll booth you pass through while traveling, it probably makes sense to create a few separate iPhoto Library folders.

iPhoto Library Manager, a freeware program, lets you do just that. You can download it from *http://homepage.mac.com/bwebster/iphotolibrarymanager.html,* among other places.

You can use the program to create and manage multiple libraries, set permissions on those libraries, and even keep separate sets of keywords for each library. You can also write AppleScripts that let you specify which library to use when you open iPhoto.

9-14   Libraries on Removable Hard Drives

If you use the previous hint to point iPhoto at a library that's stored on a removable drive, like an external FireWire drive, you may have problems if you run iPhoto when that drive is no longer connected. For example, suppose you've stored the iPhoto Library folder on a FireWire disk named Photos Drive.

Now suppose you disconnect this drive—take it to the office, for example. When you next run iPhoto, you'll find no pictures at all. Not too surprising, given that the library location no longer exists. But since you know you'll have the drive back tomorrow, you go ahead and import some new photos from your camera. Let's call these the Barbecue Pix.

Tomorrow rolls around, you return home with the hard drive, plug it in, and open iPhoto. It will show you only the small batch of Barbecue Pix; your main collection is gone. Your brain reels. Why don't you see your whole collection? After all, the original iPhoto Library folder is now back where the Mac expects it to be—on the Photos Drive.

• **The Explanation.** (If you're not especially interested in the techie innards of this problem, skip down to The Solution.)

Mac OS X maintains icons for all your hard drives (except the startup drive) in the /Volumes folder. (This folder is normally invisible, but you can see its contents if you choose Go→Go to Folder, type */Volumes*, and then press Enter.)

When you first plugged in the Photos Drive, Mac OS X created an icon for it in the /Volumes folder. When you unplug the drive, the icon disappears.

Later, when you open iPhoto while the drive is absent, iPhoto decides that, since the specified library folder doesn't exist, it had better create one. iPhoto once again adds a Photos Drive icon to the /Volumes folder, and then puts its iPhoto Library folder inside it. Any new pictures you import while the FireWire drive is absent go into this folder. If you were to open /Volumes in the Finder again, you'd see a normal folder icon for the newly created Photos Drive folder (rather than the special drive icon used for the original Photos Drive).

When you return home and plug in the FireWire drive, the Finder tries to create an icon in /Volumes for it, but finds that the name Photos Drive is already in use. So, smart little software that it is, Mac OS X names the newly reunited drive *Photos Drive 1*. When you launch iPhoto, it only sees the Photos Drive folder; the FireWire drive now has a new name, as far as iPhoto is concerned.

- **The Solution.** Quit iPhoto, if it's running, and disconnect the FireWire drive. Open the /Volumes folder in the Finder by choosing Go→Go to Folder, typing */Volumes,* and pressing Enter.

Now rescue the Barbecue Pix photos by dragging the "new" Photos Drive folder out of the /Volumes window onto, say, your desktop. Next reconnect the FireWire drive, which now proudly bears the correct name, Photos Drive (not Photos Drive 1). Open iPhoto, which now displays all of your older photos and albums again.

All that's left is to drag and drop the Barbecue Pix batch of photos from the folder on your desktop into the iPhoto window to reimport them.

Film Rolls

Each time you import a batch of photos, iPhoto groups them into what it calls a *film roll,* stamped with a roll number, the import date, and the number of photos in the import.

9-15   Faster Scrolling Through Creative Collapsing

In iPhoto 2, you turn on film-roll grouping by choosing View→Film Rolls (or by pressing Shift-⌘-F). The result is shown in Figure 9-4.

Next to each film roll is a flippy triangle that collapses, or hides, all the photos in that group. Or, to collapse (or reveal) all of your film rolls at once, Option-click the flippy triangle next to any film roll.

Collapsed rolls make scrolling in iPhoto *much* faster, since the program doesn't need to process all the image data. You may find it useful to leave the current roll in an expanded state, with all older rolls collapsed until you need them.

Figure 9-4:
The flippy triangle to the left of the film-roll icon lets you collapse or expand the display of photos for that batch. (Working with collapsed rolls is much easier, of course, if you name them as described in the next hint.)

9-16 Changing a Film Roll's Title, Date, and Comments

It's well worth taking the time to change a film roll's name ("Disneyland vacation" instead of "Roll 135"). To do so, just click its existing name and then edit the information that appears at the lower-left corner of the screen, below the album list. (If you don't see any information fields, click the small "i" button in the lower-left corner of the main window.)

You'll find that you can edit not only a roll's name, but also its comments and even its date—a great opportunity to rewrite history.

9-17 Selecting a Whole Film Roll

An easy way to select all the pictures in a film roll—in readiness to create a book, slide show, or whatever—is to just click the roll's header (its name). You've just highlighted *all* of its photos; you can now remove certain pictures from the selection by Shift-clicking or ⌘-clicking them.

To unselect all the images in a roll, Shift-click the film-roll header.

Albums

The best part of iPhoto is the way it lets you organize your photo collection into smaller subcollections called *albums*, which appear in the list at the left side of the window. (They're almost exactly like *playlists* in iTunes.) The following hints help you tackle each of these organizing tasks as painlessly as possible.

9-18   Drag Photos to Create a New Album

You probably assume that you create an album by (a) clicking the + button below the album list (to create a new, empty folder), and then (b) dragging the desired photos into it. (You can select a group of photos all at once, by dragging a selection box around them, or one at a time, by ⌘-clicking them.)

You *could* do it that way. But you can save a step by dragging a batch of photos directly onto a *blank* spot in the album list. When you release the mouse, a new album is born (Figure 9-5).

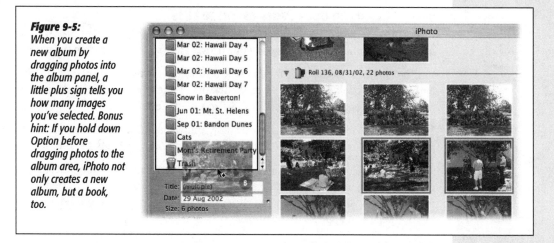

Figure 9-5:
When you create a new album by dragging photos into the album panel, a little plus sign tells you how many images you've selected. Bonus hint: If you hold down Option before dragging photos to the album area, iPhoto not only creates a new album, but a book, too.

If the white space is all taken up, drag the photos nearly to the end of the album list, as shown in Figure 9-5. As you drag over the trash icon, a black outline appears around it. If you now drag upward just slightly, the entire album box appears in outline, as shown at lower-left in Figure 9-5. iPhoto creates a new album when you release the mouse.

9-19   Selecting Multiple Photo Albums at Once

Want to create books from, and add keywords to, multiple albums all at once? How about burning multiple CDs at the same time? In iPhoto 2, you can select multiple albums by ⌘-clicking album names (to highlight names that aren't adjacent in the list), or clicking the first, Shift-clicking the last (to select a batch of consecutive names). The main photo display area now shows all of the photos in the *combined* albums.

9-20 Merged Albums

The previous hint provides a quick trick for creating a new, merged album from two or more other albums. After simultaneously selecting all the albums you want to combine, select all the images in the main photo display area (⌘-A), and then drag them en masse into a blank spot in the album list (or onto a new album you've created).

Books

iPhoto lets you create *books* from your albums. While an album is simply a digital collection of pictures, a book is, well, an actual, physical, gorgeous, hardbound book. You have the luxury of designing your own cover and laying out the individual pages from among the design schemes iPhoto offers you. A couple of clicks later, and your book design is uploaded to a professional bindery, which delivers your finished book in about three days.

9-21 Exporting Book Pages as Image Files

If one of your book pages is a particularly arresting masterpiece, you may want to print out only that page to hang on your fridge. Here's how to separate the pages.

In iPhoto's book mode, click the Preview button. The program displays a preview within iPhoto itself. But if you *Option*-click the Preview button, the book opens in the Preview program (the basic Mac OS X graphics viewer).

In Preview, select the single page you want, and then choose File→Export. In the dialog box that opens, choose a file format, such as JPEG, and then press Enter.

A warning appears. It blathers on about exporting to a format that does not support multiple pages; in small print it says, "Only the current page will be exported." This is exactly what you want. When you click OK, you have a spanking new JPEG image of your page as it appears in the book.

9-22 Many Book Pages, One Layout Style

The iPhoto Book mode lets you specify different page designs for each page of your book. Using the Page Design pop-up menu (at the bottom of the window), you can select a cover page, an introduction page, and a certain number of images per page (Figure 9-6).

Normally, your selection from this pop-up menu affects only the page you're working on. But if you want all the pages to look the same, hold down Option as you pick a design. iPhoto applies that design to all pages in the book. (Needless to say, this business involves re-laying out all of your pages, *even* those that you'd locked.)

9-23 Edit the Album as You Go

Even when you're working in Book mode, you can still rotate photos, rename them, change their dates, or delete them—just as you would thumbnails in Organize mode. You don't have to flip back to Organize mode to perform these tasks.

9-24   Intro Pages Anywhere

An Introduction page (one of the choices in the Page Design pop-up menu) doesn't have to be first page of the book (after the cover). You can turn *any* page into an Introduction page. Such pages make great section dividers.

They're especially useful in designs that use the Picture Book theme and that would otherwise have no text at all. Whatever you type or paste into the Introduction page can set the scene and explain the following (uncaptioned) pages of pictures.

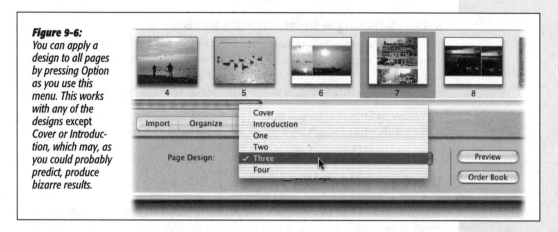

Figure 9-6:
You can apply a design to all pages by pressing Option as you use this menu. This works with any of the designs except *Cover or Introduction, which may, as you could probably predict, produce bizarre results.*

9-25   Printing Books as PDF Files

Books you order from Apple can get pricey: A 10-page book costs $30, and you pay $3 more per additional page. If cash is tight these days, you can always do the job yourself.

1. **Create a book. While in Book mode, choose File→Page Setup. In the Page Setup dialog box, make sure that the correct orientation is selected (it should be landscape mode rather than portrait).**

   The layout is probably right, but if you don't check, a real mess may result.

2. **Click OK. Choose File→Print.**

   The Print dialog box appears.

3. **At the bottom of the Print dialog box, click Save as PDF.**

   Don't click the Preview button by mistake. It forces all pages to portrait layout, which creates a horror show in your beautiful landscape-layout book.

4. **When the Save dialog box appears, give your new book a name and choose a location for saving it (such as the desktop).**

   iPhoto takes a moment to create the PDF file.

5. Switch to the Finder. Open and print your PDF file using Adobe Acrobat Reader.

Particularly if you're using an inkjet photo printer with glossy paper, the results look quite a bit like the finished product you could have bought from Apple—minus the hardbound cover, of course, and with slightly different dimensions.

As a bonus, you now have a handsome "virtual book" that you can email to friends, post on a Web site for downloading, burn to a CD for distribution, and so on. Baby pictures never had it so good.

9-26   Switching Between Organize and Book Modes

Normally, when you click a photo album in the album pane, you view that album's contents in Organize mode. But if you Option-click the album instead, you switch to the album in Book mode. Once in Book mode, you remain there as you select other albums—a nice feature if you're planning on working on more than one book.

To return to Organize mode, either click Organize, or Option-click an album. In other words, Option-clicking a different album in the list always switches into the mode you're *not* currently in: Organize or Book.

Working with Other Programs

iPhoto doesn't work in a vacuum. It's perfectly happy to shoot your photos to an email program for sending, a graphics program like Photoshop or GraphicConverter for editing, and so on. It's a great feature—and a great source of hints like these.

9-27   The Email Program

You can send selected photos to interested parties by email, provided that you use one of the Big Four programs: Mail, Entourage, Eudora, or America Online. (You can set your preferred program in iPhoto→Preferences.)

And even if you use another mail program, like Mailsmith, PowerMail, or QuickMail Pro, you're still not out of luck.

Fortunately, the freeware iPhoto Mailer Patcher, which you can download from *http://homepage.mac.com/jacksim/software/imp.html*, solves that problem neatly. As promised, it patches the program so that you can use any email program under the sun. It then replaces the Email icon at the bottom of the screen with that of your chosen program, and installs a new AppleScript to handle the mailing duties.

Tip: iPhoto Mailer Patcher includes a Restore function that returns iPhoto to its original, more limited condition. You should use this feature before you install new versions of iPhoto as they come along.

9-28   Shorter URLs for Exported Slide Shows

You don't have to have a .Mac account to create handsome online slide shows from your iPhoto photos. If you have a Web site, you can use the File→Export command to build equally great-looking online slide-show files. The result is a folder on your hard drive containing a folder full of thumbnail images, an HTML "home page" to display them, and folders full of Web pages and full-size images that will appear when a visitor clicks one of the thumbnails.

Trouble is, the home-page document isn't called index.html. It's called whatever you named the export folder—Vacation, for example. As a result, your visitors will have to do a lot of typing—something like *http://www.earthlink.net/Vacation/ vacation.html*—just to see your slide show home page. (They have to specify both the Vacation folder and the Vacation.html file inside it.)

Here's how to save them some headache. After you choose File→Export, click the Web tab, and set up your show, click the Export button. In the Save dialog box, click the New Folder button to create a new folder named *index*. Export your slideshow to it; iPhoto uses *index* as the basis of all the files and folders inside.

Before you upload the whole *index* folder to your Web site, give it a name better suited to its purpose (Vacation, for example). Because it still contains a document called *index.html,* your visitors will see the startup page for your slide show (the index.html file) when they type only *http://www.earthlink.net/Vacation* into their browsers.

The beauty of this hint is that it lets you create as many slide shows on your site as you like. Each has a nice, short URL, thanks to the index.html file nestled inside each slide-show folder.

The Other iApps

S ure, iTunes and iPhoto may be the Big iKahunas as far as hints are concerned. But it takes a whole iVillage of iApps to make a digital hub, and the rest—iCal (calendar), iChat (online conversation), iMovie (digital movie creation), and iDVD (DVD authoring on SuperDrive machines)—have a few tricks up their own sleeves.

iCal

iCal offers several advantages over paper calendars. For example:

- It can automate the process of entering repeating events, such as weekly staff meetings or gym workout dates.

- It can give you a gentle nudge (with a sound, a dialog box, or even an email) when an important appointment is approaching.

- iCal can share information with your Address Book program, with Mail, with your iPod, with other Macs, with "published" calendars on the Internet, or with a Palm organizer. Some of these features require a $100-per-year .Mac account, and some require iSync. But iCal also works just fine on a single Mac, even without an Internet connection.

10-1   Multiline Entries

When you type in a new calendar entry—what iCal calls an "event"—and then press Return, the program adds the event to your calendar. But what if you want your event to appear on multiple lines? See Figure 10-1.

10-2   Moving Events from One Calendar to Another

Just as iTunes has *playlists* that let you organize songs into subsets, and iPhoto has *albums* that let you organize photos into subsets, iCal has something called *calendars* that let you organize appointments into subsets. One person might have calendars called Home, Work, and TV Reminders. Another might have Me, Spouse 'n' Me, and Whole Family. A small business could have categories called Deductible Travel, R&D, and R&R. They can be anything you like.

Figure 10-1:
By holding down Option before you press Return, you force iCal to wrap your entry onto two (or more) lines; you've just inserted a line break. This trick is handy for making lists.

To create a calendar, double-click any white space in the Calendar list (below the others), or click the + button at the lower-left corner of the iCal window. Now type a name that defines the category in your mind.

What if you want to reassign an event to a different category? Figure 10-2 tells you how.

Note: This hint moves an event altogether, and although you'd think iCal would let you *copy* an event from one calendar to another, you'd be wrong. The program does not currently include such a feature.

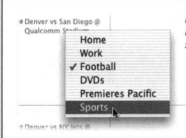

Figure 10-2:
If you Control-click an event, a menu pops up with a list of your calendars; select one, and iCal moves the event to that calendar.

10-3 Simulating a "Go to Date" Function

iCal lets you jump to today's date, but—big oversight on Apple's part—it doesn't include a "Go to Date" function that takes you anywhere else. Here's a workaround that will have to suffice until Apple's engineers get on the ball.

Start by creating a new event on, say, the fifteenth of any month, and enter a unique description—*zzzz,* for example. Next, change the "from" date back to the earliest year that you need to search, as shown in Figure 10-3.

Figure 10-3:
Although iCal doesn't include a "Go to Date" function, you can outwit the program with markers and recurring dates. The trick is to plant a "handle" of sorts on one day each month.

Finally, in the recurrence options, set the event to repeat monthly on the fifteenth, and repeat it either forever or as far forward in time as you need to go.

You now have a series of events that you can use as jumping "handles." For example, to bop from today to March 23, 1999, type *zzzz* (or whatever name you used) in the Search box. A list of many matching events appears; click March 15, 1999, and then just click March 23 on the monthly calendar. It clutters up your calendar, but it works.

10-4 Useful Calendars from Apple

To become really organized using iCal, download a few of the free calendars Apple offers at *www.apple.com/ical/library.* You can choose from such tasty treats as holiday schedules, NBA and NFL schedules, and movie and DVD release dates, among many others.

Of course, you might like to view these calendars before you download them. Here's the secret decoder trick: On a calendar's "subscribe" page, replace "webcal" with "http" and drop ".ics."

For example, to see the U.S. holiday calendar, change *webcal://ical.mac.com/ical/US32Holidays.ics* to *http://ical.mac.com/ical/US32Holidays.* The calendar appears right in your browser, for your perusal pleasure.

Tip: You'll find dozens more preloaded calendars at *www.icalshare.com,* ready to import into your own copy of iCal.

10-5   Merging Calendars

As noted in hint 10-2, iCal lets you create multiple calendars (categories) that you can hide and show at will. But what if you've subscribed to the season calendars for the Tampa Bay Devil Rays *and* the Green Bay Packers, and you want just one unified calendar called Sports?

Here's how to combine calendars, using the Devil Rays/Packers situation as an example.

In the Calendars list (upper left of the iCal window), click the Packers calendar, and then choose File→Export. Name the file something memorable (perhaps "Packers Export"), press ⌘-D to choose the desktop as the destination, and then click Export. Switch to the Finder, and then drag your newly exported file and drop it onto the Devil Rays calendar in iCal—that is, directly onto its name in the calendar list. You've now got one merged calendar.

To rename the merged calendar something more appropriate, double-click the calendar's name.

Note: You can merge more than two calendars. In fact, there's no limit to the number of calendars you can merge by dragging them *onto* a calendar in iCal, but you still have to export them one at a time.

10-6   Opening Public Calendars from any Browser

If you use a Web browser other than Internet Explorer, you may not be able to subscribe to Apple's public calendars. The fix is easy, but you have to use Internet Explorer to do it.

Open Explorer and choose Explorer→Preferences. In the window that opens, scroll down the left-side bar to the Network section, click Protocol Helpers, and then click Add. In the "Helper for" field, type *webcal* (all lower case), then click Choose Helper. Highlight your iCal program (it's in your Home folder, in Applications), and then click Open. Click OK to close the Protocol Helper Editor, and then close the Preference panel and quit Explorer.

You can now subscribe to iCal calendars from any browser.

10-7   Replacing iCal's Dock Icon

On a brand-new Mac, iCal's Dock icon displays July 17 as the date—an icon that makes no sense 364 days of the year. Each time you open iCal, Mac OS X updates its Dock icon to the *current* date. That's fine, too, but it still means that you're stuck with an out-of-date date unless you open iCal once a day.

One way to solve the problem is to paste in a custom icon of your own choosing. In fact, Apple (perhaps anticipating your dissatisfaction with its icon design) has given you a blank calendar icon to work from, as shown in Figure 10-4.

Figure 10-4:
Use the blank calendar icon (third from left) if the icon with varying dates annoys you.

Here's how to swap in the blank calendar icon:

In the Finder, open your Applications folder, Control-click iCal, and then choose Show Package Contents from the contextual menu. Open the Contents→Resources folder, find the file named "iCal-Empty.icns," and copy it by clicking it once and choosing Edit→Copy (⌘-C).

In the open Resources window, open the English.lproj folder. Choose Edit→Paste (or ⌘-V) to paste the copy of the empty icon file.

If you view the Resources window as a list view, the file you just pasted appears directly after something named iCal.icns, which you should rename to iCal_OLD.icns (or any other name that will remind you that this was the original). Finally, rename iCal-Empty.icns to iCal.icns.

To see your unconfusing new icon, either log out and log in again or restart the Mac.

10-8   Setting Identical Window Sizes

iCal lets you view your calendar by day, week, or month, and it remembers the window size for each mode independently. There *is* some logic to that feature—Day probably doesn't require as much real estate as Month—but you may find the size change distracting when you jump from one mode to another.

Yes, you could take the time to drag all three windows to the same size—just make sure you've got half an afternoon and a bottle of Advil handy before you start. A more precise way to create three identically sized windows is to edit iCal's preference file. Here's how:

1. **Set the Day view window to the size you'd like to use for all three views, and then quit iCal.**

   Behind the scenes, you've just implanted certain window dimensions, in iCal's preferences file.

2. **In the Finder, open your Home→Library→Preferences folder. Find the file called com.apple.iCal.plist, and drag it onto the icon of TextEdit.**

See page 4 for details on this technique. You may wish to make a copy of the file first, and save it to your desktop or somewhere else easy to find, just in case something goes wrong.

In the text file filled with codes that now opens before you, look for the first <dict> tag a few lines from the top. Just below that, you should see something like this:

```
<key>1-day view window rect</key>
<string>{{640, 265}, {846, 742}}</string>
```

The text between the <string> tags will probably be different on your machine, because it reflects your window size and location.

3. Carefully select and copy the text between the <string> and </string> tags.

   Press ⌘-C, for example.

4. Find the *<key>7-day view window rect</key>* line slightly farther down in the file. Directly below that, replace the text between the <string> tags with the stuff you just copied in the previous step.

   That is, select the text you want to replace, and then press ⌘-V to paste. You've just set the Week view window to the same size as the Day view window.

5. Find the *<key>monthly view window rect</key>* line. Once again, replace the text between the subsequent <string> tags with the stuff you just copied in step 3.

   You've just set the Month view window to the same size as the Day view window.

6. Save the file, quit the text editor, and reopen iCal.

   You now have identically sized windows in all three views.

Note: If you change one of the windows, it will stay changed. Doing so blows away your carefully established new all-one-size dimensions. But it was still worth doing; after all, you learned something, right?

---

iChat

iChat is Apple's version of AIM, America Online's Instant Messenger program. With iChat, you can carry on typed conversations with other people, share pictures and documents with a quick drag-and-drop move, and while away weeks at a time.

If you've signed up for Apple's $100-per-year Mac.com account, you already have an iChat user name—it's your .Mac email address, minus the *@mac.com* part. If you don't use Mac.com, you can still use iChat by signing up for a free AIM screen name. You don't need to be a member of AOL to receive an AIM name; just go to *www.aol.com/community/directory.html* and follow the link that says, "Try AOL Instant Messenger now for FREE."

10-9   Creating Your Own Image Icon

iChat lets you associate an icon with your screen identity. Anyone you chat with will see this picture, so they can see what you look like—or what you'd *like* them to think you look like.

The screen identity icons are 32 pixels square. You *could* create one using a graphics program, taking the time to trim your photo to fit this square. Or you can use iChat's built-in tool for this very task.

Drag a graphics file of any size onto the iChat Buddy List window and drop it on the icon to the right of your name. A new window opens up, revealing your image behind a small, clear square. Edit the result as described in Figure 10-5. The clear stuff in the middle will become the icon; the program crops out the rest.

Figure 10-5:
Drag your image around to get the part you want aligned with the clear square. Use the blue slider dot below the image to resize it.

When you're finished, click Done. Your newly created icon appears next to your name.

Note: Unfortunately, you can't easily save the icon you just created. So if you drag in another image for a while and then decide to return to your original, you'll have to start from scratch again.

10-10   Spell Checking

A key benefit of Cocoa programs (page 99) is that they include automatic, on-the-fly spell checking. iChat, however, comes with this feature turned off (probably because most chat text would freak out any self-respecting spelling checker: "AFK!"…"dont have time for chating now"… "ROTFL!").

Still, if you're chatting with a more literate partner, you can turn on the checker by choosing Edit→Spelling→Check Spelling As You Type. From now on, incorrectly spelled words appear with a red underline beneath them, just as in other Cocoa programs.

(You can also turn on auto–spell checking this way: Type some text into the iChat input line, Control-Click it, and choose Spelling→Check Spelling As You Type from the contextual menu.)

If the red underlining distracts you, turn the automated feature off. You can always spell-check an individual word now and then by Control-clicking it (Figure 10-6).

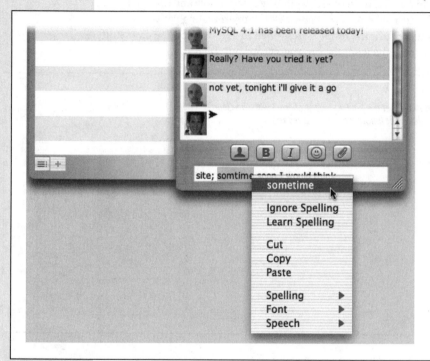

Figure 10-6:
If you Control-click a word you think might be misspelled, iChat displays alternative spellings and offers to learn or ignore the word. What you're witnessing here, of course, is Mac OS X's system-wide spelling checker at work.

10-11   Chat Rooms for Group Discussions

Although iChat specializes in one-on-one messaging, it can also create "rooms" for conversations among many people. For example, if your siblings live in seven different cities, and you want to involve everyone in a discussion about whether to buy Dad a vintage Yugo for his birthday, you can create a "Birthday Business" chat room, and save yourself the trouble of talking to each sister and brother individually.

To create a new chat room, choose File→Go to Chat and enter a name for your new room. (If you type a chat room name that's already in use somewhere in cyberspace, you join that room instead of creating a new one.) Once you've built the new room, tell everybody else (by phone or email, for example) to fire up iChat, choose File→Go to Chat, and enter the same room name. (Because iChat does not provide anyone with a list of existing rooms, you can assume that strangers won't enter your conversation.)

The room hangs around until every participant has closed the chat window.

Note: If you run a small company, chat rooms can be a good way to keep in touch with your customers. Tell them that they can find you on Monday from 3 p.m.–5 p.m. in the chat room named "XYZ Company Complaints and Compliments," and then spend a couple of hours talking with whoever stops by.

10-12 Changing the Chat Background

For kicks, you can choose which the image iChat will use as the background for chat windows. Choose View→Set Chat Background, and navigate around your machine to pick a pic you like.

For an even more hilarious time, you can change the background for the current chat only: Just drag a graphics file into that chat area, either from an open Finder window or even from iPhoto. The current background changes instantly. (Any new windows you open will use the picture you designated in Set Chat Background.)

10-13 Opening Transferred Images

When somebody sends you a graphic via iChat, it appears in your chat window as a small version of itself. To view it full size, drag it to the desktop and then double-click it to open it.

This is a perfectly fine system for people who are retired, unemployed, or imprisoned and have time to rename and file the desktop leftovers, or move them to the Trash.

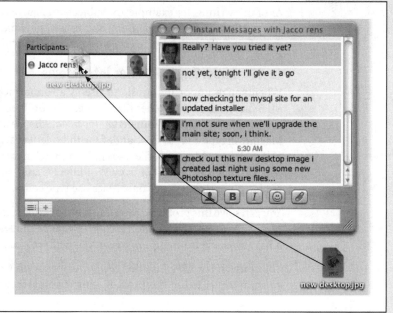

Figure 10-7:
When you drag an image or document directly into the main iChat window, the program sends it right away. But if you drag the file onto the Participants panel (or the main Buddy List window), iChat asks if you'd like to send the file, and the recipient can either accept or reject your transmission. Sometimes, this method works better for sending big things.

You can skip the desktop step, however, and simply drag the transferred image to the Dock icon of your favorite graphics program. Presto! The image opens without appearing on your desktop. Now you can rename it and save it in one neat step.

10-14   Transferring Large Files

One of iChat's most brilliant and useful features is something that never even occurs to most people: It presents no limit to the size of the files you can transfer. The 20-megabyte PowerPoint file that would choke almost anyone's In box if sent by email sails through just fine when sent iChat to iChat.

Instead, try dragging your file onto the recipient's name in the Participants panel (or the Buddy List window), as shown in Figure 10-7. (You could also drag files into the actual iChat window, but that method doesn't always work well for very large files.)

iMovie

iMovie can turn footage from your digital camcorder into very professional-looking movies that you can then share as QuickTime files, save onto CDs, or burn onto a DVD for the world to enjoy. Here are a few tips that will make you the maestro of iMovie.

10-15   Free Add-Ons

With each release of iMovie, Apple stocks its Web site *(www.apple.com/imovie)* with useful freebie plug-ins and add-ons.

As of this writing, for example, the subject-to-change listing includes dozens of professionally recorded sound effects and music, plus special-effects plug-in samplers from four different software companies. Grab 'em while they're still available.

10-16   Importing MP3 Files into iMovie

When you're importing music to use as a soundtrack, iMovie sometimes rejects MP3 files from sources other than iTunes. The problem: Not all MP3 files come with the behind-the-scenes, four-letter *type code* that iMovie requires. (Think of the Macintosh type code as a variant of the three-letter identifying suffixes on Windows files and many Mac OS X files—as in Letter to Congress.doc.) In fact, MP3 files that you get from the Internet or from Windows PC users almost certainly *don't* have the necessary type code, since only Macs use type codes.

You can solve this problem by setting the type code on the file you want to import to *MPG3*. One way to go about it is to drag your MP3 files onto a shareware utility like XRay (available from *http://www.brockerhoff.net/xray*).

Power users: If you've installed the Developer Tools CD that came with Mac OS X, you may prefer to use this procedure in Terminal instead.

Let's say you have a ditty named CarChaseJam.mp3 in your Home→Music folder, and you want to import it into iMovie. Open Terminal (page 5) and type these lines (pressing Enter after each one):

```
cd ~/Music
SetFile -t MPG3 CarChaseJam.mp3
```

These commands break down like this:

- **cd** is the Unix command for *change directory*—that is, "direct your attention to the following folder."

- **~/Music** refers to the Music folder in your Home folder. (The ~ is Terminal shorthand for "my Home folder.")

- **SetFile –t MPG3** means "change the Type code to *MPG3.*"

- **CarChaseJam.mp3** tells Terminal *which* file to change.

You can now use iMovie's Import feature to make CarChaseJam.mp3 part of your movie.

Note: If you want to change the type code for *all* MP3s to the correct one for iMovie, use this command: *SetFile -t MPG3 'find . -name "*.mp3"'* . Doing so doesn't otherwise affect your MP3 files in any way.

10-17 Stopping Ken Burns I

One of iMovie 3's most ballyhooed features is the "Ken Burns effect." It turns still digital photos into *movies,* panning and zooming across them like an over-caffeinated fighter pilot. You can use it to add pizzazz to your projects, even if all you're doing is showcasing 2,352 stills of little Jimmy sleeping.

That's the good news.

The bad news is that iMovie 3 applies the Ken Burns effect to *every single photo you import.* And it introduces huge lags into your work routine—since iMovie 3 must render (process) each photo, instead of just slapping it into your movie like iMovie 2 did.

The simplest solution is to press ⌘-period just after iMovie starts rendering a photo you've imported. As in so many other places on the Mac, ⌘-period means "halt!"; in this case, it stops the rendering and leaves you with a still clip that has a duration you can edit.

10-18 Stopping Ken Burns II

You can also tell iMovie *never* to apply the Ken Burns effect on imported photos. The trick: Edit the secret iMovie preferences file. Here's how:

Quit iMovie. Then, in the Finder, open your Home→Library→Preferences folder, and find com.apple.iMovie 3.plist.

Drag this file onto the icon of a text editor, like TextEdit or BBEdit Lite. Using the Find command (⌘-F), conduct a search for the phrase *ApplyPan*.

You've just highlighted some text that's part of these lines:

```
<key>Option autoApplyPanZoomToImportedStills: %d </key>
    <true/>
```

Change the *<true/>* tag on the third line to *<false/>* and save the file. The next time you open iMovie, the program will no longer insist on paying tribute to PBS's most famous documentary maker every time you import a photo.

Tip: You can still use the Ken Burns effect whenever you want it. Just select a still image in your movie, switch to the Photos section, set your Ken Burns settings, and then click Apply.

10-19 Synchronizing Still Images

If you're working on a movie project that contains a lot of still images (a slide show with sound and fancy transitions, for example), and you want each still to hang onscreen for the same amount of time, you can set the duration a few ways.

The best way is to decide, and set it, *before* you import the photos. Beneath the clip shelf area, click the Photos icon. Change the number displayed in the Duration box (either by typing into the box or by adjusting the slider just above it). You've just specified the standard time-onscreen duration for any photos you now import.

Of course, if you want to modify a set of stills you've already imported, that feature isn't much help.

In that case, you can use either of two solutions, both of which require you to change the duration of only one photo at a time:

- Click the photo's icon in the movie track (at the bottom of the window), and then drag the Speed slider right or left, as shown in Figure 10-8. The still photo's timing doubles or halves with each notch in the slider.

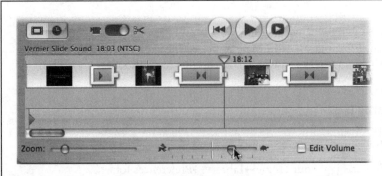

Figure 10-8:
Need to adjust the duration of certain stills in iMovie 3? Start by Shift-clicking to select all the images, then just drag the speed slider to the left (reduce the duration) or right (increase the duration). When you move the slider, all of the selected images will be affected.

- For more precision, click a still photo to which the Ken Burns effect has been applied (see hint 10-17), then click the Photos button. Use the Duration slider to specify the timing you want (or type a number into the Duration box) and then click Apply.

If the Ken Burns effect has *not* been applied (because you turned it off or ⌘-perieded it), double-click the icon of the photo (or click it and choose File→Get Info). The resulting dialog box offers a Duration box whose numbers you can easily edit.

10-20   Hiding iMovie while It Renders

One of the nice side effects of running iMovie in Mac OS X is that you can switch out of the program while it's *rendering* (processing) transitions, titles, and effects. iMovie takes a fair amount of time to render this stuff (some title sequences require many minutes), so you'll appreciate being able to check your email, surf the Web, or work on your screenplay in the meantime.

If you start a lot of renders, though, your machine can get a case of the blahs. The cursor may jerk across the screen, and the multicolored, spinning "please wait" cursor may rear its twirly head a lot.

To prevent such sluggishness, hide iMovie (choose iMovie→Hide iMovie). The system is now much more responsive because it doesn't have to update the iMovie window.

Note: To check in on the rendering progress, click iMovie's Dock icon to bring iMovie to the front. If the program is still toiling away, just rehide it and return to researching player trades in your fantasy football league.

10-21   iMovie 2 Sound Effects in iMovie 3

If you were a fan of iMovie 2, you may remember the sound effects Apple tossed into the program—stuff like a cat's meow, crickets chirping, crowds clapping and cheering, a drum roll, and so on. iMovie 3 comes with a nice assortment of sound effects—what Apple calls the Skywalker Sounds—but they don't include crickets or meows.

If you upgraded your copy of iMovie 2 to version 3 (rather than trashing iMovie 2), your old favorite chirps and bleeps are still around; they're just hidden. To reactivate them, follow this procedure:

1. **Quit iMovie 3. Create a folder named Sound Effects inside your Home→ Library→iMovie folder.**

   You may find that the folder already exists, which is fine.

2. **Inside the Sound Effects folder, create another folder called, for example, *iMovie 2 FX*.**

   Actually, you can name it whatever you want.

---

3. **Control-click iMovie. From the contextual menu, choose Show Package Contents.**

   The program's secret package window (page 3) opens.

4. **In the new window, open the Contents→Resources→Sound Effects folder.**

   It contains folders for Skywalker Sound Effects and Standard Sound Effects, along with a bunch of loose AIFF files with names like Dog Bark and Forest Rain. These unfiled files are your old iMovie 2 sound effects.

5. **To make the old sounds work in iMovie 3, copy them from their current location into the iMovie 2 FX folder you created in step 2.**

   Open iMovie 3, click the Audio button, and then select the iMovie Sound Effects pop-up menu. You'll find your iMovie 2 FX folder listed there, ready to use.

10-22 Removing Extraneous iMovie 3 Help Files

Unless you are a spectacular polyglot, you probably don't need help for iMovie 3 in fourteen languages. But that's exactly what the program comes with, eating up over 50 MB of hard-drive space in the bargain.

The iMovie help files live in your hard drive's Library→Documentation→iMovie folder. You can delete the folders for the languages you never speak by dragging each of them to the Trash.

iDVD

iDVD is the perfect partner to iMovie. It turns your newly created film masterpiece into a professional-looking DVD, complete with moving menus and background sound effects, able to leap tall buildings in a single bound, and ready to play on nearly any DVD player.

10-23 Making iDVD Fonts Available in Other Programs

iDVD comes with a number of interesting fonts, including Bank Gothic, Cracked, Santa Fe, and so on (Figure 10-9). Too bad they're the property of iDVD. Sure would be nice to have these fonts available in your other programs, too.

BANK GOTHIC MEDIUM

Cracked

Santa Fe

Handwriting - Dakota

Figure 10-9:
iDVD includes a collection of high-quality fonts with bold strokes good for viewing on television sets. Here's just a small sampling of the fonts, which you can make available to use in other programs, like Mail and TextEdit.

Make it so! In the Finder, Control-click iDVD, choose Show Package Contents from the contextual menu, and then open the Contents→Resources→Fonts folder. Select the fonts you want. Option-drag any one of them onto your Home→Library→Fonts folder. (Option-dragging creates a duplicate, so iDVD won't freak out if it can't find the fonts where it expects them to be.)

You now have access to the iDVD fonts from any Mac OS X program.

Note: To see the fonts in other programs, you must quit and restart any programs that were already running when you made the copies.

10-24 Using Apple's Theme Movies in Custom Themes

Many of iDVD's *themes* (canned design schemes)—Global, Family, and Wedding, for example—feature full-motion background videos. They really make your DVD look professional, but it's just too bad that you can't use these motion backgrounds in your own homemade themes.

Or can you?

Start by designing your theme; specify the fonts, sizes, buttons, and colors you want to use. Next, click the Settings tab so that you can see the Image/Movie well in the Background section (see Figure 10-10).

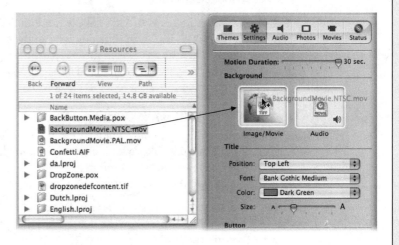

Figure 10-10:
By navigating into the packages containing Apple-supplied themes, you can use any background movie in any iDVD theme you wish. Just drag and drop the movie into the Image/Movie well as shown, and you'll have the movie you want in the theme you wish to use.

Switch to the Finder, Control-click the iDVD program icon, choose Show Package Contents from the contextual menu, and then open the Contents→Resources folder. You're almost ready to raid Apple's canned themes on your quest for their background movies.

For example, to appropriate the background movie from the Global theme, Control-click the icon called 20-1 Global.theme, and again select Show Package Contents from the contextual menu. Now open *its* Contents→Resources folder; inside are two files that start with the words BackgroundMovie (one apiece for NTSC and PAL, the American and European television formats).

Position this window so that you can also see the Image/Movie well in iDVD, and then just drag the movie into it. You now have one of Apple's standard moving image backgrounds behind your custom theme.

Note: If you carry out this procedure often, consider copying the animated backgrounds from *all* themes to a new location so that you can reach them with a lot less clicking around.

10-25   Burning Projects to DVD-RW Discs

iDVD lets you burn your movies onto DVD-R discs (single-use DVD-Recordable) only. If you hope to save a little money by trying to burn a movie onto a DVD-RW (rewritable—that is, erasable and reusable) disc instead, iDVD tells you to fuggedaboudit.

This hitch can lead to some expensive experiments. If you want, for example, to test a new menu layout for your DVD, or if you just want to see how your project looks on the big screen, you have to keeping burning new DVD-Rs, throwing away perfectly good money each time.

If you don't want to blow your kid's college fund on DVD-Rs, you can fool iDVD into using a DVD-RW disc. In the burning stage of the project, insert a DVD-R disc when requested. Then, as iDVD is in the "Preparing" stage, eject the DVD-R (hold down the Eject key on your keyboard), and insert a DVD-RW. iDVD, none the wiser, now happily burns your project to the DVD-RW disc.

10-26   Hiding iDVD while Burning a Disc

iDVD is perfectly happy to burn your DVDs in the background—a delightful feature, since DVD burning takes a long time. But you might never know it: If you try to choose the iDVD→Hide iDVD command, you'll have a hard time getting iDVD's attention, given that it's totally focused on preparing and encoding your project.

The solution: As soon as you start the encoding process, click over to the Finder and choose Finder→Hide Others. You can then make other programs visible by clicking their Dock icons one at a time.

Other Apple Goodies

The iApps described in the previous chapters are great programs, and do very well as the heart of the Apple digital hub software suite. But enough about the iApps; what about the aApps, bApps, cApps, and so on? They deserve equal time when it comes to undocumented shortcuts and secrets—and in this chapter, they get it. Open your Applications folder, peruse the list of free programs, and read on.

Address Book

Mac OS X's Address Book is a central repository where you can enter people's contact information just once and then use it in a slew of programs. Mail and iChat may be the only program that draws upon it so far, but others will soon join in.

11-1   Quick Entries from Mail

One of the most enjoyable and efficient ways to add an email correspondence to the Address Book is to do so from within Mail. Just highlight a message and then choose Message→Add Sender to Address Book—or just press ⌘-Y. The sender is instantly added to your Address Book, no questions asked.

11-2   Sharing Palm Contacts with Address Book

If you've been using Palm Desktop, the free Rolodex program provided with every Palm organizer, you might be looking longingly at Address Book. After all, Address Book is equally good at synchronizing your little black book with a Palm organizer (thanks to the free iSync program), but much more useful because it talks to Mail and can be shared via a .Mac account.

Fortunately, you can get your Palm Desktop names and addresses into Address Book—just not directly.

Instead, you have to begin in the Finder. Create a desktop folder to serve as a temporary transfer station for your information. Next, in Palm Desktop, select the contacts you want to export; once they're all selected, drag any one of them out of the Palm Desktop window and onto the folder you just made. (Behind the scenes, you've just created what are known as virtual business cards, or *vCard* files.)

Now open this folder. Press ⌘-A to highlight all of the vCards, and then drag them en masse straight into the Address Book window, where they now appear as safely ensconced addresses (Figure 11-1).

Tip: This technique works for any program that can export vCard files.

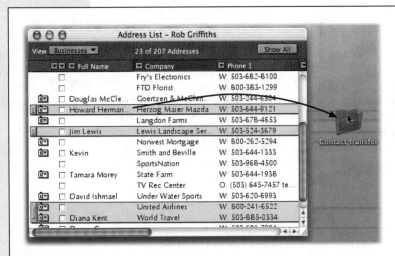

Figure 11-1:
Need to move a bunch of contacts from Palm Desktop to Apple's Address Book? It's easy, but it's a two-step process. Start by highlighting all the addresses you wish to transfer in Palm Desktop. Then, as shown here, drag them into a new temporary folder. From there, you can drag them directly into the Address Book window.

11-3   Viewing Group Members while Creating a Group

Groups are collections of email addresses stored under one name. They're very useful if you frequently email two or more contacts at the same time—like your family, your sewing circle, or your poker game buddies. Instead of typing each email address, you can simply type the group name ("Family," "Sewing Circle," "Poker") for everyone in it to receive your message.

Creating a group, alas, isn't quite as easy as you might have hoped. When you choose File→New Group, Address Book gives you an empty group to name. Once you've named it, you have to click All to see your entire contact list, so that you can drag the names of the group members onto the name of the group—but now you can no longer see the names you've already added to the group. Back and forth you go, clicking All to see your full address book, and then clicking the group name to see who you've already added.

The better way is to use the New Group From Selection command, as illustrated in Figure 11-2.

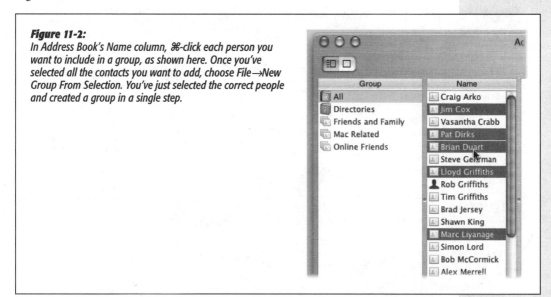

Figure 11-2:
In Address Book's Name column, ⌘-click each person you want to include in a group, as shown here. Once you've selected all the contacts you want to add, choose File→New Group From Selection. You've just selected the correct people and created a group in a single step.

11-4   Maps and Other Nifty Tricks

If your Mac is online, you can summon a map that shows the precise location of anyone in your Address Book (at least, anyone who lives within the United States). It's a really cool trick.

All you have to do is click the word "work" or "home" next to a street address (not one that you're currently editing). A contextual menu appears (even though you did not, technically, Control-click); choose "Map of," as shown in Figure 11-3. Your Web browser appears and, after a moment, displays a map showing the chosen address.

11-5   Phonetic Name Fields

It happens to everyone: You need to look up Fred Graczynwyzniki's phone number, but you can never remember whether that's an *i* or a *y* after the *w*. All right, the truth is, you haven't the faintest memory of how to spell his name. So how are you supposed to look it up?

Easy one: phonetically.

That's the purpose of the Card→Add Field→Phonetic First/Last Name command. It inserts, onto the currently selected Address Book card, text boxes called First Phonetic and Last Phonetic. If you take the time to fill in these fields now (with a spelling that will help you remember the pronunciation), you'll be able to search for this person using that phonetic spelling later.

Tip: Come to think of it, the Card→Add Field command contains a couple of other useful options: a Birthday field and Instant Messaging user names for systems like MSN and Yahoo.

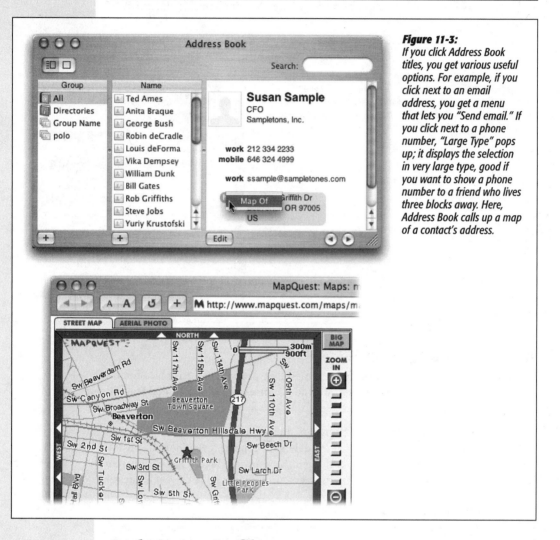

Figure 11-3:
If you click Address Book titles, you get various useful options. For example, if you click next to an email address, you get a menu that lets you "Send email." If you click next to a phone number, "Large Type" pops up; it displays the selection in very large type, good if you want to show a phone number to a friend who lives three blocks away. Here, Address Book calls up a map of a contact's address.

Apple System Profiler

Apple System Profiler is like a little X-ray machine for your Mac. It reveals all kinds of useful details about your computer, including information about its hard drives, memory, attached peripherals, and so on. If you—or a tech-support person you have on the phone—ever have a question about what's inside your machine, System Profiler is a good first stop on Geekland's solution trail.

Apple System Profiler resides in Applications→Utilities.

11-6 Quick Access to Apple System Profiler

Instead of burrowing into your Applications→Utilities folder to open System Profiler, it's usually faster to use this trick: Choose →About This Mac. In the resulting dialog box, click the More Info button. Boom—Apple System Profiler opens.

11-7 Viewing System Logs

Behind the scenes, your Mac maintains a secret diary, a record of the traumatic (and mundane) events that it experiences from day to day. These are the system logs, and they include useful information for the technically inclined. For example, they include *crash logs*, which are detailed technical descriptions of what went wrong when various programs crashed, and what was stored in memory at the time.

If you're the kind of geek who thrives on reading the system logs, you're probably used to using the program called Console (also in Applications→Utilities) to read them. That, after all, is its primary purpose. Unfortunately, in Console, each program log opens in its own window, and you have to use the file browser to find the logs you want. Plus, all the entries for each program are presented at once, which leaves you staring at a jumble that's hard to read.

Better to use Apple System Profiler. Its Logs tab contains a tidy list of your Mac's logs, each of which you can expand with a simple click on its flippy triangle (see Figure 11-4). When you click a specific event's triangle, you get the actual log entry that the system created at the time of the event.

Tip: To open (or close) all of the entries for a given program, Option-click the flippy triangle instead.

Figure 11-4:
When you use the Apple System Profiler to view crash logs (by clicking the Logs tab at the top of the main window), you can see them all in one location.

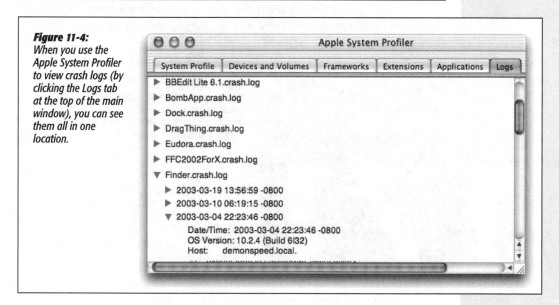

Calculator

You may feel a tiny twinge of shame for using your expensive Macintosh for its pocket-calculator features—but don't. The Calculator program looks good, works well, and even has a few impressive tricks up its sleeve.

Before you read them, however, make sure you know the two most basic Calculator secrets of all:

- The calculator has two modes: Basic and Advanced (a scientific-calculator mode). Switch between them by clicking the appropriate button just underneath the calculator readout.

- You can operate the calculator by clicking the onscreen buttons, but it's much easier to press the corresponding number and symbol keys on your keyboard.

11-8   The Talking Calculator

You can make your calculator speak each key you press—a glamorous feature that can really be useful. It ensures that you don't mistype as you keep your eyes on the receipts in front of you, typing by touch.

Just choose Speech→Speak Button Pressed to turn this feature on or off. (You choose the voice in the Speech panel of System Preferences.)

11-9   Large-Type Calculations

You probably don't often need to see your calculator results in type big enough to view clearly from Mars. But when you're trying to make a mathematical point to, for example, a colleague across the room, Control-click anywhere in the results window and choose Large Type (the only option) from the pop-up menu. The result is something like Figure 11-5.

Figure 11-5:
Seriously *large type. To display figures for the world to see, Control-click anywhere in the results window. To get back to a normal perspective on things, just click the mouse.*

11-10 Unit Conversion, Currency Conversion

One of the coolest new features in Calculator is the Convert menu, which lets you perform unit conversions (feet to meters, Celsius to Fahrenheit, and so on) in a mess of different categories, including Pressure, Power, Speed, Length, and Temperature. Figure 11-6 shows you the full list of possible conversions.

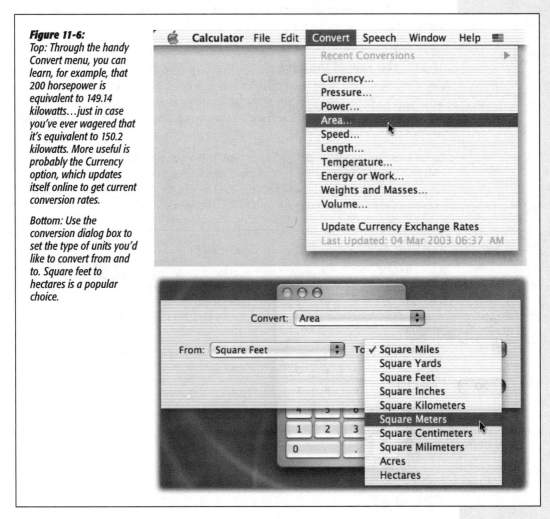

Figure 11-6:
Top: Through the handy Convert menu, you can learn, for example, that 200 horsepower is equivalent to 149.14 kilowatts...just in case you've ever wagered that it's equivalent to 150.2 kilowatts. More useful is probably the Currency option, which updates itself online to get current conversion rates.

Bottom: Use the conversion dialog box to set the type of units you'd like to convert from and to. Square feet to hectares is a popular choice.

To convert one unit to another, enter the number you want to convert, and then choose the appropriate command from the Convert menu. A dialog box appears, as shown in Figure 11-6, so that you can choose the specific units you want to convert from and to. Set the units, and then click OK. The calculator now displays your converted number.

Currency is one of the more useful conversion tools, and it let you choose from more than 30 monetary units. Even better, if you're online and you choose Convert→Update Currency Exchange Rates, Calculator downloads up-to-the-minute exchange rates for all its currencies.

Note: The Convert menu has a useful submenu, Recent Conversions, that makes it easy to repeat, say, several currency conversions in a row.

11-11   The Tale of the Tape

Calculator keeps track of your calculations as you go, thanks to its virtual "paper tape." If, after 43 calculations, your income for 2003 works out to negative $145,675, the paper tape lets you go back and see whether you mistyped a number (or whether you need a new job).

To see a session history, click the Paper Tape button on the calculator's face; the tape slides out to the side (Figure 11-7). It includes a time and date stamp, and you can copy text from it, which is handy if you want to display your calculations in a Keynote or PowerPoint presentation or a Word document.

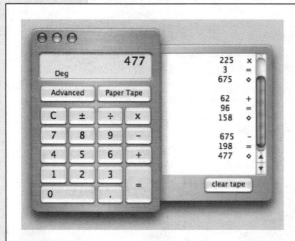

Figure 11-7:
You can select text from the tape area, copy it (Edit→Copy or ⌘-C), and then paste it into another program. Amazingly, you can actually edit these numbers, even long after a calculation is over; the total will update itself when you press Enter.

Disk Copy

Disk Copy may be the most heavily used program on your machine, and you probably don't even realize it. That's because, every time you double-click a .dmg file (a disk image file, like the ones you may have downloaded from the Web), Disk Copy is the background program that whirls into action, turning that file into a virtual disk icon on your desktop.

Beyond this essential skill, however, Disk Copy also has a number of other very useful functions, including the ability to create new disk images, or to create an image from a mounted CD or a folder. You can find Disk Copy in Applications→ Utilities.

11-12 Dragging Your Way to Disk Images

The quickest way to create a disk image of your own is to drag a folder or disk directly off your desktop and onto Disk Copy's icon (either the one in the Applications→Utilities folder or one you've put in the Dock—if you've put it there). Disk Copy opens and then presents an Options dialog box for the image you're about to create:

- If you choose "read/write" from the Image Format pop-up menu, your disk image file, when double-clicked, will turn into a superb imitation of a hard drive. You'll be able to drag files and folders onto it, drag them off of it, change icons' names on it, and so on.

- If you choose "read/only," the result will behave more like a CD. You'll be able to copy things off it, but not make any changes to it.

- The "compressed" option is best if you intend to send the resulting file by email, for example, or if you'd like to preserve the disk image on a backup disk for a rainy day. It takes a little longer to create a simulated disk when you double-click the resulting disk image file, but it takes up a lot less disk space than an uncompressed version.

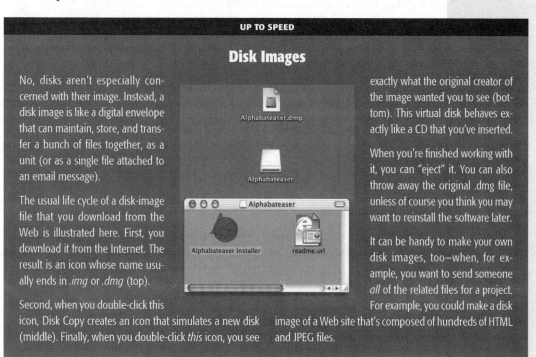

UP TO SPEED

Disk Images

No, disks aren't especially concerned with their image. Instead, a disk image is like a digital envelope that can maintain, store, and transfer a bunch of files together, as a unit (or as a single file attached to an email message).

The usual life cycle of a disk-image file that you download from the Web is illustrated here. First, you download it from the Internet. The result is an icon whose name usually ends in *.img* or *.dmg* (top).

Second, when you double-click this icon, Disk Copy creates an icon that simulates a new disk (middle). Finally, when you double-click *this* icon, you see

exactly what the original creator of the image wanted you to see (bottom). This virtual disk behaves exactly like a CD that you've inserted.

When you're finished working with it, you can "eject" it. You can also throw away the original .dmg file, unless of course you think you may want to reinstall the software later.

It can be handy to make your own disk images, too—when, for example, you want to send someone *all* of the related files for a project. For example, you could make a disk image of a Web site that's composed of hundreds of HTML and JPEG files.

• Finally, choose "DVD/CD master" if you're copying a CD or a DVD. The resulting file is a perfect mirror of the original disc, ready for copying onto a blank CD or DVD when the time comes.

Change the options if necessary, click Save, and let the program go to town. It doesn't get much easier than this.

11-13   Erasing Rewritable Disks

If you have Mac OS X 10.2 or later, you can use Disk Copy to erase your CD-RWs and DVD-RWs. (In previous versions of Mac OS X, you had to use the Disk Utility program to accomplish this task.) After inserting the erasable disk, open Disk Copy and choose File→Erase CD/DVD-RW Disc (or press Control-⌘-E).

11-14   Speed-Mounting Disk Images

Whenever you double-click a disk image, a progress bar appears, indicating that it's verifying a disk image's *checksum* before mounting. The Mac is taking this time to compare the data in your copy of the file with a special code in the original to make sure that nothing got scrambled during the download.

The trouble is, all of this verification business is a relic from the days of relatively unreliable floppy disks. Today, it's basically a waste of time. If the download truly did get garbled—an exceedingly remote possibility—then Mac OS X just won't turn the .dmg file into a virtual disk at all. No harm done.

So when that "checksum" dialog box appears, feel free to click Skip to save yourself some time.

In fact, you can make Disk Copy *always* skip that verification business. To do so, open Disk Copy, choose Disk Copy→Preferences, click the Verifying tab, and turn off Verify Checksums.

11-15   CD-Free Laptop Gaming

If you play games that require the original CD to be in the drive as you play, Disk Copy may be able to lighten your load when you're on the road with your laptop. In essence, you can use Disk Copy to create a simulated CD directly on your hard drive. And as a bonus, you can relax on the road, knowing your original CDs are safe and sound at home.

1. **Insert a CD containing a game you want to play. Open Disk Copy and choose File→New→Image From Device.**

   A dialog box opens like the one in Figure 11-8.

2. **After selecting the disk, click the Image button.**

   A dialog box like the one in Figure 11-8.

3. **Once you've specified a name, location, and format (usually CD/DVD Master), click Save, and prepare to wait.**

The process will take between five and fifteen minutes, depending on the speed of your machine and the size of the image.

When the imaging process is complete, you can test your new CD-free solution.

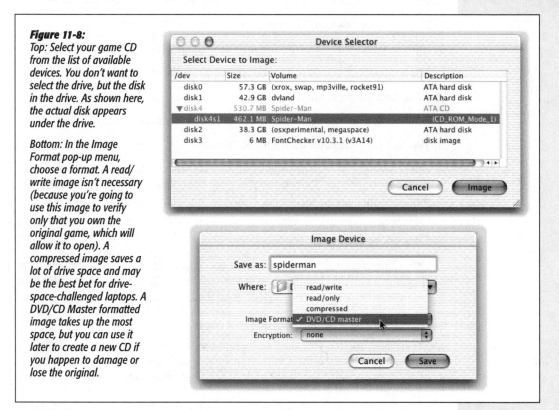

Figure 11-8:
Top: Select your game CD from the list of available devices. You don't want to select the drive, but the disk in the drive. As shown here, the actual disk appears under the drive.

Bottom: In the Image Format pop-up menu, choose a format. A read/write image isn't necessary (because you're going to use this image to verify only that you own the original game, which will allow it to open). A compressed image saves a lot of drive space and may be the best bet for drive-space-challenged laptops. A DVD/CD Master formatted image takes up the most space, but you can use it later to create a new CD if you happen to damage or lose the original.

4. **Remove the original CD. Double-click the new image.**

   The disk image turns into a simulated disk on your desktop.

5. **Double-click your game to see if it runs.**

   If it does, raise your fist in victory. If not, just drag the image to the Trash and sigh dejectedly; some games use the presence of the CD as a form of copy protection, and therefore don't respect the magnificence of this trick.

11-16 Password-Protect a Folder

All right, the name in this hint is a come-on. You can't really password-protect a folder in Mac OS X.

But you can password-protect a disk image—and you can turn a folder *into* a disk image easily enough.

1. Drag the folder onto the Disk Image icon.

   In the dialog box that appears, you're offered some fascinating options.

2. From the Encryption pop-up menu, choose "AES-128 (recommended)."

   That means, "password-protect this baby."

3. Choose a name and location for your new image file.

   The name you choose here doesn't need to match the original disk or folder name.

4. Click Save (or press Enter).

   After a moment, the Mac asks you to make up a password.

5. Type the password you want into both boxes.

   Nobody will be able to open your disk image without the password—not even you. (If you turn on "Remember password," you'll be able to open the file without typing the password, but only when it's on your own Mac and you've logged in with your own master password.)

6. Click OK.

   Disk Copy creates the image and then encrypts it. Your work is complete here. Now if you double-click the resulting image file, you'll be asked for the password before it turns into a virtual disk on your desktop.

11-17   Burning a Multisession CD

Most people think that you need a program like Roxio Toast to record a CD-R disc more than once in Mac OS X. On the contrary, Disk Copy lets you burn a single CD as many times as you like! That's right, regular cheapie CD-R discs, *not* CD-RW (rewriteable).

What you'll create here is a *multisession* disc. Each time you burn more material onto it, you create a new disc icon that will appear separately when you insert the CD. Figure 11-9, for example, shows a disc that's been burned twice.

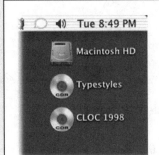

Figure 11-9:
A folder called Typestyles was burned to the CD first. Then, a week later, a folder called CLOC 1998 was burned onto the same disc, creating a second session (disc icon).

Here's how to go about it:

1. **Prepare the material you intend to burn the first time.**

   For example, put it all into a folder on your desktop.

2. **Open Disk Copy. Choose File→New→Image from Device or Volume. When prompted, navigate to, and select, the folder you want to burn, and then click Image.**

   You're asked to name the disk image you're creating.

3. **Type a name for the image, specify a location (like the desktop), and then click Save.**

   In this example, suppose it's called Typestyles.dmg.

4. **When you're ready to burn, open Disk Copy. Choose File→Burn Image. Navigate to the disk image (Typestyles.dmg), and click it once. Then click Burn.**

   The Burn Disc dialog box appears. Expand the box as shown in Figure 11-10.

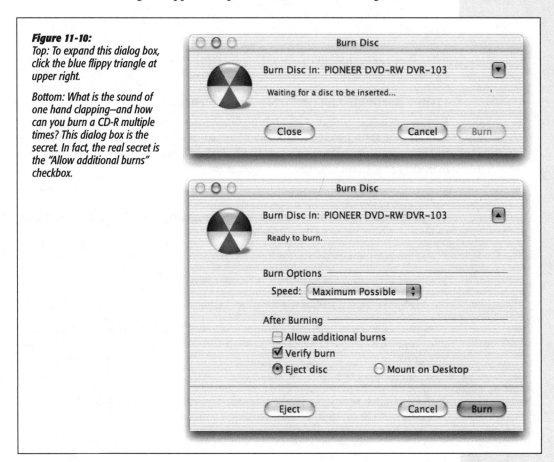

Figure 11-10:
Top: To expand this dialog box, click the blue flippy triangle at upper right.

Bottom: What is the sound of one hand clapping—and how can you burn a CD-R multiple times? This dialog box is the secret. In fact, the real secret is the "Allow additional burns" checkbox.

5. Turn on "Allow additional burns." Click Burn to record the material onto the CD.

Disk Copy does its thing, burning your CD as though it's the first and last time. But boy, do you have a surprise for it.

6. When it comes time to add new material to that disc, repeat steps 1 through 4.

This time, in the expanded dialog box shown in Figure 11-10, you'll see that "Allow additional burns" is still turned on. Instead of Burn, though, the lower-right button now says Append. That's your clue that Disk Copy understands what it's about to do: add information to an existing CD, resulting in a second disk icon on the desktop containing only the new material.

7. Click Append.

You've just created a multisession disc!

You can repeat steps 7 and 8 over and over again, adding more and more material to a disc—or at least until it's full.

Keynote

Keynote is Apple's new presentation (slide show) software, a PowerPoint killer designed to let you create fancy audio/video presentations.

11-18   Borrowing Images from Apple's Themes

Keynote includes a number of high-quality, professionally designed *themes*—collections of graphics, fonts, and colors designed to look good together. It's just too bad that you can't use these professionally designed pictures in other programs, or in themes of your own design.

At least not without doing this:

1. In the Finder, Control-click the Keynote program's icon. From the contextual menu, choose Show Package Contents.

The program's package window opens (page 3).

2. Open the Contents→Resources→Themes folder.

This folder contains all of the Keynote themes.

Apple has given each theme a number followed by the theme name and its size. In other words, 05_Letterpress_8x6.kth is the fifth theme, named Letterpress, and it's sized for an 800 x 600 pixel monitor. (Graphics sized for a 1024 x 768 screen say "10x7.")

3. Control-click the theme you're interested in borrowing images from. From the contextual menu, choose Show Package Contents.

In the new window that opens, you can see all the graphics used in that theme.

4. **Copy the graphics files to a different folder (don't *move* them).**

   To copy the images, Option-drag them to any convenient location, perhaps somewhere in your Documents folder.

   You can now use the copied images in your own themes, iMovie projects, Web pages, and so on.

Preview

Preview is Mac OS X's built-in graphics viewer. When you double-click the icon of a graphics file whose "parent" the Mac can't identify (maybe something you grabbed from a Web page or scanned in), Preview takes over. It does the work of opening and displaying the image onscreen.

Preview works with pictures saved in a wide variety of formats, including less commonly used formats like BMP, PNG, SGI, TGA, and MacPaint, as well as the typical JPEG, TIFF, GIF, and PICT images. Preview can even open Photoshop files and multipage PDF documents.

11-19 Browsing Multiple Images at Once

Among other things, Preview makes an excellent viewer for batches of graphics. It's preferable to iPhoto, in some regards, because iPhoto makes a copy of every graphic you view and lodges it in your pictures Library.

In the Finder, select all the images you'd like to see, and then drag them onto the Preview icon (either on the Dock or in your Applications folder), as shown in Figure 11-11.

Figure 11-11:
You can use Preview to open JPEG, PDF, TIFF, Photoshop, BMP, and even MacPaint pictures.

Preview opens a display window with a Thumbnail drawer on the side. You can switch among images by clicking the thumbnails, by using the Backward and Forward buttons on the toolbar, or by using the up and down arrow keys.

11-20 Navigating PDF Documents

In general, the free Acrobat Reader is the best program to view PDF files, because it offers a full-screen mode, a Search command, a Copy command, and access to the interactive features built into some PDF files—bookmarks, hyperlinks, forms, and so on.

But if you find yourself opening a PDF file in Preview anyway—perhaps unintentionally—you're not out of luck. The program works just fine for reading them, as long as you master the keyboard shortcuts.

If, for example, you're used to using the arrow keys to scroll down a page, you may be surprised to find that these keys now jump from one thumbnail to the next in Preview. In addition, if you press Page Down, Preview takes you to the bottom of the current page, and you can't press it again to go to the top of the following page. It's all very disconcerting.

Here's the lay of the land:

- If the page doesn't fit the window (that is, the vertical scroll bar appears), you can scroll within the page with the Page Up and Page Down keys.

- If the page fits entirely inside the window (that is, the vertical scroll bar isn't visible), you can change from one page to the next by pressing the Page Up and Page Down keys.

- If you press End, you jump to the bottom of the document; similarly, Home takes you to the first page.

- To move from the bottom of one page to the top of the next, use the down arrow key (you can then use Page Down to scroll on that page).

- If you turn on continuous scrolling (choose View→Continuous Scrolling), Page Down and Page Up jump from page to page.

  If you have a scroll-wheel mouse, this setting also allows the scroll wheel to cross page boundaries.

- If your mouse has a scroll wheel, you can scroll *horizontally* by pressing Shift as you turn the scroll wheel.

11-21 The Image Format Factory

If you need to convert an image from one format to another (say you have a high-resolution TIFF file and you want to throw it on your Web site as a low-resolution JPEG graphic), Preview is especially handy.

Just open the image you want to convert, and then choose File→Export. As shown in Figure 11-12, Preview lets you convert the graphic to a long list of formats, including Windows' bitmap (BMP) and the ancient MacPaint format.

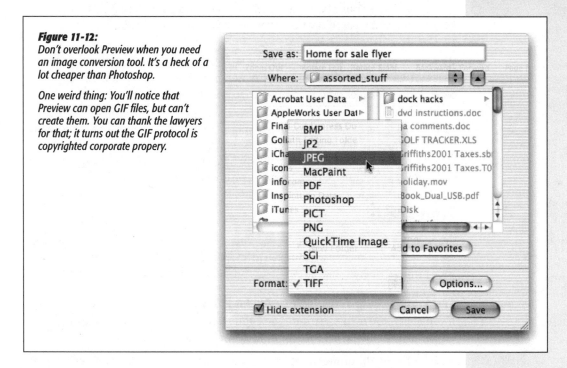

Figure 11-12:
Don't overlook Preview when you need an image conversion tool. It's a heck of a lot cheaper than Photoshop.

One weird thing: You'll notice that Preview can open GIF files, but can't create them. You can thank the lawyers for that; it turns out the GIF protocol is copyrighted corporate propery.

11-22 Clipboard Graphics

If you've copied a graphic to the clipboard—perhaps a screenshot that you'd like to email around as a JPEG file—you can use Preview to save the clipping in the graphics format of your choice.

Once you've copied the picture to the clipboard, switch to Preview and choose File→New From Pasteboard. A new window appears with the contents of the clipboard, and you can then choose File→Export to save the image in any format Preview knows (see the list in Figure 11-12).

11-23 Extracting One Page from a Multipage PDF Document

You may occasionally download a large PDF document, like an instruction manual, and find you only regularly use a few pages of it. You learn the hard way that PDF files can take awhile to open, as can navigating to the pages you need, every time you refer to the document. Monks have the patience for that; you don't.

Instead, use Preview to create small, easy-access PDF documents just for the sections you need. Here's how:

Open your gigantic PDF document in Preview and locate the first page that you'd like to keep. Open the Print dialog box (File→Print or ⌘-P). In the Pages section of the dialog box, click From, and then enter the page range you want to extract. Click Save as PDF, give your new file a name, and then click Save. Repeat this process for each section you want to save. You can't do *that* in Acrobat Reader!

Tip: Similarly, you can convert a single page of a PDF file into a TIFF graphics file. That's a handy workaround when you want to use part of that PDF in graphics, word processing, or page layout programs that don't accept PDF files. (Microsoft Word, for example, can accept TIFF graphics, but not PDFs.)

To extract a page, use the usual File→Export command, making sure to choose the new file format from the pop-up menu. You may be warned that only the currently selected page of your PDF document will be converted. (That's because there's no such thing as a multipage JPEG graphic, or whatever. But you already knew that.)

Print Center

Print Center (in your Applications→Utilities folder) is Apple's printer management tool. Print Center opens each time you print something, so that you can micromanage your printers, queues (lists of waiting printouts), and individual print jobs.

11-24 Dragging Print Jobs Between Printers

If you have more than one printer, and you send a print job to the wrong one, Print Center may be able to help you reroute the wayward job (see Figure 11-13).

First, knock out the printer to which you misrouted the job: In Print Center's Printer List, double-click the printer, and then click Stop Jobs. (If the Printer List isn't visible, choose Printers→Show Printer List.)

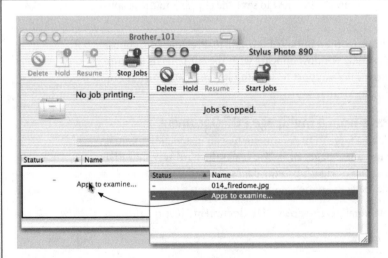

Figure 11-13:
Rerouting a printout to a more appropriate printer is as simple as dragging it from one printer window to another. Clearly, you have to do that before *it* prints out on the original printer; the ability to mess with the time-space continuum isn't expected until Mac OS X 10.5.

Next, double-click the name of the printer you've stopped. Now you see a list of the waiting printouts, including the one you misrouted. To reroute it, double-click the correct printer's name to open its window alongside the current printer's window, and then drag the print job into the correct printer's window, as shown in Figure 11-13.

Stickies

Stickies lets you create virtual Post-it notes that you can stick anywhere on your screen—a triumphant software answer to the thousands of people who stick notes on the edges of their *actual* monitors.

You can use Stickies to type quick notes and to-do items, paste in Web addresses or phone numbers you need to remember, or store any other little scraps and snippets of text you come across. Your electronic Post-its show up whenever the Stickies program is running.

11-25 Sticky Notes Within Other Programs

You're surfing the Web, and unearth a site that lists Eleanor Roosevelt monuments in the mid-Atlantic states that you may want to visit next summer. Later, you receive an email from your spouse with a reminder to polish the silverware before your tax-resistors league comes for dinner tonight. What do you do?

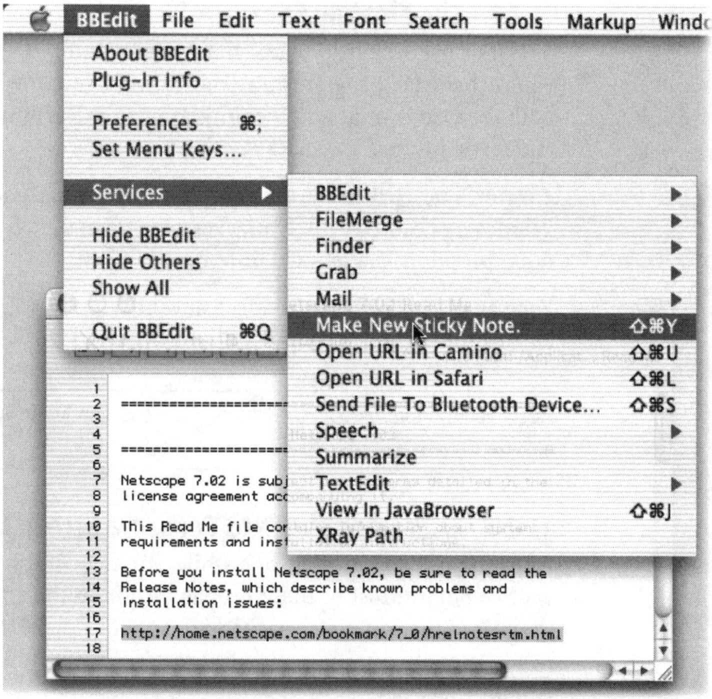

Figure 11-14:
Within a program that has a live Services menu, select some text, and then choose from the Application menu Services→Make New Sticky. Or just press Shift-⌘-Y to save yourself a trip through the menu. A new Sticky note appears with your selected text. That's it!

The twentieth-century answer: You write down the stuff you want save on a slip of paper, and then promptly lose the note. You wind up vacationing at Lake Mosquitoville for the fifth year in a row, and your spouse seethes about serving veal medallions with plastic cutlery.

The twenty-first-century answer: You create a note in Stickies, which hangs around your desktop until you delete it, reminding you to buy a map of New Jersey, and get out the silver polish already. Stimulating travel *and* family harmony ensue.

To create Sticky notes without having to open Stickies first, all you have to do is choose the proper command from any program's Services menu, as shown in Figure 11-14. Unfortunately, the Make New Sticky command is dimmed in most Carbon programs (page 99), but at least it works in most Cocoa applications—Mail, TextEdit, iTunes, Safari, and so on.

11-26 Calling All Stickies!

If you switch to Stickies by clicking its Dock icon, Mac OS X brings all the program's windows to the foreground. But if you switch to Stickies by clicking on a visible note, then only that note comes forward.

What to do if you're already in Stickies, and you want to bring all its notes forward? Just click its Dock icon; all background Stickies windows jump to the foreground. In other words, Stickies works just like all programs, if you consider each sticky note as a "document window."

11-27 The Floating Sticky

Stickies can really help when you're trying to follow instructions for using one of your other Mac programs. Instead of arranging the windows so that you can see both the instructions and the program you're learning, or struggling to switch back and forth, just use a Stickies *floating note.*

To create one, click inside the note you want to float, and then choose Note→Floating Window (or Shift-⌘-F). Now, even when you switch out of Stickies and into some other program, the selected note stays in front.

You can even choose Note→Translucent Window (Shift-⌘-T), which lets you read any text that appears behind a floating note.

Note: You can turn off both the Floating Note and Translucent Windows options in the Stickies Note menu.

11-28 Collapsing Notes to Conserve Screen Space

After you've used Stickies for a while, you may find your screen socked in by a blizzard of notes. Most of these probably contain information that you don't need to see every time you switch to Stickies, and they make it hard to find the notes you do need. After all, do you really need to see directions to your cousins' place in Perth Amboy every day?

Solve the problem by collapsing old stuff into one-line summaries, as explained in Figure 11-15.

Tip: When you create a new Sticky, make sure to start it off with a meaningful first line. If you ever collapse the note later, that's the only part that will show (Figure 11-15).

Figure 11-15:
If you double-click the title bar of any note, it shrinks up and displays only its first line. To expand the note, double-click it again.

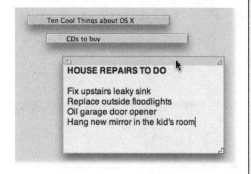

11-29 Back Up Your Stickies Database

Although you should absolutely, positively, really, truly have a backup strategy for your entire Mac, you may want to go out of your way to back up the Stickies database even more often. Why? Because as far as Stickies is concerned, closing a note deletes it forever. It's all too easy to close—and lose—a note you intended to save.

Backing up the database is a snap. Just open your Home –> Library folder, and then Option-drag StickiesDatabase into a backup folder or drag it onto a backup disk. (Option-dragging creates a duplicate of a file.) In case of disaster, all you'll have to do is drag the backed up file back into the Home→Library folder.

11-30 QuickTime Movies in Stickies

You may know that Stickies lets you drag and paste graphics into your notes, but you may be surprised to learn that it can also handle QuickTime movies. This feature is not terrifically practical. But it is totally cool.

Create an empty new note, and then drag a QuickTime movie into it. The Mac asks if you want to copy the movie or just create an alias (Figure 11-16). In general, you'll want the Alias option, which works fine and takes substantially less drive space.

When you drag a movie onto a note, the note does not resize automatically, and the movie appears all squinched up. Drag the lower-right corner of the note to make it big enough to view the movie; as you do so, the QuickTime scroll bar becomes visible, too.

To wow your friends right out the door, drag a movie onto a note, resize the note, and then choose Note→Translucent Window to make the window semi-transparent. Now press Play (or press the Space bar) and watch your QuickTime movie in all its semi-transparent glory. Figure 11-16 at bottom shows you this trippy combo.

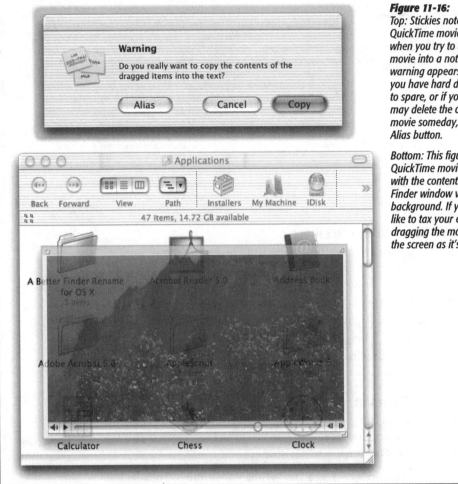

Figure 11-16:
Top: Stickies notes can hold QuickTime movies, but when you try to drag a movie into a note, this warning appears. Unless you have hard drive space to spare, or if you think you may delete the original movie someday, click the Alias button.

Bottom: This figure shows a QuickTime movie playing—with the contents of a Finder window visible in the background. If you really like to tax your eyeballs, try dragging the movie around the screen as it's playing.

TextEdit

TextEdit is a very simple word processor with some surprisingly complete formatting controls built right in. (There's even a multiple-level Undo command.)

11-31   Editing HTML Documents

If you drag an HTML (Web page) document onto the TextEdit icon, the program shows you the page as it's designed to *look*—like a Web page—rather than displaying the behind-the-scenes *HTML commands*.

That can be something of an annoyance if you're trying to use TextEdit to edit the raw HTML code. In that case, you have two options:

- **Change the way TextEdit handles all HTML documents.** Choose TextEdit→Preferences, and turn on "Ignore rich text commands in HTML files." Close the dialog box. All future HTML files will open as documents you can edit.

- **Specify how HTML pages open on a document-by-document basis.** Choose File→Open. In the dialog box that appears, select the document you want to open, and then turn on "Ignore rich text commands," as shown in Figure 11-17. TextEdit dutifully opens the file with all HTML codes visible and ready to edit.

Figure 11-17:
In the File→Open dialog box, turn on "Ignore rich text commands" to prevent TextEdit from displaying an HTML file in its designed mode.

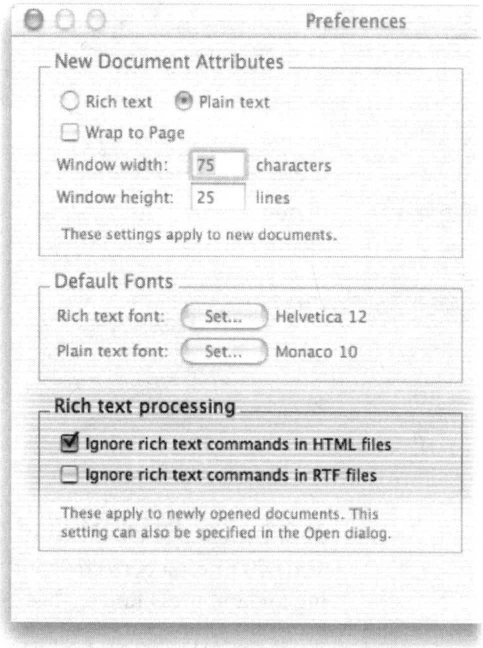

11-32 The Secret Zoom Command

TextEdit lacks a general zoom feature to let you increase or decrease the display of your current document—unless, weirdly enough, you're working on a document in *Rich Text Format* (a standard word processor export format that maintains some formatting).

Figure 11-18 explains how to capitalize on this quirk.

Note: To return to your normal editing mode (which sets the display back to 100%), just select Format→Wrap to Window.

11-33 Navigation Shortcuts

TextEdit recognizes some of the very same keyboard shortcuts found in Microsoft Word. For example, you can advance through documents one word at a time by pressing Option-left arrow or Option-right arrow. Adding the Shift key to those key combinations lets you *select* one whole word at a time. You can also use the Control or ⌘ key in conjunction with the right and left arrow keys to jump to the beginning or end of a line.

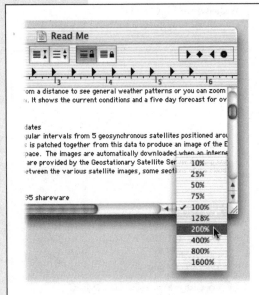

Figure 11-18:
Open a document, and make sure you're in Rich Text mode by choosing Format→Make Rich Text (if the menu command reads Make Plain Text, then you're already in Rich Text mode). Next, choose Format→Wrap to Page, which opens a page view that includes the margins and a zoom controller in the lower-right corner of the window, as shown here.

11-34 The Quickest Kind of Search

TextEdit offers a perfectly good Find command—press ⌘-F, type what you're looking for, and press Enter—just as you might expect.

But if you're looking for other occurrences of something that's already in your document, there's a much faster way. Just highlight the text as it appears in your document, and then choose Edit→Find→Use Selection for Find (or press ⌘-E). This command searches for the next occurrence of whatever text you've already selected *in your document,* without even opening the Find Panel. Select one occurrence of the word you want to look for, press ⌘-E, and then press ⌘-G to jump to each new occurrence of that word.

Web Browsers

A s a Mac OS X devotee, you enjoy a wealth of choices when it comes to Web browsers, some of which run only on Mac OS X. Internet Explorer is the best-known Mac browser, but Apple's own Safari is coming up fast—and if you crave even more variety, you can use Mozilla, Netscape Navigator, OmniWeb, Camino, Opera, iCab, or even a couple of browsers that work in Terminal (like *links* and *lynx*).

No two browsers are created equal; they all have quirks and strengths. Choose one based on the features you like (or your desire to use the fewest Microsoft products possible—you know who you are).

Note: The "alternative" Web browsers appear in new versions more often than you blink. The hints in this chapter were tested on the very latest at the time of writing: Mozilla 1.3, Netscape 7.01, OmniWeb 4.1.1, Camino 0.7 (March 6, 2003), Opera 6.0b2, iCab Preview 2.8.2, and Safari beta 2.

As these browsers evolve—especially Mozilla, which is slated for a radical overhaul at the end of 2003—your mileage may vary when you try these hints.

Hints for all Browsers

Except as noted, the following hints work on all of the browsers listed above. You may be surprised at some of the cool tips you've been missing.

12-1   Dragging and Dropping URLs

When you want to copy a URL (a Web address) from a browser into another program, like your word processor or mail application, here's the hard way to do it: Highlight the URL in the address bar, press ⌘-C to copy it, switch to the other program, and then press ⌘-V to paste it. (OK, the *really* hard way is type out the URL. But nobody would ever do that...would they?)

Here's the easy way: Highlight the URL in the address bar, and then drag it to the program where you'd like it to appear.

If your browser displays a small symbol in front of the URL (the @ sign in Internet Explorer, the symbol in Camino, and so on), dragging that instead of highlighting the full address, as shown in Figure 12-1, is sometimes easier—and sometimes produces slightly different results. For example, dragging the address itself into Word copies the URL there; dragging the @ symbol inserts the name of the Web page and turns it into a blue, underlying link.

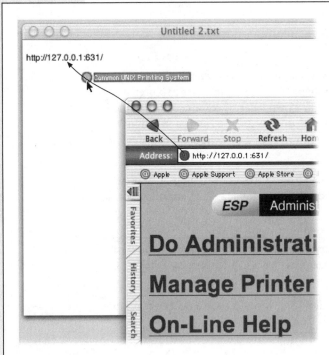

Figure 12-1:
As you drag, some browsers display the name of the page instead of the URL itself. This feature is handy if you have the memory span of a fruit fly and you forget exactly which Web page you're dragging.

12-2   Dock-Launched Web Pages

Once you've mastered the art of dragging URLs, here's a nifty trick: Create a Web Shortcuts folder, install it on your Dock, and then drag your favorite URLs into it. Now you have instant access to your most beloved Web sites.

A few Web browsers (Internet Explorer, OmniWeb, iCab, and Camino, to be specific) even let you drag URLs directly onto the Dock, where they appear as individual icons.

12-3   Address Bar as Launcher

You're sitting in front of your Web browser and you suddenly realize you need to look up an appointment in iCal. What do you do?

If you're content to join the unwashed masses in laborious application launching, then click into the Finder, navigate to your Applications folder, then double-click iCal.

But the elite do it this way: Just type *ical://* in your browser's address bar and then press Enter. This supercool trick also works for iChat (*ichat://*), Address Book (*addressbook://*), and Sherlock (*sherlock://*).

12-4   Open Multiple Web Sites at Once

If you're like most people, you have a set of favorite Web pages that you visit each day, perhaps first thing in the morning. Unfortunately, that usually involves clicking your way through a million or so bookmarks, waiting for each to load.

A much better way: Let AppleScript do the work for you.

Open Script Editor (a program in your Applications→AppleScript folder). Type this:

```
open location "http://www.nytimes.com"
open location "http://www.macosxhints.com/"
```

Continue building this list, adding as many additional Web addresses as you like, one per line.

Choose File→Save. Choose Application from the Format pop-up menu, name the script *Web Faves* or whatever you like, and save the file onto your desktop.

From now on, whenever you double-click the Web Faves desktop icon, your browser opens a new window for each site, loading up the pages you requested as you're relaxing and sipping coffee.

Tip: If you designate this little AppleScript as a Login Item (open System Preferences→Login Items), your browser will do its morning ritual automatically when you log in.

12-5   PDF Files in Your Browser

When you want to view a PDF (Acrobat) document from a Web site, the ritual usually goes like this: Your browser downloads the file, you wait a moment, and then the file opens up in Preview or Acrobat Reader. What to do when you just want a bit of information from the PDF document and don't need the whole thing on your machine?

PDF Browser Plug-in to the rescue. This free plug-in lets you view PDF files right in the browser window, which means you can preview them before deciding whether to save to your hard drive. It also makes viewing PDF documents a much speedier operation. (PDF Browser Plugin works with all browsers except for Opera.)

You can download PDF Browser Plug-in from *www.Schubert-it.com/plugin*. Install it by dragging it into your Home→Library→Internet Plug-Ins folder. If this folder doesn't exist, just create it first (name it exactly as shown here). Quit and reopen your browser.

When you surf, the plug-in is invisible. When you try to open a PDF page, however, the PDF plug-in jumps to life at the top of your scroll bar. Figure 12-2 shows the difference between the dormant plug-in (on the left), and the active plug-in (in the middle).

You can navigate the PDF document once it's on your screen either with the mouse or by pressing the arrow keys. As you read, the program displays page numbers in the lower-right corner of the PDF window.

Figure 12-2:
Left: Your browser's scroll bar.

Middle: Your browser's scroll bar with the PDF plug-in.

Right: The plug-in's secret pop-up menu.

12-6   Keyboard Control of Links

In Internet Explorer, Mozilla, and OmniWeb, you can jump to any text link on a Web page by typing the first few characters of its name. When the browser finds a link that matches what you've typed, it highlights the link. If you press Enter, the linked page loads. (This doesn't work, of course, if the insertion point is currently in the address bar. In that case, the browser interprets typing as an attempt to input a Web address. It also doesn't work in Internet Explorer if you've chosen Internet Explorer→Preferences, clicked Browser display, and turned on "Tab to just text fields.")

For example, if you're on a page with text links for Search and Site Map, type *Se* to highlight the Search link. If you type *Si*, the browser highlights Site Map.

Note: Typing to select links works great on smaller pages. But if you're on a longer page, it can be tricky. If you start typing *Si* in order to get to the site map, you could wind up at a link for Sibling Rivalry Specialists, which comes up alphabetically before Site Map. On a page with a lot of text links, be prepared for the browser window to jump around as you type.

12-7   Favorites on Your Personal Toolbar

Web surfing would be a drag without bookmarks. You'd have to remember the URLs for your favorite sites (is it *ConsumerReports.org* or *ConsumerReports.com*?), or worse, write them down on paper. Of course, browsers let you store bookmarks in a series of folders, usually called Favorites. And in most browsers, you can place about ten ultra-special bookmarks on a Favorites toolbar. (If you don't see the toolbar in your browser, look for something like View –> Favorites Bar.)

But what if you're a Web sophisticate with *more* than ten Very Important Bookmarks? In every browser except Opera and *lynx,* you can place *folders* on your Favorites bar, which you can then fill with individual links. The folders then act like pop-up menus of the links inside. Not only can you add many more faves this way, but you can organize them, too.

The exact method of creating a folder varies by browser, but the basic process is the same: Start by bringing up the bookmark-editing window, create a new folder, and then drag that folder into your Favorites folder. If you then drag individual links into the new folder, they're instantly available on your Favorites bar.

12-8   Google Searching in Your Browser

Google.com, as almost everybody knows, is the world's greatest Web-searching tool. It's so great that Apple installed a Google search bar right there on the toolbar of the Safari browser.

If you use any other Web browser, consider installing the Google *bookmarklet.* (Bookmarklets are little programs that run as extra features in your browser.) The Google bookmarklet sits as a link on your Favorites bar; when you click it, a search windows pops up (Figure 12-3). If you type in your search and then press Enter, your browser jumps to a Google page with your search results.

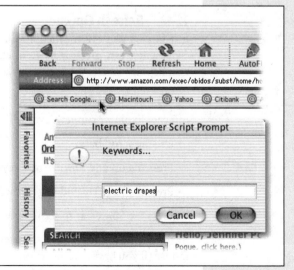

Figure 12-3:
Save yourself a lot of extra clicking around by adding the Google bookmarklet to your toolbar. From now on, you don't have to go to Google to search Google; you can fire off a search no matter where you are.

Another useful bookmarklet behavior: If you have any text selected on a page, when you click the Google bookmarklet, your browser automatically brings up the Google results page for those words—without even making you use the input dialog box.

You can find the Google bookmarklet at *www.bookmarklets.com/tools/search/srchbook. phtm.* (Bookmarklet.com also offers a bevy of other useful search tools, calculators, design helpers, and navigation aids.) To install it into Internet Explorer, just drag it (the "Search Google" icon) right off the Web page and onto your Favorites bar.

If just dragging the bookmarklet doesn't work (some browsers are a bit recalcitrant), proceed like this:

Define a new bookmark and give it a meaningful name like "Google search." In the Address portion of the bookmark definition screen, enter the following text, allon one line (or copy it from the file at *www.macosxhints.com/book/scripts.html):*

```
javascript:Qr=document.getSelection();if(!Qr){void(Qr=prompt
('Keywords...',''))};if(Qr)location.href='http://google.com/
search?query='+escape(Qr)+'&num=20'
```

Type all of that as one continuous line, with no spaces at all. After entering the code, save the bookmark and then (for truly fast access), place it on your Favorites bar.

Internet Explorer Hints

Internet Explorer has been around for the Mac for years. Because it's the one that comes preinstalled on the Dock, it's the browser of choice for many people—many of whom may not be aware that they even *have* a choice.

If you use Internet Explorer, the following hints may teach you a few tricks you didn't know your browser was capable of performing.

12-9   Refresh Options

Just in case you ever needed a fourth method of *refreshing* a Web page—beyond clicking Refresh, pressing ⌘-R, or choosing View→Refresh—pressing the F5 function key also causes the current page to reload.

12-10   A Good Scrolling Trick

Internet Explorer runneth over with ways to scroll a long Web page:

- Use the scroll bars

- Press the up and down arrow keys

- Press the Page Up and Page Down keys

- Press the Space bar to scroll down a page; Option-Space to scroll up a page

By far the most satisfying way, however, is to turn the little wheel on the top of your mouse (if you have a scroll-wheel mouse). This method gives you exact control over how much you scroll, and when.

Even if you haven't bought a non-Apple mouse, however, you can emulate one by holding down ⌘ as you drag inside any empty area of the Web page. It's a very big target, and a very fun tip.

12-11   A Warning about Web-Page Printouts

If you've highlighted some text on a Web page, the highlighting remains visible when you print the page or save it as a PDF document.

Feature or bug? It's your call.

12-12   Tricks for Opening New Windows

If you ⌘-click a link on a Web page, Internet Explorer opens that link in a new window. This is a hugely important tip to know when, for example, you're exploring a list of search results, trying to find the one Web page that interests you. Rather than clicking the Back button repeatedly after each exploration, you can just close the newly created window; you'll find yourself happily deposited back at the list of search results.

Most people don't realize, however, that you can do the same thing in the address bar. That is, if you type in a Web address and then press ⌘-Enter (instead of just Enter), Internet Explorer opens the specified Web page in a new window.

12-13   Starting Downloads

There's more than one way to skin a cat, and there's more than one way to download a file from a link on a Web page in Internet Explorer.

- If you Control-click a link, and then choose Download Link to Disk from the contextual menu, a Save dialog box opens. Specify a file name and destination, and then click Save to let the download rip.

- You can drag a link to your Downloads window.

- You can drag a link directly to the desktop, or into a folder where you like to store your downloads.

- Option-click a link. (The downloaded software winds up in whatever folder you've specified in the Internet Explorer→Preferences dialog box.)

In each case, Internet Explorer begins transferring the specified file, no questions asked.

12-14   Downloading Files with Long Names

Although Mac OS X permits up to 255 characters in a file name, certain Mac OS 9 programs that have been *Carbonized* (page 99) can only deal with a few dozen characters. Internet Explorer is one such program, at least when it comes to downloading files.

If you download something whose name is longer than 31 characters, Internet Explorer truncates the name at the thirty-first position. This behavior can cause problems if the file name extension gets lopped off (.exe, .doc, .sit, and so on). For example, StuffIt Expander doesn't know how to expand files without extensions.

The solution: In the Finder, rename the download to match its original name on the Internet (or just add the proper extension to the shortened name).

12-15   Icons on the Button Bar

The Internet Explorer button bar is the row that contains buttons for Forward, Backward, Stop, Refresh, and so on. But you can also place icons on that row that, when clicked, jump directly to your favorite Web sites, as shown in Figure 12-4. It's a great way to capitalize on all the otherwise wasted space on the button bar, create a bigger target for your mouse, and provide a handy visual reminder of a site's contents.

You can create these icons two ways: the lucky way and the unlucky way.

Figure 12-4:
*Icons make great
shortcuts to your
utmost favorite sites.*

The lucky way

Open the page you want to keep in the button bar. Try to find a graphic on the page that loads the site's *index page* (its home page or welcome page). On the Macosxhints.com site, for example, the main logo links to the home page. When you find such a graphic, you're in luck: just drag it up onto the button bar. Internet Explorer obediently makes a button out of it.

The unlucky way

If you can't find a graphic that links to the home page (the CNN logo in Figure 12-5 is one such image), you can still make this hint work; you just have to edit a preference file by hand.

1. **On any Web page, find a graphic that you'd like to serve as your button. Drag it onto the button bar.**

   It doesn't matter what the graphic links to.

2. **Quit Internet Explorer and open TextEdit.**

   See page 4 for details on the TextEdit ritual you're about to enjoy.

3. **Choose File→Open. Navigate to your Home→Library→Preferences→Explorer folder, and open the file called English.Toolbar.xml.**

   You've just opened a window of code (XML, as it turns out) that stores the technical information about your toolbar. Your job now is to find the scrap of text that refers to the graphic you pasted.

4. **By scrolling or by using the Find command, look for something that should be in the name of the graphic you pasted in step 1, like part of the domain name.**

In the case of the CNN logo, a search for "CNN" finds this section of the file:

```
<button>
<command>OURL</command>
<url>http://i.cnn.net/cnn/.element/img/1.0/logo/cnn.gif</url>
<title>CNN.com</title>
<imageenabled>http://i.cnn.net/cnn/.element/img/1.0/logo/
cnn.gif</imageenabled>
</button>
```

5. **Replace the stuff between the <url> tags, shown italicized above, with the actual URL you want the icon to link to.**

For the CNN logo, you'd probably use the CNN home page address, like this:

```
<url>http://www.cnn.com</url>
```

Tip: You can also use "mailto://" or "ftp://" links to put email and FTP sites in the button bar.

6. **Change the button name, if you like.**

You can edit the name that appears under the button by changing the stuff between the <title> tags.

Note: At this point, the <imageenabled> tag indicates that the graphic you're using isn't actually on your hard drive, but is rather being dished out by the Web page from which you swiped it. If you'd rather use a graphic on your hard drive (either a saved copy of that same button or even another graphic), replace the "http://" stuff between the <imageenabled> tags with "file:///" followed by the full path to the image on your hard drive. For example, if it's a picture in your Home→Pictures folder, replace the "http://" line with *file:///~/Pictures.* (See page 297 for more on path notation.)

Figure 12-5:
With a bit of work, you can create customized icons in the Internet Explorer button bar, as seen here. Just click the logo to jump to each site.

7. When you're done editing, save the preference file, quit TextEdit, and reopen Internet Explorer.

Check out your newly customized button bar.

12-16   PNG Files in New Windows

PNG stands for Portable Network Graphic—a newish image format that beats the JPEG format in terms of file size (smaller) and image quality (better). As a result, PNG files are starting to crop up around the Web.

Internet Explorer loads and displays these images as it should—unless you're trying to view a PNG image by itself. For example, if you Control-click a PNG image and choose Open Image in New Window from the contextual menu, Internet Explorer offers you the useful error message shown in Figure 12-6.

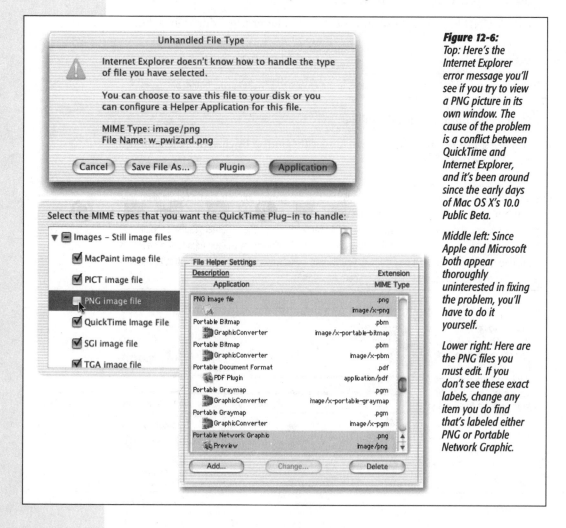

Figure 12-6:
Top: Here's the Internet Explorer error message you'll see if you try to view a PNG picture in its own window. The cause of the problem is a conflict between QuickTime and Internet Explorer, and it's been around since the early days of Mac OS X's 10.0 Public Beta.

Middle left: Since Apple and Microsoft both appear thoroughly uninterested in fixing the problem, you'll have to do it yourself.

Lower right: Here are the PNG files you must edit. If you don't see these exact labels, change any item you do find that's labeled either PNG or Portable Network Graphic.

Luckily, the problem is relatively easy to fix, thanks to a tweak discovered by *Macosxhints.com* reader Matthew H. Rothenberg.

Open System Preferences, and then click the QuickTime icon. On the Plug-In tab, click MIME Settings. In the dialog box that opens, click to expand the triangle next to Images. Turn off "PNG image file," as shown at middle in Figure 12-6. Click OK, and close the QuickTime preference panel.

Return to Internet Explorer and choose Explorer –> Preferences. In the left-hand frame, scroll down to Receiving Files and click File Helpers. On the right side, scroll down until you find the two PNG entries (they're both highlighted at bottom in Figure 12-6). Highlight the first one, click Change, and in the Handling box, choose "View with Browser" from the pop-up menu. Click OK to save the change, and then repeat the process with the second PNG file helper.

Close the preference panel. Now, when you Control-click a PNG image and choose Open Image in New Window, Internet Explorer will obediently do what you asked.

12-17   Page Holder I

Internet Explorer has a handy sidebar called Page Holder. If that name means nothing to you, join the confused masses. But don't overlook the feature, because it's actually very cool; see Figure 12-7.

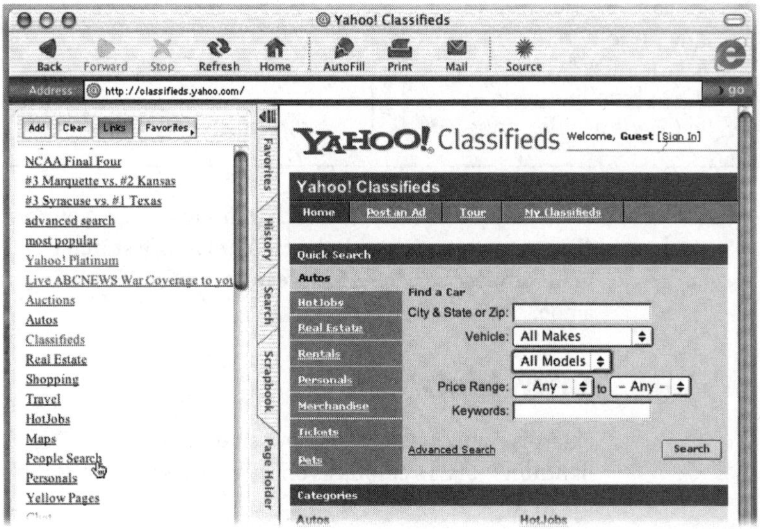

Figure 12-7:
The Page Holder is a sidebar that lets you click link after link on, say, a Results page from a search. The main part of the window reflects the pages you're summoning, while the sidebar's original page stays put. Page Holder can display just the hyperlinks on a page, concealing all of the irrelevant filler (click the Links button atop the sidebar). It even has its own Favorites department (click Favorites).

Page Holder is worth a thousand clicks when you're searching a Web site with lots of branches and levels. Here's how it works:

In Internet Explorer's main window, open a page you want to use as a base for some surfing (Yahoo.com, for example). Open the Page Holder sidebar (it's the bottom tab on the left-hand side of the window). If you click Add, the main page loads in the sidebar. Once it's in the sidebar, you can click the links there, and they open in the main window without changing what's in Page Holder.

12-18   Page Holder II: Google

One obvious use for Page Holder is to display Google search results—and Google, Inc. is way ahead of you on this one. Go to *www.google.com/ie,* open the Page Holder sidebar, and then drag the @ symbol from the address bar into the Page Holder area, as in Figure 12-8.

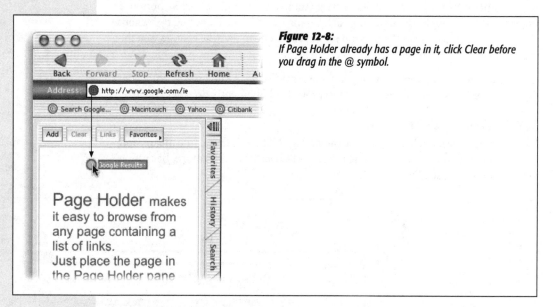

Figure 12-8:
If Page Holder already has a page in it, click Clear before you drag in the @ symbol.

Now, whenever you enter search terms in Google, your results appear in Page Holder. (If you try this trick with the regular Google search page, your results appear in the main browser window.) This feature is worth the savings in Back and Forward clicks alone.

Safari Hints

Safari is Apple's new Web browser, designed from Day One to load Web pages like lightning. Safari's emphasis on speed is a welcome addition to the browser battle on the Mac.

At this writing, Safari is still a beta product and may not work well with every site you visit. In fact, some of the hints in this section may not work in newer versions. Still, the program looks cool and works hard, making it worth a try.

12-19 The Master Keyboard Shortcut List

Deep in the guts of Safari is a formatted page listing nearly every keyboard shortcut you could ever use in Safari.

To view this extensive list, open the Finder and Control-click the Safari icon. Choose Show Package Contents from the contextual menu, and then in the new window, open Contents→Resources→English.lproj (shown in the background in Figure 12-9). Finally, drag the icon called Shortcuts.html into the Safari browser.

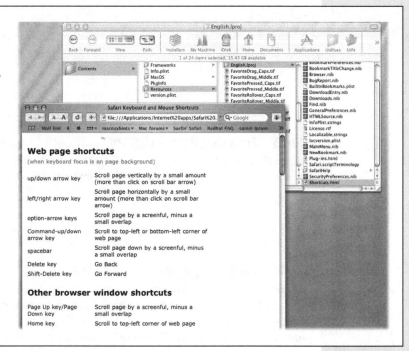

Figure 12-9:
Safari spills the beans about its secret keyboard shortcut list. Keep this list near at hand by dragging its URL from the address bar to your Bookmarks bar.

12-20 Default Window Size and Position

Close all your open Safari windows. Open a new window, and then move it and make it the size you'd like for new windows in the future. Quit Safari. When you open the program again, new windows jump to the location and size you just specified.

12-21 Quick Address Selection I

Highlighting the URL in the address bar is the first step in a number of important Web-browsing tasks. For example, you'll want to highlight the whole thing before typing a new address over it. You also have to highlight the address before copying it so that you can paste it into another program.

In any case, Safari offers a clever shortcut for highlighting the entire address. One of them is strange but true: Position your cursor at the very upper edge of the address-bar text box. (The tip of the Arrow should literally be on the top line of the box and it should no longer look like an insertion point.) Now just click to highlight the entire address.

12-22 Quick Address Selection II

If you enjoyed the previous hint, you'll love this one. It's another way to highlight the entire address very quickly, ready for copying or pasting; see Figure 12-10.

Figure 12-10:
Select a whole URL with just one click—on the small icon on the left edge of the address bar.

12-23 Browsing Recent History

If you Control-click (or click and hold) either the Back or Forward button and wait a moment, Safari produces a pop-up menu listing all your recently visited sites by name.

Tip: If you'd prefer to see URLs instead of names, Option-click either arrow.

12-24 Navigating a Site via the Title Bar

As you dig your way down into a Web site, it can sometimes be a little tricky to get back to the original page. You can use the Back button, of course, but you either have to press and hold it to see the list of prior pages, or click it repeatedly to go back one page at a time. Luckily, Safari offers another method for backtracking.

If you ⌘-click the title bar (centered just above the address bar), Safari displays a list of each page you've visited in the current site (Figure 12-11). To navigate back, just click the page that you'd like to see.

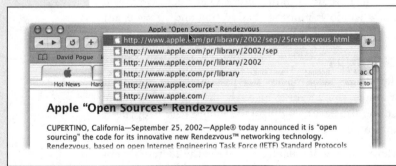

Figure 12-11:
This secret menu shows a hierarchical trail of the pages you crossed to get here. It works even if you didn't actually burrow here step by step—that is, if you jumped here directly by typing this page's address in its entirety.

12-25 Google Search Features I

Safari has a handy "search Google" box in the main toolbar (if you don't see it, choose View→Google Search). Make it even more useful by employing these little-known tricks:

- If you click the small magnifying glass on the left side of the search box, it displays a list of your recent Google searches, as shown in Figure 12-12.

- If you highlight a word or phrase on any Web site and then Control-click it, the pop-menu gives you an option for "Google search." Choose it to run a search directly.

Figure 12-12:
Top: The magnifying glass is your portal to Google searches past.

Bottom: Click an entry in the list to run that search again. (The Clear Entries command, of course, erases the list to cover your tracks so that employers or spouses won't know what you've been doing.)

12-26 Google Search Features II

If you run a search via the Google box, the results page lets you do an internal search: Press ⌘-F to bring up a small search box that has your search terms in it already, so that you can search the page itself.

12-27 Bookmark Folders

Safari's bookmark folders (Bookmarks→Add Bookmark Folder) can help you keep your shortcuts bar (that is, your Favorites bar, Bookmarks bar, whatever you want to call it) nice and organized.

To create a bookmark folder, choose Bookmarks→Add Bookmark Folder, which creates an untitled folder and opens the Collections window on the left-hand side of the screen (if it's not already open). Type a name for the folder. Now you can fill those folders with bookmarks that you drag from the main bookmark window area as shown in Figure 12-13, or from the other folders in your Collections list—or you can just save new Web sites into it as you surf.

On the Bookmarks Bar, a folder icon looks just like a regular bookmark icon, except that a triangle sits to its right. If you click a folder's name, it pauses and then displays the sites stored within it. If you click the little triangle, you eliminate the delay, and a list of the folder contents drops down immediately.

12-28　A Keyboard Shortcut for the Bookmarks Bar

You can easily reach the first nine icons on your Bookmarks Bar by using an unusual keyboard shortcut: ⌘-1 to open the first bookmark, ⌘-2 to open the second, and so on.

This trick doesn't work for *folders* on the Bookmarks Bar; it skips over them.

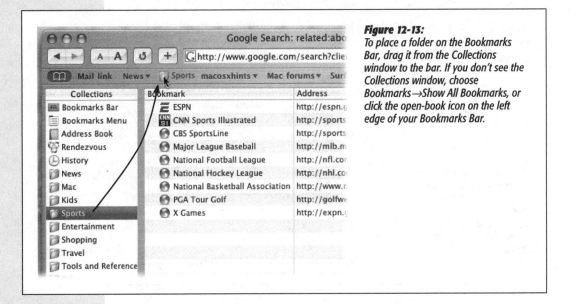

Figure 12-13:
To place a folder on the Bookmarks Bar, drag it from the Collections window to the bar. If you don't see the Collections window, choose Bookmarks→Show All Bookmarks, or click the open-book icon on the left edge of your Bookmarks Bar.

12-29　Searching History and Bookmark Folders

If you bookmark a ton of Web pages but your collection is slightly less organized than, say, the Library of Congress, Safari can help make trips into your bookmarks and history folders less intimidating.

Click the bookmark icon at the left end of the shortcuts bar; choose Edit→Find→Find (or press ⌘-F), and type your search term. Safari highlights the first entry, among your bookmarks, that contains a match. Use Edit→Find→Find Again (or ⌘-G) to find the next occurrence of your term. You can even jump backward with Shift-⌘-G (Edit→Find→Find Previous).

12-30　Bookmarking Folders for Fast Access

If you generally save all your downloads into one particular folder, you can create a toolbar icon for it, giving you one-click access to its contents. The idea is to end forever the annoying "I know I downloaded it—what the heck happened to it?" syndrome so familiar to millions of surfers.

In Safari's address bar, type *file:///* (note the three slashes), followed by the path to the folder. (See page 297 for details on path notation.)

Note: If you have more than one hard drive or partition, type *Volumes/* immediately after the three slashes but before the folder path.

Once you've typed in the full path, don't press Enter! Instead, highlight it and drag it onto Safari's bookmark folder, as in Figure 12-14.

Figure 12-14:
To bookmark a folder on your hard drive, type file:/// in the URL bar, followed by the full path to the folder. Don't press Enter at that point; just drag the address to the Bookmarks Bar.

When Safari prompts you, enter a meaningful short name (something like "Downloads") and then click OK.

From now on, you can click the Downloads icon on the shortcuts bar whenever you like. Safari instantly switches to the Finder and opens a new window showing its contents. (Of course, you can stash *any* folder's icon onto the bar, not just your Downloads folder.)

12-31   Status Bar for Full Link Information

When you mouse over a link on a Web page, most browsers display its corresponding URL, which is a good way to find out where a click will take you. Safari displays this info in the Status Bar, a one-line metallic row at the very bottom of the browser window (Figure 12-15). If your browser has no evident Status Bar, choose View→ Status Bar (or press ⌘-\).

Figure 12-15:
The status bar shows you what will happen when you click the link under the current mouse pointer location.

When you hover over a link, the Status Bar puts "Go to http://…" before the URL, which is the program's way of telling you that clicking the link will take you there. But:

- If you press ⌘, the Status Bar says, "Open 'http://xyz' in a new window." Click to do so.

- If you press Shift-⌘, the Status Bar says, "Open 'http://xyz' in a new window behind the current window." Click to do so.

- If you press Option, the Status Bar says, "Download 'http://xyz'." Click to download the file identified by the link, to your hard drive.

- If you press Control, the Status Bar says, "Display a menu for 'http://xyz'." This message just tells you what you already know: Control-clicking a link brings up a handy contextual menu (from which you can open the link in a new window, download it to your hard drive, copy it to the clipboard, or add it to your bookmarks).

12-32 Deleting Entries from Safari's History

The importance of being able to delete individual entries from your History list is illustrated by the following fable.

Your favorite site is EthernetRules.com. You visit often, and you don't have any other bookmarked sites that start with "et," so you usually just type *et* and let Safari autocomplete the URL. Then you press Enter to load the site.

But one day, someone sends you an email telling you about ETphonehome.com. So you check it out, but it's really not anything you want to visit regularly. A bit later, you decide to visit EthernetRules.com, but your usual *et* shortcut now loads ETphonehome.com. The problem: Safari uses the first matching entry in your History list to offer autocompletion—which, in this case, is a Web site you only visited once.

To solve this problem, click the book icon at the left end of the Bookmarks Bar, and then click History. Click the triangle next to today's date, and then select the entry for ETphonehome.com. If you press Delete, Safari removes the URL. Close the bookmark manager. You can now use your old "et" shortcut again.

12-33 Clearing Favicon.ico Files

Ever heard of a Favicon.ico file? Figure 12-16 tells all.

Once Safari gets a hold of favicon.ico files, it's loath to give them up. Even choosing Safari→Empty Cache doesn't force them to reload, which makes it quite hard to test a *new* favicon.ico file in Safari—a particular problem for Web designers.

If you're among the few, the proud, and the frustrated, here are two ways to nix your not-so-favorite icons:

- **Trash them all.** Unlike everything else in Safari's cache (which you can find in Home→Library→Caches→Safari), favicon.ico files live in Home→Library→Caches→com.apple.WebKit. To force a favorite icon to reload, delete this entire folder.

  Unfortunately, this action tosses *all* your favicon.ico files in the Trash. Fortunately, they simply reappear when you visit sites that have them.

- **Clear them selectively.** A neat piece of freeware, Safari Icon Manager (*www.ircandy.com/openmac/sim/*), lets you choose which favicon.ico files to remove from the cache.

Figure 12-16:
It's all about branding: Here's the favorites icon for Shashdot.com. The small logos that appear in the Safari address bar and bookmarks folder are designed by the Web page creators themselves. They're called favorites icons or favicon.ico files. (They appear in other browsers, too.)

12-34 Emailing URLs from Safari I

Some Web browsers include a handy "Mail this page" feature that sends the current URL to a recipient you specify. Not Safari. But if you use Apple's Mail program, you can simulate this feature.

Start by highlighting the URL (see hint 12-21), and then choose Safari→Services→Mail→Send Selection. A new mail message opens with the selected URL in the body. Type an email address and a subject header, and click Send.

12-35 Emailing URLs from Safari II

If you send URLs to your friends every 37 seconds, consider creating a "Mail this page" shortcut for your Safari toolbar.

Get in touch with your inner Web developer, and type the following line of JavaScript (a Web-page programming language) into Safari's address bar—all on one line, no spaces:

```
javascript:location.href='mailto:?SUBJECT='+document.title+
'&BODY='+escape(location.href)
```

Now drag the icon next to the word "javascript" to the Bookmarks Bar. Safari asks you to name the bookmark; type something fitting like *Mail URL* or *Mail Link,* and then click OK.

You now have an easy-access button that, when clicked, opens a new message in your email program, fills the Subject line with the title of the page, and adds the URL in the body (see Figure 12-17). All you have to do is add a recipient, click Send, and smile smugly.

Figure 12-17:
With a one-line JavaScript bookmark, you can create a "Mail this page" feature that Apple engineers would be proud to call their own. Make this feature even easier to use by dragging the mail link to the leftmost spot on your Bookmarks Bar, so that you'll be able to trigger it from now on just by pressing ⌘-1 (see hint 12-28).

12-36 Minimum Font Size

Some Web designers are evil. They use fonts so small that no amount of squinting can make them readable. (If they're not evil, they may just be using Windows, whose standard screen resolution isn't the same as the Mac's. That's why so many Web pages have tiny type on Macs, but normal-size type when viewed on a PC.)

Many browsers let you specify a minimum font size for your Web pages. Safari doesn't come with such a feature, but you can specify a minimum size in either of two ways:

The easy way

Download Safari Enhancer *(http://gordon.sourcecod.com/sites/safari_enhancer.php)*, a free program that lets you specify the smallest permissible font size, and more.

The homemade way

If you're stranded on a desert island without a cable modem (and you therefore can't download Safari Enhancer), you can achieve the same thing like this:

Quit Safari. In the Finder, open the Home→Library→Preferences folder. Find the icon called com.apple.Safari.plist and open it by dragging it onto the TextEdit icon (page 4). Click just after the <dict> tag that's near the top, press Return, and then type these new lines:

```
<key>WebKitMinimumFixedFontSize</key>
<integer>13</integer>
```

```
<key>WebKitMinimumFontSize</key>
<integer>14</integer>
```

Replace "13" and "14" with your preferred font sizes; the first number is for mono-spaced fonts (fonts in which every letter is exactly the same width, like Courier), and the second is for proportional fonts (fonts where letter widths vary, like this one).

Save your changes and restart Safari. Fonts no longer appear any smaller than the minimum size you specified.

12-37 Jump Between Tabs With The Keyboard

To move between tabs in Safari, you can either use the mouse to click each one (slow, painful, removes hands from keyboard), or just hold Command and Shift and then click the left or right arrow keys to move, well, left or right between tabs.

12-38 The Debugging Menu

It could happen to you: You visit a favorite Web site, which sends out a little invisible signal to find out which Web browser you're using. (Many Web sites do this so that they know which Web page to show you, and the unfortunate result is the fact that different Web browsers display Web pages differently.)

But because you're using the relatively unknown Safari browser, your otherwise be-loved Web site tells you: "Sorry, browser not supported."

One quick solution is to turn on the Debug menu in Safari. Its user-agent option makes Safari masquerade as some other browser, successfully fooling diva Web sites into letting you in.

To turn on the debug menu, there's once again an easy way and a Terminal way.

The easy way

Download Safari Enhancer, as described in the previous hint. It offers a simple checkbox that turns on the Debug menu.

The homemade way

First quit Safari, and then open Terminal (page 5). Type this line, and then press Enter:

```
defaults write com.apple.Safari IncludeDebugMenu 1
```

Quit Terminal. When you open Safari again, the new Debug menu appears right next to Help. Most of its commands are designed to appeal mostly to programmers, but a few are useful for a wider audience.

- **Use Back/Forward Cache** lets you turn on and off the cache, which is a speed trick in which Safari, like most Web browsers, *caches* each Web page you visit. (In other words, the browser makes a copy of it on your hard drive so that it won't have to download the page the next time you visit.)

- **Keyboard and Mouse Shortcuts** opens up the master page of Safari keyboard shortcuts, saving you the effort of following the steps in hint 12-19.

- **Populate History** fills your History menu with the names of bogus Web sites (wittily called *bogus page 1, bogus page 2,* and so on). The idea, of course, is to let programmers try out the various features of the history list without actually having to visit ten pages to fill it up.

- **User Agent** is the command that lets Safari masquerade as a different browser. Choose User Agent→Mac MSIE 5.22, for example, to assume the identity of Internet Explorer.

If you ever want to eliminate the menu, just repeat the above instructions, but replace the "1" at the end of the command with a "0."

Note: The Debug menu might not be available in the final release of Safari.

12-39 Open All Bookmarks Within A Folder

You can open all the sites within a folder on your Bookmarks bar just by ⌘-clicking it. The sites listed in that folder will fill your current window, one site per tab. If you do this by accident, hit Safari's Back button.

On a related note, ⌘-clicking any individual link on your Bookmarks Bar opens that link in a new tab, without changing the "focus" from your current window.

12-40 An End to Brushed Metal

Safari joins Apple's tribe of programs, including QuickTime, Address Book, and iTunes, that look like they've been built out of brushed aluminum. If you prefer the Aqua appearance common to most Mac OS X programs (see Figure 12-18), you can switch Safari over, using either of two methods.

Method 1: If you've installed Developer Tools

This method is for people who have installed the Developer Tools CD (page 6).

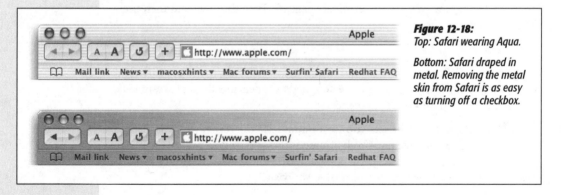

Figure 12-18:
Top: Safari wearing Aqua.

Bottom: Safari draped in metal. Removing the metal skin from Safari is as easy as turning off a checkbox.

Quit Safari and make a copy of it (just in case). Control-click the copy, and choose Show Package Contents from the contextual menu (page 3). In the new window, open the Contents→Resources→English.lproj folder. Double-click the Browser.nib file, which opens into a program called Interface Builder (a program used by programmers to design their software).

In the Browser.nib window, click Window. Press Shift-⌘-I to bring up the Inspector window. As Figure 12-19 shows, the very last option is Textured Window. Turn off this box, save your changes, and launch your copy of Safari to see its full Aqua glory.

Method 2: Doing without Developer Tools

If you prefer a hands-off approach, download Unsanity's free Metallifizer program from *http://unsanity.com/haxies/metallifizer/*. This little application removes (or adds) the metal appearance from (or to) any Cocoa program.

OmniWeb Hints

The Omni Group, creator of OmniWeb, has been programming for Mac OS X for years—even before there was a Mac OS X. That's because the company developed OmniWeb for the NeXT operating system, on which Mac OS X was eventually based.

OmniWeb is a Cocoa program, so it automatically includes nice features like system the Services menu, a customizable toolbar, and spell checking.

12-41   Web Pages as PDF Files

As you know, Mac OS X can create a PDF file from anything you can print; just open a print dialog box and click Save as PDF.

OmniWeb includes a keyboard shortcut to make this procedure even easier. If you hold down Option as you choose File→Save As, the menu item becomes Save As PDF. It's a great way to preserve a receipt, driving directions, or some other important Web info.

12-42   Opening a New Window Containing the Current Page

Every now and then, you might want to open an exact copy of the page you're currently viewing. For example, if it's a site that's heavy on links, you may wish to follow a story on the main page, and yet keep the original page open to revisit again when you're done reading.

In OmniWeb, you can double-click the small blue lightning icon next to the site's name in the URL bar, as shown in Figure 12-19. You open a duplicate of the first Web page, ready for link-following.

12-43   Scrolling One Page at a Time

If your mouse has a scroll wheel, you can use it to zoom forward and backward through a long Web page one screenful at a time, without ever having to involve the keyboard. The technique: Turn the wheel while pressing it down.

This feature may not work if the mouse came with its own special software. If you have such an animal, use its System Preferences panel or its configuration program to disable its special features when you're using OmniWeb.

Tip: Of course, if you prefer the keyboard, you can use the Page Up and Page Down keys, or Option-up and -down arrow keys.

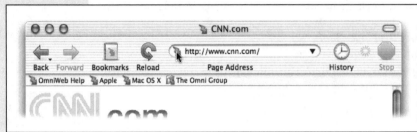

Figure 12-19:
Want to open a new window containing the exact page you're viewing now? If so, just double-click on the icon next to the URL, as shown here.

12-44   Shortcuts

OmniWeb comes with a few predefined shortcuts that can save you some address typing. One of the best is the one for Google, which, instead of just loading the page, lets you type search terms in the address bar, like this: *google Icelandic tomatoes* (or *google whatever you're looking for*). When you press Enter, OmniWeb loads the Google page with your search results.

You can see the predefined shortcuts by choosing OmniWeb→Preferences→ Shortcuts. But since you're the kind of person who likes to do things Your Way, you'll be most interested in the + button at the bottom of the panel, which lets you add your *own* shortcuts.

When you click the +, OmniWeb creates a shortcut called "somewhere" and associates it with a URL of *http://www.somewhere.com*. To make it your own, simply double-click each field to rename the shortcut and enter the real URL, as shown in Figure 12-20.

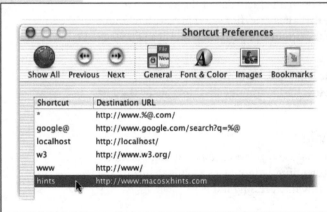

Figure 12-20:
In this example, the "hints" shortcut will let you type hints to load Macosxhints.com.

Tip: If you visit Apple's site every day, create an "A" shortcut (or "a"—OmniWeb distinguishes uppercase from lowercase shortcuts) for ultra-fast access.

12-45 Death to the Pop-Up Ads

Sure, everyone knows that ads help to pay for the rich goodness we call the Web. But there's no law stating that annoying and invasive advertising should be allowed to take over your browsing experience. Thankfully, OmniWeb makes it relatively easy to turn off some of the most annoying advertisements: the ones that appear in their own pop-up or pop-under windows (which appear in front of or behind your main window, respectively).

Choose OmniWeb→Preferences, and then click the Javascript icon. In the section marked "Scripts are allowed to open new windows," click "only in response to a link being clicked," as shown in Figure 12-21. OmniWeb now blocks any window that was not explicitly called when you clicked a link.

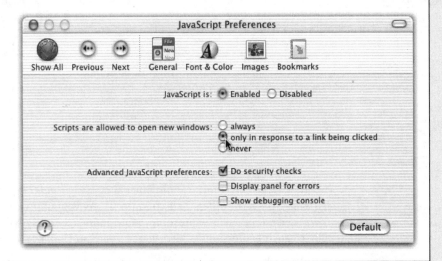

Figure 12-21:
When you activate "only in response to a link being clicked," you fend off most pop-up and pop-under ads.

12-46 Death to On-Page Advertisements

In addition to letting you turn off pop-up and pop-under ads, OmniWeb also can block ads directly on Web pages.

Choose OmniWeb→Preferences, and click the Privacy icon. Turn on the "Don't load anything from sites matching these expressions" checkbox (Figure 12-22). That simple step eliminates a large percentage of the ads you typically see.

Now, at the bottom of the Privacy panel, consider the two checkboxes next to "Don't automatically load images." If you turn on "whose sizes match the standard sizes for ads," OmniWeb compares each image on a Web page with standard advertising image sizes, as defined by the International Advertising Bureau. If an image matches, and it's hyperlinked, OmniWeb blocks it.

If you turn on "that aren't from the site which loads them," OmniWeb blocks images that pop up on the page *you're* trying to read that actually come from some *other* Web site (a common method for serving ads). Unfortunately, although this feature eliminates most ads, it also tends to eliminate many legitimate graphics, as many Web sites today are created by multiple servers.

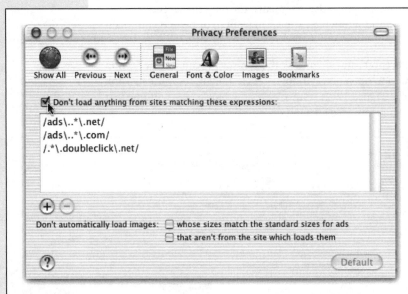

Figure 12-22:
OmniWeb includes three predefined filters (the weird-looking lines in the window) that check for anything coming from an "ads" directory on a .net or .com site, as well as a more general filter for anything coming from Doubleclick.net, one of the largest online advertising placement services.

Finally, you can even block certain other sites using *regular expressions* (Unix codes that create powerful filters and conditions). As you can see from the predefined filters, however, regular expressions could more accurately have been named "totally irregular expressions" unless you're a veteran Unix hound or Perl puppy.

OmniWeb's help page for the Privacy panel includes a primer on regular expressions. Choose Help→OmniWeb Help, and then click Customizing OmniWeb in the left-hand panel. When the customization page loads, click Privacy Preferences for a tutorial on building your own strings.

12-47   Just Saying No to Cascading Windows

When you surf using OmniWeb, you'll probably open multiple windows as you find sites of interest ("Whoa, kitchen appliances made of Lego? I gotta open a new page here!"). The program is set up so that each new window opens slightly below and to the right of the previous window, leading to the cascading effect shown in Figure 12-23.

Some people find cascades a useful way of organizing pages, and others find them an annoying waste of screen space. If you're in the latter camp, OmniWeb has a hidden preference for turning off the feature.

Quit OmniWeb, open Terminal, and type this:

```
defaults write com.omnigroup.OmniWeb OAWindowCascadeDisabled -
bool YES
```

Enter the command as one line, and make sure to insert a space between "OmniWeb" and "OAWindow." Press Enter, and then quit Terminal.

Now fire up OmniWeb, open a few windows, and discover that they sit right on top of each other.

If you ever decide you want the old behavior back, just quit OmniWeb, open Terminal, and repeat the command above, changing "YES" to "NO."

Tip: This nugget of information is buried in the OmniWeb release notes, but it can also be found in the Complete Defaults List, a document that offers a passel of settings you can change only in Terminal. To view the list, choose Help→OmniWeb Help, click Advanced Topics for System Administrators, and then click Complete Defaults List.

Figure 12-23:
When you open multiple OmniWeb windows, they cascade down the screen. If you'd rather they all pile up on top of one another like a rugby scrum, you can set that behavior using a hidden preference field.

12-48 Learning HTML Techniques

OmniWeb is great for learning the intricacies of HTML (the behind-the-scenes page description language of the Web). The next time you're facing a page that makes you ask yourself, "I wonder how they did that?" choose Browser→View in Source Editor. Click Reformat, which makes it easier to read.

OmniWeb color-codes the HTML tags, and, for the benefit of student Web designers, it flags HTML coding errors with various colored blocks over the text (unclosed tag pairs, illegal attributes, invalid <form> constructs, and so on).

Take your education a step further by making some changes in the HTML code, and then clicking Redisplay to see what's changed on the page. The beauty of OmniWeb is that it lets you edit the source HTML code, not just look at it. (Of course, you're just fooling around with a copy of the original page; you can't actually make changes to a page that's online.)

Mozilla, Netscape, and Camino

If you want something done right, you have to do it yourself. At least that's what thousands of volunteer programmers all over the Web—part of the volunteer *open-source* movement—were thinking when they decided to build their own Web browser.

What they came up with was a core Web browser "engine" proudly called Gecko. From there, various groups worked to create finished Web browsers that are today called things like Mozilla *(www.mozilla.org)*, Netscape *(www.netscape.com)*, and Camino *(www.mozilla.org/projects/camino)*.

The group responsible for Gecko, Mozilla.org, is a virtual company composed of programmers all over the world. Still, many of its team members are paid. For example, Netscape (the company) hired software engineers to create Netscape (the browser) by adapting Mozilla.

Netscape and Mozilla look pretty much the same. But the Netscape company tends to hang back and use more established versions of the software, so in general, the Mozilla browser is a revision or two ahead. For example, 1.2.1 is the current version of Mozilla, while Netscape 7.0.1 is based on Mozilla 1.0.2.

Camino, an open-source Cocoa Mac OS X browser, is a much newer cousin of Mozilla and Netscape. In fact, its 1.0 version isn't even finished yet. (Until March 3, 2003, Camino was known as Chimera.)

Although Camino uses the Gecko engine, it looks nothing like either Mozilla or Netscape. On the other hand, it's still in its infancy, and it's hard to say what it will look like when it's an adult browser.

Bear in mind that Camino is subject to growth spurts, so some of the following hints may not work on later versions of the software.

Hints for Gecko-Based Browsers

The following hints work on all three of the Gecko-based browsers.

12-49   Tabbed Browsing

One annoying aspect of Web surfing is that windows open and cover your screen as you go. Before you know it, you're awash in screen clutter, and when you want to find a particular window, you have to dig halfway to China.

Fortunately, all three Gecko-based browsers offer a feature called *tabbed browsing*, which has nothing to do with the Tab key. It's described in Figure 12-24.

Here are some tab browsing tips:

- If you Control-click any link, a contextual menu pops up; you can choose Open Link in New Tab.

- If you press ⌘-T, the cursor jumps to the address bar, where you can type a URL to open a new tab.

- If you press ⌘-W, your browser closes the active tab.

- Use Control-Page Up and Control-Page Down to switch between the tabs.

If you find yourself getting addicted to tabbed browsing, you can make the windows even easier to create. If you use Mozilla or Netscape, choose Mozilla→Preferences or Netscape→Preferences. In the Navigator list on the left, click Tabbed Browsing. You can modify four settings here as follows:

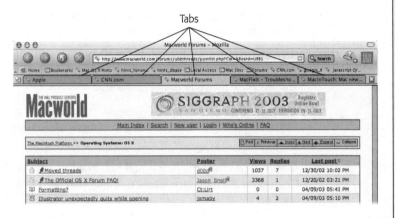

Figure 12-24:
In tabbed browsing, a browser displays all your Web pages in one window, using tabs at the top of the window to distinguish individual pages. Once you've tried browsing with tabbed pages, you'll never go back to the multiwindow system again.

- If you turn off "Hide the tab bar when only one tab is open," your browser always keeps the "tab row" visible at the top of the main window, even if it contains only one tab. That way, the tab row won't appear and disappear as you add and remove tabs, making the Web-page display area bounce up and down annoyingly.

- If you turn on "Command+click or Command+Return on links in a Web page," ⌘-clicking a URL forces it to open in a new tab instead of a new window. This option might be the most useful of the batch.

- If you also turn on "Load links in the background," then these new tabs open *behind* the active tab, waiting for your visit later on. This is a great setup, because it lets you read a primary article, flagging the links that look good as you go (by ⌘-clicking), without losing your place. You can always investigate the tabs you created later, when you're finished reading the main story.

- If you turn on "Command+Return in the Location bar," when you type a URL and then press ⌘-Enter, your browser opens that URL in a new tab. This behavior is a handy complement to the one that opens new tabs when you click links.

Note: The language of these options varies slightly according to the browser you're using.

If you use Camino, choose Camino→Preferences, then click the Navigation icon, and then click Tabbed Browsing. Here you can set ⌘-click to open either a new window or a new tab. And you can make all windows and tabs open in the background.

12-50   Tab Groups

The best thing about the Web is that you can find thousands of sites to satisfy your craving for news, information, and entertainment.

The worst thing about the Web is that you can find thousands of sites to satisfy your craving for news, information, and entertainment.

If you have a glut of like-minded sites that you typically search one after another—say eleven sites that analyze weather patterns in your town—a *tab group* can help you organize them for easier browsing.

A tab group is a collection of Web pages that opens in one window (each site gets its own tab), giving you fast access to a collection of related sites. All Gecko-based browsers let you create tab groups. Here's how:

Open a new browser window and load the first site you'd like to place in the group. Then press ⌘-T to open a new tab, and load the second site. Press ⌘-T again, and load the third site. Repeat until you've loaded each site on its own tab.

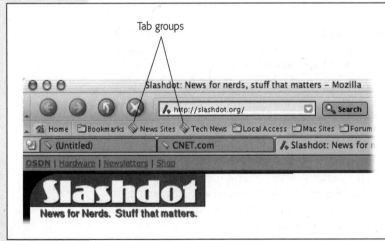

Tab groups

Figure 12-25:
"OS X Sites" and "News sites" have tab group icons, which look like a bunch of stacked pages or stacked ribbons (depending on your browser). Normal bookmarks look like a single piece of ribbon, or a folder.

Next, in Mozilla or Netscape, choose Bookmarks→Bookmark This Group of Tabs (in Camino, choose Bookmarks→Add Page to Bookmarks). In the dialog box that appears, enter a descriptive name for the tab group (*Weather Obsession*) and specify where, in your Bookmarks, you want it saved (in Camino, also turn on "Bookmark all tabs"). When you click OK, your browser creates the new tab group.

Make tab groups even handier by saving them in your personal toolbar folder, giving you one-click access. When you place a tab group in your personal toolbar, your browser gives it a different icon from a normal bookmark, as shown in Figure 12-25.

Tip: For the ultimate in power surfing, create multiple tab groups and open a new window (⌘-N) for each one. This arrangement gives you the best of both worlds—only two or three open windows (easy to manage), each containing ten or more subject-related, tabbed Web pages (lots of sites within easy reach). So instead of needing several dozen mouse clicks, you can use just three to open the 30 sites you normally visit each morning.

12-51 Internet Shortcuts

You can place ten or so of your most-often visited sites on your personal toolbar; putting folders on the toolbar greatly increases that number. But if you have enough favorite sites that you can't remember where you've filed some of them, *Internet shortcuts* can save you both frustration and mouse movement.

An Internet shortcut is a short name that you assign to any bookmark. When you type the short name into the address bar and press Enter, your browser loads the full URL for you. So instead of typing *http://www.nytimes.com* or mousing into your favorites subfolder News→World→Current, you could just type *nyt* and press Enter to call up the *New York Times* site.

In all three browsers, you must first bookmark any page you want to shortcut. Once you've done that, open the bookmark management window (in Netscape and Mozilla, choose Bookmarks→Manage Bookmarks; in Camino, choose Bookmarks→Manage Bookmarks in Sidebar, or click the Sidebar icon in the toolbar). In this window, highlight the URL you want to shortcut, Control-click it, and then choose Properties (Netscape and Mozilla) or Get Info (Camino) from the contextual menu.

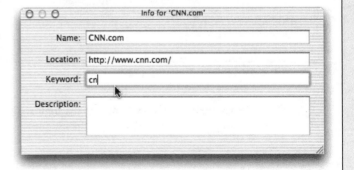

Figure 12-26:
Here, cn will become the shortcut for CNN.com. The typing you save could be your own, even though you're cutting out what little exercise you once got at the computer.

The dialog box that opens is slightly different in each browser, but pretty straight-forward in all of them. Figure 12-26 shows the dialog box as it appears in Camino; in all three browsers, the box you want to fill in is labeled Keyword. Type the letter or combination of letters that you'd like to use as a shortcut (Camino requires two-letter keywords; Netscape and Mozilla both work fine with one letter), and then close the dialog box.

No more hunting through subfolders to click a URL—from now on, you need to type only your shortcut and press Enter to load your favorite page.

How you remember the shortcuts is another matter entirely. The classic solution: Write them down on a piece of paper that you stash under your keyboard.

12-52 Killing Pop-Ups and Pop-Unders

Pop-up and pop-under ads can surf you to distraction. As hint 12-45 explained, it's easy enough to block them when you use OmniWeb. This hint shows you how to do so for the Gecko-based browsers.

All three browsers have different methods of accomplishing the same basic task, as the dialog boxes in Figure 12-27 illustrate.

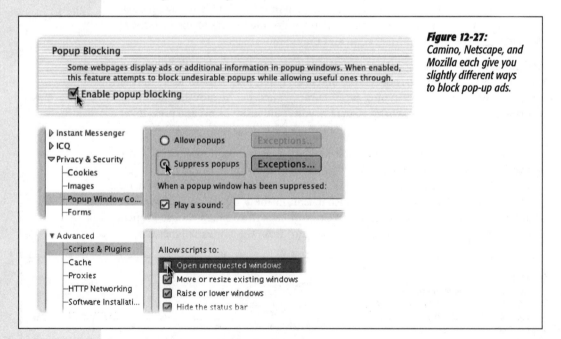

Figure 12-27:
Camino, Netscape, and Mozilla each give you slightly different ways to block pop-up ads.

Here's the lowdown on each:

- **Camino.** Camino attempts to distinguish pop-up boxes that you *want* to see (like login boxes or catalog pages) from pop-up boxes you don't want (ads).

To turn on this feature, choose Camino→Preferences and then click Web Features. In the section called Popup Blocking, turn on "Enable popup blocking" (if it's not already on). Close the panel and relish your ad-free Web world.

- **Netscape.** Netscape doesn't try to tell good pop-ups from bad; it just squashes all windows that you haven't expressly requested by clicking a link.

  To turn on this feature, choose Netscape→Preferences, click the Privacy & Security section, and then click Popup Window. Turn on "Suppress popups" to prevent unrequested windows from appearing.

Tip: If your bank or favorite online store uses pop-ups for logins or other important information, click Exceptions and add its address to the list.

Netscape can also play a sound and/or display an icon in the status bar when it blocks a pop-up ad (the setting is in the Popup Window panel). This feature is useful when you hit a site that displays important information in a pop-up box (a login window, for example), and you can't open it. The sound or icon tells you what's going on—and at other times, gives you the rosy, smug feeling of knowing that you've just smushed your foot into some slimy advertiser's face.

- **Mozilla.** Mozilla's ad blocking works much like Netscape's.

  Choose Mozilla→Preferences. On the left-hand side of the panel, click the triangle next to Privacy and Security, and then click the Popup Windows section. Turn on "Suppress popups" to prevent all pop-up windows from appearing. Once again, if some sites you visit legitimately display pop-ups, click Exceptions to add their addresses.

12-53 Tabbing Around a Page

When you're filling out an online form, pressing the Tab key moves your insertion point from one text input field to the next, skipping over things like pop-up menus and radio buttons. If you'd rather Tab to those screen elements, too—so that you can use the keyboard to complete an entire form—you have only to modify a preference file.

To do so, start by quitting the browser.

You want to modify a file called "user.js," which holds settings that you can't change through the standard preference panels. This file lives in your account's browser profile folder.

- If you use **Netscape or Mozilla,** open Home→Library→Mozilla→Profiles→ *profile_name*→*mtxjr7zs*.slt folder. "Profile_name" is the name you created when you first ran the browser. (As for that randomly named *.slt* folder, its name is random; yours probably isn't named mtxjr7zs.slt, but something equally random.)

• If you use **Camino**, open the Home→Library→Application Support→ Chimera→Default folder.

If you find "user.js" in this folder, drag it onto the TextEdit icon (see page 4) to open it.

If not, open a new, blank TextEdit document.

Either way, type this at the end of the document:

```
user_pref("accessibility.tabfocus", 1) ;
```

See the final 1 inside the parenthesis? That's Mozilla code for, "Tab takes me only to text boxes." But you can change this number to:

• 7 if you want to tab your way to text boxes, other form elements (like pop-up menus and checkboxes), and links.

• 3 if you want to tab only to text controls and form elements.

Save your changes. (If you created a new file, save it into the *profile_name* folder described above, giving it the name *user.js*.)

You're ready to try out your newly enhanced browser.

Note: To restore the original setting, repeat the steps above but change that number back to a 1.

Mozilla and Netscape Hints

The following hints work in both Mozilla and Netscape but not in Camino.

12-54 Jumping to Your Home Page

To get from your current Web page to your home page—your preferred startup page—press ⌘-Home (if your keyboard has a Home key, that is). (You specify your favorite startup page by choosing Mozilla→Preferences→Navigator or Netscape→ Preferences→Navigator.)

This keyboard shortcut doesn't appear in the menu Go→Home, but it works fine in both Mozilla and Netscape.

12-55 Filling Out Forms

Both Mozilla and Netscape let you save information for forms that you fill out frequently, making future completion of the same form a snap. The FTD flower site, for example, makes you re-enter your name, address, and other information every darned time you visit it. Ditto with sites whose "Email this page" links request your name and email address every time you click it. But now you can fight back with software.

The next time you fill out the form manually, just choose Edit→Save Form Info to capture all your info. Now the *next* time you visit the form, you can choose Edit→Fill In Form to complete the whole thing.

But what if you don't want the whole form to fill in with your saved info? Maybe, for example, you want to put in your name and email address but not your complete address.

The solution is surprisingly easy. Rather than choosing Edit→Fill In Form, click inside (or Tab into) each field that you'd like to fill in with your saved value, and then double-click inside it. The rest remain blank, so you can single-click inside them to fill them with any nonsense you like.

Tip: On shortish forms, you may also find that a series of three or four double-clicks is faster than moving the mouse up to choose Edit→Fill in Form.

12-56   Browser Interior Decoration

You can change the look of Mozilla and Netscape by changing their *skins* or *themes* (canned design schemes). If you have a customization compulsion, this feature is not to be missed.

Mozilla comes with two skins: Modern and Classic (the preset choice). Modern is the new look for Mozilla; Classic exhibits Mac OS X–like pinstripes. Figure 12-28 shows what each skin looks like and explains how to change them.

Figure 12-28:
Mozilla's Modern (top) and Classic themes (bottom). To switch skins, choose Mozilla →Preferences, expand Appearances, and then click Themes. Click a theme; restart the program.

You can also download more skins. To install them, choose Mozilla→Preferences, click the triangle next to Appearances, and then click Themes. At the bottom of the pane is the link to Get More Themes. If you click it, Mozilla opens a Web page that, in turn, offers two sites for installing themes.

The two sites offer many of the same skins, but if you want to make sure you're familiar with every possible choice, visit them both. As Figure 12-29 shows, you can get a variety of different looks, ranging from elegant to oddball.

On both sites, if you click a theme's link ("Pimpzilla," for example), you get a window that previews the skin (in this case, lots of leopard print) and an option to install it.

Tip: Themes are version specific. If you're running Mozilla 1.3, and Pimpzilla is only available for 1.2.1, you're out of luck. Check the version key find out if a theme will work with your version of Mozilla or Netscape.

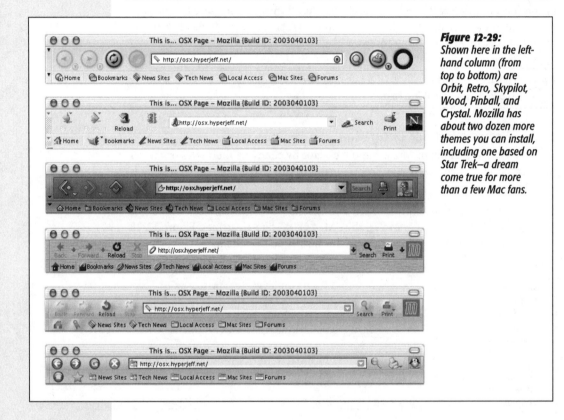

Figure 12-29:
Shown here in the left-hand column (from top to bottom) are Orbit, Retro, Skypilot, Wood, Pinball, and Crystal. Mozilla has about two dozen more themes you can install, including one based on Star Trek—a dream come true for more than a few Mac fans.

Once you've chosen a compatible and pleasing theme, simply click Install, watch the twirly circle come and go, and then quit and restart your browser. Shazzam! It's funkadelic.

12-57   Mouse Magic

Imagine if you could open new windows, switch tabs, scroll up and down, reload pages, minimize a window, and more, all just by *moving* the mouse in specified directions. (Ever try dragging your stylus straight up a Palm organizer's face to summon the Graffiti cheat sheet? Same idea.)

Mouse Gestures is an add-on that provides just such features for Netscape and Mozilla. Once you've installed it, you can maneuver with gestures like these:

• Drag the mouse straight up the page to open a new tab.

• Drag up-right or up-left to cycle between open tabs.

• Drag a Z shape to close a current tab or window.

Mouse Gestures includes roughly 30 defined actions, and you can find a complete list at *http://optimoz.mozdev.org/gestures*.

To install Mouse Gestures, download it from the same Web site. To make it "take," quit and restart your browser. (Cocoa Gestures, a program described in Chapter 14, adds similar features to Camino.)

You can customize the gestures by choosing Mozilla/Netscape→Preferences, clicking the triangle next to Advanced, and then clicking Mouse Gestures to reach the panel shown in Figure 12-30.

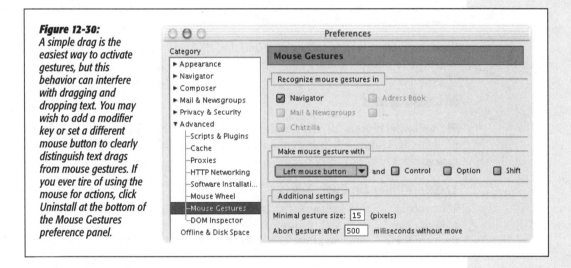

Figure 12-30:
A simple drag is the easiest way to activate gestures, but this behavior can interfere with dragging and dropping text. You may wish to add a modifier key or set a different mouse button to clearly distinguish text drags from mouse gestures. If you ever tire of using the mouse for actions, click Uninstall at the bottom of the Mouse Gestures preference panel.

12-58   Using an External Mail Program

If you use Mozilla or Netscape as a browser, you probably experience a small fit of annoyance whenever you click a Send Email (*mailto:*) link, and your browser launches its own mail program instead of the one you've specified in System Preferences→Internet→Email. (The MailTo command opens a blank email message, addressed to whomever is specified in the link.)

You can, of course, send a message from the browser's own mail program. But it won't have any of your settings (special fonts, signature, and so on), and it won't file itself in your regular mail program's Sent folder.

You can change your browser's behavior—and save some Advil over the course of your lifetime—by editing one simple text file.

Quit Mozilla or Netscape. The file you want to edit is in your Home→Library→ Mozilla/Netscape→Profiles→*profile_name*→*mtxjr7zs*.slt folder. (As noted earlier in this chapter, for *profile_name*, you'll see whatever name you provided to Mozilla or Netscape the first time you ran the program; it may simply be "default." And *mtxjr7zs*.slt is a folder named with random characters followed by .slt—yours may not be called exactly "mtxjr7zs.slt.")

- If you see a file there called *user.js*, you're home free. Drag it onto the TextEdit icon to open it (page 4). Type a new line that says (complete with semicolon): *user_pref("network.protocol-handler.external.mailto", true);*

Save your changes.

- If you don't see a user.js file, open TextEdit. In a new blank document, type that magic code: *user_pref("network.protocol-handler.external.mailto", true);*

  Choose File→Save. Name the file *user.js* and save it into your Home→Library→ Mozilla/Netscape→Profiles→*profile_name*→*mtxjr7zs*.slt folder.

When you restart your browser, you'll find that clicking a MailTo link now launches your regular mail program.

Mozilla Hints

The following hints work only for Mozilla, not Netscape or Camino. (Still, all three products are continually being enhanced. Some of the following may work on future versions of the other two browsers.)

12-59   Killing On-Page Ads

You probably want to see most of the pictures on the Web pages you visit. But a few graphics may be irrelevant or worse (who needs a highly annoying flashing advertisement for the latest and greatest offshore casino?). Mozilla offers two methods for managing Web pics.

The preference panel method

Choose Mozilla→Preferences, click the triangle next to Privacy & Security, and then click Images. Under Image Acceptance Policy, you can specify how Mozilla handles graphics.

The program comes set to "Accept all images," but you can set it to "Do not load any images," or to "Accept images that come from the originating server only." If you turn on the last option, Mozilla blocks graphics from Web sites other than the one you're visiting (a common method for serving ads). Alas, this feature may also block a few legitimate graphics.

You can also control those infuriating animated GIF graphics—looping animations. You can stifle them completely, or specify that you want them to play only once, so that you can admire the designer's artistic prowess, and then stop.

The contextual menu method

The second method of controlling on-page images is through a contextual menu. If you Control-click any graphic, you can choose a menu option to Block Images from this Server, as in Figure 12-31.

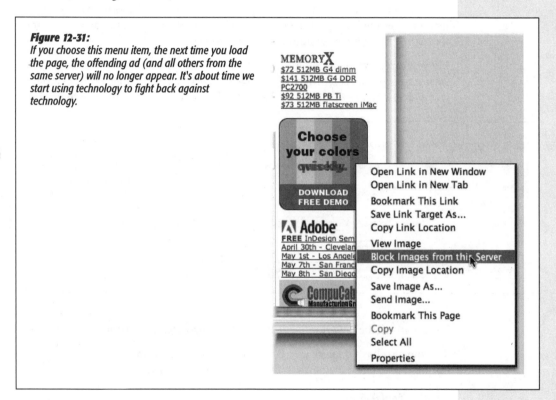

Figure 12-31:
If you choose this menu item, the next time you load the page, the offending ad (and all others from the same server) will no longer appear. It's about time we start using technology to fight back against technology.

One you've chosen the menu option, Mozilla blocks *any* graphics from the server that delivered that picture.

If you ever wish to allow pictures from the blocked server, you have two choices. You can Control-click a spot that should hold an image from that server; if there's a blocked picture there, choose Unblock Images from this Server.

A much more reliable method, however, is to choose Mozilla→Preferences, click the triangle next to Privacy & Security, and then click Images. In that panel, click Manage Image Permissions, which opens a window displaying all the servers you've blocked; highlight any you want to restore, and click Remove Site.

Tip: This technique doesn't work on Flash-based ads (an especially annoying type of flashing, jittering, noisy animation). Still, you can even stifle those, if you're willing to read a long article and type in some code. The full story, complete with reader comments, embellishments, and more, awaits at this Web page: *www.macosxhints.com/article.php?story=20021127061854547*

12-60   Installing a True Aqua Theme

Although the Classic theme for Mozilla looks a lot like Aqua (the overarching Mac OS X design scheme), it's not a true Aqua interface. Mozilla draws its own interfaces instead of letting Mac OS X handle the job. The disadvantage of this arrangement is that Mozilla draws new windows relatively slowly.

But you can download the "Pinstripe" theme for Mozilla that looks similar to Classic but uses the speedier Mac OS X Appearance Manager to draw the background and widgets. Figure 12-32 shows the subtle differences between the two themes.

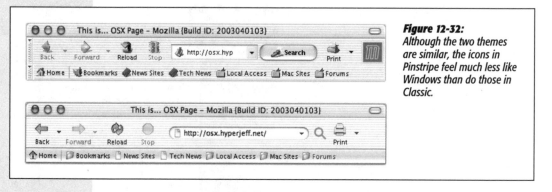

Figure 12-32:
Although the two themes are similar, the icons in Pinstripe feel much less like Windows than do those in Classic.

You can install the Pinstripe theme from *http://kmgerich.com/pinstripe/pinstripe.html*.

The site also has Graphite and Blue versions available to match either of the two standard Mac OS X themes; install either or both as you see fit.

12-61   MultiZilla

If you like the tabbed browsing feature in Mozilla (hint 12-49), you're gonna love the open-source MultiZilla add-on. Available at *http://multizilla.mozdev.org*, MultiZilla lets you do a world of cool things in tabbed browsing, including:

• Renaming tabs.

• Specifying a group of tabs to open when you launch your browser.

• Moving the tab bar to the bottom of the browser window.

• Hiding the tab bar completely.

• Copying tabs by dragging them to empty locations on the tab bar.

- Learning the status of any tab just by glancing at the color of the icon on the tab's left edge—a yellow dot means the page is opening, a red dot means the page is loading, and a green dot means the page is ready.

When you install it, MultiZilla places a toolbar just under your Favorites bar. The new toolbar includes a menu for Mozilla's preference settings, which you can otherwise reach only by choosing Mozilla→Preferences and then clicking the specific setting you want to change. Figure 12-33 shows this menu in action.

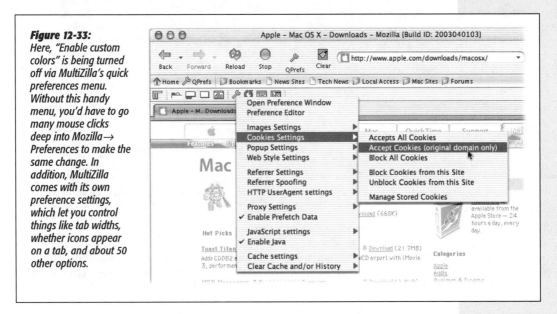

Figure 12-33:
Here, "Enable custom colors" is being turned off via MultiZilla's quick preferences menu. Without this handy menu, you'd have to go many mouse clicks deep into Mozilla→Preferences to make the same change. In addition, MultiZilla comes with its own preference settings, which let you control things like tab widths, whether icons appear on a tab, and about 50 other options.

MultiZilla also adds a small menu at the right side of the toolbar with buttons that let you close the current tab, all tabs other than the current tab, or all tabs.

A cautionary note: MultiZilla has no uninstaller. Furthermore, note that you must delete your Home→Library→Mozilla folder before you install MultiZilla. So before you rush through the installation process, make a backup copy of your Home→Library→Mozilla folder, so that you can reinstate it if you decide to return to your pre-MultiZilla days.

Note: Mouse Gestures (see hint 12-56) and MultiZilla don't play nicely together. You have to choose one or the other.

12-62   MultiZilla and Google

Once you have MultiZilla up and running, consider adding the GoogleBox Widget. This one-line toolbar sits on the MultiZilla bar, and lets you search Google (even advanced and specialized searches) without first jumping to the Google Web site.

Complete instructions for downloading and installing it are at *http://multizilla. mozdev.org/features/googlebox.html.*

As Figure 12-34 shows, the GoogleBox Widget provides a box for entering searches and a pull-down menu for choosing Google options.

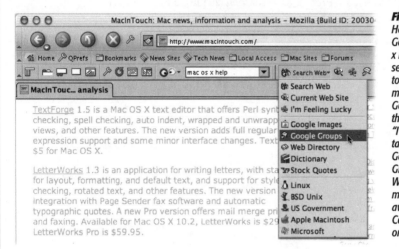

Figure 12-34:
Here, you're searching Google groups for "mac os x help." If you enter a search and click the buttons to the right of the pop-up menu, you search specific Google sites. In this figure they are, from left to right: "I'm Feeling Lucky" (which takes you to the top page Google returns), Google Groups, and the Google Web Directory. You can modify the assortment of available buttons by Control-clicking anywhere on the GoogleBox toolbar.

In the unlikely event that you ever tire of the GoogleBox, you can uninstall it by clicking the Google eyeball icon to the left of the search box and then selecting Uninstall.

A Camino-Only Hint

12-63 Copying Tabs

If you have a bunch of tabs going in Camino, you can do-si-do them around as follows:

- If you drag an existing tab to the very edge of the tab bar (the empty part), using the small icon next to its name as a handle, you create a new tab of the same site, as in Figure 12-35.

Figure 12-35:
Dragging the Apple tab to an empty spot (far left) creates a new tab for the same site. It's now very easy to branch off to a second page of that site.

- If you drag one tab over another, you overwrite the second one and create a copy of the first.

A Camino-Only Hint

- If you drag a link from a Web page to the empty edge of the tab bar, you create a new tab that opens the URL you just dragged into place.

GEM IN THE ROUGH

Path Notation

Sometimes a Unix tentacle pokes through the user-friendly Aqua interface. Every now and then, you find a place where you can use Unix shortcuts instead of the mouse—including many of the hints in this book that direct you to use *path notation*.

One classic example is the Go→Go to Folder command (Shift-⌘-G). It brings up a simple "Go to the folder:" box.

The purpose of this box is to let you jump to a certain folder on your Mac directly by typing its Unix *folder path*.

For example, if you want to see what's in the Documents folder of your Home folder, you could choose Go→Go to Folder, type this:

```
/Users/mjones/Documents
```

Then click Go or press Return. (In this example, of course, *mjones* is your short account name.)

In other words, you're telling the Mac to open the Users folder in your main hard drive window, then your Home folder inside that, and then the Documents folder inside *that*. Each slash means, "and then open." (Leaving off the name of your hard drive is optional.) When you press Enter, the folder you specified pops open immediately.

Of course, if you really wanted to jump to your Documents folder, you'd be wasting your time by typing all that. Unix (and therefore Mac OS X) offers a handy shortcut that means, "home folder." It's the tilde character (~) at the

upper-left corner of your keyboard.

To see what's in your Home folder, then, you could type just that ~ symbol into the Go To box and then press Return. Or you could add some slashes to it to specify a folder inside your Home folder, like this:

```
~/Documents
```

You can even jump to someone *else's* Home folder by typing a name after the symbol, like this:

```
~chris
```

If you get into this sort of thing, here's another shortcut worth noting: If you type nothing but a slash (/) and then press Return, you jump immediately to the Computer window, which provides an overview of all your disks, plus a Network icon.

But the Go to Folder trick *really* turns into a high-octane time-saver if you use *tab completion.* Here's how it works: After each slash, you can type only enough letters of a folder's name to give Mac OS X the idea—*de* instead of *desktop,* for example—and then press the Tab key. Mac OS X instantly and automatically fills in the rest of the folder's name.

For example, instead of typing */applications/Microsoft Office X/clipart/standard,* you could type nothing more than */ap/mi/cl/st,* remembering to press Tab after each pair of letters.

Other Applications

S ure, Mac OS X comes with a slew of iApps and utilities. But it wouldn't be a very impressive operating system if it didn't also run a world of programs from other companies—Microsoft Office, Photoshop, and so on.

This chapter's hints let you get the most out of BBEdit, Microsoft Office, Photoshop or Photoshop Elements, Snapz Pro X, and so on. These tend to be advanced programs, so these tips tend to be for advanced Mac users.

BBEdit

BBEdit (or its sibling BBEdit Lite) is a text editor that's beloved by power users, Web designers, and programmers. It's designed to handle a multitude of projects, from HTML Web pages to computer coding in PHP, Java, and other languages.

13-1   Editing System Files

If you try to edit one of Mac OS X's own system files (like httpd.conf, the settings file for the Apache Web server), you'll quickly discover that it's not so easy. Mac OS X is very protective of the files that make it up, and generally doesn't permit ordinary humans to make changes to them.

You can work around this blockade in any of three ways. First, if you know Unix, you could open Terminal (page 5) and use the *sudo* command. Second, in the Finder, you could open a Get Info window for the file, change the ownership to yourself (using the Ownership & Permissions controls), edit the file using your favorite text editor, and then restore ownership to *root* when you're done.

Or you could use BBEdit, which offers a third, and much easier, solution.

System files are typically hidden, so the first thing you have to do is *find* the file you want to edit. (The following instructions assume that you, the power user, know where your Mac keeps desired files.) Open BBEdit, and choose File→Open Hidden. In the dialog box that opens, enter the full path to a hidden folder, as shown in Figure 13-1.

When you press Enter, BBEdit opens the hidden folder in the top portion of the dialog box, showing all its hidden files.

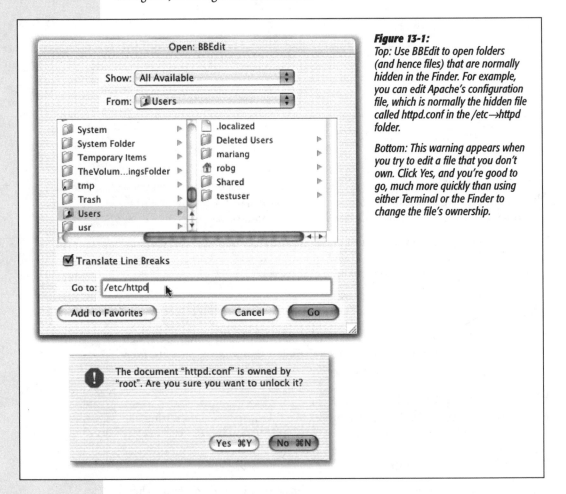

Figure 13-1:
Top: Use BBEdit to open folders (and hence files) that are normally hidden in the Finder. For example, you can edit Apache's configuration file, which is normally the hidden file called httpd.conf in the /etc→httpd folder.

Bottom: This warning appears when you try to edit a file that you don't own. Click Yes, and you're good to go, much more quickly than using either Terminal or the Finder to change the file's ownership.

Pick a file to edit by double-clicking it. When you start editing, the warning box shown in Figure 13-1 at bottom may appear.

Use your newfound power with care. If you improperly edit a system file, you can damage your Web server, FTP server, or even Mac OS X itself.

13-2 Browsing Mac OS X Package Files

As described on page 3, most Mac OS X programs come in cleverly disguised folders called *bundles* or *packages,* which have one icon but actually contain all kinds of goodies, including graphics, sounds, and settings.

In the Finder, if you Control-click a package and then choose Show Package Contents, you can view the files and folders within a bundle.

You can snoop around even more easily with BBEdit. Just drag any Mac OS X bundled program (Mail, TextEdit, OmniWeb, and so on) onto BBEdit's Dock or Finder icon. As Figure 13-2 shows, BBEdit's disk browser opens, showing you the contents of that bundle.

Note: It's wise to create a backup of any bundle you plan to edit.

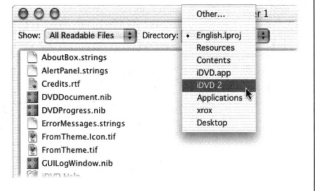

Figure 13-2:
A simple double-click opens any file that BBEdit is capable of editing. The pop-up menu shows the path to the currently displayed folder (xrox→Applications→iDVD2 bundle→iDVD.app→Contents).

13-3 Listing Files I

The previous hint explained how to use BBEdit to browse program bundles. But what if you just want a list of all the files within a bundle—say, to find an image or sound you want to borrow for another project?

Instead of dragging the bundle onto BBEdit's Dock or Finder icon, drag it into a new, empty BBEdit document. Depending on the size of the bundle, BBEdit thinks for a few seconds and then shows something similar to Figure 13-3.

Tip: Before you drag a program icon into BBEdit, turn on line numbering, which makes it much easier to count the total number of files and navigate your way about the list. Choose Tools→Add Line Numbers.

13-4 Listing Files II

An even more useful variation on the previous hint lets you create a printable list of the entire contents of a folder or hard drive. This is handy if, for example, you need a hard copy for archival purposes (maybe you're a former U.S. president, and you're expecting your files to be incorporated into a biography in 20 or 40 years).

If you drag a folder or hard drive icon into a new BBEdit document window, the program goes to work—sometimes for quite a while—and eventually displays all the files and folders inside.

Note: This process can take *forever*, especially if the folder or hard drive you're investigating includes Mac OS X itself; indeed, you could wind up with a list of more than 100,000 files. Buy stock in toner and paper companies before you print it out.

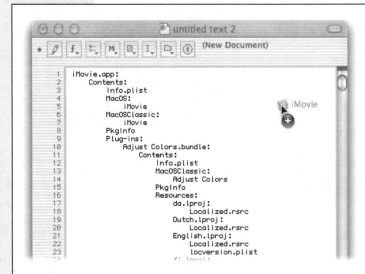

Figure 13-3:
To create a list of all the files within a bundle, including hidden files, just drag the program icon into an open BBEdit document window. Here, iMovie has been dragged into the window, resulting in a list of over 7,000 files, each on its own line.

13-5   Keyboard Scrolling

If you have a document that is wider or longer than the BBEdit window, keyboard combos are the quickest way to navigate.

- Option-up/down arrow scrolls up or down a full page.

- ⌘-up/down arrow jumps to the beginning or end of your document.

- ⌘-left/right arrow take you to the beginning/end of the current line.

13-6   Scroll Bar Acceleration

When you click one of the scroll bar arrows, BBEdit scrolls down a line at a time, as you would expect.

If you press ⌘ while clicking, the scrolling speed increases. And if you press Option, you scroll faster still.

But if you press ⌘ *and* Option, you hit fourth gear and fly through the document.

DragThing

DragThing is a program designed to help organize and launch your most-used programs (see Figure 13-4). This little shareware gem is one of the first downloads by efficiency-nut power-users.

Note: The following five hints all use AppleScript to change various hidden settings within DragThing. To implement these hints, open the Script Editor (in Applications→AppleScript), type in the script for a given hint (taking care to press Enter at the end of each line), and then click Run. You can reverse the effect of any hint by clicking Run again.

Figure 13-4:
DragThing is something like Apple's Dock, but it allows you to create many docks, each with a number of additional features, including full AppleScript capability, hot keys, and tabs.

13-7   Nix the Fades

When you hide a dock (using Scripts→Dock→Hide Dock or Hide All Docks) or show a dock (using Scripts→Dock→Show All Docks), the dock slowly fades out of or into sight. If you'd like less drama and rather it just blinked on and off, type and run the following script in Script Editor:

```
tell application "DragThing"
  set x to do not use fading
  set do not use fading to not x
end tell
```

13-8   Nix the Zoom Rectangle

When you open programs from a DragThing dock, they open with the usual zooming-rectangle animation. (An outline of a rectangle grows until the program's window fills the screen.)

If you find this feature annoying, this script turns it off:

```
tell application "DragThing"
  set x to do not use zoom rects
  set do not use zoom rects to not x
end tell
```

Canning the zoom animation doesn't actually make the programs open any faster—just a little less irritating.

13-9 Keeping the Dock Translucent

A DragThing dock is translucent until you mouse over it, at which point it becomes opaque, making it easier to see what you're doing.

DragThing docks can take advantage of Mac OS X's transparency features. To see this effect, choose Edit→Dock Options, click the Visibility tab, and turn on "Use translucency." From now on, the dock will be see-through until you mouse over it, at which point it becomes opaque so you can see the icons on it.

But what if you, a transparency fan, would prefer your dock to be see-through *all the time?* Use this script:

```
tell application "DragThing"
  set x to do not make docks opaque on mouseover
  set do not make docks opaque on mouseover to not x
end tell
```

13-10 Active-Program Hack

If you want DragThing to tell you which programs on its dock are actually open, it's only too happy to display a microscopic green dot on the corresponding icons (Figure 13-5, top). To make it so, open DragThing Preferences, click the Switching tab, and turn on "Highlight running applications in other docks."

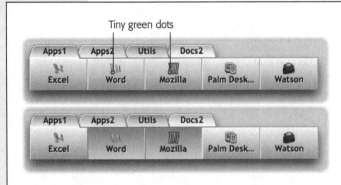

Tiny green dots

Figure 13-5:
Top: DragThing's new way of telling you a program is active: a barely perceptible green dot in the program's dock cell. Here, Word and Mozilla are active. Bottom: DragThing used to tell you a program was active by darkening its whole dock cell.

Older versions of DragThing indicated that a program was active by darkening its dock cell (bottom, Figure 13-5)—a less subtle, and some would say more useful, visual cue. Old-timers pining for the nostalgia of the old indicator need only run this AppleScript:

```
tell application "DragThing"
  set x to do not use running app badge
  set do not use running app badge to not x
end tell
```

13-11   Font Sizes for Dock Labels

Using its Preferences command, you can specify the size of the type that DragThing uses for text labels on a dock. But its pop-up menu of sizes lists only a few type sizes.

If you'd like to try a font size you don't see, use this script:

```
tell application "DragThing"
  set use Appearance font to false
set dock font size to 13
end tell
```

Of course, replace *13* with the specific font size you want to use. (The normal range is about 7 to 24.)

13-12   The DragThing Easter Egg

If you think Easter eggs are pink and yellow ovals that appear in drugstores in the spring, you're *so* last year. In the digital age, Easter eggs are hidden program features, planted in software by the programmers, that do something cool and fun. To see a useless but visually interesting Easter egg in DragThing, choose DragThing→About DragThing and leave the About box open. After about ten seconds, the image starts to get woozy and liquid.

Even better, if you switch to another program while you've got the box open, the box's blue background fades to gray. When you return to DragThing, the gray fades back to blue. Programmers have all the fun, don't they?

Microsoft Office X

Microsoft Office X is a leading software package for Mac OS X. It includes Word, Excel, PowerPoint, and Entourage (an email/calendar/address book program), providing just about everything you need to do personal or business work on a Mac.

13-13   Long File Names

Although Mac OS X lets you use up to 255 characters in file names, Office X programs are more limited.

If you open a document that has more than 31 characters (the limit in Mac OS 9 programs), edit it, and save it, Office retains the long file name. But if you create a new document, you can't give a name with more than 31 characters.

As it turns out, Office can *handle* long file names—it just can't *create* them. If you rename a document in the Finder, giving it a long file name, Office will open that document and respect its name without batting an eye.

13-14   The Treachery of Damaged Fonts

Office programs are particularly vulnerable to damaged fonts. Even when a particular font plays nicely with other programs, it may cause Office applications to crash when you open them.

Finding a corrupted font is more an art than a science. The easiest way to start is by moving all of your Mac OS 9 fonts (they're in System Folder→Fonts) and then re-launching the Office program you want to use. (Why start here? Because Mac OS X builds its font menus from several sources, starting with the fonts in your Mac OS 9 folder.)

If moving the Mac OS 9 fonts solved your problem, then you know that one of them was the cause. Unfortunately, you won't know which one.

To identify the bad font, you can use a program like Font Doctor *(www.morrison softdesign.com/fd_mac.html)* or FontAgentPro *(www.insidersoftware.com/products/fontagentpro)*. Or just put a few fonts at a time back into the System Folder→Fonts folder, restarting your Office program each time, until you pin down the culprit.

If the Mac OS 9 Fonts folder doesn't seem to be the problem, then you may have an issue with one of Mac OS X's own Fonts folders. Unfortunately, there are *three* of them:

- Your Home→Library→Fonts folder. This is your own personal stash.

- The Library→Fonts folder. These are fonts added by the Mac's administrators (page 11).

- The System→Library→Fonts folder. These are Apple's fonts, the one Mac OS X requires to run.

Unfortunately, trying to ferret out a bad font from these folders using trial and error is likely to be a real trial, fraught with errors. You may not be able to remove them for testing, for example. In this case, your best bet is to let Font Doctor or FontAgentPro turn them off and on for your testing pleasure.

13-15 Zooming Word Documents

If your mouse has a scroll wheel, you can use it to zoom in or out on an open document. Press Control and scroll up to zoom in; press Control and scroll down to zoom out. Sure beats mousing up to the Zoom pop-up menu.

13-16 Listing Word's Keyboard Shortcuts

Word contains a huge number of keyboard shortcuts, many of which require a combination of keys, and some of which are really esoteric (Toggle Master Subdocs, anyone?). Fortunately, Word contains a *macro* (a preprogrammed process) that creates a new document listing all the program's keyboard shortcuts.

Choose Tools→Macro→Macros. Near the bottom of the Macros dialog box is a pop-up menu labeled "Macros in"; click it and choose "Word commands." In the new list of macros that appears, scroll down to List Commands, highlight it, and then click Run (Figure 13-6).

A dialog box appears, asking what type of list you'd like to create; leave it set to "Current menu and keyboard settings" to get a list of just those commands that have keyboard shortcuts. When you click OK, Word generates a new document with a chart of all its keyboard shortcuts.

Figure 13-6:
This special Word macro, which you can find by choosing Tools→Macro→Macros, generates a list of all Word keyboard shortcuts in a new document. Just highlight the List Commands macro and click Run.

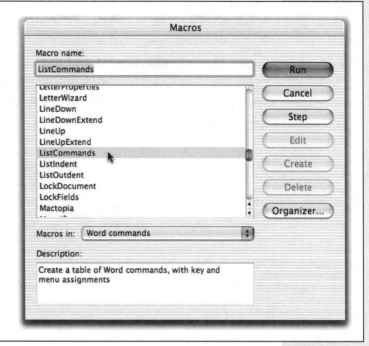

13-17   Speeding Up Scrolling

On not-quite-state-of-the-art Macs, Word documents sometimes scroll at the speed of turtles. In mud. On Benadryl.

You can speed things up by turning off *Quartz Text Smoothing*, a Mac OS X feature that smoothes onscreen fonts by softening their edges. Here's how:

In Word, choose Word→Preferences, and then in the list that appears on the left, click General. Turn off the "Enable Quartz text smoothing" checkbox, and then close the window. As Figure 13-7 shows, your text now looks a bit different, but it remains highly readable.

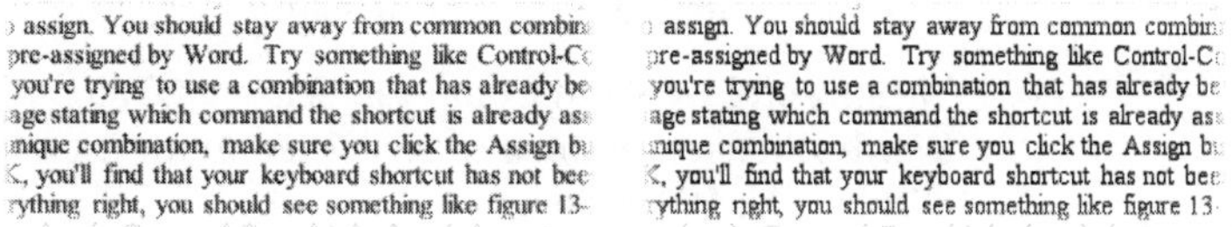

Figure 13-7:
A Word document with Smoothing turned on (left) and off (right). They scroll much differently.

) assign. You should stay away from common combin: pre-assigned by Word. Try something like Control-C(you're trying to use a combination that has already be age stating which command the shortcut is already as: unique combination, make sure you click the Assign b(<, you'll find that your keyboard shortcut has not bee rything right, you should see something like figure 13-	) assign. You should stay away from common combin: pre-assigned by Word. Try something like Control-C(you're trying to use a combination that has already be age stating which command the shortcut is already as: unique combination, make sure you click the Assign b(<, you'll find that your keyboard shortcut has not bee rything right, you should see something like figure 13

You can use this same trick to speed up scrolling in Excel and PowerPoint, too. In Excel, the checkbox is in Excel→Preferences→View. In PowerPoint, choose PowerPoint→Preferences, and then click the View tab.

A telling example from Mac os x hints: jaguar edition Labs: Scrolling one line at a time, a nine-page text document on a 500 megahertz iBook required nearly 30 seconds to scroll from top to bottom with Quartz rendering turned on. With Quartz rendering turned off, the scroll time dropped to only 12 seconds.

13-18   The Live Word Count Problem

Word's Live Word Count feature can slow down Word in a big document on a slow Mac, too. That's the counter shown in Figure 13-8.

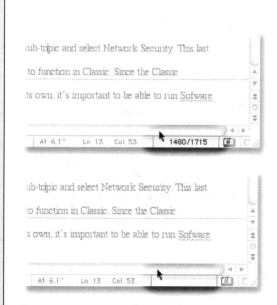

Figure 13-8:
Left: The Live Word Count feature–a Macintosh-version exclusive–displays the total number of words in a document and the number up to where the insertion point is.

Right: When Live Word Count is turned off, this section of the status bar goes blank and your work goes faster.

It sounds innocuous, but this constant word counting can use lots of your available computing horsepower while Word is sitting idly in the background.

To learn how much of your computer's attention Word commands while it's running in the background, open a long document, and then open Process Viewer (in Applications→Utilities). Scroll down in Process Viewer until you see the entry for Word, and look at the "% CPU" column. If it's higher than 10 percent or so, Word is probably contributing to your machine's laggardly ways.

Turning off Live Word Count can help a lot. You can turn it on and off by choosing Word→Preferences, then clicking View in the list that appears on the left, and then clicking Live Word Count.

Tip: Wait a minute after you turn off the feature before you check Process Viewer. Word has to integrate the change, and the CPU usage spikes in the meantime.

13-19   PowerPoint 4.0 Files in PowerPoint X

Unfortunately, PowerPoint X can't open presentations you created only a couple of Office versions ago—files in PowerPoint 4.0 format, to be precise.

They're not necessarily consigned to the dustbin of your hard drive, however. You can salvage them using Office 98, if you can rustle up a copy.

In PowerPoint 98 (which runs in Classic; see page 99), open the presentation you'd like to convert. Choose File→Save As, set the format to Presentation Template, and then save the file. Quit PowerPoint 98, open PowerPoint X, and open the converted 4.0 presentation.

You may find that you've lost some font information and formatting, but at least you can see and edit most of the presentation.

13-20   Importing Entourage 2001 Data into Entourage X

Sure, Entourage X can import your old Entourage 2001 data—hey, there's an Import command right in the File menu. There's only one problem: It doesn't work if you don't still have a *copy* of Office 2001 installed.

Instead of reinstalling Entourage 2001, just insert your original Office 2001 CD into your CD-ROM drive. The import program now sees Entourage 2001 on the CD-ROM, and it runs the process without any more backtalk.

(This is only half a hint, really: If you no longer have Office 2001 at all, you're truly out of luck.)

Figure 13-9:
Create a new blank Stickies note, and then switch to Entourage, making sure you can still see the new Stickies note. Highlight the Entourage note you want to transfer, but don't open it. Now drag it from Entourage onto the empty note. The contents go along for the ride (but without graphics, alas).

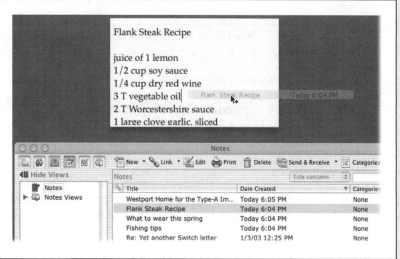

13-21 Entourage Notes to Stickies

If you want to convert an Entourage note to a new note in Stickies—perhaps you're uninstalling Entourage, or maybe a particular Entourage note is just crying out to appear with its compatriots in Stickies—you could open the note in Entourage, select all the text, copy it, switch to Stickies, and then paste.

But there's an easier way, as shown in Figure 13-9.

13-22 Easy Email Attachments

Normally, to send an attachment, you'd switch to Entourage, open a new email, address it, add some explanatory text, and then attach the file. But life's *way* too short for that.

The next time out, try this shortcut: Just drag the attachment onto Entourage's Dock icon. A new message window opens with the file attached, ready for you to enter a recipient and subject.

Tip: This hint also works with Mail, Eudora, and several other mail programs.

Photoshop/Photoshop Elements

Photoshop is the 800-pound gorilla in the graphics world. It's a complicated, hardcore program best left to trained professionals wearing protective garb. Elements is a lite version of Photoshop, providing about 80 percent of the big program's features for about 15 percent of the cost. These hints apply to both programs.

13-23 Zooming with a Scroll-Wheel Mouse

Here we go again with the scroll-wheel mouse: If you press Option as you turn the little wheel, you magnify or reduce your Photoshop document, zooming in or out.

Tip: The program is set to zoom in 100-percent increments (you jump from 100 percent to 200 percent to 300 percent, and so on). But you press Option *and* Shift, you can zoom in much finer, smoother increments.

13-24 Speeding Up Batch Conversions

Photoshop's File→Batch Processing command lets you apply resizing and formatting changes to a large number of files at once, while you sit back and leaf through a magazine.

To speed up your batch conversions, send Photoshop to the background. When it's not the frontmost program, Photoshop doesn't bother to redraw the screen as it opens and modifies every file in the batch, which results in much faster processing.

Snapz Pro X

Snapz Pro X is a shareware program *(www.ambrosiasw.com)* that lets you create great-looking snapshots of the screen—or even movies of the screen. It greatly improves Mac OS X's built-in screen-grabbing feature (hint 4-14) by adding a choice of file formats, movie capturing, naming options, on-the-fly previews, and border creation. It's a godsend for anyone who writes about computers, teaches computers, makes Web sites about computers—or publishes books of Mac OS X hints.

13-25   Saving Screenshots to any Location

Snapz Pro X lets you save your captured screen graphics anywhere you like—as long as it's the desktop, the clipboard, the printer, or your Pictures folder.

But what if you want to save all your images in another location? Here's a fiendishly simple solution.

Create an alias of the desired folder, and drag it to your Pictures folder. As Figure 13-10 shows, any alias you place in your Pictures folder shows up in Snapz Pro X as a location for saving your screenshots.

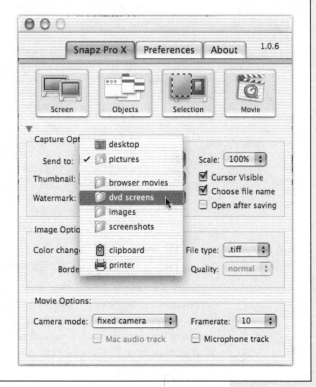

Figure 13-10:
In this figure, book project, browser movies, dvd screens, images, and iPhoto library are all aliases. If you choose one of them during a Snapz Pro X capture, the program saves the screenshot in the specified folder.

13-26   DVD Screenshots

It's a strange quirk of computer graphics cards: If you try to take a snapshot of a DVD movie you're playing (by pressing Shift-⌘-3, for example), you'll find that you've photographed a ghost. The resulting graphic shows nothing but an empty black space where the movie image should have been.

There *is* a sneaky workaround, but the steps depend on which video card your Mac has installed. To find out which card you have, open Apple System Profiler (in Applications→Utilities), click the Devices and Volumes tab, and look under PCI. Then proceed with one of the tips shown here:

- **nVidia card.** If your PCI reading says that Card Type is *NVDA,* you have an nVidia graphics card. You can capture a frame of a DVD movie using Snapz Pro like this:

  Install Snapz Pro on your Dock, and click it to make sure it's running. Open DVD Player, and pause the movie on the frame you want to capture.

  Now press the Snapz Pro activation keys (the ones you assigned when you set up the program). *Don't* click the DVD Player window; if you do, you will have to relaunch Snapz Pro.

  If you've done everything right, the Snapz Pro window capture menu comes up. Anything you capture now will include the DVD image.

- **Another kind of card.** See hint 14-26.

13-27   Going Pro

This hint is courtesy of Andrew Welch, author of Snapz Pro X. His advice will help you create screen captures that look better in print and on the Web.

- If you're taking a picture of an entire window, set the clipping border to Small (on the Preferences tab) and use a Fade to White image border (on the Snapz Pro X tab). If you're planning to place the image on a Web page with a black background, then use a Fade to Black image border.

- If you're capturing just a portion of a screen object (like a window, word, or picture), choose Fade to White (or Fade to Black), and then drag the selection box until it's roughly eight pixels wider than the desired capture area.

13-28   Smoother "Follow Cursor" Movie Captures

In Snapz Pro X's Follow Cursor movie-recording mode, you select a region of the screen to capture. As you move the mouse during the recording, the selection rectangle moves around, keeping the mouse centered within the window at all times. The idea is a compromise, designed to address the fact that a QuickTime movie of your *entire* screen (1900 x 1200 pixels, or whatever) may not be such a hit with the people you email it to.

To create movies in this mode, move the mouse smoothly and evenly across the screen: Any jumpiness in your mouse movements translates directly into jumpiness in your finished movie.

Better yet, don't move the cursor with the mouse at all. Instead, use the keyboard. Open System Preferences, click Universal Access, and then click the Mouse tab. Turn on Mouse Keys, and then set the Initial Delay slider to Short.

Once you've started recording the capture, you can move the cursor around the screen by pressing the eight keys that surround the 5 key. For example, press the 9 key to move the cursor diagonally up and to the right. If you hold one of these keys down continuously, the cursor, after a pause, begins to move smoothly in that direction—according to the way you have adjusted the sliders called Initial Delay and Maximum Speed.

The 5 key acts as the clicker—hold it down for a moment to "click the mouse," do that twice to double-click, and so on. Press the 0 key to lock down the mouse button, and the period key to unlock it. (The amount of time you have to hold them down depends on how you've set the Initial Display slider.)

Add-Ons Worth Adding

M ac OS X provides a great experience—and huge number of features—
right out of the box. But the most exciting feature of all may be the fact
that it's based on Unix, a familiar operating system to many of the world's
programmers. At the same time, it's a new operating system, with plenty of holes to
be plugged and polish to be added. Taken together, these two factors help to explain
the explosion of free and shareware add-ons (programs, utilities, and preference
panels) that can make the system even more useful—and fun.

This chapter is a bit of a nonconformist in this book. Rather than providing hints,
its purpose is just to let you know that these add-ons exist and to show you how they
can enhance—or solve problems in—Mac OS X.

Most of the programs fall into one of these categories:

- **Shareware programs.** You pay for these on the honor system, *after* you download
  them and try them out. If you like what they do for you, you send a small amount
  ($15 or so) directly to the programmer. In return, you usually get a code that
  unlocks more features or turns off nagging reminders to pay up.

- **Freeware programs.** These are free. Use them with the programmer's compliments.

- **Donationware.** These are a lot like shareware, except that the amount you owe to
  the programmer is left up to you.

Make Mac OS X Feel Like Mac OS 9

If you come to Mac OS X from an earlier version of the Mac operating system, you may find your initial foray a little disappointing. Old friends like the Application menu, the customizable menu, folder labels, and window shades are missing, and other features' behaviors have changed. But with the help of shareware, you can restore, and even enhance, nearly every feature that you miss from your Mac OS 9 days.

14-1 The Mac OS 9 Menu

If you were a big fan of the customizable menu in Mac OS 9, you're probably mighty disappointed by Mac OS X's noncustomizable version. If the Mac OS X alternative (the Dock) doesn't float your boat, try FruitMenu from Unsanity Software *(www.unsanity.com),* a leading provider of software for the Mac OS 9 fan in transition (see Figure 14-1).

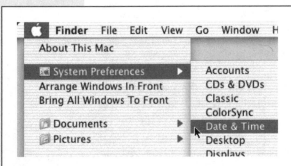

Figure 14-1:
Using FruitMenu, you can easily add your own folders and subfolders to the menu. You can also set up a number of very useful predefined commands, like "Bring all windows to front" or "IP Address."

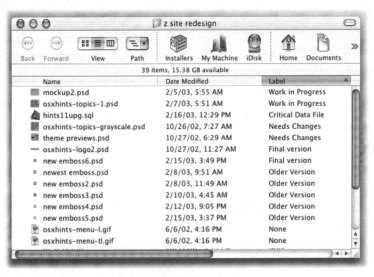

Figure 14-2:
The list is sorted by label, so that all files at a similar stage of completion are listed together. In addition, the colors make it easy to see each group with a quick glance at the screen. As each file progresses, a quick label change moves it to the next relevant group. The ability to label files allows quick and easy project management.

14-2   Folder Labels

Folder labels were a favorite Mac OS 9 feature that didn't make the leap to Mac OS X. If you never tried them, you probably don't realize what you're missing. Folder labels let you assign a color-coded text tag to any file, folder, or program on your hard drive. You can flag one batch of files with a label called "First Drafts," another with a label "Urgent," another "Back me up," and so on. You could then search and sort by these labels, making it very easy to manage large projects even if their files were scattered all across your hard drive.

You can assign both label color and name, *and* you get a handy contextual menu to do so. If you select multiple icons, you can apply a label to the whole batch. Figure 14-2 shows labels in action: a book project with chapters in various states of completion.

If you haven't used labels before, give Labels X a test drive. Your mileage may vary, but you could find yourself wondering how you functioned without them.

14-3   Sound Sets

A sound set, in Mac OS 9, was a collection of sounds that could be attached to different actions. You would hear a little zip when you scrolled, a little scratch when you emptied the trash, a little whoosh when you collapsed a window, and so on.

Although Mac OS X's Sound preference panel includes a "Play user interface sound effects" button, it's a very crude affair compared to the options Mac OS 9 gave you. Mac OS X doesn't give you any choice of sound themes—only On or Off—and it produces only two tiny sound effects.

Figure 14-3:
If you like to hear your machine chirp, hiccup, breep, scratch, and click as you go about your work, give Unsanity's Xounds a whirl. Xounds brings back the best of Mac OS 9's sound sets; think of it as a Top 40 Chirps feature.

Once again, Unsanity has an offering to plug this hole. Xounds (Figure 14-3) applies sounds to menus, windows, controls, and the Finder, and includes a tool to help you download, convert, and install older Mac OS 9 sound sets from *www.soundset central.com.*

14-4   Window Shades

In Mac OS X, clicking the yellow globule in the upper-left corner of the window (or pressing ⌘-M) *minimizes* a window, getting it out of your way by shrinking it onto a Dock icon. In Mac OS 9, you were supposed to manage window clutter by window-shading windows that were in your way. You would double-click their title bars, causing the body of the window to collapse upward into the title bar itself, which remained on the screen like the smile of the Cheshire cat.

WindowShade X, yet another Unsanity product, brings back window shades—with a vengeance. You can specify precisely what happens when you click the Minimize button, double-click the title bar, or press ⌘-M. For example, you can make a window semi- or completely transparent, hide a program, or minimize a window to the Dock. You can control how shadows are applied (if at all) to your active and shaded windows. And you can control all of these settings on a program-specific basis.

14-5   The Application Menu

In Mac OS X, the Dock serves as a list of all of your open programs. In Mac OS 9, the Application Menu at the upper-right corner of the screen took care of this function.

If you miss the Mac OS 9 method of program switching, the solution is Application Switching Menu, or ASM *(www.vercruesse.de)*. Once you install it as a new panel in System Preferences, ASM returns the program menu to the top right of the screen (Figure 14-4). You can also tell ASM to include any Dock submenus in its menus,

Figure 14-4:
With ASM, you can reach any program's windows through a menu, and you can also control things like icon size, program switching modes, and custom settings on a program-specific basis.

making ASM a complete replacement for the Dock's program-switching role (you can still use the Dock, of course).

ASM also includes some window-switching options. For instance, in single-program mode, ASM automatically hides the windows of all programs except the one you're currently in. You can also switch to Classic window mode, so that whenever you click a window, all windows of its program come to the front. (In Mac OS X, only that single window comes to the foreground, sometimes resulting in, for example, a Microsoft Word document window being sandwiched between two Internet Explorer browser windows.)

14-6 The Print-Window Command

Many Mac OS 9 devotees miss the ability to print a list of a folder's contents directly from the Finder—and great way to create "liner notes" for a backup CD, for example. You can do it in Mac OS X, but it's a more complex operation. (Highlight the icons in the folder, press ⌘-C to copy them, paste the list into a word processor, then print it. It's a sure recipe for carpal tunnel syndrome.)

Print Window *(www.swssoftware.com)* is a much better idea. When you double-click it, a dialog box opens (Figure 14-5), containing a number of options for your printout that go well beyond the basic print function available in Mac OS 9.

Figure 14-5:
This dialog box lets you include multiple subfolders in a printout and change from a full listing to just a name listing. With a name listing, you can create a multicolumn layout (saving paper when you print long folder listings), and include a header row and icons of various sizes.

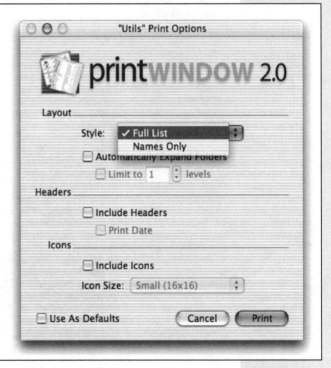

Tip: If you install Print Window in your Applications folder, it will install a Print File Listing command in your Services menu, which means you don't have to launch the program to print. (After installing Print Window, log out and back in again to see it.)

You can even set up Print Window to respond to the ⌘-P keystroke, just as in the old Mac OS 9 Finder. To do so, launch the program and open its preference panel. Turn on "Respond to ⌘-P in Finder."

While you're in the preference panel, also consider turning on "Launch at Startup" and "Finder to Front" so that Print Window is always running and ⌘-P always works.

14-7 "Share Any Folder" File Sharing

Although Mac OS X lets you share files in your Public folder, you can't easily share any other folder on your machine. SharePoints, from HornWare *(www.hornware.com)*, aims to make it nearly as easy to share 'em as it was in Mac OS 9. See hint 6-12 for details.

14-8 Putting that Old Scanner Back to Work

If Mac OS X has a sore spot, it's scanners—an especially painful fact considering the fact that the Mac's core audience includes artists and graphic designers. Many scanner manufacturers simply haven't bothered to write Mac OS X drivers for their older scanner models.

Figure 14-6:
VueScan offers three levels of complexity, letting you choose your level of expertise. Depending on your scanner, you may have different options for Basic, Intermediate, and Advanced. In Basic mode, you control very few options; in Advanced mode, shown here, you control them all.

Fortunately, you may not even need them. VueScan, a set of shareware scanner drivers *(www.hamrick.com)*, is just the ticket that lets hundreds of older scanners work with Mac OS X. The full list of compatible models appears on the Web site, but it includes many scanners from UMAX, Nikon, HP, and even the Apple Color OneScanner.

The full version costs $40—considerably less than the price of a new scanner, leaving you with cash to buy something really critical like, say, a copy of SimCity. (There's a free trial version, too.)

VueScan offers three levels of complexity, letting you choose your level of expertise. Depending on your scanner, you may have different options for Basic, Intermediate, and Advanced. In Basic mode, you control very few options; in Advanced mode, as shown in Figure 14-6, you control them all.

14-9 Professional Charts

Although it's more a presentation tool than a charting tool, many people use PowerPoint to create charts. But for organization charts, network diagrams, and floor plans, OmniGraffle is a much better choice *(www.omnigroup.com)*.

The program's main work area resembles a sheet of graph paper. Off to the side is a Palettes window that stores premade shapes for easy use in your chart. Figure 14-7 shows the main work area along with the Network 3D object palette. OmniGraffle comes with over fifteen object palettes, and you can download additional palettes from the company's Web site.

Figure 14-7:
OmniGraffle's palettes let you place premade professional-grade images in your charts. The program includes over fifteen unique object palettes, including Boolean gates, flow chart symbols, networking symbols, computer images, 3D network icons (shown here), and equipment racks. You can download additional palettes from the Web, or create your own.

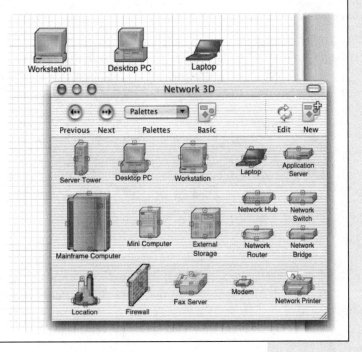

Information windows control up to nine areas of every chart, including object size, shape, style, alignment, and lines. You can open as many of these info windows as you need and change the category of information displayed in each to meet your needs. OmniGraffle also includes layers, transparency, flexible lines that move as you rearrange your chart's objects, and the ability to create a multipage layout.

Note: Because of its heavy use of graphics, OmniGraffle runs best if you've got a newer G4 with a Quartz Extreme–capable video card. But it runs on anything that's capable of running Mac OS X.

14-10   Mighty Morphing

Morphing is a movie special effect in which one face or object magically transforms itself into another. You've seen it a million times—it's how, for example, the cat in *Harry Potter and the Sorcerer's Stone* visibly transforms into Professor McGonagall (Maggie Smith).

Morphing is a good way to demonstrate the progression of a project from "before" to "after"; think home remodeling, painting your car, changing from Bill Bixby into the Incredible Hulk, and so on. You probably don't need morphing software every day, but if you ever do, here's a freeware program that'll create the intermediate images.

MorphX *(www.orcsoftware.com/~martin),* is very simple to use, despite the seriously complex math it uses to execute your commands (see Figure 14-8).

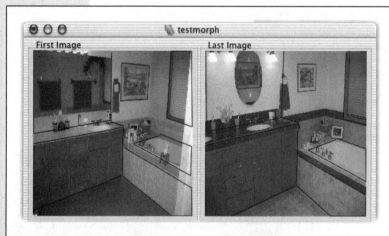

Figure 14-8:
As you outline an area in the left-side image, the program automatically adds the same lines to the right-side image. Once you've outlined a region in the left-side image, move to the right-side image and adjust the lines as necessary to outline the same region in the "after" image. Outline a few major areas of the image, lining up the "before" and "after" sections as closely as possible.

When you're ready to create the morphed images, choose File→Save Morph Frames. A dialog box appears, asking questions about the image size, number of frames you'd like to generate, and the playback rate (in frames per second). If you want a two-second morph that plays at 20 frames per second, you need to create 40 frames (twenty frames per second, times two seconds). The more frames you create, the longer the morph-creation process takes.

Once you've set your options, click Save, and then…wait. Morphing calculations are very complicated, and if you've asked for a lot of large images, the calculation process can literally take hours.

The result of the morph can be either a still image (like the "bastard children of unnatural celebrity couplings" comedy segment on the Conan O'Brien show) or a movie. Making a movie out of your MorphX frames, however, requires the assistance of another program, like QuickTime Player Pro ($30).

Program Launchers and Switchers

The Dock is Mac OS X's combined program launcher and switcher. It's also a spot for storing often-used documents and folders and minimized windows (on the right side). That's a lot of tasks for one lonely program. Luckily, a number of great third-party launchers and switchers can take some of the strain off your Dock. Here are a few of the best for your consideration.

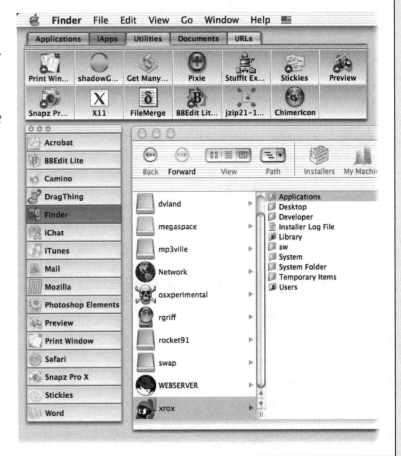

Figure 14-9:
Using DragThing, you can create docks with multiple tabs, letting you store many programs and documents in a small space. In addition, you can view one dock that lists all running programs, and another that shows your hard drives. DragThing is also fully AppleScriptable, and it can pull off some other tricks, like putting the Trash on your desktop and hiding all windows when switching between programs.

14-11   Replacing the Dock's Program Launcher

After you've customized your Dock half to death, you may discover that having 35 available icons makes it hard to find the program you want to open. Instead of fighting the left side of the Dock, consider working around its limitations—and one way is to find a non-Apple Dock replacement to use as your launcher.

Some people find that the Dock works much better in its role as an open-programs *manager*—displaying their icons, managing their windows, and switching among them—than as a launcher. If you share that view, consider using a dedicated program launcher for opening programs. You'll find yourself thinking of the Dock as a friend rather than a potential enemy.

Many good launcher programs exist, including DragThing (see Figure 14-9), PocketDock, LaunchBar, and DropDrawers. Most of the launcher programs are "try before you buy" shareware, so experiment and find one you really like before committing your money.

Once you've found a launcher you like, remove all your stored programs from the Dock (except for perhaps the new launcher itself), and use the shareware replacement launcher instead. Most launcher programs provide a keyboard shortcut to bring them forward, like the Dock's ⌘-Tab, so you can use them from any application.

14-12   Keyboard Launchers

If you're a keyboard power user, you'll love LaunchBar *(www.obdev.at/products/launchbar/index.html)*. This program launcher lets you open any program or document with only a few keystrokes.

Once installed, LaunchBar places an icon in your main menu bar, and then hides itself until needed. You can open LaunchBar by moving the mouse onto its icon in the menu bar, but of course the whole purpose of the exercise was to avoid using the mouse. Fortunately, you can press ⌘-Space instead.

Figure 14-10:
As you type, LaunchBar displays a list of all the programs and documents whose names match what you've typed so far. This process continues until you score—at which point you press Enter to open the program or document. Here, typing Te brings up TextEdit.

Once open, LaunchBar drops a data-entry box just below the menu bar and waits for you to start typing the name of the program or document you'd like to open, as shown in Figure 14-10.

Tip: You can force LaunchBar to learn your own shortcuts. For instance, if you want *Te* to open TextEdit and not TextEdit Plus, just use the arrow keys to select TextEdit once or twice after typing *Te*. In the future, LaunchBar will offer TextEdit as the selection after you type *Te*.

14-13 Storing Stuff in Drawers

DropDrawers *(www.sigsoftware.com/dropdrawers/index.html)* is an innovative launcher and storage program that lets you create "drawers" for storing programs (the launcher), or nearly any other type of data you can envision (Figure 14-11).

In addition to the launcher drawers, which hold programs, drawers can also hold text clippings, which you can insert into programs using keyboard shortcuts. Drawers can also hold sound files, movie files, graphics, and so on. The program also has a special Process drawer that shows all running programs, so DropDrawers can also function as a program switcher.

What really makes DropDrawers unique is the way that its drawers stay out of the way until you need them. As Figure 14-11 shows, you can normally see only the tab of a drawer.

Figure 14-11:
When you mouse over a tab, its drawer slides out from the edge of the screen, revealing the contents. If you don't want the drawer to slide shut again, click its tab to make it stay open. You can position drawers on any side of the screen, and they don't have to be right next to one another.

14-14   LiteSwitch X: The Power of Switching

Proteron's LiteSwitch X is a simple program that focuses on one task and does it extremely well *(www.proteron.com)*. LiteSwitch X is a program switcher that works by placing a semitranslucent menu of all running programs across the center of your screen.

Once open, LiteSwitch X displays Dock-like switching icons in the center of your screen. The program makes it easy to toggle between two programs, because it always displays their icons in order of last use, from left to right. By contrast, the Dock lets you switch between two programs, but it leaves them in their assigned spots, which makes it tougher to see which program you're about to activate.

In addition, you can use the program's preferences to control window behavior (whether, for example, all windows of a program are brought forward when switching, or just one) and window hiding (single program mode, for example, hides all other windows every time you switch). The program also has modifier keys that perform certain actions on the selected program (for example, press F twice to force quit the chosen program).

14-15   Keyboard Maestro

If LiteSwitch X represents the simple butter knife of program-switching programs, then Michael Kamprath's Keyboard Maestro is the Swiss army knife of switchers *(www.keyboardmaestro.com)*.

In addition to providing full control over program (and window) switching, Keyboard Maestro includes an excellent macro feature through its Hot Keys (keyboard shortcuts of your own choosing). As Figure 14-12 shows, you can turn on predefined

Figure 14-12:
Keyboard Maestro lets you specify a keystroke to open one program, to bring all of a program's windows forward, and so on. It even has a predefined set of Hot Keys for controlling iTunes, including commands to pick a random song or jump to next song.

hot keys or create your own. For example, maybe you want Control-W to open Microsoft Word, Control-S to open Safari, and so on.

Keyboard Maestro also offers a Clipboard Switcher that lets you copy various bits of text and graphics out of various programs, ready for pasting at any time in any sequence.

Expanding Your Mac OS X Experience

Another set of popular Mac OS X add-on utilities is designed to turn on hidden preferences, change aspects of the Dock's behavior, and provide additional information on running programs. Here are a few tools to get you started on the path of tweaking.

14-16   Hidden System Preferences

Want to move your Dock to a corner of the screen instead of having it centered? Want to remove the zooming rectangle effect when a file opens? Want double scroll arrows at both ends of all your scroll bars? Mac OS X has features like these, but you can usually only set them by typing a cryptic command in Terminal.

TinkerTool, a free program from *ww.bresink.de/osx*, however, lets you employ a more Mac-like way of doing things. This free program installs itself into System Preferences, giving you direct access many settings (Figure 14-13).

Figure 14-13:
TinkerTool lets you set a number of hidden Mac OS X preferences from the comfort of a graphical interface. The Fonts tab, shown here, lets you change the standard Mac OS X screen fonts (although some programs ignore these settings).

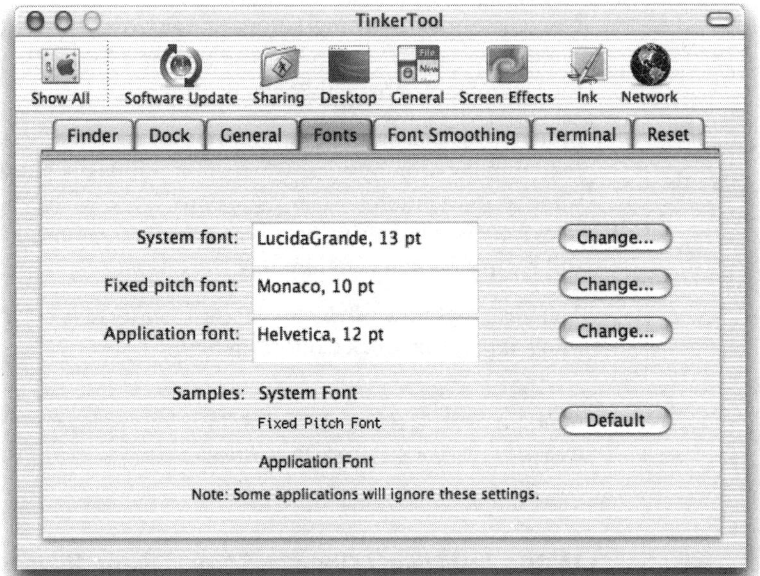

14-17   Searching Google from the Menu Bar

Google is among the most popular search tools on the Web. But getting to Google to start your search can be time-consuming: switch to your browser, open a new window, click your Google shortcut, type what you're looking for, and then press Enter. Half an inning has passed before you're done.

The remarkable, free program Searchling (*http://web.ics.purdue.edu/~mthole*) changes that long process into a simple click-and-type operation (see Figure 14-14).

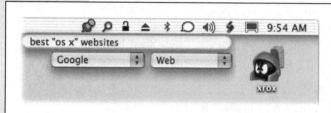

Figure 14-14:
Searchling sits on the menu bar as a G icon. When you click the icon, a one-line input box and two pop-up menus appear. Enter your search terms and press Enter; Searchling opens your browser and loads the Google results page for your search.

You can also set a few preferences with Searchling. To reach the preferences screen, Control-click the G icon (right-clicking, if your mouse has more than one button, doesn't work). A dialog box appears, letting you turn the pop-up menus on or off and determine whether Searchling should automatically check for program updates.

14-18   The Silence of the Dock

As you're probably aware by now, Dock icons bounce up and down excitedly whenever you're opening a program, as though to demonstrate their delight at being chosen to serve you. If you find this animation a bit much, you can turn it off through the Dock panel of System Preferences.

Much to your chagrin, however, you may soon discover that you have only stifled that jumping-icon business when applications open. When background programs want your attention—when the printer jams, when your email program has new mail for you, when your browser in the background has reported an error—they still try to alert you with jumping Dock icons.

The free program Dock Detox (*www.unsanity.com/haxies/dockdetox*) does only one thing: it prevents Dock icons from bouncing.

Note: The downside of Dock Detox, of course, is that if a program really needs you to do something like dismiss a dialog box or respond to an error message, you won't know about it until you switch to the program.

14-19   Improving Open and Save Dialog Boxes

Default Folder X (*www.stclairsoft.com*) offers power-user features that enhance the Open and Save dialog boxes. For example, it lets you assign keyboard shortcuts for your often-used folders, execute common commands like Move and Rename right there in the dialog box, specify which folder the Open or Save dialog box presents first, add and remove programs and documents from Favorites, and much more (see Figure 14-15).

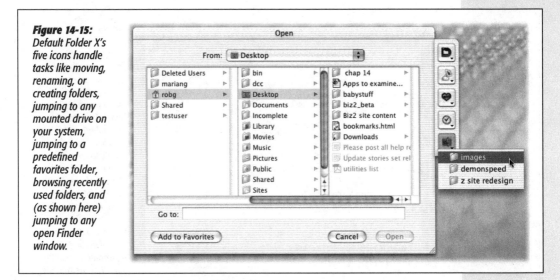

Figure 14-15:
Default Folder X's five icons handle tasks like moving, renaming, or creating folders, jumping to any mounted drive on your system, jumping to a predefined favorites folder, browsing recently used folders, and (as shown here) jumping to any open Finder window.

14-20 Power to the File Renaming Process

Although renaming files and folders isn't the most exciting task you can perform with Mac OS X, it may be one of the most frequent. Most of the time you need to rename only a file or two, and the process isn't especially complicated. But when you have a batch of 50 or 60 files that you want to modify, hand-editing their names can take longer than curing a ham. If you know Unix, you can perform this sort of magic in Terminal. For mere mortals, however, a more Mac-like solution is A Better Finder Rename *(www.publicspace.net)*, or ABFR for short.

Once you've installed it, you'll see a new menu item, called Better Finder Rename, in the contextual menu that appears whenever you Control-click selected icons in the Finder. This command opens ABFR, which offers an array of choices for renaming files and folders (see Figure 14-16).

Then you specify what to change in the selected files' names. As Figure 14-16 shows, a Replace dialog box offers a variety of options, including time and date stamp.

14-21 Customized Pop-Up Menus

MaxMenus *(www.proteron.com/maxmenus)* places a small semitransparent circle in each corner of your screen, which, when clicked, produces a pop-up menu. The top-left circle displays your recently used programs and the contents of your Applications folder; the top-right corner pops up a list of your active programs, drives, and desktop icons. The bottom left-hand corner displays the contents of your Documents folder and any recently used documents, and the bottom right-hand corner displays all of your System Preferences panels for quick access. Considering the fact that pressing Shift, Option, ⌘, or Control changes the contents of a menu, you actually have a total of 20 menus at your mouse tip!

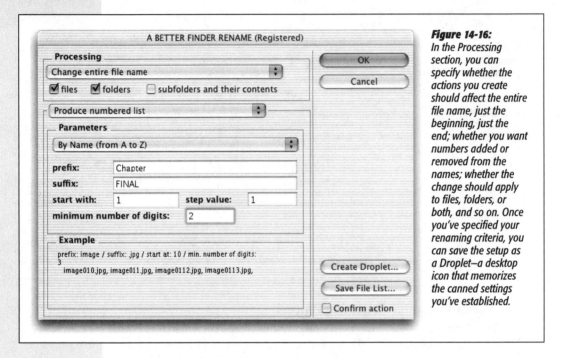

Figure 14-16:
In the Processing section, you can specify whether the actions you create should affect the entire file name, just the beginning, just the end; whether you want numbers added or removed from the names; whether the change should apply to files, folders, or both, and so on. Once you've specified your renaming criteria, you can save the setup as a Droplet—a desktop icon that memorizes the canned settings you've established.

If these tricks were all that MaxMenus did, it would be a very useful accessory. But its real power-user features lie in its System Preferences panel, where you can either modify the existing menus' contents or create your own menus from scratch (Figure 14-17).

By assigning a hot key, you can make your custom menu accessible from anywhere on the screen.

MaxMenus lets you drag files, folders, and programs from the Finder to create your menus. For example, if you were writing a book and wanted fast access to any chapter, you could create a Control-B menu, and then drag into it the Word documents that make up each chapter. Or you could create a fast-launch menu for your Web browsers by dragging each of them into a Control-W customized menu.

MaxMenus has a lot of features, and the learning curve can be steep. Happily, it comes with an excellent manual, and it's worth mastering.

14-22 Program Priorities

You may be able to gain computing speed in some programs by changing what's called the *nice value,* a Unix element that controls how much attention your machine devotes to each application (the *priority* it gives them).

Assigning a program's nice value, rather than letting the system do it, can be useful when, say, you're processing a complex series of Photoshop operations on a batch of images. You want to make sure that Photoshop gets as much power as possible.

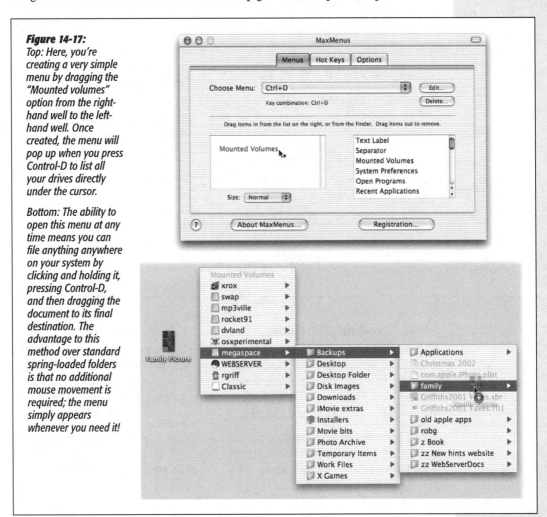

Figure 14-17:
Top: Here, you're creating a very simple menu by dragging the "Mounted volumes" option from the right-hand well to the left-hand well. Once created, the menu will pop up when you press Control-D to list all your drives directly under the cursor.

Bottom: The ability to open this menu at any time means you can file anything anywhere on your system by clicking and holding it, pressing Control-D, and then dragging the document to its final destination. The advantage to this method over standard spring-loaded folders is that no additional mouse movement is required; the menu simply appears whenever you need it!

ProcessWizard *(www.lachoseinteractive)* sits on your menu bar; when you click its icon, you get a list of all running programs (as well as all background programs) in a window. Next to each program is a small slider, which you can drag to adjust the program's priority (Figure 14-18). When you release the mouse button, the program asks for your administrative password—and the deed is done.

Note: If you do a lot of processor-intensive work or play 3D games, you can see a tangible improvement in performance if you increase the program's priority levels. Be aware, however, that there's no such thing as a free lunch. The speed you're adding to one program comes at a price: you're slowing down other programs in the bargain.

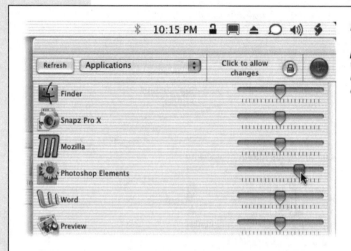

Figure 14-18:
Why drag right to increase a program's priority? Weirdly, the lower the nice value (they range from −20 to +20, and 0 is the default) the more attention your computer gives to that program.

14-23   Replacing the Finder

Path Finder *(www.cocoatech.com)* is a Finder replacement, a Cocoa program with a number of features you won't find in the standard Mac OS X Finder (which is actually a Carbon application): folder labels; full control over font families, colors, and sizes; window transparency; a preview drawer; and a full selection of contextual menu options, all shown in Figure 14-19.

If you come to love Path Finder, you can actually use it to replace the standard Mac OS X Finder completely. To do that, open Terminal (page 5). Assuming you've put Path Finder into your Applications folder, the necessary command is as follows:

```
defaults write com.apple.loginwindow Finder
/Applications/Path\ Finder.app
```

After entering the command, press Enter, quit Terminal, log out and then back in again. You'll find yourself in the Path Finder world rather than the standard Finder.

If you ever wish to return to Apple's Mac OS X Finder, just open Terminal and type this:

```
defaults delete com.apple.loginwindow Finder
```

After you log out and log in again, the original Finder is back in action.

Note: Even if you've set Path Finder to open instead of Apple's Finder when you log in, certain programs (including OmniWeb) may automatically relaunch the original Finder. If that behavior gets on your nerves, consider adding a Quit menu item to the Finder (hint 2-20).

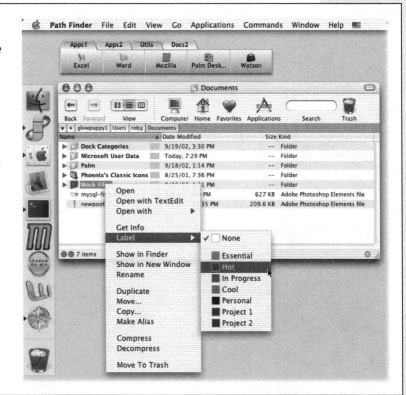

Figure 14-19:
Path Finder is a Cocoa-based replacement for the Finder, with an array of useful features. It features the full complement of normal Finder features, including spring-loaded folders, three views, a customizable toolbar, server connections, and more. Since Path Finder is just another Mac OS X program, you can use it even while the Finder is running.

14-24 More Than One Clipboard

If you've spent more than about ten minutes using a Mac, you're probably familiar with the Clipboard shuffle. This dance occurs when you copy and paste more than one piece of information between the same two programs.

For example, suppose you want to copy several different sections of a Web page to your word processor. So you start in the browser, copy a paragraph, switch to the word processor, paste, return to the browser, copy the next section, return to the word processor, paste, and repeat until you've got everything you want. The reason you must go through this dizzying process, of course, is that Mac OS X has only one clipboard for storing copied items.

PTHPasteboard, an excellent freeware program *(www.pth.com/PTHPasteboard/)*, can put a quick end to the clipboard shuffle. It lets you open an unlimited number of clipboards (it starts with 20). You can even create permanent clipboards for storing bits that you use all the time—your return address, driving directions to your house, your favorite *Star Trek* quotes, or whatever.

As Figure 14-20 shows, PTHPasteboard makes it very easy to copy any old selection to the clipboard.

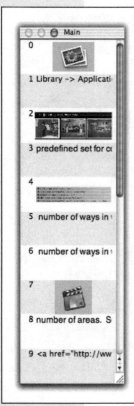

Figure 14-20:
Using PTHPasteboard, you can store 20 (or more) cut or copied bits on your clipboard at one time, which become accessible through this simple scrolling window. You can even assign hot keys that paste stuff to any of the first ten slots without taking your hands off the keyboard.

Instead of flipping back and forth when you need to copy and paste multiple selections, use PTHPasteboard to copy them all, then switch to your destination program and paste them all in one step.

Other Programs

As you gain experience with Mac OS X, you may find other things you wish to do that can't be handled by the Apple programs and utilities. For example, you may want an easy way to copy your existing Mac OS X installation to a new hard drive, or you may want to take some DVD screen grabs, or you may want to run a more robust FTP server. The following programs solve those problems and more.

14-25 Creating a Bootable Backup

Everyone agrees that backing up is massively important, and yet many people find it too difficult or time-consuming to do regularly. However, if you have an external hard drive (or a spare partition on your main one), Carbon Copy Cloner (CCC) can take care of the difficult part *(www.bombich.com)*. This program copies your entire hard drive onto another hard drive, creating an exact mirror-image copy. As Figure 14-21 shows, CCC has a very simple dialog box.

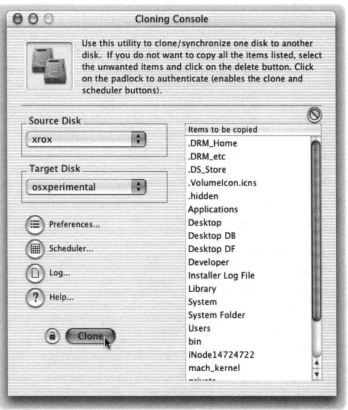

Figure 14-21:
Specify the existing copy of Mac OS X in the Source Disk box, identify the destination disk in the Target Disk box, click Clone, and provide your password when asked. CCC gets to work creating an exact duplicate of your existing Mac OS X installation.

CCC can even keep the two disks synchronized (add a file to a folder on Drive A, and it's automatically added to the same folder on Drive B) using a Unix tool called *psync*, and it offers a scheduling tool to make sure they get done regularly.

14-26 DVD Screen Grabs on ATI-Video Card Macs

If you try to capture a screenshot of a DVD movie (hint 4-14), you'll find that it's like trying to photograph a ghost: When you look at the resulting film (that is, the Picture 1 file), you'll find that it's completely blank.

Hint 13-26 demonstrates how you can capture DVD movie screenshots using the shareware Snapz Pro—but that trick works only if you're Mac has an nVidia graphics card in it. If you have an ATI video card, however, that trick doesn't work; you'll still get blank screen captures.

There is, however, a workaround.

VideoLAN Client *(www.videolan.org)* is a program that can display MPEG video on your Mac—like the video from a playing DVD—that's actually being played on another machine across the network.

To take a screenshots of a DVD, quit DVD Player if it opened when you inserted your DVD. Next, open VideoLAN Client, and choose File→Open Disc, which opens a dialog box displaying the DVD. When you click OK, the movie begins playing. (VideoLAN Client ignores the menu system built into most DVDs.) Use the controller to fast-forward to the section of the movie you want to capture, click Pause, and then use any of the standard screen capture tools (see hints 4-14 or page 311) to take your screenshot. The result is exactly what you'd expect: a screenshot of the frame you had selected.

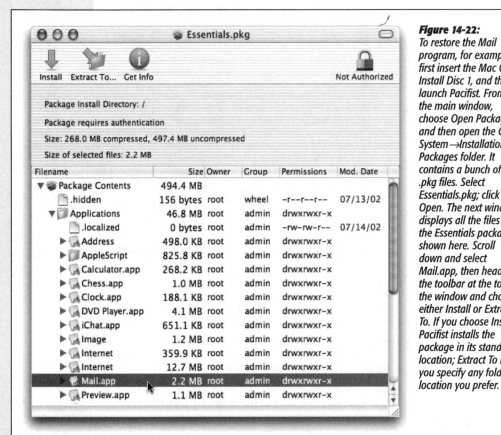

Figure 14-22:
To restore the Mail program, for example, first insert the Mac OS X Install Disc 1, and then launch Pacifist. From the main window, choose Open Package, and then open the CD's System→Installation→ Packages folder. It contains a bunch of .pkg files. Select Essentials.pkg; click Open. The next window displays all the files in the Essentials package, shown here. Scroll down and select Mail.app, then head to the toolbar at the top of the window and choose either Install or Extract To. If you choose Install, Pacifist installs the package in its standard location; Extract To lets you specify any folder location you prefer.

Note: You probably won't want to use VideoLAN Client to actually watch a DVD, as it's not quite as good as the Apple player. Its playback isn't as smooth, it offers fewer controls, and so on.

14-27   Installing Individual Programs from the Mac OS X Discs

If you accidentally delete your copy of Mail, how would you get it back?

If you look through your machine's software discs, you'll discover they include no disc for Mail. It's also not available for download from Apple's Web site. The only obvious solution is to reinstall Mac OS X in its entirety—possibly less appealing than root canal surgery.

Luckily, CharlesSoft *(www.charlessoft.com)* has developed Pacifist to handle precisely this problem. As it turns out, the Mac OS X CDs are actually, behind the scenes, composed of many individual installers called packages. Pacifist lets you browse the Mac OS X packages and extract individual pieces as you need them. Figure 14-22 explains how it works.

14-28   Installing a Full-Featured FTP Server

If you have a full-time Internet connection—a cable modem or DSL, for example—one click on the Sharing panel of system preferences can turn your Mac into an FTP server (a software-download site on the Internet). Unfortunately, this built-in feature is fairly limited: only people with accounts on the machine can connect, and without advanced Unix knowledge, it's not easy to permit anonymous connections.

The solution: CrushFTP *(www.crushftp.com)*, a full-featured FTP server that lets you configure and manage your server, capitalizing on a huge constellation of settings and features for both connecting accounts and the server itself. Figure 14-23 shows but one example.

Figure 14-23:
CrushFTP lets you set maximum login and idle times, download speed restrictions, and much more.

CrushFTP account names and passwords don't exist in Mac OS X itself, only in CrushFTP— which is a tremendous advantage over Apple's FTP server, which requires every person who connects by name to have a Mac OS X account.

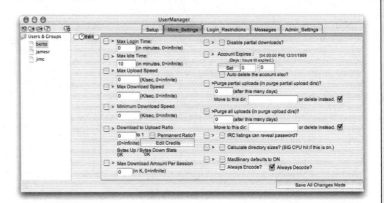

Note: CrushFTP isn't a beginner's FTP tool. If you misconfigure the settings, you might find that your machine is open to intruders from the Internet, which could either be a minor annoyance or a major disaster. If you have some experience with FTP servers, however, CrushFTP offers all the power of the command line variants with a much simpler interface.

14-29   Mouse Gestures

A mouse gesture (see hint 12-57) is an action that's triggered by a specific movement of the mouse, usually in combination with dragging and/or a modifier key. For example, an up-down-up drag motion could open a new window, save a file, or scroll a window. For some people, mouse gestures feel more natural than choosing commands from menus or memorizing obscure keyboard shortcuts.

Cocoa Gestures *(www.bitart.com)* lets you add mouse gestures to any Cocoa program, including Mail, Chimera Navigator, TextEdit, and so on.

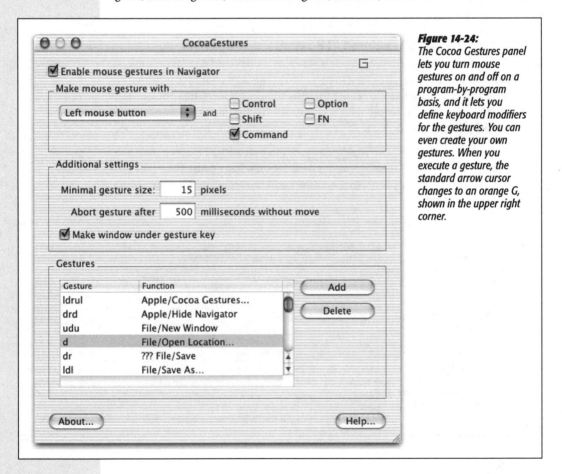

Figure 14-24:
The Cocoa Gestures panel lets you turn mouse gestures on and off on a program-by-program basis, and it lets you define keyboard modifiers for the gestures. You can even create your own gestures. When you execute a gesture, the standard arrow cursor changes to an orange G, shown in the upper right corner.

Once you've downloaded Cocoa Gestures, drag the Input Managers folder to your Home→Library folder (or to your hard drive's Library folder if you want everyone who uses your Mac to have access to the program). From that point on, any newly launched Cocoa program will have a Cocoa Gestures command in its program menu, usually just below Preferences. When you open Cocoa Gestures, the panel shown in Figure 14-24 appears.

Gestures start out turned off in every program, so your first step should be to turn on "Enable mouse gestures in this program" (shown in the figure). "Make mouse gesture with" lets you define which combination of mouse buttons and modifier keys create the gestures. You can even specify *no* mouse button by choosing the "Modifier only" setting from the pop-up menu.

Explore the Possibilities

Although a good number of problem-solving programs is described in this chapter, the universe of programs is vast. Mac OS X is a young operating system, and new stuff comes out for it every day. The best way to keep up with the latest and greatest is to pay regular visits to one of the software tracking sites (*www.versiontracker.com, www.macupdate.com, www.macosxapps.com*) and see if anything on the new release lists seems interesting. If you install a program you don't like, you can always drag it to the Trash.

A final note: If you wind up adopting any shareware programs, do pay the authors the requested fee for their efforts! Doing so will inspire those programmers to create even cooler stuff for you and millions of others.

Useful Unix Hints

T he Unix engine at the heart of Mac OS X may seem completely foreign to
you. It may even seem intimidating and completely unnecessary. You're for-
given if the presence, in this day and age, of a *command line*—a system of
controlling the Mac by typing cryptic commands instead of using menus—strikes
you as a blast from the DOS-ish past.

And you'd have good company. The vast majority of Mac OS X fans live long, happy
lives without ever touching Terminal or even realizing that the Mac OS X sports car
rides on Unix, a venerable, highly polished 30-year-old Unix chassis.

But an extremely important minority lives, eats, and sleeps in Terminal. This is where
the more advanced crowd of major league geeks can compile open-source programs,
connect to remote computers, and perform magic with strings of commands like
grep, sed, and *fdisk.*

These people enjoy a world of power and control usually enjoyed only by dictators
and Hollywood stars. They're the people who, admiring the handsome plumbing of
Mac OS X, are writing cool new programs for it, bringing it into corporations, and
helping fan the flames of Mac passion.

This chapter and the next are dedicated to helping you get the most out of Terminal
(which awaits in your Applications→Utilities folder). Some of the tricks are simple
enough for anybody. Others require some experience in Unix. But all of them involve Terminal.

Unix Basics

The first time you see it, you'd swear that Unix had nothing in common with the traditional Mac OS (see Figure 15-1).

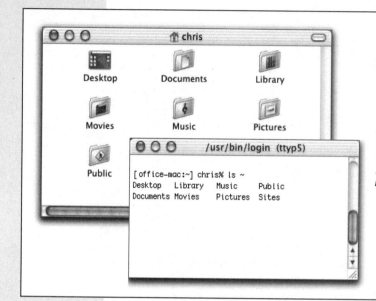

Figure 15-1:
Top: What most people think of when they think "Macintosh" is a graphic interface—one that you control with a mouse, using menus and icons to represent files and commands.

Bottom: Terminal offers a second way to control Mac OS X: a command line interface, meaning you operate it by typing out programming codes.

What the illustration at the bottom of Figure 15-1 shows, of course, is a *command line interface:* a place where you can type out instructions to the computer itself. This is a world without icons, menus, or dialog boxes. Even the mouse is almost useless.

The first time you open Terminal, you'll notice that there's not much in its window except the date and time of your last login, a welcome message, and the *command line prompt* (Figure 15-2). It breaks down like this:

- **office-mac:** This is the name of your Mac (at least, as Unix thinks of it).

- ~ The next part of the prompt indicates what folder you're "in" (see Figure 15-2). It denotes the *working directory*—that is, the current folder. (Remember, there are no icons in Unix.) Essentially, this notation tells you where you are as you navigate your machine.

The very first time you try out Terminal, the working directory is set to the symbol ~, which is shorthand for "your Home folder." It's what you see the first time you start up Terminal, but you'll soon be seeing the names of other folders here; *[office-mac: /Users]* or *[office-mac: /System/Library]*, for example. (The slashes show you the progression of folders-in-folders.)

- **chris%** This part of the prompt begins with your short user name. It reflects whoever's logged into the *shell* (see the box below), which is usually whoever's logged into the *Mac* at the moment. As for the % sign: It's a *prompt*, the Mac's way of saying, "OK, I'm ready. Tell me what to do."

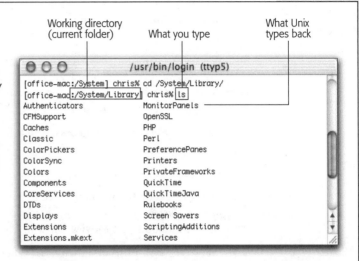

Figure 15-2:
On the Web, Mac OS X's Terminal is one of the most often discussed elements of Mac OS X. Dozens of step-by-step tutorials for performing certain tasks circulate online, usually without much annotation as to why you're typing what you're typing.

It works on a call-and-response system. You type a command (often pertaining to the files in the working directory) and press Enter; Terminal either performs something or types something back to you.

Working directory (current folder)

What you type

What Unix types back

```
●●●                    /usr/bin/login (ttyp5)
[office-mac:/System] chris% cd /System/Library/
[office-mac:/System/Library] chris% ls
Authenticators          MonitorPanels
CFMSupport              OpenSSL
Caches                  PHP
Classic                 Perl
ColorPickers            PreferencePanes
ColorSync               Printers
Colors                  PrivateFrameworks
Components              QuickTime
CoreServices            QuickTimeJava
DTDs                    Rulebooks
Displays                Screen Savers
Extensions              ScriptingAdditions
Extensions.mkext        Services
```

UP TO SPEED

Of Terminal and Shells

One-Unix program runs automatically when you open a Terminal window: *tcsh* (pronounced "T.C. Shell").

Technically, a *shell* is a Unix program that interprets the commands you've typed, passes them to the *kernel* (the operating system's brain), and then shows you the kernel's response.

But more practically, the shell is the Unix Finder. It's the program that lets you navigate the contents of your hard drive, see what's inside certain folders, launch programs and documents, and so on.

The *tcsh* shell has one of the most extensive manuals of all time. If you type *man tcsh*, the program produces more than 100 pages, covering topics including basic interac-

tion, customization, date and time formats, and programming. Reading these manual pages will help you understand many elements of the Unix operating system.

There are several different shells available in Unix, each with slightly different command syntax. A few others–like *sh,* the Bourne shell; *bash,* the Bourne Again Shell (hey, that's good!); *zsh;* and *csh*–come with Mac OS X. Read the *man* pages for each shell to determine which one you might like to use. See hint 16-23 for instructions on how to change from *tcsh* to one of the others.

You can open additional Terminal windows by choosing Shell→New. Each window runs independently of any others. For proof, try opening several windows and then running the *cal* command in each.

This isn't a book about Unix. A gentle, two-chapter introduction appears in *Mac OS X: The Missing Manual,* and a full-length exploration of Terminal appears in O'Reilly's *Learning Unix for Mac OS X.* But here's the absolute minimum you need to get by:

- Unless you've fiddled with Terminal's preferences, the insertion point looks like a tall rectangle at the end of the command line. It trots along to the right as you type.

  The ritual is: Type a command at the % prompt (capitalization matters in Unix) and then press Enter. Terminal does what you asked, and then shows another % prompt.

- You can't see any icons for your files and folders, so you're supposed to work with them by asking Unix to tell you what folder you're looking at (using the *pwd* command), what's in it (using the *ls* command), and what folder you want to switch to (using the *cd* command).

  For example, if you type *pwd* and press Enter, Terminal may show you something like this:

  ```
  /Users/chris/Movies
  ```

  Terminal is revealing the working directory's *path*—a list of folders-in-folders, separated by slashes, that specifies a folder's location on your hard drive. */Users/chris/Movies* pinpoints the Movies folder in Chris's Home folder.

  If you now type *ls* (for *list*) and then press Enter, Terminal responds by showing you the names of the files and folders inside in a horizontal list, like this:

  ```
  Desktop Documents Library Movies Music Pictures Public Sites
  ```

  In other words, you see a list of the icons that, in the Finder, you'd see in your Home folder.

  To make Terminal "think about" a different folder, you'd type the *cd* (for *change directory*) command, like this: *cd /Users/chris/Pictures.*

- As you can tell by the *cal* and *ls* examples, Unix commands are very short. They're often just two-letter commands, and an impressive number of those use *alternate hands* (l-s, c-p, r-m, and so on).

  The reason has partly to do with conserving the limited memory of early computers and partly to do with efficiency, since most programmers would just as soon type as little as possible to get things done. User-friendly it ain't, but as you type these commands repeatedly over the months, you'll eventually be grateful for the keystroke savings.

Terminal Shortcuts

The hints in this first batch are so safe and so easy, you'll wonder why anyone ever used "Terminal" and "intimidating" in the same sentence.

Notes: Many of the hints in this chapter work only if your Mac OS X installation includes the software chunk known as the *BSD Subsystem.* But the only reason you wouldn't have it is if you explicitly turned its checkbox *off* when you installed Mac OS X.

15-1   Specify a Path by Dragging

Instead of using the geeky *cd* command to tell Terminal what folder you want to work with, try this: *drag the icon* of the folder you want to specify directly into the Terminal window. Figure 15-3 should make this clear.

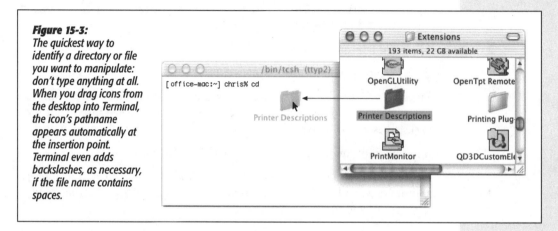

Figure 15-3:
The quickest way to identify a directory or file you want to manipulate: don't type anything at all. When you drag icons from the desktop into Terminal, the icon's pathname appears automatically at the insertion point. Terminal even adds backslashes, as necessary, if the file name contains spaces.

15-2   When to Use the Mouse

The mouse isn't very useful at the command line. You generally move the cursor only with the left and right arrow keys.

You *can* use the mouse, however, to select text from anywhere in the window (or other programs) and paste it in at the prompt.

Furthermore, you can use the mouse to position the insertion point, although there's a trick to it. That's lucky because no matter how stellar a typist you are, occasionally you're going to commit a typo in a very, very long Terminal command. You could fix it using keyboard commands (call up the bad command with the up arrow, and then use the cursor positioning shortcuts like Control-A to jump to the beginning of the line, and so on). If the command is long enough, however, this routine is an incredible drag.

To use the mouse to position the insertion point, start by choosing Terminal→Window Settings to open the Terminal Inspector. From the pop-up menu at the top, select Emulation. Turn on "Option click to position cursor" and close the Inspector.

Now, you can *Option-click* inside a command to plant the insertion point there. For example, when you want to correct a typo, press the up arrow to repeat the last command you typed, move the cursor over the typo, and Option-click to edit at that spot.

15-3   Tab Completion

You know how you can highlight an icon in a Finder window by typing the first few characters of its name? Terminal's tab-completion feature works much the same way. Over time, it can save you miles of finger movement.

It kicks in whenever you're about to type a pathname. Start by typing the first letter or two of the path you want, and then press Tab; Terminal instantly fleshes out the rest of the directory's name. As shown in Figure 15-4, you can repeat this process to specify the next directory-name chunk of the path.

Some tips for tab completion:

- Capitalization counts.

- Terminal will add backslashes automatically if your directory names include spaces, $ signs, or other special characters. But you still have to insert your own backslashes when you type the "hint" characters that tip off tab completion.

- If it can't find a match for what you typed, Terminal beeps.

    If it finds *several* files or directories that match what you typed, Terminal beeps and shows you a list of them. To specify the one you really want, type the next letter or two and then press Tab again.

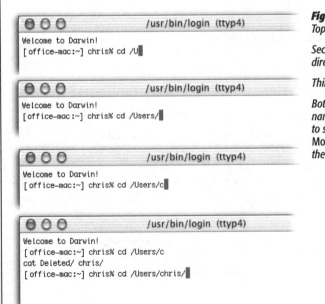

Figure 15-4:
Top: You type cd /U *and then press Tab.*

Second from top: Terminal finishes the directory name Users *for you.*

Third from top: You type c *and then press Tab.*

Bottom: Terminal finishes the home-directory name, chris. *You can also use tab completion to specify file names, as when you type* ls -l Movies/R *and then press Tab; Terminal finishes the name* Reviews.doc.

15-4   The History

You may find yourself at some point needing to run a previously entered command, but dreading the prospect of re-entering the whole command. Retyping a command, however, is never necessary. Terminal (or, rather, the *shell* it's running—see the box on page 343) remembers the last 150 commands you entered. At any prompt, instead of typing, just press the up or down arrow keys to walk through the various commands in the shell's memory. They flicker by, one at a time, on the same line as the % prompt.

15-5   Wildcards

Wildcards are special characters that represent other characters—and they're huge timesavers.

The most popular wildcard is the asterisk (*), which means "any text can go here." For example, to see a list of the files in the working directory that end with the letters *te,* you could type *ls *te.* Terminal would show you files named Latte, BudLite, Dynomite, and so on, and hiding all other files in the list.

Likewise, to see which files and directories begin with "Old," you could type *ls Old** and press Enter. If you add the asterisk before *and* after the search phrase, you'd find items with that phrase *anywhere* in their names. Typing *ls *jo** will show you the files named Johnson, Mojo, Major Disaster, and so on.

15-6   Directory Switching

A hyphen (-) after the *cd* command means, "take me back to the previous working directory." For example, if you changed your working directory from *~/Movies/Movie 1* to *~/Documents/Letters*, simply enter *cd -* to change back to *~/Movies/Movie 1*. Use *cd -* a second time to return to *~/Documents/Letters*. (Note the space between *cd* and the hyphen.)

Tip: On the other hand, if you're doing a lot of switching between directories, you should probably just open and switch between two Terminal windows, each with a different working directory.

15-7   Special Keys

The *tcsh* shell (page 343) offers dozens of special keystroke shortcuts for navigation. You may recognize many of them as useful undocumented shortcuts that work in any Cocoa application (see page 99), but even more are available (and useful) in Terminal.

Keystroke	Effect
Ctrl-U	Erases the entire command line you're working on.
Ctrl-A	Moves the insertion point to the beginning of the line.
Ctrl-E	Moves the insertion point to the end of the line.
Ctrl-T	Transposes the previous two characters.
Esc-F	Moves the insertion point to the beginning of the next word.

Esc-B	Moves the insertion point to the beginning of the previous word.
Esc-Delete	Erases the previous word (defined as "anything that ends with a space, slash, or most other punctuation marks; periods and asterisks not included"). You have to press and release the Esc key and *then* the Delete key; repeat for each word.
Esc-D	Erases the word following the insertion point.
Esc-C	Capitalizes the word following the insertion point.
Esc-U	Changes the next word to all uppercase letters.
Esc-L	Changes the next word to all lowercase letters.

To see all of the available key bindings, type *bindkey,* which generates a list something like this:

```
Standard key bindings
"^@"→set-mark-command
"^A"→beginning-of-line
"^B"→backward-char
"^C"→tty-sigintr
... ... ...
```

(The ^ symbol denotes the Control key.)

If you see an explanation that you don't understand, like *tty-sigintr,* use *bindkey -l,* which produces a list of the possible key bindings, along with a slightly more detailed description.

Tip: You can change any key bindings by setting the value in your environment.mine file, as described in the box on page 351.

15-8　Turning off Autocorrection

In *tcsh,* when you make a typographical error, as in the first word here:

```
pinge 192.168.1.100
```

...the shell nicely suggests a correctly spelled alternative, like this:

```
OK? ping 192.168.1.100?
```

If you press *y* at this point, *tcsh* executes the command it suggested.

If this behavior makes you crabby, add the following two lines anywhere in your environment.mine file. (This instruction should become clear after you read the boxes on pages 350 and 351):

```
unset autocorrect
unset correct
```

If you ever want the correction function back, change *unset* to *set,* save the file, quit the editor, and then type *source ~/Library/init/tcsh/environment.mine* to activate your changes.

15-9   File Names That Contain Spaces

You may find it frustrating in Terminal dealing with a file whose name contains spaces. For example, if you type *cd Summer Design Sketches* to see what's in that folder, Terminal responds with *cd: Too many arguments.* (Remember: In Terminal's strict little head, anything after a space is an *argument* of a command.)

You can deal with this mumbo jumbo three ways.

- If you type *cd* and a space, you can drag a folder from the Finder—yes, right off the desktop—into the Terminal window. Terminal autocompletes the line and displays the full path to the dragged folder. Press Enter, and you've now navigated to that folder in Terminal.

- You can also precede each space with a backlash, like this: *cd Summer\ Design\ Sketches;* or you can enclose the entire thing in quotes (*cd "Summer Design Sketches"*).

- Use autocompletion. Start typing the directory name and then press Tab before you reach the first space, like this: *cd Summ* [Tab]. When you press Tab, Terminal automatically completes the folder name, including the backslashes. Press Enter.

Tip: If you work in Terminal regularly, keep your file names simple. Avoid spaces and other characters that have special meaning in Unix: ~, !, @, #, $, %, &, *, parentheses, and brackets. You'll avoid confusing Terminal—and yourself.

15-10   Going Back Home

You've been exploring Terminal and navigating various folders and subfolders for hours. You're miles from where you started and seriously lost. You want to get back to your Home directory quickly and easily. Here are your options:

- **Long:** Type *cd /Users/chris/* (*cd* is the change directory command, and *chris* is your Home account).

- **Quicker:** Type *cd ~* (the tilde is shorthand for *Users/UserName*).

- **Quickest:** Type *cd* and press Enter.

15-11   Change Directories in a Snap

In the course of a typical Terminal session, you probably use the *cd* command more than any other, and it can get annoying to type *cd /path/to/some/directory* every time you want to jump to a new directory. You can use Tab to autocomplete the path (see hint 15-3) or drag an icon into the Terminal window (hint 15-1), but you still have to type *cd* every time.

But by taking advantage of a predefined *shell variable* (a keyword that the Terminal recognizes), you can save those three keystrokes.

After reading the box on page 351 for full instructions, add this line anywhere in your environment.mine file:

```
set implicitcd
```

(Get it? "Implicit *cd*," as in, "when I type a path, *assume* that I want you to *cd* to it.")

Save the file, quit the editor, and then type *source ~/Library/init/tcsch/ environment.mine* to activate your changes.

You can now switch to any directory by typing only the path to that directory. For instance, typing *~/Documents* executes the *cd* command and places you in your Home→Documents directory.

GEM IN THE ROUGH

Setting Up for Better Hints

Unix comes in many flavors, each of which may have a slightly different means of establishing settings for its Terminal program. Mac OS X is no exception; it lets you establish your settings in a number of different ways. "Settings," in this case, means important Unix concepts like these:

The prompt. When you first open up Terminal, the % symbol is the prompt—the sign that tells you, "I'm ready to do your bidding, master. Type something." But it doesn't have to be the % symbol; you can change it.

Paths. You need to tell Terminal where it's supposed to find all of Mac OS X's executable Unix files (programs) by specifying a *path* (a folder hierarchy).

Aliases. A Unix *alias* is a text shortcut for a longer command.

When you first install Mac OS X 10.2, though, some preference files (*shell configuration files*) that enhance the factory settings aren't installed, leaving you deprived of many shortcuts that can make Terminal a lot easier to use.

Fortunately, it's very easy to add back these missing functions. Just type each of the following lines into the Terminal, pressing Enter after each. (Each single command appears on two lines here, but you should type each on a single line, without a space after *tcsh/*):

```
echo "source /usr/share/tcsh/
    examples/rc" > ~/.tcshrc
echo "source /usr/share/tcsh/
    examples/login" > ~/.login
echo "source /usr/share/tcsh/
    examples/logout" > ~/.logout
```

These three commands create three new, invisible files (called .tcshrc, .login, and .logout) that help to put in place all of the prompt, path, and alias settings you'll need for some of the hints in this chapter. They contain Unix commands that help customize your working environment, and that get executed (loaded) each time you open a new Terminal window.

While you're at it, you should also take a moment to issue this command:

```
mkdir -p ~/Library/init/tcsh
```

You've just created two folders: one, inside your Home→Library folder, called *init;* and another, inside *that* folder, called *tcsh*. Right now, the *tcsh* folder is empty, but Mac OS X will put certain key files into it as you work on some of the hints in this chapter—files called aliases.mine, completions.mine, environment.mine, path, and rc.mine. You'll be reading more about these in the relevant hints and in the box on the facing page.

If you happen to have a directory name that matches the name of a Unix command, be aware that *implicitcd* takes priority over the command name. So if you have a directory named *ls*, and you turn on *implicitcd*, typing *ls* will take you to the *ls* directory instead of executing the *ls* command.

If you decide you liked your Unix world the way it was originally, you can turn off the *implicitcd* feature. Open your environment.mine file again (page 351), delete the *set implicitcd* line and save the file.

The next time you open a new Terminal window, you'll once again have to use the *cd* to change directories.

UP TO SPEED

Editing the Environment Variable Files

Many of the hints in this chapter and the next direct you to modify one of the four key setup files described in the box on the facing page: alias.mine, environment.mine, path, and rc.mine. It would probably help if you had some instructions for doing so.

Mac OS X's Unix personality comes with three different text processors—like the Unix version of TextEdit or BBEdit. Of course, in Terminal, you won't be using your mouse, you won't see any graphics, and you won't have a choice of fonts and sizes. But you'll be perfectly equipped for making changes to text files like those setup files (properly called *environment variable* files).

The three Terminal text editors are known by their Unix-command names: *emacs, vi,* and *pico.* Of these three, *pico* is easiest for beginners.

To use *pico,* make sure you've used the *cd* command to direct Terminal's attention to the proper directory (page 344), and then type *pico groceries.txt* (or whatever the file name is). Or skip the *cd* business, and just type *pico ~/Documents/groceries.txt* (or whatever the path to your file is). Either way, you see something like the display shown here.

To edit a document, move the insertion point by pressing the arrow keys. (If you're a mouse diva, see hint 15-2.) Then just type to insert text, press Delete to backspace over text, and so on. (You can't drag to select text in *pico*.)

pico lists the most important commands right across the bottom of the screen. Once you've entered or edited the text as directed, hit Control-O (Write Out—that is, Save) to save your changes. Then hit Control-X (Exit) to quit the editor and return to the regularly scheduled Terminal window.

In this chapter, you'll be editing the four environment variable files called aliases.mine, environment.mine, path, and rc.mine. In other words, proceed like this:

First, type *cd ~/Library/init/tcsh* to switch to the proper directory. (This folder exists if you followed the instructions in the box on the facing page.)

Second, type *pico aliases.mine* (or whatever the name of the file is). Edit the text in this file as described in the hint.

Third, press Control-O to save your changes, and Control-X to quit *pico*. Finally, type *source aliases.mine* to activate the changes.

15-12   Mouse-free Copying

You're working away in Microsoft Word X when you realize that you need to paste a Unix directory list (*ls*) into the document. You could switch to Terminal, type *ls -al*, then grab your mouse and *then* carefully select all the *ls* output, switch back to Word, and press ⌘-V to paste.

You'd save a lot of time, however, if you used the *pbcopy* command to load the clipboard, like this:

```
ls -al | pbcopy
```

This line takes the output of the *ls* command and sends it to the *pbcopy* command. *Pbcopy* places the output on the clipboard. When you switch back to Word, press ⌘-V to paste the clipboard contents.

15-13   Mouse-free Pasting

Speaking of mouse-free copying and pasting: You can move clipboard contents in the other direction using *pbpaste.* This trick is most useful for creating a new file from a selection of text.

Open a document in some Mac OS X program, select the text that you'd like to use, copy it, then switch to Terminal and type *pbpaste > somefile.txt.* (Replace *somefile.txt* with a file name of your choice.) *Pbpaste* creates a text file called somefile.txt in the current Terminal directory, filled with the current Clipboard contents. (If you're not sure what directory you're "in," type *pwd* and press Enter.)

Window Administration

The Terminal has some tricks up its sleeve to make your time at the command line a little less black-and-white, a little more productive, and even a little more fun.

15-14   Changing Window and Font Colors

If you're bored, and you want to change the window and font colors in Terminal, you can choose Terminal→Window Settings. In the pop-up menu at the top of the dialog box, select Color, and then click the area of the screen you want to change. Finally, choose a color to use.

In fact, this method is your only choice if you want to change the color of text you've selected. For changing all other color settings, however, Terminal gives you another method.

First, make sure you can see normal text, bold text, some of the screen background, and the cursor on the screen. (The easiest way to see all this stuff is to view the manual pages for a program. For example, type *man tcsh,* which displays the manual for *tcsh,* a techy program you'll probably otherwise never encounter.)

Now choose Font→Show Colors (or press Shift-⌘-C) to bring up the color wheel. Change the color of anything in the Terminal window by setting the color you'd like to use in the color wheel, and then dragging that color from the sample swatch (next to the magnifying glass, above the wheel) onto the text or background you want to change, as in Figure 15-5.

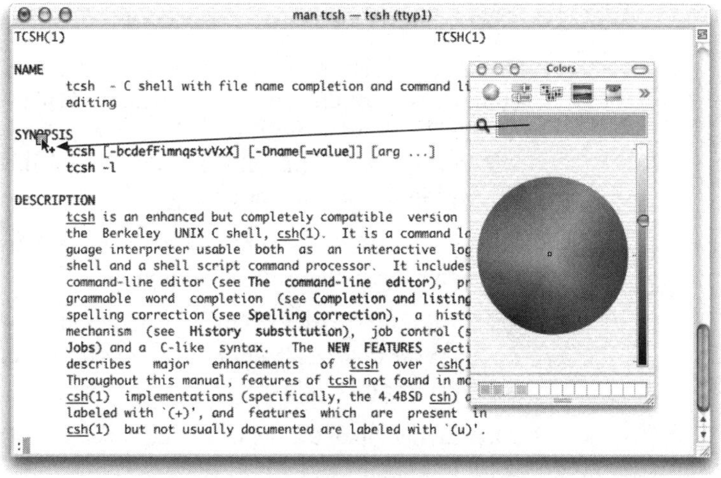

Figure 15-5:
Here, a color swatch is being dragged onto the bolded word SYNOPSIS. When the mouse is released, all bold text will take on the dropped color. You can also drag color swatches onto the background, normal text, and even the block representing the cursor.

Once you have a color scheme you like, choose select File→Use Settings As Defaults to make your eye-popping colors appear in all new Terminal windows.

15-15 Insta-Double-Clickable Terminal Commands

Terminal is your rabbit hole into a wonderland of cool commands, but if you come to rely on it, you may come to resent all the red tape involved just in preparing to run a command.

For example, suppose you want to run *top -u 20*—a handy command that lists the top 20 most processor-intensive programs running at the moment, all in a tidy list—so that you can see where all your memory and processor power are going. First you have to open or switch to Terminal, then maybe open a new Terminal window if you don't want to lose what you're currently working on. You then must size and place it, perhaps set background and font colors and sizes, and then type the command and its options.

Wouldn't it be cooler to just double-click a file in the Finder to do the exact same thing?

You can. Once you've adjusted a window's fonts, colors, and sizes, you can use Terminal's special Save command to enshrine them as an icon on your desktop. You can then open a customized window at any time by double-clicking that saved file in the Finder.

This feature makes it easy to customize windows for various commands. For instance, you can create a blue and white window for *ssh* sessions (hint 6-9), a yellow and black window for *top* sessions (hint 15-53), and a green and black window for editing sessions. Then, even when you have 20 windows open on your screen, you can tell at a glance which has the command you want to jump to.

Here's how it works:

1. **Open a new Terminal window and set it up the way you like it.**

   Position it where you'd like it on the screen, set its width and height (perhaps by running as a test the program that will be displayed in the window), and choose Terminal→Window Setting to bring up a dialog box that lets you customize the window. Use the Terminal Inspector (File→Show Info or ⌘-I) to change the display, color, and window settings.

2. **Once you've set all your options, choose File→Save As, and then pick a location and name for your Terminal window.**

   Terminal wants to save the file in your Application Support folder, but you may find it easier to locate later on if you save it in your Home folder. (Alternatively, see the next hint.)

3. **After saving, open the file in TextEdit (see page 4).**

   BBEdit works well, too, from the Finder, or you can use one of the Terminal editors, like *vi* or *pico*.

4. **Search for the section of the file that contains these lines:**

   ```
   <key>ExecutionString</key>
   <string></string>
   ```

5. **Between the two "string" tags, insert the name of the command you'd like Terminal to execute.**

   For example, for that *top -u 20* command, you'd type:

   ```
   <string>top -u 20</string>
   ```

6. **Save the file. Test your new command launcher in the Finder by double-clicking the new Terminal file.**

   If all went well, Terminal opens with the settings you specified in the screen location you chose and it launches your command.

If the program doesn't start as expected, try including the full path (*/usr/bin/top*) instead of just the command name between the string tags in step 5.

15-16 Opening Saved Terminal Windows in the Dock

Using the same methods as described in the previous hint, you can create a saved Terminal session that opens *pre-minimized in the Dock* instead of opening a new window. This arrangement is handy if, for instance, you use Terminal to download email from a remote host, but you use Mail to read your messages on your current machine. In that case, you really don't need to *see* the Terminal window.

Create the saved session as you did in the previous hint, and then open it to edit. Search the file for this section:

```
<key>IsMiniaturized</key>
<string>NO</string>
```

Replace NO with YES and save the file. Your Terminal session now starts minimized in the Dock.

15-17 Dragging Text Between Terminal Windows

You can drag and drop text from one Terminal window to another. (How's *that* for a quickie?)

Note: Oddly, when you drag and drop text from one Terminal window to another, the first window remains the active window.

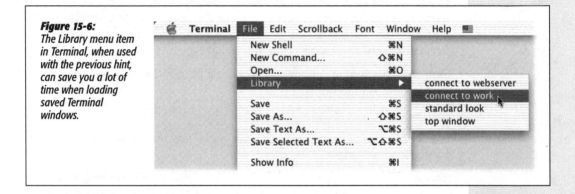

Figure 15-6:
The Library menu item in Terminal, when used with the previous hint, can save you a lot of time when loading saved Terminal windows.

15-18 A Library of Terminal Windows

Terminal comes with a very useful menu item, File→Library, grayed out. This menu can provide easy access to the customized windows you created using the previous hint, as shown in Figure 15-6.

Here's how to turn on File→Library.

Quit Terminal and open your Home→Library→Application Support folder. Create a new folder here called Terminal. Then, in the Terminal program, choose File→Save As, and note that the save location is your newly created Terminal folder.

If you save your open Terminal window (before you make any changes to it), the File→Library menu item turns on, and its submenu shows the name of the file you just saved. To make this submenu really handy, use your new Terminal folder to save the customized windows you created in the previous hint.

For easy access to this menu, consider putting an alias of the Application Support→
Terminal folder on your Dock. (Just drag the Terminal folder to the right side of the
Dock.)

Manipulating Commands

The Unix shell can make your command time more productive in a googol of different ways. The shell can keep track of what commands you've run, help you fix typos
you've made, and even allow you to create entirely new commands with ease.

15-19   The Master List of Commands and Programs

Want to see a master list of every Unix command Terminal knows about—your
master vocabulary of magic words?

At the % prompt, press Control-X, and then Control-D. Terminal displays a list of
every executable program anywhere on your path—hundreds and hundreds of them,
most of which explain themselves when you use the *man* command (hint 15-57).

15-20   Scrolling Through Command Completions

When you're trying to remember one of the seemingly infinite Unix commands,
you'd probably find it helpful if Terminal prompted your memory with some hints.
You're in luck: By using the *bindkey* function, it can.

Using the *pico* editor as described in the box on page 351, add the following line to
your environment.mine file:

```
bindkey "^I" complete-word-fwd
```

Save the file, quit *pico,* and then type *source ~/Library/init/tcsch/environment.mine*
to activate your changes.

From now on, if you type *a* and then press Tab, Terminal scrolls through all commands that begin with *a*. If you type *po* and then press Tab, you scroll through all
commands that being with *po*. And so on. This trick is very useful when you're sure
the command you're looking for starts with a certain letter, but you don't remember
the rest.

But wait. There's more!

Suppose Unix has 1,649 commands that start with *a*. The Tab trick isn't going to
help you much. Here's a way to narrow down the list.

If you type *a* and then press Control-D, Terminal displays a list of all commands
that start with *a*, followed by the % prompt with your *a* still sitting there, ready for
more letters of the command. Add *c* after *a*, press Control-D again, and Terminal
presents you with a list of commands that start with *ac*.

You can also use this behavior with the *ls* (list) command to make directory lists for
deeply buried subfolders. Type *ls,* press Space, press Tab, and you'll see each of the

current directory's subfolders pop into the display. When you see the one you'd like to list, hit the right arrow, then hit Tab again. This time, the second level subdirectories (folders within folders *within* folders) will start appearing. Hit Tab until you see the one you want, and then hit the right arrow again.

For example, if you want to list everything in the Documents→Projects→2002→ Remodeling→Basement→Kids Room directory, you could do it by typing *ls [Tab until Documents appears] [Right Arrow] [tab until Projects appears] [Right Arrow] [tab until 2002 appears] [Right Arrow]*…and so on. (It's much harder to describe than it is to use.)

When you arrive at the level you'd like to see, press Enter to execute the *ls* command.

Tip: This exact keystroke sequence works with the *cd* command as well, which makes it very simple to move down a directory tree.

If you get tired of this behavior, remove the *bindkey* line from your environment.mine file, and then close and reopen Terminal or repeat the *source* command.

15-21 Saving Keystrokes with the History File

When you execute commands in the *tcsh* shell, Mac OS X adds them to a file named *.tcsh_history*, which sits in your Home folder. If you followed the advice in the box on page 351, you have access to a powerful set of tools that lets you easily find and use previous commands—even if you quit Terminal and don't return to it until days later.

Note: *.tcsh_history* is updated only if you use *exit* to end your shell session! If you just press ⌘-Q or click the close button, the commands from your session won't be added to the History file.

For example, if you press Control-R, Terminal displays a *bck:* indicator below the current line, like this:

```
bck:
```

If you then begin to type a command, it shows up on the *bck:* line, and the nearest alphabetically matching command appears on the command (%) line. You've just recalled a command from your Terminal history, which (if Terminal guessed it correctly) you can execute just by pressing Enter.

For example, if you had recently executed both a *cd ~/Documents* command and a *cat recipes.txt* command, pressing Control-R followed by *c* causes Terminal to display *cd ~/Documents* on the command line. If you then type *a,* the command changes to *cat recipes.txt.*

15-22 Finding Old Commands via History

In Terminal, the left and right arrow keys move you forward and backward through a command to make corrections; the up and down arrow keys move you sequentially through the History list, one command at a time. Even if you'd already started typing a command when you press the up arrow, Terminal replaces the new command with the last one.

But if you want to re-execute a command starting with *de* that you issued hours ago, it would be useful if, when you typed *de* and pressed the up arrow key, the system showed only those commands in History that started with *de*. Otherwise, you'll have to scroll through hundreds of commands one line at a time, and you'll be bored.

UP TO SPEED

Meet the *sudo* Command

Normal and Administrator aren't the only kinds of accounts in Mac OS X. There's one account that wields ultimate power, one person who can do anything to any file anywhere. This person is called the *superuser.*

Unix fans speak of the superuser account—also called the *root* account—in hushed tones, because it offers absolutely unrestricted power. The root account holder can move, delete, rename, or otherwise mangle any file on the machine. One wrong move—or one Internet hacker who manages to seize the root account—and you've got yourself an Apple-logoed doorstop. That's why Mac OS X's root account is completely hidden and, in fact, deactivated.

Some of the things the root account holder can do include: seeing the thousands of crucial system files that Mac OS X ordinarily renders invisible; manipulating the files within the System folder's Library folder; and executing certain powerful Unix system commands in Terminal.

In Terminal, you can enjoy most root-like powers without actually turning on the root account. There's a simple command—the *sudo* command—that simulates root powers without you actually having them.

sudo is a great command name. Technically, it's short for *superuser do,* which means that you're allowed to execute any command as though you had logged in with the root (superuser) account—but without actually having to turn on the root account, log out, log back in again, and so on.

It's also a great command name because it looks as though it would be pronounced "pseudo," as in, "I'm just *pretending* to be the root user for a moment. I'm here under a pseudonym." (In fact, you pronounce it "SOO-doo," because it comes from *superuser do.* In the privacy of your own brain, though, you can pronounce it however you like.)

The first time you run *sudo,* you're treated to the characteristic deadpan humor of programmers worldwide: "We trust you have received the usual lecture from the local System Administrator. It usually boils down to these two things: 1) Respect the privacy of others, and 2) Think before you type."

In other words, *sudo* is a powerful tool that lets you tromp unfettered across delicate parts of Mac OS X, and you should therefore proceed with caution. At the outset, at least, you should use it only when you've been given specific steps to follow, as in this chapter.

Now *sudo* asks you for your usual login password, just to confirm that you're not some seventh-grader up to no good. If you are indeed an administrator, and your password checks out, *sudo* gives you a five-minute window in which, by prefacing each command with *sudo,* you can tromp around as though you're the all-high, master root account holder. (If you don't use *sudo* again within a five-minute span, you have to input your password again.)

Using the *bindkey* function, you can easily set Terminal to display a smart history of your commands. Using the *pico* editor as described in the box on page 351, add these two lines to your environment.mine file:

```
bindkey -k down history-search-forward
bindkey -k up history-search-backward
```

Save the file, quit the *pico* editor, and then type *source ~/Library/init/tcsh* to activate the changes.

From now on, the up and down arrow keys pay attention to any characters that you have already typed, and Terminal displays *only* commands that match. Simply start typing the command you want to find, and then press the up arrow key.

To undo your work, remove the two lines from your environment.mine file, and then close and reopen Terminal.

15-23   Running the Previous Command as the Superuser

Sooner or later, you're going to execute a command as your Normal account that you intended to execute as the superuser (via *sudo;* see the box on page 358). Instead of hitting the up arrow and editing the previous line to insert the *sudo* command, just type *sudo !!.* The two exclamation points (*!!*) are a shortcut for the previous command (which you can redisplay thanks to the History file).

For more tricks based on previous commands, search the Terminal shell manual for History substations (type *man tcsh /History substitution*). Repeat the search (just press slash again) until you find the right section. It describes a bunch of shortcuts including *!**, which takes the arguments from the prior command and gives them to the current command.

15-24   Fixing Errors in the Previous Command

While trying to change to the Web server's documents directory, you goof and type *cd /Library/WebbServer/Documents.* The shell nicely tells you that no such directory as "WebbServer" exists, so you press the up arrow to recall the previous command, use the left arrow (or cursor-positioning keys; see hint 15-7) to move back, delete the extra "b" from *WebbServer,* and press Enter.

Here's how to save a bunch of keystrokes the next time you need to fix a typo: Just type *^bb^b,* and then press Enter. The shell pulls up the previous command (thank you, History!), finds the first instance of *bb,* replaces it with *b,* and then executes the resulting command.

You can't fix numerous complex typos with carets, but they're perfect for fixing simple mistakes.

15-25   Merging History Files

If you're using the History file and it seems not to remember everything it should, *it's* probably the one with the memory problem, not you. Here's the deal.

If you use Terminal with more than one window open (most people do), then every time you use *exit* to close a Terminal window, Mac OS X overwrites the existing History file with a new one. As a result, you lose the list of commands you've recently created.

You can change this behavior, if you like. Using the *pico* editor as described in the box on page 351, add this line to your environment.mine file:

```
set savehist = (500 merge)
```

Replace 500 with the number of previous commands that you would like the shell to search. The *merge* option tells the shell to combine (sorted by time stamp), rather than overwrite, the History files from multiple windows.

Note: Remember that you must exit each window by typing *exit* or pressing Control-D in order to successfully update the History file!

15-26 New Commands Using Aliases

Unix *aliases* aren't the same thing as Mac aliases. They're shortcuts, but instead of serving as shorthand for files and programs, Unix uses them as shorthand for existing *commands*.

For example, if you frequently open certain programs from the command line, aliases can make the process easier. The long *shadowGoogle* launch command described in hint 15-38, for instance, can be reduced to *sg*—just two keystrokes.

Here's an experiment to help you understand Unix aliases. If you've set up your Unix environment as discussed in the box on page 351, the command *word* is an

---

TROUBLESHOOTING MOMENT

Help! My Terminal History File Stopped Working

You're making great progress learning the shell, and you've created some customized environment files to help make the shell work for you (see the box on page 351). But now, your History file isn't working. You can no longer use the up arrow key or Control-R to get at previous commands, and you can't figure out why.

More than likely, the problem is an error in one of your environment files in your Home→Library→init→tcsh folder. Try turning off these files temporarily (a good way to do so is to quickly rename them using, for example, the command *mv aliases.mine aliases.bad*, and then close and open the Terminal window) and see if your History file works as expected.

If it does, you need to spend some time figuring out what section of which file is causing the problem. This process is one of trial and error; start by making sure only one script is loading (leave the others renamed), and then *comment out* (by placing a "#" sign at the front of each line) or remove one line at a time and see if your History file remains functional.

Test the changes by opening a new Terminal window while leaving the editing window open. Repeat the process until you find the culprit, and then either permanently remove or fix the offending command. Repeat as necessary through the other four files in the directory (path, rc.mine, completions.mine, and environment.mine).

---

alias. If you type *word hello,* you get a list of words that all contain "hello."

To learn how this alias works, type *alias* at the % prompt, which generates a list of *tcsh*'s predefined aliases. Near the end of the output is the entry for *word*:

```
word grep !* /usr/share/dict/web2
```

word is the alias—shorthand for the longer command that appears to right of it. The *grep* search program looks for the text you supply (*!** is the place holder for that text; in the example above, you searched for "hello"), and the search looks in the file */usr/ share/dict/web2*. (That file, incidentally, is Webster's Second International dictionary, right there on your hard drive. Who knew?)

Aliases can also be handy for combining commands you often use together. For example, suppose you have a remote computer that you connect to often using *ssh* (hint 6-9). Some computers require that you specify a particular *port number* (networking "keyhole") as part of the *ssh* command. So your *ssh* line becomes rather lengthy, something like this:

```
ssh -p 5022 chris@www.earthlink.com
```

Instead of typing that every time you want to connect, you can create an alias called *sshwork* that runs the whole command.

By looking through the existing aliases, you can get a sense of what's possible. For a good example of combined commands, pay close attention to the *wordcount* alias, which uses two *cat* commands, the *tail* command, and the *awk* command.

Here's how to create your own alias:

1. **Using the *pico* editor as described in the box on page 351, open aliases.mine.**

   The *pico* text processor opens it up on the screen.

2. **Add the alias as a new line anywhere in the file.**

   To add this line, note that the first word must be *alias*; next is the name of the alias (abbreviation) you want to create; and then, in quotes, is the longer command or commands that you want to execute.

   For example, if you were to recreate the *word* alias, you'd type:

   ```
   alias word ''grep \!* /usr/share/dict/web2''
   ```

   You need the backslash to remind the shell that here, the exclamation point is a special character (*!** is a special code that means, "anything following the command on the same line").

   To create the *ssh* alias described above, you'd type:

   ```
   alias sshwork ''ssh -p 5022 chris@www.earthlink.com''
   ```

(Of course, substitute the real port number and email address.)

To create the shadowGoogle alias described above, you'd type:

```
alias sg ''open -a /Applications/My\ Utilities/
shadowGoogle.app''
```

Tip: Avoid giving one of your aliases the same name as an existing Unix command (*ls,* for example). If you
did that, you'd be missing out if Apple ever quietly updated the "official" version with a new, improved,
supercharged version. Your alias would continue to intercept your typing of *ls* (or whatever), and you'd
miss out on the goodies.

Administering the Mac

The Unix shell can help you keep a close eye on the performance of your Mac—in
ways that no "real" Mac OS X program can. For example, did you know you can
pause an application that's running in the background so that it won't take any of
your precious CPU cycles while you're not using it? If you read this section, you'll
know that and much more.

15-27   Your Mac's True Unix Heritage

During the normal boot-up sequence for Mac OS X, you see a gray logo in the
middle of the screen with a progress wheel spinning just below it. But if you ever
want to see what *really* happens when your machine boots up, hold down ⌘-V just
after you press the power button or the reset switch. This key combo reveals the
underlying process and is known as *verbose mode booting.*

Figure 15-7:
Tail-*ing the Apache
logs helps you see
what's happening
on your site in real
time. For instance,
on April 12 at
23:43:22 (the first
line), somebody
whose Mac was at
IP address 24.138.47
.140 did a "GET" on
the geeklog.rdf file
(that is, loaded it).
You can even see
that this person's
MacReporter
program asked for
the page.

Some ugly white text on the black background shows you exactly what Unix is doing to boot your machine. The messages go by very quickly, but you can see them once the boot process is finished.

Unfortunately, the messages aren't likely to make more sense to you when you can actually read them. But if you're curious, do this: Launch Terminal and type *dmesg | less* (the *less* command makes the long *dmesg* results scroll one page at a time).

15-28 Log Files in Real Time

If you like to see what's going on with your machine as it happens, you can use the *tail* command.

Type *tail -f /var/log/system.log,* for example, to watch the system log being recorded in real time. The system log is a file that records certain activities that other applications send in its direction. Although much of what you may see in the log looks like technical gibberish, studying it might lead you to discover that one certain program is constantly saving data to the file—a sign that it's misbehaving, slowing down your machine, and worth troubleshooting.

(The *-f* flag tells *tail* to read the end of the log file and then keep reading it as the log is updated. Without the *-f* flag, *tail* would just display the last lines of the file and then quit.)

You can also watch the Apache logs, which track visitors and activity on any Web pages you serve with Personal Web Sharing. To do that, open a Terminal window, type *tail -f /var/log/http/access_log* or *tail -f /var/log/http/error_log,* shrink the Terminal window, and position it so that you can see it while you work on other things. Now you have an always visible real-time activity monitor (Figure 15-6).

15-29 Pausing CPU-Hungry Background Programs

Many Carbon programs, including Explorer, iTunes, Acrobat, and the Office applications, eat up a ton of computing power even when they're running in the background. Even while it's doing nothing, for example, Microsoft Word can scarf down 10 percent or more of your CPU's (central processing unit's) attention all by its big fat self.

If you want to leave such a program running when you're not using it—maybe you have a lot of windows open that you don't want to close and reopen—but you need the CPU's energy for other tasks, you can pause the offending program. While paused, the program's CPU usage drops to zero. Its windows remain open, but you can't use it. Unpausing is easy and doesn't require relaunching the program and its windows.

To pause a program, you need what's called its *process ID* (PID). You can find a PID by typing *ps ax | grep "Microsoft Word"* or whatever the program name is (you don't need the quotes if it's just one word). When you press Enter, the PID is the first number on the line that appears.

Suppose the program's PID is 791. You can pause it by typing:

```
kill -STOP 791
```

To restart the paused program, use:

```
kill -CONT 791
```

15-30   Maintenance Scripts on Demand

Mac OS X runs a series of maintenance scripts designed to clean out system logs, update things like the *locate* and *whatis* databases, and perform a number of other tasks. These scripts are scheduled to run on a daily, weekly, or monthly basis. You can see what these scripts are set to do by typing these commands:

```
cd /etc
cat daily | less
cat weekly | less
cat monthly | less
```

After each *cat* command, you'll see the contents of the corresponding file go flowing by on the screen. If you're new to Terminal, you probably won't understand most of what scrolls up your screen. But their purpose is to remove temporary files, log files that Mac OS X no longer needs, and compress other older routine tracking files to save drive space. Each is set to run on a different schedule. To find out exactly when these scripts are scheduled to run, type *cat /etc/crontab*. The end of the resulting output looks like this:

```
. . .
#min hour mday month wday command
. . .
#
# Run daily/weekly/monthly jobs.
15 3 * * * root periodic daily
30 4 * * 6 root periodic weekly
30 5 1 * * root periodic monthly
```

Although you might not realize it at first glance, the last three lines reveal the times at which the maintenance scripts run—for example, the daily script runs at 3:15 a.m.

Here's how to read that: The first column is minutes; the second column is the hour (in 24-hour mode); and the asterisk in the third column means every day. Similarly, the weekly script runs at 4:30 a.m. on Sunday morning (in the fifth column, days are numbered from 0 on Monday through 6 on Sunday), and the monthly script runs at 5:30 a.m. on the first day of every month. (For more information on the *crontab* command, see hint 16-1.)

If you leave your Mac on (and not sleeping), the scripts run at their appointed times. But a constantly running computer is not necessarily good for your Mac or your energy bill. If, like most people, you put your Mac to sleep when you're not using it, you can run the scripts on your own schedule. You don't need to do so every day, but if your Mac sleeps when you do, it's a good idea to occasionally run the cleanup scripts by hand.

You can use regular Mac OS X program for this task—Cronnix, for example (*www.koch-schmidt.de/cronnix*)—or you can do it from Terminal. You simply need to execute the scripts in the */etc* directory. Assuming you are not currently in the */etc* directory, just type:

```
sudo periodic daily
sudo periodic weekly
sudo periodic monthly
```

Each command runs for a while and then returns you to the command prompt. Obviously, there's no need to run the *monthly* script any more often than monthly, the *weekly* script any more often than weekly, and the *daily* script any more often than daily.

15-31   Complete Backups

If you want a complete backup of your files, it's not enough just to drag your Documents folder onto a backup disk. You also have to worry about endless invisible files and settings: resource forks, ownership, and permissions, Unix aliases, and so on. If you don't get all of it into a backup copy, your documents and programs won't work properly when restored.

The two obvious options, copying files in the Finder or using the *cp* command in Terminal, don't cut it. If you drag a folder in the Finder, you copy the resource forks (see hint 15-42) but not the hidden files. If you use *cp* in Terminal, you copy the hidden files but not the resource forks. Either way, some of your backup files might be rendered useless.

Happily, Mac OS X includes a program called *ditto* that can make an exact duplicate of a directory—*all* of it, even the settings and invisible files. This program is great for completely backing up your Home folder, which is probably where most of your personal documents and preferences live.

Just use the command in this format:

```
sudo ditto -v -rsrcFork /folder /Backupdrive/folder
```

It breaks down like this:

- **-v** tells *ditto* to spew out one line of output for each file.
- **-rsrcFork** tells *ditto* to copy the Mac's resource fork data (see hint 15-42) as well as the file itself.
- **folder** is the folder you want to back up (it can be any folder path).
- **Backupdrive** is the path of the backup drive and destination folder.

So suppose you have another hard drive named Backups, your name is Chris, and you want to back up your Home folder. You'd type:

```
sudo ditto -v -rsrcFork /Users/chris/Volumes/Backups/chris
```

(Mac OS X thinks of all its disks as being in the invisible Volumes folder.)

When backing up is this simple, you have no excuse not to do it regularly.

Tip: Type *man ditto* for more information on the program and all its options.

15-32 Identifying Generic Files

The *file* command can help you identify mystery files that appear after you download something from the Internet. *File* uses a combination of methods to guess what type of file you've asked about, and it responds if it finds a match.

For example, this command:

```
file download.php
```

returns this information:

```
download.php: gzip compressed data, deflated, last modified: Fri
    Jul 12 18:17:34 2002, os: Unix
```

In this case, the file was compressed with a program called gzip, and should be expandable by StuffIt (or the command line if you prefer, using *gzip -d*).

Tip: If you want to learn how *file* matches your unknown files to known file types, try *man file* for some good information on the subject.

15-33 What Version of Mac OS X?

When connecting to another Macintosh via *ssh* (hint 6-9), you might want to find out what version of Mac OS X the machine uses. Type *sw_vers* to get a short readout of the relevant information that looks something like this:

```
ProductName: Mac OS X
ProductVersion: 10.2.1
BuildVersion: 6D52
```

You can also find out which version of the *Darwin kernel* it has (that is, which version of the underlying Unix) by typing *uname -a*. You get something like this:

```
Darwin demonspeed.local. 6.1 Darwin Kernel Version 6.1: Fri Sep
    6 23:24:34 PDT 2002; root:xnu/xnu-344.2.obj~2/RELEASE_PPC
    Power Macintosh powerpc
```

In the above example, the Darwin kernel version is 6.1 and the system updated it on September 6, 2002.

15-34 Managing Type and Creator Codes

Mac OS X, has no built-in tool for changing your files' *type code* or *creator code* (see hint 10-16). But if you've installed the Developer Tools (page 6), you can use *GetFileInfo* and *SetFile* to view and modify this file information.

For example, the command *GetFileInfo MyHomework.cwk* yields:

```
file: ""/path/info/for/MyHomework.cwk""
type: ""CWWP""
creator: ""BOBO""
attributes: avbstclinmed
created: 6/09/2002 07:41:19
modified: 8/13/2002 20:54:46
```

The type code is CWWP (ClarisWorks word processor), and the creator is BOBO (that is, AppleWorks).

Using *SetFile,* you can easily change any of these attributes. The command on its own (*SetFile*) explains how it is used:

```
SetFile [option...] file...
-a attributes # attributes (lowercase = 0, uppercase = 1)*
-c creator # file creator
-d date # creation date (mm/dd/[yy]yy [hh:mm[:ss] [AM | PM]])*
-m date # modification date (mm/dd/[yy]yy [hh:mm[:ss] [AM |
PM]])*
-t type # file type
... ... ...
```

For example, to change a downloaded TIFF image file so that Mac OS X will recognize it as a Photoshop Elements TIFF file when double-clicked, you'd type *SetFile -c 8BIM -t TIFF myImage.jpg.*

Finder-Terminal: A Joint Venture

Mac OS X includes a number of handy integration tools to make the transition from the Terminal to the Finder and back as easy as possible—as you're about to find out.

15-35 Opening the Current Directory in the Finder

If you type *open .* (note the trailing period) in Terminal, the Finder opens the folder (directory) you were perusing in Terminal. If you type *open ..,* the Finder opens the directory's *parent* folder (the folder that contains it).

You can also type *open* plus the full path to any directory; once again, the actual corresponding Finder folder pops open. This trick is especially useful for opening folders that are typically hidden from view in the Finder, like */var/etc* or */var/httpd*.

For example, the following command opens the */var/etc* folder in the Finder:

```
open /var/etc
```

15-36 Opening URLs from the Command Line

You're working along in Terminal when you suddenly remember that you want to check the new QuickTime trailers on Apple's Web site. You could grab the mouse, move to the Dock, click your Web browser's icon, click in the address bar, and then type the URL.

But you could also pull an Amazing Kreskin–type move and just type *open http://www.apple.com/trailers/*. Your Web browser opens and loads the page whose address you typed.

15-37 Opening Onscreen URLs in Terminal

You can also ⌘-double-click any Web address that appears as a URL in Terminal to visit that page in your Web browser.

15-38 Opening Files from the Command Line

The *open* command performs many tricks beyond simply opening URLs. You can also use it to open programs as if you had double-clicked them in the Finder. For example, try one of the following:

```
open -a Mail
open -a iChat
open -a Microsoft\ Excel
```

(The *-a* flag means you're referring to an "application.") If typing just the program's name doesn't work, specify the full path to a program like this:

```
open -a /Applications/Utilities/shadowGoogle.app
```

Using the *-e* flag, you can tell *open* that you'd like to use TextEdit to edit a file, like this:

```
open -e RatatouilleRecipe.txt
```

Mac OS X attempts to open the file with an appropriate program for the file name you specified (according to its file name extension). For example, if you type *open Salaries.doc,* the system launches Word and opens your Salaries document; *open Salaries.xls* launches Excel and opens your Salaries spreadsheet.

15-39 *locate* I

While the Mac OS X Finder includes a great search tool, if you're already working in Terminal, it's sometimes more convenient to search there. To find any file anywhere on your hard drive, use the *locate* command, like this:

```
locate filename
```

(Of course, type the name of the file you want instead of *filename.*)

When you press Enter, Terminal immediately starts listing files that match. (If Terminal produces a blank list, yet you're positive the file exists, the *locate* database may not yet have been created on your machine. The next hint tells you how to overcome that glitch.)

Locate returns any file whose pathname includes your search string. Thus, if you have a hard drive named HTML (all right, an absurd example, but it's making a good point), and you execute *locate HTML,* you get back a list of every single item on the HTML hard drive! If this result is not what you wanted, use a pipe to narrow the search results, like this:

```
locate HTML | grep "/Volumes/HTML/Client_WebSites"
```

The *locate* command returns files whose names contain *HTML,* and the pipe combines that search with the *grep* command, which restricts the search to files that live in the Client_WebSites folder.

15-40 *locate* II

The same weekly maintenance script that updates the *whatis* database (see hint 15-63) also updates the *locate* database. So if the *locate* command isn't working on your machine, try forcing it into existence with this command:

```
sudo /usr/libexec/locate.updatedb
```

Depending on the size of your hard drive, the system may take a while to establish the *locate* database. Go get yourself a bowl of cereal, and don't be surprised if you hear the drive spinning for up to five minutes. Once the command prompt has returned, the *locate* command should work as expected.

Note: As you add programs and files to your system, run the above command again to update the *locate* database with the new information. If you don't, then the *locate* results will only contain data that were present when you first established the database.

15-41 *grep:* Finding a Text String

To find any *text string* (sequence of characters) in a text file or command output, use *grep,* a beloved Unix search program. *Grep* stands for "global regular expression print"—a thoroughly confounding name for an amazingly powerful program.

The basic format for using the command is as follows:

```
grep -options "text to find" "files to look in"
```

For instance, take a look at this command:

```
grep -l "font" *.html
```

The *-l* option builds a list containing the name of any file or files in the current directory that contain the text "font" and whose name ends in ".html."

If you have some spare time and want to see how *grep* can search your entire hard drive, type the following (and replace "*text to find*" with something you'd actually like to look for):

```
cd /
grep -lr "text to find" *
```

These commands send *grep* looking for "text to find" in every file in every directory on your machine, and then lists the results. The *-r* flag tells *grep* to *recursively search* directories (that is, to search all directories *in* the specified directories), which it does starting with your hard drive's folder. This search takes a while, given that Mac OS X is made up of over 26,000 files! Many of these files are programming code and appear as a bunch of meaningless characters when *grepped*. When it finishes, however, you have a lovely list of every file that contains the search string.

Grep really shines when you use it in conjunction with other commands, as it can help narrow the output from another command down to just the specific data you want to see or use.

15-42   Checking for Resource Forks

If you could inspect certain traditional Macintosh files with the software equivalent of a CAT scanner, you'd see that their single icon might actually house two chunks of computer code, which the geeks call the *data fork* and the *resource fork*. (Data refers to, well, data—stuff you type, or the programming code that makes up an application. Resources are programming components like icons, windows, toolbars, and other pieces of your applications.)

This fork business is news to Unix, however. When you use the *cp* command (or *mv,* described later in this chapter), Unix copies or moves only the data fork—the one it knows about. Most non-Cocoa programs (AppleWorks, Word, and so on) will be rendered useless, having lost many of their essential resources.

POWER USERS' CLINIC

Regular Expressions

grep, along with many other Unix and Mac OS X programs, understands something known as regular expressions, or *regex* for short. A regex is simply a certain pattern of text. In hint 15-41, for example, "text to find" is the regex.

Regex strings can be complex and powerful. Here's one that checks to see if a certain blob of text is a correctly formatted email address (by checking for spaces, illegal characters, the @ sign, and so on):

[a-z0-9_-]+(\.[a-z0-9_-]+)*@[a-z0-9_-]+(\.[a-z0-9_-]+)+

And here's a regex string, used with *grep,* that searches all .htm and .html files in the current directory for references to either a serif font or a 12-point font, and then produces a list of those files:

% grep -irl ']*(face="serif"|size="12")' *.htm *.html

The *-i* option tells *grep* to ignore case, *-r* triggers recursive searching, and the text between the two single quotes is the regex.

To learn more about regex string, try *man regex*, read up on the Web, or consult a book like O'Reilly's *Mastering Regular Expressions.*

To see if the files in your current directory have any resources, just type *ls -al */rsrc* for a list. If any resource forks exist, Terminal returns a message something like this:

```
-rw-r—r—1 robg admin 0 Aug 27 06:48 Internet
Explorer.app.sit/rsrc
```

Finder-Terminal:
A Joint Venture

Once you know you have resource forks in the current directory, you may opt to switch back to the Finder to move or copy those files.

Alternatively, you can use the Unix programs *CpMac* and *MvMac*, which are just like *cp* and *mv* except that they copy or move all forks of any file they copy. The standard Mac OS X installation doesn't include these commands, however; they're available only if you install the Developer Tools (see page 6).

The *ditto -rsrcFork* command also ensures that you don't lose the resource fork data, as explained in hint 15-31 (Complete Backups).

Note: *CpMac*—an Apple-only variation on the *cp* (copy) command—also takes care to copy all forks of a file. However, *CpMac* also resets file ownership and modification times, making it not so good for backups (because it means you'll no longer be able to tell if the backed-up file is older or newer than the one on your hard drive). In those cases, you'd want to use *ditto* instead.

15-43 Screenshots from Terminal

Just as you can capture screenshots in the Finder, you can also take them from Terminal. Simply type *screencapture* for a list of options.

For example, if you type this—

```
screencapture ~/bigpic
```

—you'll capture a full-screen PDF graphic, which gets saved as a file named *bigpic* in your Home folder. The program also lets you capture regions or windows using the mouse using *screencapture -i*. For information on this, and other options, just type *screencapture—help*.

15-44 Downloading Files from Terminal

If your home Mac has a permanent connection to the Internet, and you've turned on Remote Login (System Preferences→Sharing→Services tab), you can pull off a sneaky three-way file maneuver. You can connect to your home box remotely via *ssh* while you're away at, say, the office, and start downloading large files from the Web that would otherwise have to wait for you to arrive home. So instead of waiting an hour after arriving home for that new 150 MB Castle Wolfenstein Multiplayer demo or the 200 MB Illustrator 10 demo to download, you can start them during your lunch break at the office by remote control.

The *curl* command can help you out. Use it like this:

```
curl -O ftp://name.of.site/name_of_file.ext
```

Curl works with any kind of address that you'd type into a browser, including ftp, http, and telnet. The *-O* option tells *curl* to write the file to the same name as that of the provided URL. For instance, if the demo you wished to download comes from *www.megagames.com* and was named 3d_ultramaze.dmg, you would grab it with this command:

```
curl -O http://www.megagames.com/3d_ultramaze.dmg
```

When the download finishes, you'll have the .dmg file saved on your home Mac. Disconnect your *ssh* session with *exit*, drive home, and start playing the new demo within minutes of walking in the door. (See hint 16-17 for a corollary tip about the *screen* command.)

Tip: The *curl* command is very powerful and can do a lot of other things; type *man curl* to get a look at all its features. As one example, if you need to download 100 sequentially numbered image files from an FTP server, it's as easy as *curl -O ftp://ftp.somesite.com/filename[1-100].txt.*

15-45 Software Update in Terminal

Software Update is a handy way of keeping your computer up to date. But if you use or administer more than one Mac and you prefer to test all the software updates yourself before installing them, you can't use the "Automatic update" option. Instead, you have to test the updates and then walk to each machine to physically install them. Which would be fine if the day were 124 hours long.

Here's a glimmer of hope: If you have remote access to all your Macs, you can run all the updates from Terminal (although still one Mac at a time).

Use *ssh* to connect to the other Mac (see hint 6-9) and then type *softwareupdate*. If the remote machine has any updates to be installed, Terminal displays something like this:

```
Software Update Tool
Copyright 2002 Apple Computer, Inc.

Software Update found the following new or updated software:

3171
  Security Update 2002-08-23 (1.0), 6000K - restart required

To install an update, run this tool with the item name as an
  argument.
  e.g. 'softwareupdate <item>…'
```

Thinking you can follow instructions, you promptly type *sofwtareupdate 3171*, only to be informed "softwareupdate: Must be run as root." If you get that annoying message, try *sudo softwareupdate 3171*.

Note: You can also use *softwareupdate* on your own machine, but it doesn't have any particular advantage over the front-end program.

15-46 Which Files Did Software Update Modify?

Finder-Terminal: A Joint Venture

Occasionally, you may run Software Update and find that it purports to fix something on your machine but you don't get much detail on exactly what it's up to. For example, what does a Security Update do?

Luckily, Mac OS X keeps track of installed packages, including everything that comes in through Software Update. You can find details by looking in the */Library/Receipts* directory, which is where Software Update keeps a record of the various patches that it has installed.

Change into this directory by typing *cd /Library/Receipts*. If you issue an *ls* command, the system displays a list of installed packages something like this:

```
AdditionalApplications.pkg Essentials.pkg
August 2002 Dev Tools 10.2 Update.pkg Mac Mac OS X Log.txt
BSD.pkg  Microsoft Mouse.pkg
BSDSDK.pkg NcFTP 3.1.4.pkg
BaseSystem.pkg SecurityUpd2002-08-23.pkg
... ... ...
```

Each of the .pkg files is a directory containing additional directories, at least one of which should contain a file name that ends in .bom. BOM stands for Bill of Materials, and those files can provide details on what you've installed.

To find all the .bom files in your Receipts folder, you can use the *find* command (see hint 16-12 for more on *find*) by typing:

```
find . -name ""*.bom""
```

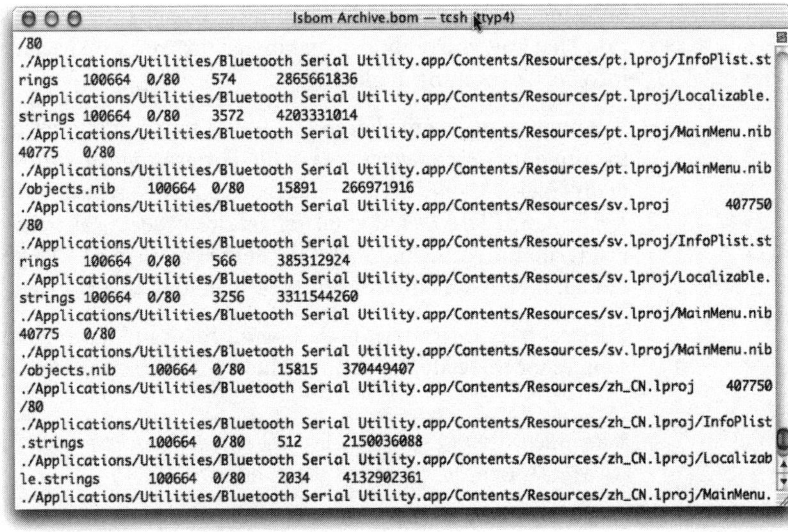

Figure 15-8:
As you can see, a narrow Terminal window and lsbom output do not make for easy reading. Widen the window, reduce the font size, and you'll be able to see exactly what was installed where by the chosen update. You can even see that this person's MacReporter program asked for the page.

Once you have the list of files, you can read any one of them by typing *lsbom name_of_bom*. For example, to see what was installed in the August 2002 Security Update, type:

```
lsbom ./SecurityUpd2002-08-23.pkg/Contents/Archive.bom | less
```

The | *less* at the end is not required, but it helps; most .bom files are quite lengthy, and the *less* command gives you paging control, making them easier to read. (Widening your Terminal window all the way would probably help, too, since each line in the file can be quite wide, as seen in Figure 15-7.)

The output of the *lsbom* command shows one line for each file modified during the update. By studying the names and paths, you can get a very good understanding of just which files were modified by the installer.

15-47 System Preferences

If you're curious about how Mac OS X stores preferences, you can use the command *defaults* to view a list of programs with preference files. Just type:

```
defaults domains
```

This command inelegantly displays every program for which the system has stored preferences—a massive blob of text that scrolls on forever. To view the preferences for a certain program in the list, just type:

```
defaults read com.apple.iChat
```

Replace *com.apple.iChat* with whatever example you like from the massive blob that appeared when you used the *defaults domain* command.

Although you can change preferences using *defaults write* in Terminal, you're better off using a program's own Preferences dialog box (or System Preferences) when you can. That way, you're almost guaranteed that you won't accidentally set some setting incorrectly, resulting in glitches.

You might find Terminal useful, however, for changing settings that don't appear in the program's preferences area at *all*. For example, if you wanted to show the normally "invisible" files in the Finder, you could just type *defaults write com.apple.finder AppleShowAllFiles ON*. If you later get sick of seeing all those normally hidden files, just rerun the command with *OFF* at the end instead. (There's no on/off switch for hidden files in System Preferences, as you may have noticed.)

The real trick, of course, is finding all these hidden preference settings. The best sources for these are the various Mac OS X Web sites—and the pages of this book.

Note: Before changing settings via Terminal, review *man defaults* for details on how the system works and any caveats regarding programs already running.

15-48 A Quickie Batch File Renamer

When you operate on your files and folders in Terminal, you can use *wildcard characters*—asterisks that, in a search-and-replace operation, mean, "any characters can go here." For example a search for *pea** would show you a list of of files containing the words pea, peas, peak, peaks, pearl, pearls, peat, peats, and so on.

So it would stand to reason that you could use wildcards to *rename* a bunch of files. For example, you'd expect that the *mv* command, whose syntax is this:

```
mv oldfilename newfilename
```

could change the word *hand* in all JPEG files (handball.jpg, handsome.jpg) to *foot* (football.jpg, footsome.jpg) like this:

```
mv hand*.jpg foot*.jpg
```

But you'd be wrong. The *mv* command isn't designed to rename more than one file at a time. Trying to manipulate multiple files like this would either produce an error message or, worse, erase some of the files you're trying to rename.

Using a mix of commands, however, you can build a file renamer that works on a bunch of files at once. Alas, it doesn't work right if your file names have spaces in them. If you have space-free names, though, it can save you a lot of time.

The command looks like this (type it all on one line with a space between *sed* and '*s*):

```
ls hand*.jpg | awk '{print("mv "$1" "$1)}' | sed
 's/hand/foot/2' | /bin/sh
```

The above is a complex, compound Unix command, but the basics go like this:

- **ls hand*.jpg** command just outputs the list of files that start with "hand" and end with ".jpg."

- **| awk.** The pipe symbol passes this list to *awk*, a very powerful, very complex pattern-matching and action language. In other words, it can find patterns in things and then take actions based on the patterns. Here, it won't actually look for a pattern, but it will take an action, represented by the commands inside the curly braces (the $1 is a stand-in for the values passed to it by *ls*).

- **sed "s/hand/foot/2"** is a simple search and replace, where *s* indicates "find," the / is a delimiter between search and replace terms, *hand* is the text to find, *foot* is the replacement text, and *2* means only replace the second occurrence of each found string. The *2* is the real trickery here, as it prevents the first file name from being modified.

- **/bin/sh** passes the string of commands to the shell, which then executes each command one at a time. You won't see any output from the command at all, though a quick *ls* (which shows you a list of the files in the folder) will prove that it worked to rename your files, as follows:

```
ls fo*
foot1.jpg foot2.jpg foot3.jpg
```

If you're using this command for yourself, of course, replace the file names with those that match your needs, but keep everything else the same.

If your file names *do* contain spaces, by the way, here's an alternative command. It's not as easy to remember, and it doesn't work if the same word appears twice in a file name (hand in hand.jpg), but it's otherwise a beauty. Type it all on one line (there's a space after *sed*):

```
ls hand*.jpg | awk '{print("mv \""$0"\"" " \""$0"\"")}' | sed
's/hand/foot/2' | /bin/sh
```

Tip: If you find yourself using this hint often, consider creating an alias for it (see hint 15-26).

Cool Commands

If all you knew of Unix was what you'd read so far in this chapter, you might assume that it's a pretty utilitarian, programmery sort of language. But it has its cool side.

15-49 Checking Dates

Unix has a calendar command, *cal,* that's handy when you're in Terminal and you want to know which day of the week a given date falls on, or which of your future birthdays fall on weekends.

On its own, *cal* displays a calendar for the current month, like this:

```
October 2003
 S   M Tu  W Th  F   S
     1  2  3  4
 5   6  7  8  9 10 11
12  13 14 15 16 17 18
19  20 21 22 23 24 25
26  27 28 29 30 31
```

If you add a year (*cal 2006*), *cal* displays a twelve-month calendar. If you add a month *and* year (*cal 4 2006*), *cal* displays that particular month and year.

15-50 The Command Line Calculator

When you're working in Terminal and you wish you had a calculator handy, you could switch to Apple's Calculator program. But that requires using the mouse and leaving Terminal, which is for sissies.

Instead, use Terminal's freeware calculator, *bc.* Type *bc* to start the program, and then type your equations (the program presents no prompt for entering new equations, just a blank line).

For example, try something like this: *3+4*(5-2)+10,* and then press Enter to get the result: 25. Try *50/4*(10*10)* to get 1200.

Type *quit* to end the program.

Tip: In a new Terminal window, type *man bc* for a very detailed explanation of the program and its features.

15-51 How Long Has Your Machine Been Running?

Barring any restarts for software updates, Mac OS X is perfectly happy to run for weeks or months at a time. If you want to find out just how your machine has been running since you last rebooted, use the *uptime* command—just *uptime,* nothing more—which generates something like this:

```
11:50AM up 19 days, 17:33, 3 users, load averages: 0.83, 1.08,
    1.10
```

That's a long time without a crash. Good old Mac OS X!

The "users" figure tells you how many people are logged in, although having multiple Terminal windows open will also inflate this figure. The "load average" figures give you a rough measure of how hard your computer has been working over the last 1, 5, and 15 minutes, respectively; it can range from nearly 0 all the way up to 4, although load averages under 2 are much more common.

15-52 A Simple Benchmark Test

The *openssl* program is a cryptography toolkit, but that's not important for this hint's purposes. Instead, you can use it for its built-in benchmarking program which compares different machines' speeds. (Unfortunately, the program doesn't take into account different operating systems, so you should use it only to compare Macs running the same OS.)

Open Terminal and type *openssl speed.* Then wait…and wait…and wait. The openssl program is generating encrypted keys (passwords). You don't actually care *what* it's doing, though; you're just happy that it's giving your Mac's speed a real workout, and can repeat the exam on another machine.

After half an eternity, the program displays its final results, which look something like this:

```
sign verify sign/s verify/s
rsa 512 bits 0.0034s 0.0003s 296.4 3138.9
rsa 1024 bits 0.0197s 0.0011s 50.7 921.5
rsa 2048 bits 0.1306s 0.0039s 7.7 256.8
rsa 4096 bits 0.8850s 0.0140s 1.1 71.4
  sign verify sign/s verify/s
dsa 512 bits 0.0032s 0.0039s 313.7 256.1
dsa 1024 bits 0.0109s 0.0126s 91.7 79.4
dsa 2048 bits 0.0373s 0.0456s 26.8 21.9
```

The higher the number in the far right column of each row (think of the output as several different benchmark tests), the faster your machine is.

15-53 *top* and Other System Speed Indicators

When you type *top* and press Enter, you get a handy table that lists every process (program and background operation) that's currently running on your Mac, including the obscure background ones you may not even know exist (Figure 15-9). (To be more specific, you get the top 20; make the window taller to see the rest.) You also get statistics that tell you how much memory and speed (CPU power) they're sucking down.

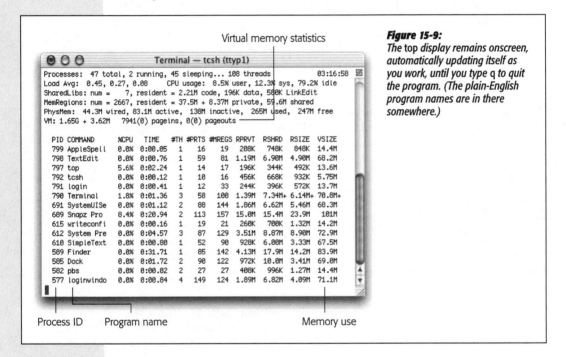

Virtual memory statistics

Process ID   Program name   Memory use

Figure 15-9:
The top *display remains onscreen, automatically updating itself as you work, until you type q to quit the program. (The plain-English program names are in there somewhere.)*

Top has a number of command line options. For example, if you type *top -u,* you get a list sorted by CPU usage, meaning the power-hungry programs are listed first. If your Mac ever seems to act sluggish, checking *top -u* to see what's tying things up is a good instinct.

You can also include a number at the end of the command, which restricts *top* to displaying only that number of processes. So if you want to view the top fifteen CPU-hungry processes, type *top -u 1,* and your screen fills with something like this:

```
Load Avg: 1.81, 1.19, 0.97 CPU usage: 64.1% user, 27.2% sys, 8.6% idle
SharedLibs: num = 129, resident = 31.1M code, 2.75M data, 8.71M LinkEdit
MemRegions: num = 14339, resident = 530M + 17.2M private, 259M shared
PhysMem: 129M wired, 659M active, 473M inactive, 1.23G used, 19.6M free
VM: 7.29G + 70.8M 44962(0) pageins, 13110(0) pageouts

PID COMMAND %CPU TIME #TH #PRTS #MREGS RPRVT RSHRD RSIZE VSIZE
3149 Microsoft 16.9% 44:58.90 6 105 571 44.9M+ 71.6M 33.8M+ 239M+
```

```
2829 Photoshop 12.7% 3:27:00 4 86 1383 90.7M 48.1M 60.3M 322M
3517 top 10.0% 0:01.73 1 14 18 360K 340K 656K 13.6M
198 Window Man 8.9% 3:35:21 2 682 2456 15.9M- 86.5M+ 81.4M+ 224M+
515 iTunes 5.5% 3:59:22 8 140 417 13.0M 16.4M 19.4M 144M
3516 MSN Messen 3.4% 0:15.19 10 96 157 2.95M 13.7M 8.60M 128M
1123 Terminal 3.1% 8:15.80 6 119 625 3.91M 19.9M 10.7M 151M
771 DragThing 2.7% 16:34.00 1 61 172 3.89M 25.5M 4.63M- 145M
... ... ...
```

The display has a lot of information buried in it, some of it about as interesting as the list of ingredients in a can of Raid. So skip the header and look at the list of running programs to see what's eating up your computing power.

In this example, some Microsoft program is taking up 16.9 percent of your CPU's energy, Photoshop is hogging 12.7 percent, and so on.

As the display updates, keep an eye on processes near the top of the list that may be taking up more than their fair share of the CPU's attention. For example, Mozilla occasionally slows down dramatically as it processes text and displays pages. If *top* tells you that Mozilla is using more than 60 percent of the CPU, you know something is wrong beyond wrong. Quit and restart Mozilla to clear the problem, and check *top* to make sure the browser's CPU usage is back to normal.

Troubleshooting via Terminal

Because it offers a direct connection to the Unix core of Mac OS X, Terminal can help troubleshoot problems that may not be resolvable on the graphic side of the system.

15-54 Help! I Can't Empty My Trash!

In Mac OS X 10.2, the "My Trash is permanent" problem tends to crop up much less often than it did in prior versions. But if you happen to have a file stuck in the Trash, it can be hard to get rid of. The problem is usually related to permissions, and Mac OS X doesn't like you messing with those settings.

You can head to, for example, *www.versiontracker.com* to download any of several free tools for fixing the problem (such as Force Empty Trash, BatChmod, or Super Empty Trash). You can also try booting in Mac OS 9, if you have a pre-2003 Mac, and deleting the file there.

And you have a Terminal alternative. Try this command:

```
sudo chflags nouchg ~/.Trash/*
```

The *nouchg* keyword in the command tells *chflags* to turn off the *user immutable* file flag, thereby unlocking the file. Now you should be able to delete anything in Trash through normal means.

If this doesn't work, then the problem file is not in the Trash on your boot disk, but was trashed from another drive. In this case, you must remember which disk you trashed the file from, then execute the above command—but within that disk on a folder named *Trash*.

For example, if you have a disk named MyMusic, and that's where the file in question lives, the command would be *sudo chflags nouchg /Volumes/MyMusic/Trash/**.

15-55   Finder or Dock Problems

On occasion, your Finder or Dock may stop responding. The Finder may not respond to mouse clicks (or even the Option-⌘-Esc "force quit" keystroke), or the Dock may refuse to add new items. If you have a Terminal window accessible, you can use the *ps* command to force either program to restart, which often clears the problem.

In order to kill (exit) either the Dock or the Finder, you need to know its *process ID number*, or PID. So how do you find that out?

In Terminal, type *ps -ax | grep Finder* or *ps -ax | grep Dock*

(*ps* is the process status command, and it shows the status of all open programs on your machines. The -*a* option asks *ps* to display information on everything the Mac is doing, while the -*x* asks for jobs that aren't associated with an active Terminal window—in other words, tasks running in the Finder.)

You might see something like this (using the Dock example):

```
1810 ?? S 1:34.80 /System/Library/CoreServices/Dock.app/Cont...
  3560 std R+ 0:00.00 grep Dock
```

The PID is the first number displayed in the output (1810 in the example).

Now you can force the Finder or Dock to restart by typing *kill 1810* (of course, replace *1810* with the PID you just located). Make sure you type the correct number, as the *kill* command terminates whatever process is associated with the PID you provide.

After you enter the *kill* command, the Finder or Dock restarts and, you hope, runs just fine.

Tip: If you can't get to Terminal, and your Finder is unresponsive, your only recourse may be to press the reset button—which causes you to lose any unsaved data. Better to keep Terminal aliases in places other than the Finder.

If you use a launcher like DragThing or LaunchBar, keep an alias there and in your Dock. Or just keep Terminal running all the time.

15-56   Help! ^M Characters in Text Files

The *cat* command gives you an easy way to open up a text file to read it (*cat ~/ Documents/README.txt*, for example).

But if you ever *cat* a file and discover a whole bunch of ^M characters, chances are someone forgot to save the file with Unix line breaks. This can be bad, because it can render many scripts inoperable, and you won't know why. The *vi* and *emacs* editors, for example, won't show the ^M characters, so you'll have trouble debugging the script.

You can use BBEdit, if you have it, to convert the line breaks. (Choose File→Save, click Options, then set Line Breaks to UNIX). But if you're working in Terminal, you can also fix the bad files with this one-line command:

```
perl -pi -e 's/\r\n?/\n/g' file_name.txt
```

This one-line script (in the Perl programming language) searches the file whose name you specify, and changes all the Mac line breaks to Unix line breaks. It even works on batches of files, so you can fix a bunch of files in one pass by using a wildcard, like this: **.txt* or **.php.*

You don't have to know why it works—but if you're interested, here's the breakdown. Translated into English, the command reads, "Substitute every Mac return or line-break combination in the named file with just a new-line character."

The *-p* option tells *perl* to take action on every line in the file; the *-i* option tells *perl* to send the output of the command back to the same file it came from, and the *-e* option tells *perl* to execute the following text, which is surrounded by single quotes, as if it were a script.

The *s* is the substitution command, which accepts data in the format of *s/ what_to_find/replace_with/*. So the first slash, called a *delimiter,* just turns on the substitution command. After that, *\r\n?* finds Mac line breaks (*\r*) that are also paired with Unix line breaks (*\n?*) and replaces them (after another slash delimiter) with just a Unix line break (*\n*). After the last slash delimiter, the *g* indicates that this change is global, meaning it should be applied to the full file. The last part of the line is just the name of the file.

Since it's a pain to remember and type this command all the time, consider creating an alias (see hint 15-26) to make it easier to use. Because the command itself includes single quotes, you need to use double quotes to enclose the alias in your aliases.mine file, like this:

```
alias alias_name "perl -pi -e 's/\r\n?/\n/g' "
```

You can, of course, name the alias whatever you wish. If you name it "fixit," you could modify future files by simply typing *fixit file_name.txt.*

Terminal Help

An enormous number of programs have been written for Unix, and hundreds of them come with Mac OS X. You never see their icons, because they don't *have* icons; they're Unix programs, invisible until you type their names into Terminal and press Enter.

Each Unix command generally calls up a single one of these programs (or *processes*, as geeks would say) that opens, performs a task, and closes.

The most important way to learn about them is to try them out—but the following tips help quite a bit, too.

15-57   The Built-in Unix Manual

If you're new to Unix, the most powerful command you can put to immediate use is *man. Man* stands for manual, and it displays the Unix system manual (that is, online help). You can type, for example, *man uptime* to find out what the *uptime* command does.

That's the good news.

The bad news is that the manual pages for some commands are missing, incomplete, or confusing. Still, in most cases, the manual provides you with at least the basic information required to use a command.

The first manual you should read is probably that for the *man* command itself, which explains the various command line options available and gives a couple of simple examples:

```
man man
```

One of the first things you'll notice is that the manual stops at the end of the first screen with a : character. This symbol is your first interaction with a *pager,* a command that controls scrolling for long documents in Terminal. Simply press the Space bar to view each subsequent page.

Tip: Type *man ascii* for a chart of the first 128 ASCII characters in hexadecimal, octal, and decimal formats.

15-58   The *less* Pager

When you read *man* pages, each screen scrolls by and then stops at a : character. The program controlling this paging activity is known as *less,* and its options can come in handy. Some of the more useful commands include *b* for back one page, *f* for forward one page, and /, which searches for whatever text you type after the slash. During a search, *n* takes you to the next occurrence, and *N* returns to the previous occurrence.

You can get help two easy ways with *less.* Either type *h* while sitting at a colon prompt, or just type *man less* in the shell. (The *h* gives you a "Reader's Digest" version of the manual; *man less* gives you the full story.)

15-59   Printing Unix Manual Pages I

If you have a PostScript printer, you can print a nicely formatted *man* document from the command line using *lpr.* For instance, to print the *man* page for *ftp,* the file transfer protocol program, type:

```
man -t ftp | lpr
```

The *-t* option passes the manual through a second program named *troff,* which converts the pages into PostScript format (which is why a PostScript printer is required). The *pipe* symbol (|, which you produce by pressing Shift-backslash) tells the shell to take the output of the command to its left and pass it as input to the command on its right.

So the output from *man -t,* a PostScript -formatted manual page, is passed on to *lpr,* the file printing utility. If everything works as expected, your printer generates a nicely formatted hard copy of the manual page you specified.

15-60 Printing Unix Manual Pages II

Although this isn't technically a Unix hint, you're most likely to use it while working in Terminal. If you want to print a manual page but you don't have a PostScript printer, you can use a program that runs on the regular side of your Mac.

Several freeware programs can open and print Unix manual pages from the Finder. ManThor *(www.blackmac.de/manthor/)* and ManOpen *(www.clindberg.org/projects/ ManOpen.html)* do the best job of maintaining the original page's formatting and spacing when printed. Launch the program, type in the name of the manual page, and select Print.

UP TO SPEED

Pipes

A pipe is a means of stringing two or more independent commands together to perform a desired action. In the printing example (hint 15-60), two commands (*man, lpr*) are combined to send a manual page to a printer.

You can use pipes to combine an infinite number of commands. For example, occasionally you may need to quit and restart the Dock. In Terminal, you do so by finding the *process ID* of the Dock (that is, the ID number given to it, behind the scenes, by Mac OS X) and then executing a *kill* command. This process requires two commands, not to mention scanning a long list to find the Dock's job number. By using a pipe, you can do pull off this trick with one command:

```
kill `ps -axc | grep "Dock" |
    cut -c1-6`
```

This command uses two pipes to send the output of *ps* (a list of running *processes,* or programs) to *grep,* a powerful search program, which searches for the word Dock. The

result of these first two commands is then sent to *cut,* which clips everything except the first six characters on the line. Finally, the *kill* command is executed on the remaining data, which is just the job number of the Dock.

The backticks (`) around the piped commands (press the upper-left key on your keyboard) send the results of the entire backticked sequence to the *kill* command (the backticks are like parentheses for the command line). Without the backticks, the shell would try to run "kill ps -axc ...", which is not a valid option for *kill.* With the backticks, the program first evaluates the expression inside them, and then sends the results of that expression (the job number) to kill.

Since pipes can prevent you from easily identifying the end result of the command chain, a great way to learn how they work is to execute the first piece of code, then add the first piped command, execute the command again, and repeat until you have the full command.

15-61   Help for Programs Without Man Pages

If you've tried executing a *man* command for a given program and received a response like "No manual entry," you can try two other things.

First, try typing the name of the program by itself, which may generate a simple help file. If not, you can also try either of the following commands, substituting the program's name for *program* here:

```
program -help
program --help
```

You can see an example of these steps in action if you try to get help for *bzcat*. The *man* command reports that there is no help available, but typing *bzcat* on a line by itself generates this response:

```
bzcat: I won't read compressed data from a terminal.
bzcat: For help, type: 'bzcat -help''.
```

Take the program's own advice and use *-help* to generate a basic but informative help page. (If you're wondering why the program is bright enough to suggest something that you should type to get help, yet not bright enough to simply *provide* that help in the first place, you're not alone.)

15-62   The Developer Tools

If you're going to do much work at all with Terminal, you may wish to install the Developer Tools, which are described on page 6. Although intended primarily for programmers, the Developer Tools let you convert a large library of Unix *source code* (the raw computer code) into *compiled* programs (versions particular to your computer type—like a Mac). In addition, the Developer Tools include some useful programs for the regular side of Mac OS X, as well as some interesting sample programs.

Once you've installed the Developer Tools, you wind up with a Developer folder on your hard drive. Inside, there's a Tools folder (which contains programs that you'll use in Terminal) and an Applications folder (regular, double-clickable Mac OS X programs).

After the installation, you may need to add the folders from the Developer Tools' installation to your *path* in order to use the additional Unix tools.

The path is a pointer that tells Terminal where your Unix programs are on the hard drive—usually in various invisible folders like */bin*, */usr/bin*, and */usr/sbin*. Terminal doesn't yet know about the Developer Tools folder, though.

To solve this problem, you must edit the *path* file, using the *pico* editor as described in the box on page 351. Once you've opened the *path* file, type this line anywhere in the file before you:

```
set path=( $path /Developer/Tools /Developer/Applications)
```

Press Control-O (the equivalent of the Save command), press Enter to accept the file name, then press Control-X to exit the editor.

Back at Terminal's command line, type *source ~/Library/init/tcsh/path* to activate your modified path. From now on, you'll be able to use any of the programs in the Developer Tools package just by typing its name.

15-63   *whatis* I

If you find yourself needing to know what a certain Unix command does, try the *whatis* command, a command that explains others. In other words, *whatis* tries to figure out which command might do what you're looking for, based on the word you provide. For example, if you were interested in programs that dealt with printing, you might type:

```
whatis print | grep "(1"
```

The *whatis* command looks for stuff related to *print*, since that's the word you gave it. Next comes a pipe (see the box on page 383), which directs the output from *whatis* to the command on the other side of the pipe. In this case, that's *grep*, a Unix search command. *Grep* is going to search for "(1" anywhere in the results of your *whatis* command.

Why is *grep* looking for "(1"? In short, the Unix man pages are broken down into distinct sections, each identified by a number. In most varieties of Unix, the main sections are as follows:

• Section 1 covers commands people can execute.

• Sections 2–4 cover *C libraries, system calls,* and *error numbers.*

• Section 5 covers configuration files.

• Section 6 covers Terminal games.

• Section 7 covers miscellaneous documentation.

• Section 8 covers *system manager's* commands.

Of all of these, the only one the typical Unix user is likely ever to be interested in is section 1. Section 1 contains information on commands that you can run from the Terminal prompt.

So the purpose of the *grep* "(1" after the pipe is to restrict the answers to commands in the first section of the manual. In other words, this will ensure that *whatis* returns only commands that you, the user, can actually use.

When you hit Return after typing in the command above, you see output like this:

```
arch(1) - print architecture type
banner(1) - print strings in large letters
bpwhoami(1) - print the output of a bootparams whoami call
cat(1) - concatenate and print files
diffpp(1) - pretty-print diff outputs with GNU enscript
domainname(1) - set or print YP domain of current host system
[listing continues…]
```

This is a list of all commands that you can run whose short description contains the word *print*.

You can get the same explanations by using two other commands: *apropos keyword* or *man -k keyword*. For example, *apropos print* and *man -k print* would both return identical output to what you see here. If these commands generate an error message on your machine, see the next hint for the fix.

15-64   *whatis* II

If you try the hint above and get an error message that says, "apropos: no whatis databases in /usr/share/man," then you don't have the *whatis* database installed. The fix is simple.

The list of words that *whatis* understands is built by your system from the programs installed on your machine. When you first install Mac OS X, this list, or database, does not exist. If you leave your machine on for at least a week—without turning it off at all—a weekly maintenance script quietly creates the database in the background. But if you'd like to create it immediately, type:

```
sudo /usr/libexec/makewhatis
```

After you enter your administrative password, your Terminal window sits for a couple of minutes before returning the command prompt. Thereafter, *whatis* should work as expected.

15-65   **Compressing *man* Pages to Save Drive Space**

The *man* command can read compressed files, but the *man* pages included with Mac OS X come in a space-wasting uncompressed format.

You can compress the *man* pages, after which they'll take longer to expand when you want to view them. But if you're looking to save hard drive space, you can recoup about 20 MB—and the tradeoff might be worthwhile.

Try the *gzip* command, like this:

```
gzip -f /usr/share/man/man1/*
```

Repeat for each of the other *man* directories, replacing *man1* with *man2*, *man3*, and so on up through *man9*.

Fun Stuff

You've been working hard (or hardly working), and now it's time for a break. Welcome to the lighter side of Terminal.

15-66 Customizing Terminal's Welcome Message

When you open Terminal, it displays a friendly "Welcome to Darwin!" message every time (a reference to the particular flavor of Unix that Mac OS X uses). What if you'd like it to say something more meaningful or entertaining—like "Cower in Fear, All Ye Who Enter Here"?

The trick is to edit the file */etc/motd*, using the *pico* editor as described in the box on page 351. But because Mac OS X officially owns this file, you're not allowed to edit it—unless you blast past the security by using the *sudo* command (see the box on page 358). The complete command, then, is this:

```
sudo pico /etc/motd
```

Enter an administrative password when asked.

Replace the stock wording in this file with a message of your choice, and save your changes. Now you're connecting to "Tina's Terrific G4 Tower of Terror!" instead of Darwin.

Tip: In today's age of hackers, constant Internet connections, and big litigation over very small things, you may wish to consider a warning message, something like: "This computer system is private. Unauthorized usage is strictly prohibited, and all activity is logged. If you are here by mistake, please close your connection window now."

While this message may not do much to stop a hacker, it may be useful if you were to ever reach litigation with someone who had hacked your system.

15-67 Removing Terminal's Welcome Message

If you'd prefer not to see *any* message when you open Terminal—Tina's Tower of Terror or otherwise—type *touch ~/.hushlogin*.

The next time you launch Terminal, the first thing you see is the command prompt. To return to the normal startup message, just delete the *.hushlogin* file in your Home folder.

15-68 Terminal as a Reference Resource

Ever wondered where the 80521 zip code is? Or the airport code for Charlotte, North Carolina? Or the birthstone for July?

Normally, you'd hit Google or some other search engine to find your answers. But bizarre as it may seem, Mac OS X includes, as part of Unix, files filled with such information. If you're working in the Terminal anyway, you may find that it's just as easy, and probably faster, to just use the tools under your nose.

Open Terminal. Type *cd /usr/share/misc*.

Now you'll use the *grep* command—which searches the specified folder—to find the data you want. Here's how it works:

The command *grep 80521 zipcodes* gives you this result:

```
zipcodes:80521:Fort Collins, CO
```

and there's your answer.

Similarly, the command *grep -i Charlotte airport* produces this:

```
CLT:Charlotte/Douglas International
```

And typing *grep -i July birthtoken* gives you that month's birthstone and flower:

```
July:Ruby:Larkspur
```

(The *-i* option tells *grep* to ignore capitalization.)

If you find some files that don't seem current (such as Denver International Airport listed as Stapleton Airport), you can find updates at:

www.openbsd.org/cgi-bin/cvsweb/src/share/misc/

Click the version number of any file, and then click the Download link to transfer the file to your machine. The */usr* folder is owned by *root* (Mac OS X itself), so you have to use *sudo* to copy the files after downloading, like this:

```
sudo cp ~/Desktop/airports /usr/share/misc/airports
```

15-69   Converting from Meters to Feet

Ever need to convert 73 inches to centimeters? Or want to know how many kilometers there are in 648 miles? You could open up the Calculator program, of course. Or you could do it the macho way.

Here's a typical "conversation" with the *units* command. What you type is shown in bold; what the Mac types back appears in regular type.

```
% units
501 units, 41 prefixes

You have: 4 inches
You want: cm

*10.16
/ 0.098425197
```

The first line of the output is the result: 10.16 cm. (The second line is a factor that, when divided into 1, gives the same answer. Don't ask.)

Press Control-C to exit the program and return to the usual % prompt.

Units can work with 501 different types of units, covering categories like time, distance, mass, volume, length, wet and dry volumes, and much more. (The file even includes currency conversion rates, but they're not current, of course.) To see a list of all 501 units, type *less /usr/share/misc/units.lib* at the command prompt.

Note: One limitation of *units* is that it does only conversions that work by simple multiplication (feet * 3 = yards). Temperature conversions (like Fahrenheit to Celsius—a conversion formula involving both multiplication and addition) are therefore out of the question.

15-70   A Really Big Banner

If you have a couple minutes to blow on some meaningless fun, create a new Terminal window with a very small font size (9 pt). (Choose File→New Shell, and then choose Terminal→Window Settings. Set the top pop-up menu to Display, click the Set Font button, and then pick a small font size.)

Make the window as tall as possible, and at least 135 columns wide (as you drag the Resize box in the lower-right corner, Terminal shows you how wide the window is in the title bar of the window).

Now type *banner Hello world!,* and see what happens.

You can control the font size of the banner message with the *-w* option; *banner -w 50 Hello world!* displays a more reasonably sized banner.

What you choose to do with your newfound banner-creation skill is up to you.

15-71   Renaming the Trash Can

When you move your mouse over the wastebasket icon in the Dock, the name "Trash" pops up. If you'd like to change the word "Trash" to something more suitable ("Garbage," "The Bad and the Ugly," or "What Was I Thinking?"), you can do so without even breaking a sweat.

1. In Terminal, type the following commands, one after another:

```
cd /System/Library/CoreServices/Dock.app
cd Contents/Resources/English.lproj
sudo cp InfoPlist.strings InfoPlist.bak
sudo cp InfoPlist.strings ~/Desktop/InfoPlist.txt
```

The first two lines switch you into the directory that contains the file you need to edit. The next line creates a backup copy just in case anything goes wrong (edit your administrative password when prompted).

The last line copies the file to the desktop, where you can work on it with a friendly, non-Unix text editor like TextEdit.

Leave the Terminal window open, switch to the Finder, and proceed:

2. Open the System→Library→CoreServices→Dock.app→Contents→Resources →English.lproj folder. Double-click the icon called InfoPlist.txt.

It should open in Text Edit.

3. Change the word "Trash" to whatever you would like to call the icon instead.

Don't make any other changes.

4. Save your changes.

TextEdit tells you that the file is write-protected, but it offers to try to overwrite the file; choose Overwrite.

5. Switch back to Terminal, and type the following commands:

```
sudo cp ~/Desktop/InfoPlist.txt InfoPlist.strings
sudo chown root:wheel InfoPlist.strings
```

These commands copy your modified file back to the proper location, and set the ownership back to the proper owner (*root*—that is, Mac OS X itself).

Now quit and restart the Dock (see hint 3-6) and test your changes by dragging the mouse over the Trash can. If everything worked, the new name for the Trash should pop up.

If you'd like to get the original name back again, return to Terminal and make sure you're in the right directory (as listed in the first line of the first command in this hint), and then type:

```
sudo cp InfoPlist.bak InfoPlist.strings
```

15-72 The Secret *emacs* Adventure Game

Emacs is a powerful text editor that you run from the command line; it's included with Mac OS X. In addition to editing text with it, you can also use the program to launch an old-fashioned text-based adventure game.

Just type *emacs -batch -l dunnet* at the command prompt, and you'll soon be engrossed in a small but fun adventure game. If you grew up with text-based adventure games like Adventure or Zork, you'll feel right at home. If not, type *help* and hit Enter.

Intermediate
Unix Hints

Chapter 15 describes some basic hints for working directly with the Unix foundations of Mac OS X. In this chapter, the hints are more advanced—sometimes *very* advanced—and assume much more Terminal experience. In fact, the technical level of these hints may approach nosebleed territory for the Unix novice.

Specifically, this chapter is for people who:

- Are comfortable in Terminal, with a good working knowledge of commands like *ls, mv, cp, cd, mkdir,* and *sudo.*

- Can create a new file from scratch using a text editor like *pico, vi,* or *emacs,* add data to the file, save it, and then quit the editor.

- Can open a file in a text editor (given only the file's name and path), and insert or delete lines in it.

- Understand the concept of paths and putting programs on your path to make sure that the shell can execute them (page 350).

- Understand the location and use of aliases.mine, environment.mine, and the other related files in that directory (see the box on page 351).

Many of these hints explain how to add stuff to the Unix side of your system—new utilities packages, basic scripts to accomplish certain tasks, a Web-log analysis package, and even a cool software package for running a Web forum.

Note: You're not expected to retype all of the various scripts and commands described in this chapter. At *www.macosxhints.com/book/scripts.html,* you can download a tidy text file that contains all of these commands and scripts already typed, for your copying and pasting pleasure.

Terminal for Productivity

You may consider the Terminal only a tool for tweaking the guts of your system, but the tools in the Unix side of Mac OS X can do some things that are much less efficient in the Finder—impossible, even.

16-1 The Unix Task Scheduler

The *cron* program is a *daemon* (background program) that's always working, even when you're logged out, which gives it some amazing powers. For example, you can use *cron* to automate things like backup scripts, Web site updates, and file purging. You can even make your Mac serve as an alarm clock.

Basically, *cron* can schedule anything you can type at the command line. Unfortunately, it's cryptic, even for a Unix program. Here's how to bend it to your will.

1. **Decide what you want to schedule.**

   For example, if you're trying to build a Macintosh alarm clock, decide when you want it to go off. Say you need it to blast twice each morning, once at 6:15 a.m. and then again at 6:45 a.m. In addition, you sometimes take Saturday naps, but you want to make sure you wake up in time for your big night out, so you'd like the alarm clock to also go off at 7:30 p.m. on Saturday. After those brutal Saturday nights out, you also need the clock to wake you at 7:30 p.m. on Sunday, so that you can go to sleep again before the work week begins. You have the wake-up noise you want to use in an MP3 file on your hard drive.

2. **Using your favorite command line editor (see the box on page 351), create a new empty file (the name of the file doesn't matter), and then enter a sequence of commands that *cron* will read.**

   cron runs whether or not you're logged in, so can run the commands as any account holder. Since you can't predict what anyone else's environment variables will be (and write your script accordingly), it's a good idea to explicitly set the variables in this file, telling cron which shell to use and where things are. The good news is, the settings can be the same for most *cron* jobs you wish to create, so you don't have to remember anything other than these defaults:

   ```
   SHELL=/bin/sh
   PATH=/bin:/sbin:/usr/bin:/usr/sbin
   ```

3. **Add a comment line (beginning with #) as a reminder of the structure you want to use for the *cron* task itself (which will be the next line in the file).**

Structures adhere to the following format: minutes; hour; day of the month; month; day of the week, and the command to be followed. The comment line should always look like this:

```
#min hour mday month wday command
```

4. **Fill in the task's structure.**

The data corresponds to the headings in the comment line above, with tabs (not spaces) between each column entry, like this but all on one line:

```
15,45 6 * * 0-4 open /MyDisk/Users/MyName/
Music/weekdays.MP3
30 19 * * 5,6open /MyDisk/Users/MyName/
Music/weekends.MP3
```

These structure lines are for the alarm clock example. There are two of them because you want two distinct behaviors for your alarm clock, one for weekdays and the other for Saturdays. Here's how to read the lines:

The first column is for minutes, so in the alarm clock example, *15,45* runs the weekday task at 15 and 45 minutes past the hour. *30* runs the weekend task on the half hour.

The next column is the task's hour (in 24-hour mode), in this case 6 (for 6:00 a.m.) and 19 (for 7:00 p.m.).

The next two columns are for day of the month and the month of the year; an * indicates that your task runs every day of the month and every month of the year.

- The *wday* column indicates the days of the week your task runs; the days are numbered from 0 (Monday) to 6 (Sunday). Your weekday alarm run Monday through Friday, *1-4*. Saturday and Sunday alarms are *5* and *6*, respectively.

- The *command* column is the actual command you want *cron* to perform; it should be entered on one row (it's shown here split across two lines to fit the page). For your alarm clock, the *open* command is used to play the *weekdays.MP3* file. You must specify a full path in *cron* commands.

5. **Save the file, give it a name you can remember (like MyCronAlarms), and quit the editor.**

Now you'll feed your file of tasks to the *cron* program.

6. **Type *crontab MyCronAlarms* (or whatever your file is named), and then press Enter.**

To verify that the jobs are scheduled, type *crontab -l*. You should see your file *echoed* (printed) back to the screen.

If you'd like to set the alarm clock for other times, just change the settings in MyCronAlarms and then resubmit it to *cron*.

Tip: You can use *cron* for more complex tasks, like examining all the files in a folder and deleting those older than a certain age, then connecting to a remote host, executing a script on that remote host to run a backup, and then transferring the results of the backup to the local computer. With *cron*, all of that can happen automatically, as often as you want.

16-2   Comparing Two Text Files

From time to time, you may find yourself with two versions of a Terminal file and no memory of why you have both, or how they're different. You could open them up in an editor and try to page through to figure out what you changed from one to the other. But that requires half a day, tons of flipping back and forth, and the patience of a yogi. Instead, try using *diff* in Terminal.

The *diff* command returns the key differences between two files. For example, consider the command *diff user.php user2.php*. The first file name after the *diff* command, *user.php*, is the "from" file; *user2.php* is the "to" file. In other words, *diff* looks at *user.php* and attempts to recreate the differences between it and *user2.php*.

That command would produce a display like this:

```
24d23
< <a href=\"user.php?op=editcomm\"><img src=\"$uimages/
conf_comments.gif\" border=0></a>  \n
41d39
< if (mysql_num_rows(mysql_query("select uname from users where
uname='$uname'")) > 0) $stop = "<center>".translate("ERROR:
Nickname taken")."</center><br>";
54a53
>     # Note to self - Revise this?? subroutine next week!
```

The first line, *24d23*, breaks down like this: *24* is the line number in user.com on which you took an action; *d* (for delete) is the action that resulted in user2.com; and *23* is the corresponding line number in user2.com.

On the second line, the < symbol indicates that you deleted everything in that row from user.com.

The third and fifth lines (41d39 and 54a53) follow the format of the first line (*a* is for add), and the fourth and sixth lines follow the format of the second. (On the sixth line, the > symbol indicates that the row was added to user2.com.)

Tip: *diff* does not work on files that have Macintosh line breaks, which differ from Unix line breaks (see hint 15-56).

16-3   Setting Permissions on Multiple Files

Some Web-based Unix programs, like *phpnuke* (a Web site management system) or *phpBB* (a forum software package; see hint 16-40), require that you set the permissions on a large number of files before you can use the application. *phpnuke's* instructions, for example, direct you to "Set all files to 666 permission; set all directories to 777." You'd have to change literally hundreds of files and dozens of directories and subdirectories—and they're all mixed in the program's directory. In other words, this is not for the faint of heart or short of time.

Fortunately, you can use two Unix commands, *find* and *xargs*, to make the changes in a hurry.

For example, if you've installed *phpnuke* in Library→WebServer→Documents, you can set the required permissions with the following commands:

```
cd /Library/WebServer/Documents/phpnuke
find . -type f -print0 | xargs -0 chmod 666
find . -type d -print0 | xargs -0 chmod 777
```

The *find* command searches in and below the current directory (as specified by the "."") for files (*-type f*) or directories (*-type d*). The results of the search are then piped to *xargs,* a utility that passes a series of arguments on to a utility. In that case, that utility is *chmod,* a command for changing file permissions. So all the specified files end up set with 666 permissions, and all the directories wind up set with 777 permissions.

Note: These commands could be disastrous if you're in the wrong directory! If, for example, you were in your hard drive folder instead of in the *phpnuke* folder, these commands would attempt to change the permissions on every file and directory on your hard drive. The process has some protection built in, because you aren't running the command as the root (with *sudo*). Still, be sure you're where you need to be before executing these babies.

File-Sharing Hints

Mac OS X comes with a full set of tools and utilities for file sharing, but there's more flexibility—much more—awaiting in Terminal.

16-4   File Sharing from the Command Line

You are the featured speaker at a big industry conference, and you have been asked to give your famous speech, "Soggy in Seattle: Why Salad Dressing Should Always Be Served on the Side," along with an associated PowerPoint presenation. You stride confidently to the dais, laptop tucked under your arm, ready to boot up and knock everyone out of his or her socks.

But as soon as the laptop starts humming, you realize you forgot to transfer your presentation from your desktop computer; the laptop holds only the slides for your less famous talk, "Eleven Reasons Pizza is Better Cold." Rather than give the alternate speech, you think you'll just hop online and grab your presentation via Personal File Sharing, which you turned on (in System Preferences→Sharing) on your home machine before you left. Or did you?

When you try to reach your desktop's files, you are thwarted: You never switched on Personal File Sharing.

Fortunately, using *ssh* in Terminal, you can connect to your home machine as always, and then type */usr/sbin/AppleFileServer*. This command launches Personal File Sharing. You can now access your home computer through the Go→Connect to Server command in the Finder.

If, for some reason, you need to turn off Personal File Sharing from the command line, type *ps -ax | grep -i applefileserver,* and then press Enter. Note the job number in the first column of the output, and then type *kill job_number.*

16-5   Sharing Additional Folders with Windows

Mac OS X lets you make your Mac files visible to Windows computers on the same network—handy if you're sitting in front of a Windows machine three floors from your desk, and you need to pull up a document from your own Mac.

To make the magic work, you have to set two Mac preferences. First, open System Preferences→Sharing, click the Services tab, and then turn on Windows File Sharing. Next, on the Accounts preference panel, highlight your account, click Edit User, and then turn on "Allow user to log in from Windows." Type your password when asked. After that, you can reach your Home folder from any Windows machine on your network.

All well and good, but the Mac only shares your Home folder. What if you have an external drive and you want to make accessible the files you store on it? Two solutions let you share any folder on your Mac.

The first requires turning on SWAT, the Web-based Samba administration tool, which is covered in hint 16-36. The second solution, in which you manually add your additional folders to Samba's configuration file, is explained here.

1. **Open the Samba configuration file, with root permissions, in an editor like** *pico* **or** *vi.*

   The file is named *smb.conf,* and it lives in */etc.* To gain root permissions when you open it, type *sudo vi /etc/smb.conf* (you can substitute another editor's name for *vi*).

   The first lines of the file are all comments, denoted by the semicolon at the start of each line. Below the comments are sections labeled "[global]" and "[homes]," plus commented-out sections for "[public]" and "[printers]."

2. **To create a new share, create a new section.**

   For example, if your MP3 collection is stored on an external hard drive named MyMP3s in a folder named MyTunes, the following section would create a new share called MyGreatMusic:

   ```
   [MyGreatMusic]
   comment = My MP3 Collection
   ```

```
path = /Volumes/MyMP3s/MyTunes
browseable = yes
read only = no
create mode = 0750
```

The first line (in brackets) is the name of the folder as Windows machines will see it; you can use the *comment* to help identify the folder when it's being shared. The *path* command specifies the physical location of the folder to be shared; setting *browseable* to *yes* lets Windows machines see the folder's contents. Setting *read-only* to *no* lets the contents of the folder be changed from Windows machines.

The *create mode* setting sets up, in advance, the permission settings for any new files that get created in this folder. (Setting *create mode* to *0750* gives full privileges to the folder's owner, read-only privileges for the group, and no permissions for everybody else. This is a good default setting for *create mode,* as it gives you full access and restricts others from seeing the file.)

To share additional folders, duplicate the section above—but change the name, comment, and path for each new folder.

Once you have created all the shares you need, save the *smb.conf* file and exit the editor. Now you just need to activate your new shared folders.

3. **Turn off and restart Windows File Sharing (in System Preferences→Sharing, click the Services tab).**

You should now be able to log into your new shares from a Windows machine as easily as you can connect to your Home folder.

16-6   Protecting Your Windows' Shared Folders

If you use Mac OS X's Mac-to-Windows file-sharing services, you may wonder if your shared folders are secured from unauthorized access via the Internet.

The short answer: Somewhat. An attacker would need your account name and password to access the shared folders, which is a good start.

The long answer: You can do better. Add an additional layer of defense by restricting which computers can connect to your shared folders.

Edit the *smb.conf* file by typing *sudo /etc/smb.conf,* and look for the "[global]" section. Then add a line to the section, using the *hosts allow* option to specify (by IP number) which machines can connect to your shared folders. For example:

```
hosts allow = 192.168.1.
```

In this example, only machines on the local 192.168.1.xxx network are allowed access; use an IP range that's suitable for your internal network. Save the file, and then stop and restart Windows File Sharing in the Sharing preference panel.

Note: You can use this *hosts allow* program (and a related *hosts deny* directive) to do many more things; read all about them by typing *man smb.conf* and searching for "hosts allow."

Remote Access Hints

How do you manage a Mac that's hundreds of miles away? From Terminal, of course.

16-7   Wake a Sleeping Mac Remotely

The Mac's remote-connection features are all well and good, but they won't do you any good if your Mac's gone to sleep. Even if you go into System Preferences→Energy Saver, click the Options tab, and turn on "Wake for network administrator access," you may still not be able to wake up your machine.

You can solve the problem with Wake550, a freeware program you can download from *www.tc.umn.edu/~olve0003/wake550.html*.

Or you can hit Terminal to send a little networking pulse cutely called a *magic packet* to rouse your sleeping Mac. Harry Potter would be proud.

1. **Before you leave the premises, write down the sleeping computer's Ethernet and IP addresses.**

   To do that, open System Preferences→Network, click the TCP/IP tab. The Ethernet address is a series of six two-character letter and number combinations, like 01:34:63:be:20:ad. The IP address is four blocks of numbers, like 192.168.1.6. Write these numbers down. You'll need them when it comes time to wake the sleeping Mac remotely.

   Now suppose you've left the house, and you're at the remote machine.

2. **At the new machine, open Terminal, and then create a script like the following one in a folder somewhere on your path (for easy future access):**

   ```
   #!/usr/bin/env python
   import socket
   s=socket.socket(socket.AF_INET, socket.SOCK_DGRAM)
   s.sendto('\xff'*6+'\x01\x34\x63\xbe\x20\xad'*16,
   ('192.168.1.255', 80))
   ```

   Copy the first three lines exactly.

   As for the last line, copy this part exactly: *s.sendto('\xff'*6+'*.

   Then, after each remaining *\x*, enter the components of your Ethernet address, as in the example.

   Replace the IP address in the example with your machine's actual IP address.

   Finally, enter the port on which the magic packet will be sent; in the example, it's 80. Make sure you pick a port number that is forwarded through your router (if applicable) to the destination machine. Many Internet service providers will block some (or all) of the ports below 1024, so check with your ISP and/or system administrator if necessary to find an available port.

Save the file and exit your editor when you're done editing (name it whatever you like, of course), and then make sure it's executable (type *chmod filename 755*).

Run your script to awaken the remote machine. Once the sleeping machine is awake, you can then access it via *ssh*, Apple Remote Desktop, or any other remote-access program.

16-8 Restarting Services

If you're working on a machine remotely (or locally), and you need to restart some of the system services (like AppleTalk, NetInfo, or *lookupd*), you could use *ps* to identify the process and then *kill* to end it.

It's easier, however, to use the restart-services scripts that are already sitting dormant on your Mac:

```
/System/Library/SystemConfiguration/Kicker.bundle/Resources/
```

The folder holds a number of scripts, including *enable-network*, *restart-AppleTalk*, *restart-NetInfo*, and *restart-lookupd*. Run each script by simply typing its name. (Note: Add *./* in front of the file name if you're already in the specified directory, like this: *./ restart-NetInfo*).

FTP Hints

You can connect to FTP servers from Terminal just as you can with a Web browser. But by using the Terminal's FTP program, you can add some automation features that may save you some time.

16-9 Automating FTP Server Logins

When you use the *ftp* program to connect to servers, you must either include your user name and password in the command line or enter them when prompted by *ftp*. With help from a file named *.netrc*, however, you can make this process much easier.

Make sure you're in your Home directory by typing *cd ~*, then type *pico .netrc* (use a different editor, if you prefer). For each FTP host that you connect to, add a line in the *.netrc* file that matches this syntax:

```
machine machine_name login user_name password your_password
```

For example, if you regularly connect to *ftp.myfavoritestuff.com* with the user name *Wilson* and the password *beachplay*, the *.netrc* entry would look like this:

```
machine ftp.myfavorites.com login Wilson password beachplay
```

Add a new row for every machine you regularly connect to, and then save the file and quit the editor.

Before you can use this file with *ftp*, make sure none of the other accounts on the machine can read it, because it contains your user name and password information. Use the command *chmod 700 .netrc* to restrict the visibility of the file to just your account.

Now type *ftp ftp.myfavorites.com*; you connect without providing a name or password.

Tip: By adding the following as the last line of the file, you can also allow anonymous logins to servers that *don't* require a user name and password: *default user anonymous password your_name@your_host.com.*

16-10   Automated FTP Transfers

If you often transfer the same file to or from an FTP server (or do anything repeatedly with an FTP server), Unix and a simple script can automate the process. (You can also pull off this trick with front-end FTP programs like Fetch or Anarchie.)

The following script uploads an HTML file via FTP and makes it the new index.html file on the server. (This example uses *pico*, but you can use any shell text editor.)

1. **Use *cd* to switch to the folder where you're going to create the script.**

   Your Home folder's *bin* directory is fine, if you've created one. Anywhere in your Documents folder is fine.

   Then create the file, like this:

   ```
   pico site_upload
   ```

2. **Enter the following information into the editor:**

   ```
   #! /bin/sh
   echo Uploading the new index page...
   ftp <<**eof
   open www.yourISP.com
   cd wwwdir
   ascii
   put /Users/user_name/Documents/newindex.html index.html
   bye
   **eof
   echo FTP ended - your Web site is now marked as UP.
   ```

   Here's how the script works:

   #! /bin/sh is a shell script (as opposed to a *perl* script or some other type).

   echo Uploading the ServerUp page.... tells Terminal to display the designated text (everything after *echo*) on the screen.

   ftp <<eof** launches your FTP program and redirects all the lines between the **eof* characters to it.

This section of the file is called a *here doc,* and it simply inserts characters between the opening and closing text tags (in this case, ***eof*). These tags have to match exactly and be unique so that nothing between them could accidentally trigger the ending.

In this example, the *here doc* opens the connection, switches to the right directory, establishes ASCII mode, sends and renames the new index page, and disconnects.

You should modify these commands to match the ones you issue when you run your FTP program directly.

You should replace the *put* command with whatever you require for your own site, including the proper paths and file names. If you want to transfer more than one file, just add more commands in the *here doc* section of the file. If you need to download files instead, use the FTP command *get* instead of *put*. Anything that you can do directly on the FTP server can be included in your script, allowing for a great degree of flexibility in building timesaving scripts.

echo FTP ended - your Web site now has a new index page.... is another *echo* statement that shows up in Terminal.

3. **Save the file, quit the editor. Make your script executable with the following command:**

```
chmod ugo+x siteup.xfr
```

This command adds execute permissions to the file so that you can run the script.

4. **In your Home directory, create a file called** *.netrc.*

You need this file because FTP doesn't accept user names and passwords from a *here doc.*

5. **Add these three lines to the file:**

```
machine www.yourISP.com
login your_user_name
password your password
```

Replace the placeholders with the name of your Web site, your user name, and your password.

6. **Save the file and quit the editor.**

Now that *.netrc* has your password in it, in plain text, it's somewhat of a security hole. You should, therefore, immediately change the permissions on the file so that only you can see it.

7. **Use this command:**

```
chmod go-rwx .netrc
```

chmod, of course, is the command for changing file permissions.

8. To run the sample script from the current directory, just type:

```
./siteup.xfr
```

Alternatively, in the Finder, Control-click the script's icon, choose Open With→Other, and then select Terminal (it's in Applications→Utilities). Double-click the script in the Finder to run it.

You can also give the script with a .command extension, which makes it run automatically when you double-click it in the Finder.

Shell Hints

The following hints don't do anything for your workday productivity; they're all efficiency tips for using Terminal itself (and *tsch* in particular).

16-11 Nixing Case Sensitivity in Autocompletion

To amp up your efficiency in Terminal, you should always use the autocomplete feature described in hint 15-3. Instead of typing *cd /Library/WebServer/Documents*, you can type nothing more than *cd /Li W D*, pressing Tab after each letter to make Terminal complete the missing portions for you.

While this feature is incredibly useful, the shell is picky about what it autocompletes. If you miscapitalize any portion of what you type, you'll get a beep instead of a completed path, because the shell is case-sensitive. It thinks of w as different from W.

The easy solution: Add *set complete = enhance* to your environment.mine file (see the box on page 351).

If you ever wish to return to case-sensitive behavior, just change that line in your environment.mine file to read *set complete*.

16-12 Finding Files in the Current Directory Tree

While *locate* is a great tool for searching your entire hard drive (see hints 15-39 and 15-40), it can be cumbersome for more focused searches. To restrict *locate* to a certain directory, you have to include the full path as part of the search string. Worse, any files you created since your last database update aren't included in the search.

Using the *find* program, however, you can apply virtually any set of conditions to a search. (It's just not as fast as *locate*—not nearly.)

One of the program's basic uses is finding files that match a certain file name or file-name pattern. For example, to find all files that end in *.html* within the current directory, you can type:

```
find . -name "*.html"
```

The dot tells *find* to search from the current directory down through all its subdirectories, the *-name* variable tries to match file names with the following pattern (*.html). The * is a wildcard that tells the shell to search for any number of characters before .html (so *baby.html* and *thebabyisanalien.html* both show up in the results). For any search string that contains wildcards, you must enclose the whole thing in double quotes; otherwise, the shell tries to search for the wildcard itself.

Find lets you use a number of *operators* (like *-name*), and you can combine them with each other or with *logical operators* (*-and* and *-or* to combine conditions) to make the command more powerful. For example, say you've created a new Help folder and used it to consolidate a bunch of help files (.help) from various subdirectories. You want to find all the remaining .help files, and you don't want the list to include the documents you've already moved. By combining operators, you're in business:

```
find . -name "*.help" \! -ipath "./help/*"
```

The first part of the command finds all files that end in *.help*. But the command includes another condition: \! *-ipath ./help/**. The exclamation point says to the *find* command "not," and it needs to be preceded by the backslash (so that the shell won't interpret the ! as a special character). The "not" statement acts on the next operator, *-ipath,* which specifies the path to the new Help folder, along with any files already in it (as indicated by the wildcard). (The *i* means, "ignore capitalization.")

Translated into English, this command tells the shell to find all files in the current directory (and its subdirectories) whose name ends in .help, but that are not in the Help directory. It works only if the Help folder is in your current directory—not buried any deeper inside other folders.

If you want to go nuts, *find* can help you, for example, catalog and identify all identical files that are bigger than 20 KB. Use the following command in your Home directory. (Enter the text all on one line—not broken up as shown here. Insert a space where you see each line break here.)

```
find . -size 20 \! -type d -exec cksum {} \; | sort | tee
/tmp/f.tmp | cut -f 1,2 -d ' ' | uniq -d | grep -hif -
/tmp/f.tmp > ~/Desktop/duplicates.txt
```

Key points about this command: The *-exec* flag is a powerful feature of the *find* command. It lets you run a command on the search results. When you use the *-exec* flag, it must end in a semicolon, and those semicolons must be preceded by a backslash, which prevents the shell from interpreting the semicolon character. The empty curly brackets (*{}*) tell *find* to execute the specified command on each result of the find. The *cksum* command sizes up each file identified in the *find* command.

After the command runs, open *duplicates.txt* on your desktop. It's a list of all the duplicate files in your Home directory.

Note: For more information on the *find* command, spend some time reading *man find*; the manual pages contain a wealth of information on different ways to put the program to use.

16-13   Counting the Files in the Current Directory

Terminal gives you no obvious way to see how many files the current directory holds, which is a hassle when you're trying to determine if two different directories are identical. (Counting the number of files is a good, quick first check to make.) Using a pipe, however, you can fashion a tally command.

Typing *ls | wc -l* makes Terminal display the number of (visible) lines in the current directory listing. It works by sending the output of the *ls* command to *wc,* a word counting utility. The *-l* option on *wc* returns the number of words in the *ls* output, and a word is defined as white space between groups of characters. So a single space in a file name won't trigger an additional word count, but the tab between file names does increase the counter.

This will not work for *regressive ls* commands—that is, it doesn't work when you're using *ls -R* to list the current directory and all subdirectories inside it. (That's because the *-R* option adds a blank line and identifying row ["~/Documents/Home-work to do:"] to each directory listing. These two lines per directory throw off the total file count.) But for a quick count of files in the current directory, *ls | wc -l* works perfectly.

16-14   Authorizing Alternate Shells to Use FTP Services

In addition to the default *tcsh* shell, Mac OS X comes with the *bash, csh, sh,* and *zsh* shells—yours free inside non-specially marked packages. If you have installed another shell (such as *ksh*) on one machine, you may find that you can't FTP into other Mac OS X boxes.

The culprit is a file named *shells* that lives in */etc.* This file contains a list of shells from which the FTP server will accept connections. If your alternate shell is not listed, you won't be able to connect.

The fix is simple. Edit the *shells* file (using *sudo,* because the file is owned by root), and add a line with the full path to your newly installed shell. Save the changes. You should now be able to connect from the machine running the alternate shell.

16-15   Shell Scripts in the Finder

If you use shell scripts (if you do, you know what they are), you can easily make them launch from the Finder. Just add *.command* to the end of the script's name to turn it into a standard, double-clickable icon. (Of course, you need to make sure the script has execute permissions. Type *chmod 755 script_name* to set execute permissions.)

16-16   Trace Program Execution in Real Time

Ever wondered why a certain program takes so long to start up? What's it *doing* all that time? Or why a program makes you wait a moment after you click an object within it?

A program called *ktrace* can reveal exactly what happens while another program is executing. For example, to see what happens when you run an *ls* command, type *ktrace /bin/ls.* The resulting output is stored in a file named *ktrace.out* in the directory from which you ran *ktrace*.

You can read this file using a utility called *kdump*. The *ktrace.out* file is relatively long, so you'll probably want to read it by typing *kdump | less* to turn on stops at each page. (You could also use *kdump | grep some_search_term* to find a specific word or phrase in the file.)

Although the output of *ktrace* on the *ls* command might not be terribly interesting, you can also use *ktrace* to see what your regular Mac OS X programs are doing when they run. To see a *ktrace* on Mail, type:

```
ktrace /Applications/Mail.app/Contents/MacOS/Mail
```

This command opens Mail behind your Terminal window. Switch to Mail, do a little work, and then quit Mail. *Ktrace* now stops running, too, and you can inspect its output file.

You'll be able to see which directories Mail.app is looking at when it scours your hard drive in search of the various pieces it loads when it runs. Such knowledge can be very helpful for trying to figure out where certain icons, images, or sounds are stored, as shown in Figure 16-1.

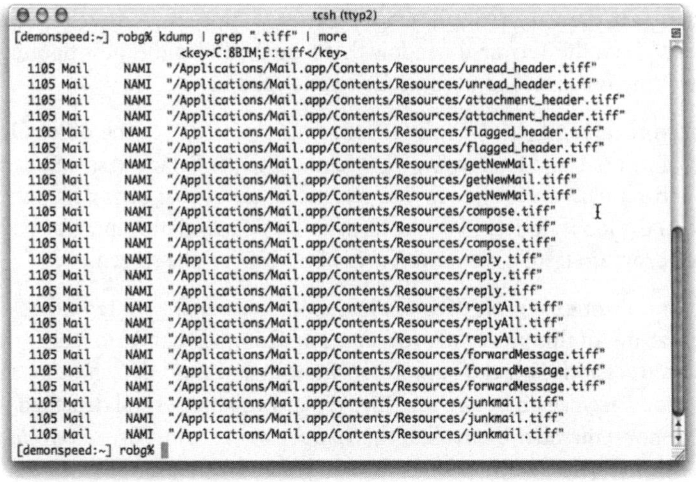

Figure 16-1:
Here, ktrace *has been run against Mail.app, and the results are being viewed with* kdump. *The output from* kdump *is sent through* grep *to find only files that contain ".tiff" in their names (and then through* more *to handle paging onscreen). This is a great way to figure out where certain icons, sounds, and images might be stored within a given application.*

(Why did you use *Mail.app* in this example instead of just *Mail?* Because as noted on page 3, a typical Mac OS X program is actually a pseudo-folder called a *bundle*— and the actual program, the icon that's really in charge, is called the *executable* inside that bundle. Page 3 explains how to open up an application's bundle icon to peruse its contents; you'll find a program's executable in the Contents→MacOS folder.)

Your *ktrace.out* files can get pretty big; feel free to delete them after inspection.

16-17 Multiple Machine-Independent Terminal Sessions

Have you ever started a task at one location, and then wished you could continue it from another? For example, you use *ssh* to connect to your Mac at home from the office, and start a large download of the latest *Lord of the Rings* movie trailer. Several hours later, the download still hasn't finished, but it's time to go home for the night. This leaves you with two options, neither of which are good. You either leave your work machine on through the night, or you shut down and start over with the download when you get home.

Luckily, Mac OS X includes a program that solves this problem. *Screen* lets you start a program in one Terminal (your work *ssh* connection in this example) and then pick it up again later in another location (at home). Through this transition, the program continues to run, never even realizing that you're pulling a fast switcheroo on it.

Starting *screen* is relatively easy, though it may seem complex at first. In this example, you would establish your *ssh* connection from your office location. Then you'd type *screen* (and hit Enter), followed by the Space bar when prompted. After you press the Space bar, the screen clears, leaving you at a very normal-looking command line prompt.

Now you can start your download as you normally would (i.e. *curl -O http://www.somesite.com/demo.dmg*). Once the download has started, press Control-A and then type *d* to detach the screen (a "[detached]" message appears). A detached screen has been "freed" from the Terminal window that launched it, and is now floating in hyperspace waiting for someone to come along and grab it.

At this point, you can end the *ssh* connection, finish your day at the office, drive home, launch Terminal, and type *screen -R* to reattach to the detached screen. *screen* will launch and return you to the job you started hours ago, showing its current progress. When the job is done and you're back at the Terminal prompt, type *exit* to end the *screen* program (you'll see *[screen is terminating]* on the screen).

This scenario is only one example of *screen* in action. Use *man screen* to understand better all the features of this powerful program. For example, there's no real limit to how many *screen* sessions you can run; if you want to start and detach more than one job, just type *screen* again before starting. When you have several detached sessions, you may not remember them all. If this happens to you, just use *screen -list* to view the detached sessions.

Amazingly, *screen* will even survive a logout and login (but not a restart). So if you think your spouse is likely to want the machine right in the middle of your download of the latest Stephen King online book, just start *screen* before you start the download. When your spouse asks for the machine, you can log out without fear, knowing that *screen* is keeping things going in the background (of course, you'll need a full-time Internet connection to pull off this trick).

16-18 A Graphic Interface for Unix

If your history in personal computing goes back a way, you may remember a DOS program called Norton Commander. It attempted to make working in DOS more fun by giving it a rudimentary graphic interface.

Unix has a cousin program, Demos Commander (DC for short), that attempts to do the same thing, as Figure 16-2 shows. If you're more comfortable with menus and a visual structure to things, you may find it easier to work in DC than in the "normal" Terminal.

Installing Demos Commander requires the Developer Tools (page 6).

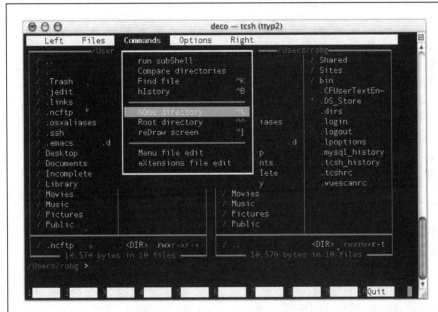

Figure 16-2:
Demos Commander provides a structured menu environment for browsing, copying, moving, and generally managing your files. It has an extensive manual that you can reach by typing man deco.

To download DC, shoot over to *deco.sourceforge.net,* click the "Download page" link, and then look for Decos Sources. Click the file name ("deco39.tgz") in the Sources section to download the program. Expand the archive using StuffIt Expander (or via the command line, if you like). You wind up with a folder called something like "deco39."

Open Terminal and use *cd* to switch into the new directory. Then type out these steps to compile and install Demos Commander:

```
./configure—mandir=/usr/local/share/man
make
sudo make install
rehash
```

Demos Commander winds up in the */usr/local/bin* directory. If you've followed the suggestions in the box on page 351, this directory will already be in your path, ready to roll.

Before running Demos Commander, set Terminal to correctly display the colors used by Demos Commander; type *set term=xterm-color.*

After typing *deco* to launch Demos Commander, you'll be faced with something like Figure 16-3. This is the main DC interface, from which you control the program. For example, hit F9 to activate the menus at the top of the screen, and then use the arrow keys to move about the menus.

When you're finished using DC, set Terminal back to its normal VT100 mode by typing *set term=vt100.*

16-19   A Command Line Dictionary Using *curl*

When, on a well-deserved break from programming, you pick up a copy of *Time* and read that Oliver Stone feels *enervated* lately, you might wish you had a dictionary handy. Of course, you have several: there's one built right into Sherlock, for example.

But if you'd rather not switch out of Terminal, you can create a dictionary feature using the *curl* program, which can retrieve documents from the Internet. Curl can speak a special protocol called *DICT,* which is designed to find definitions in a set of dictionary databases. When you ask *curl* for a definiton, it turns around and asks a public DICT server to retrieve a definition.

For example, to look up *enervated* at the *www.dict.org* dictionary Web site, you'd type:

```
curl -s dict://dict.org/d:enervated
```

The *-s* option puts *curl* in silent mode (no progress or error messages); */d:* is the *define* command in the DICT protocol, indicating you would like the definition of the word following the colon (*enervated* in this example). The command returns a definition like this:

```
220 pan.alephnull.com dictd 1.8.0/rf on Linux 2.4.18-14
<auth.mime> <893659.15971.1050180258@pan.alephnull.com>

250 ok
150 1 definitions retrieved
151 "Enervated" web1913 "Webster's Revised Unabridged Dictio-
nary (1913)"
Enervate \E*ner"vate\, v. t. [imp. & p. p. {Enervated}; p. pr.
   & vb. n. {Enervating}.] [L. enervatus, p. p. of enervare, fr.
   enervis nerveless, weak; e out + nervus nerve. See {Nerve}.]
   To deprive of nerve, force, strength, or courage; to render
   feeble or impotent; to make effeminate; to impair the moral
   powers of.
```

```
          A man . . . enervated by licentiousness.—Macaulay.
      Syn: To weaken; enfeeble; unnerve; debilitate.
      .

      250 ok [d/m/c = 1/0/20; 0.000r 0.000u 0.000s]
      221 bye [d/m/c = 0/0/0; 0.000r 0.000u 0.000s]
```

Although this output is reasonably readable, the extra glop from the DICT server means you have to ignore a lot of lines to get to your definition. To trim the extraneous info, use a modified version of the command (enter on one line, with a space after *-v*):

```
curl -s dict://dict.org/d:enervated | egrep -v
'^22.*|^250.*|^15.*'
```

How did that *egrep* bit kill the junk lines?

Egrep is a form of *grep* that can work with extended regular expressions. Here's how it breaks down: After *curl* obtains your results, the pipe symbol transfers them to *egrep*. The *-v* option tells *egrep* to invert the results of the search (in other words, find the text that does *not* match the search pattern). The next section is where the hard work is done.

The carats (^) tell *egrep* to start at the beginning of a line. The numbers (22, 250, 15) are the text *egrep* should look for. And the dot and asterisk tell it to match everything after that text.

In English, the entire phrase translates to "Find all items that do not match text that starts with 22, 250, or 15." This command effectively kills all the extra lines, leading to the clean output here:

```
Enervate \E*ner"vate\, v. t. [imp. & p. p. {Enervated}; p. pr.
   & vb. n. {Enervating}.] [L. enervatus, p. p. of enervare, fr.
   enervis nerveless, weak; e out + nervus nerve. See {Nerve}.]
   To deprive of nerve, force, strength, or courage; to render
   feeble or impotent; to make effeminate; to impair the moral
   powers of.

      A man . . . enervated by licentiousness.—Macaulay.
   And rhyme began t' enervate poetry.  —Dryden.

   Syn: To weaken; enfeeble; unnerve; debilitate.
```

Fine, you're thinking, but who's going to type out that *egrep* command just to look up a word? It's almost easier to open a paper dictionary.

Here's where a Unix alias comes in handy (see hint 15-26). To automate the lookup process, add the following command to your aliases.mine file:

```
alias dict "curl -s dict://dict.org/d:\!:1 | egrep -v
'^22.*|^250.*|^150.*'"
```

Enter the command as one line, with a single space after the -v. The only difference between the alias and the command is \!:1 after the d:. This string tells the shell that this spot is the place to insert the the word you're looking up. (\!:1 is a placeholder for the first argument—thus the 1—of the command linked to this alias). In other words, when you execute the command, place the word you're looking up next to *d:*, before sending off that URL.

Save your aliases.mine file, quit the editor, and type *source aliases.mine.* You can now type nothing more than, for example, *dict enervate* anytime you need to know a definition.

16-20   Customizing Your Shell Prompt

Using the Terminal→Window Settings command, it's easy to change the background color of a Terminal window and the color of the text.

That's a start, but it leaves the *prompt* looking fairly undistinguished from the commands you type or the output that results. Your prompt probably looks just like everyone else's, showing your machine's name, the current directory, and your user name, like this:

```
[powerbook:~/Library] chris%
```

Using this hint, you can set off the prompt in a different color font or background. You can even rewrite it, adding some juicy data like the time, date, or even the command number the shell is executing.

Note, though, that designing a new command prompt is both an art and a science. You've got a lot of nifty choices, but ancient Greek might be easier to understand than the strings that create prompts. For instance, suppose you'd like to make the standard prompt appear with a solid yellow background and blue text, to set it off from the surrounding Terminal output.

"All" you'd have to do is type out this command:

```
set prompt="%{\033[43;34m%}[%m:%~] %n%#%{\033[0m%} "
```

"Greek might actually be easier," you're probably thinking. But by the end of this hint, although you may not be fluent in a foreign language, you'll at least have some understanding of the art and science of creating prompt strings.

The first step in your education is to look at the above string piece by piece.

- **Set prompt=".** The first part of the command tells Terminal to *set* a variable (the variable *prompt*, in this case, which is designed to control, well, your prompt) equal to what follows. Then there's an opening quote for the string that will define the prompt.

- **%{.** These two characters are the first half of a special "wrapper" used to "hide" certain commands from the shell. Without the wrapper, the characters following would be displayed by the shell instead of interpreted as commands. These characters must always be used as a set of two, with the second set (*%}*) marking the end of the wrapped section. Think of them as an invisibility cloak; anything placed between the two markers will not show up in the prompt.

- \033. These characters are the Unix-command equivalent of pressing the Esc (Escape) key, a requirement at the beginning of any *ANSI color* command (read on).

- [43;34. These are the ANSI color commands. But first, a moment of history.

ANSI (American National Standards Institute) is a committee that helps to define technical standards. Back in 1979, its members defined a number of Escape-key sequences that would create colors on computer systems. To this day, you can't set the color of your prompt without using the ANSI color codes shown in the following table.

ANSI Color Sequences

0	Reset colors to default
1	Brighter text
5	Blinking text
7	Reverse video
30	Black
31	Red
32	Green
33	Yellow
34	Blue
35	Magenta
36	Cyan
37	White
40	Black background
41	Red background
42	Green background
43	Yellow background
44	Blue background
45	Magenta background
46	Cyan background
47	White background

In an ANSI color command, the first character ([) is always required, followed by one or more colors (separated by semicolons) that correspond to the table below. As shown in the chart, *43* is a yellow background, and *34* is blue (if it doesn't say "background," it's a foreground color). The final *m* character marks the end of the color definitions.

- %}. This is the end of the invisibility cloak that you applied to the ANSI color commands. Any subsequent characters will be visible in the prompt.

- [%m:%~] %n%. This will be the part of the prompt that actually appears on the screen. It consists of both regular characters (the square brackets, a colon, and a space) and special codes (*%m*, *%~*, *%n*, and *%#*). You have to precede each special code by a % sign. Each code has a particular function, as shown here:

Code	Meaning
%m	The short host name (your Mac's name)
%~	The current working directory. Your Home directory is represented by ~, and other people's home directories are denoted by ~*chris* (or whatever the name is).
%n	Your short user name, as it shows up in the System Preferences→ Accounts panel.
%#	The actual % symbol at the end of the prompt. (Don't be confused. When you see "%# here, the % is *not* the prompt that you'll see—it's the required prefix for the special code, which, here, is the # symbol. And #, believe it or not, is what makes your prompt show up as a % symbol!)

Tip: If you prefer a > prompt to a % prompt, you could replace the %# business with just the > symbol. (For very technical reasons, you don't need the % prefix for the > prompt.)

Code	Meaning
%B (%b)	Starts (*%B*) or stops (*%b*) boldface. (It's really handy to put your prompt into bold, to help set it off from your commands.)
%U (%u)	Starts (*%U*) or stops (*%u*) underline mode.
%p	The current time in 12-hour AM/PM format, with seconds.

There are many additional options, but finding them is tricky; they're buried deep in the *tcsh man* pages, in a section on (fittingly) prompts. To get there quickly, type *man tcsh* and hit Enter. When you see the : prompt at the bottom of the screen, type *80p* to make the *man* program jump to a point 80% of the way through the *tcsh* file. Nearby, you should see a section of the screen with this text:

```
Prompt  The string which is printed before reading
each command from the terminal. prompt may include any of the
following formatting sequences (+), which are replaced by the
given information:

%/  The current working directory.
%~  The current working directory, but with
    one's home directory represented by...
```

Scroll down from there (using the down arrow) to see the remaining commands.

- %{\033[0m%]. This last bit is important. Without it, you'd change not only the color of your prompt, but also of all the text on your screen! The color commands remain in force until a new color is applied. So you need to change the colors at the end of the prompt to avoid affecting the color of the commands and their output.

This time you'll build a command that specifies the color 0, which resets the colors to their default values (whatever you have chosen for your Terminal windows).

As you can see, constructing a prompt string takes some work. You'd probably rather not type that in every time you launch a new Terminal window—thankfully, you don't have to. Instead, you can add the prompt command to your rc.mine file (see the box on page 351). Once you've edited the file and added the prompt command, all subsequent Terminal windows will have your fancy new prompt string.

If you think you've got the prompt syntax mastered, try deconstructing this one, thoughtfully provided by Jody Chen:

```
set prompt =
"%B\n%{\033[1;93m%}>>>%{\033[0;93m%}[%{\033[0;37m%}\\!\!%{\033
   [0;93m%}][%{\033[0;37m%}%D%w%y%{\033[1;93m%}%P [space]
%{\033[0;37m%}EST%{\033[0;93m%}][%{\033[0;37m%}%n%{\033[0;93m%}@%{\033
   [0;37m%}%m%{\033[0;93m%}][%{\033[0;93m%}%c03]\n\n%#%{\033[0m%}
%b"
```

If you decide to blow off a whole evening and solve the mystery by typing in the string, remember to make it one long line, and replace [**space**] with an actual press of the Space bar.

If you're more interested in jumping directly to the answer, you can see the result in Figure 16-3.

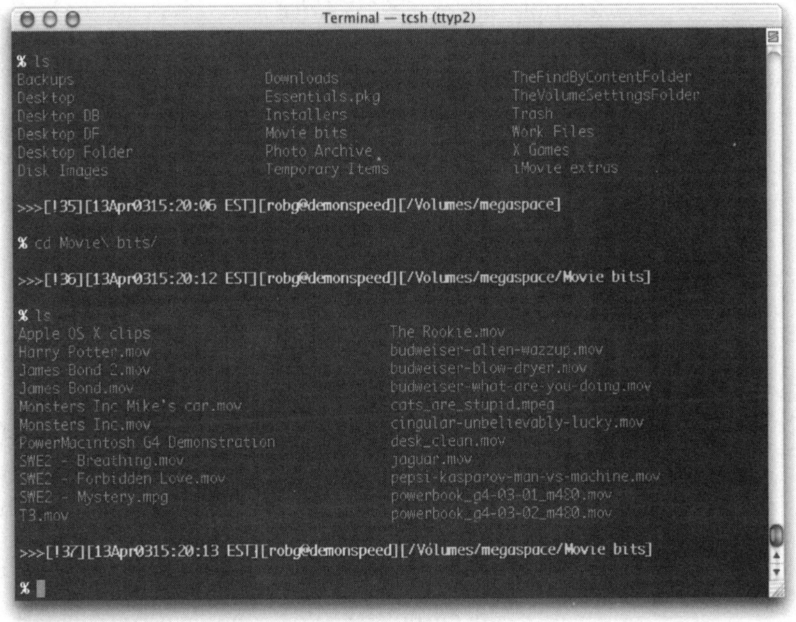

Figure 16-3:
There's a lot of information there, including the current command count (the [!90]), but the truly unique thing is that this is a multi-row prompt. In other words, anywhere you see \n in the prompt string, a new line is inserted in the shell. If this book were in color, you'd also see that this command is rainbow-hued.

16-21   Removing Spaces from File Names

As an experienced Mac hand, you're probably used to including spaces in file names. In Mac OS X, you can still do so, of course, but spaces and other special characters can get in your way in Terminal. As you know from hint 15-9, for example, you have to use various workarounds in Terminal whenever you want to operate on a file name that contains spaces (enclose it in quotes, use\ backslashes\ around\ the\ spaces\, and so on). If you're working with a lot of file names in the Terminal, this gets old in a hurry.

The following script, courtesy of James Huston, removes all spaces from every file name within the current directory:

```
#! /bin/sh
for n in *
do
 OldName=$n
 NewName='echo $n | tr -d " "'
 #NewName='echo $n | tr -s " " "_"'
 echo $NewName
 mv "$OldName" "$NewName"
done
```

Save this file somewhere in your path (*/usr/local/bin*, for example) and make sure it's executable (use *chmod 755 script_name* after entering and saving the file). If you'd rather replace the spaces with underscores, uncomment the second NewName command (remove the #) and comment out the first NewName command (place a # at the beginning of the line).

Now when you need to fix the file names in a directory, simply use *cd* to switch into that directory, and then run your script.

Note: As with most scripts that process things in batches, it's a good idea to double-check the directory you're in before you execute the script.

16-22   Terminal Window Titles

By now you're probably familiar with that famous folk dance, the Terminal Window Shuffle. It goes like this: You've opened one Terminal window for the *ssh* connection to your office, another window for another *ssh* connection to your Web hosting site, another for editing an index.html file, another for the *top* process monitor, and another for editing your aliases.mine file. Every time you want to find one, you have to shuffle through the whole batch.

To make it easier to differentiate among them, you could set a custom color for each one as you create it, but that's inconvenient. Or you could choose Terminal→Window Settings, switch to Window options, and choose "shell command name" for the Title area. But this doesn't help much when three of your windows are running *ssh* and the other two are running *vi*.

You can, however, include the full version of the current command (*ssh -l username somehost* instead of just *ssh*). To turn on this feature, add the following command as the *last line* of your aliases.mine file using *vi* or *emacs*. (Sorry, *pico* won't work in this case; it can't insert certain character codes.) All on one line, now, with a space after *-b:*

```
sched +0:00 alias postcmd 'echo -n "^[]0; `echo \!# | cut -b
1-25`^G"'
```

This command involves two special characters, ^[and ^G. The first is the equivalent of pressing the Esc key, and the second simulates pressing Control-G.

- To make these characters appear in the *vi* editor, press Control-V before pressing Escape and Control-G.

- In *emacs*, press Control-Q and then Esc or Control-G. Onscreen, they appear just as shown here, but they're special characters. (These are the strings that *pico* can't create.)

Two key things make this command work. The first is the *sched +0:00* bit, which calls on the *tcsh* shell's built-in scheduler and tells it to schedule the following command (*alias*, in this case) in zero hours, zero minutes, and zero seconds. To you, this means "do it right now"; to the shell, it means "issue the following command over and over and over." Same result.

The second is the *alias* portion, which is similar to the other entries in your *aliases.mine* file, but does more work than most/

- **postcmd** makes the alias execute after each command the shell runs.

- **echo**, along with the *-n* option, removes the trailing carriage return that the shell normally adds, and reflects back (echoes) whatever the shell sends to it. In this case, the shell sends a string that has special meaning.

- The " denotes the beginning of the string that's about to be sent.

- *^[]0;* is the special escape sequence that tells Terminal to start defining a new window title. Remember that *^[* is the special Esc character you entered in *vi* or *emacs*.

- `*echo \!# | cut -b 1-25*` is a special construct to grab the name of the current command. If you type this in the Terminal as a command (without the surrounding `), you won't see much useful information; it just displays *!#* as the output. However, when the shell processes this command as part of your window title, the *!#* is replaced by whatever command you have just executed.

Echo sends this output (the name of the command) via the pipe to *cut*, a command that cuts text from strings. Here it's cutting columns 1 through 25. Finally, the whole command is wrapped in backticks (`), which causes the shell to process the command and then pass the result (the first 25 columns of the command name) back to whatever program was run before the backticked section (that first *echo* command mentioned in the second bullet).

Save the file, quit the editor, and then close and open a Terminal window. When you type a command and press Enter, the last 25 characters of the full command name appear in the title bar of the window.

16-23 Terminal Shell Games I

If you prefer another shell over Mac OS X's *tcsh*, you can use Terminal preferences to set your choice. That setting does not, however, pull up your new shell when you use *sudo* or when you connect to your machine remotely. In those instances, the *tcsh* shell still appears.

To make sure that Terminal *always* uses your preferred shell, type:

```
sudo niutil -createprop . /users/chris shell /bin/bash
```

Replace *chris* with your account name, and */bin/bash* with the path to your preferred shell. The shell programs are all located in */bin*, and include *bash*, *csh*, *sh*, *tcsh*, and *zsh*.

16-24 Terminal Shell Games II

Actually, there's a second way to switch shells for good: Use NetInfo Manager (in your Applications→Utilities folder). Launch the program, click the lock in the lower-left corner, and then enter your administrator's password. Then proceed as shown in Figure 16-4.

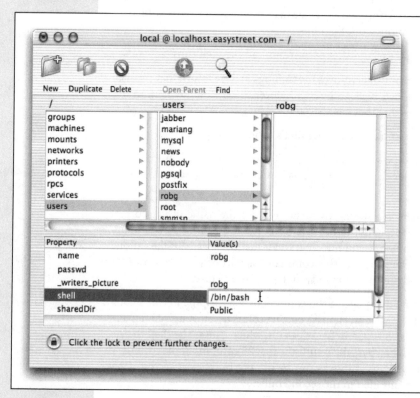

Figure 16-4:
To switch to a different shell, like bash, find the middle column, click "users," and then select your account name on the right. In the bottom pane, scroll down to the shell line, then double-click "/bin/tcsh" and replace it with the path to the shell of your choice. Quit the program (saving as you go).

Tip: For safety's sake, make a backup copy of your NetInfo database by choosing Management→Backup Domain.

That's it. You've got a new shell.

16-25 Fast Switching to Favorite Directories

In Terminal, the command most people use most often is *cd.* Moreover, most people just flip among a few directories regularly. If you develop Web sites, for example, you constantly flip between */Library/WebServer/Documents* (the directory that holds your sites) and */etc/httpd* (the location of the Apache configuration file). Even using Tab-key completion trick (hint 15-3), it gets annoying typing *cd* more often than you breathe.

If you know the secret, you can set up your system to recognize a simple command like *cd webstuff,* when what you really mean is *cd /Library/WebServer/Documents.*

To make this magic work, you need to add four lines to your aliases.mine file, courtesy of reader Michael Boyle.

1. **Create a *savedir* alias.**

   This alias will be the engine of your quick-switch feature. Type this on one line, with a space at each line break shown here:

   ```
   alias savedir 'sed "/set \!$/d" ~/.dirs > ~/.dirs1; \mv
   ~/.dirs1  ~/.dirs; echo set \!* = \"'pwd'\" >> ~/.dirs; source
    ~/.dirs'
   ```
   Enter the text on one line, with a single space instead of the line break shown here.

2. **Add an alias to the *sdirs* command, like this:**

   ```
   alias sdirs 'source ~/.dirs'
   ```

   A *source* command like this forces the shell to reread the file, so that your aliases will be immediately available to any other existing Terminal windows.

3. **Create a third alias, this time for the *showdirs* command:**

   ```
   alias showdirs 'cat ~/.dirs'
   ```

   This command displays all of your defined shortcuts.

4. **Ensure that all new Terminal windows will know about your directory shortcuts by typing this:**

   ```
   if ( -f ~/.dirs ) source ~/.dirs
   ```

   This command checks to see if the file named .dirs is a regular file. If so, it reads the file in, so that when you open a new Terminal window, your aliases will be ready to go.

5. **Save your aliases.mine file, and then return to your Home directory.**

   Type *cd ~*, in other words.

6. **Create an empty .dirs file for the savedir alias to use the first time it's called, like this:**

   ```
   touch .dirs
   ```

   You've just created an empty file. That's what the *savedir* alias expects to find.

7. **Type *source ~/Library/init/aliases.mine* to activate the new aliases and start using them.**

   From now on, whenever you find yourself in a directory you know you'll want to return to, you can create a shortcut to it by typing *savedir shortcut_name*. For example, to create the previously mentioned shortcut to the ~/Library/WebServer/Documents folder, first *cd* into that directory, and then just type *savedir webstuff*. Thereafter, you'll be able to get back to this directory just by typing *cd webstuff*.

   You can also edit the ~/.dirs file by hand if you wish. Just add additional rows for any additional shortcuts you'd like to use. The format is very simple:

   ```
   set webstuff = "/Library/WebServer/Documents"
   ```

16-26 Automatic Aliases

Using the *open* command, you can launch a program right from within Terminal—as long as you type out its entire path, like this: *open /Applications/Editors/BBEdit/BBEdit.app*. But unless your fingers desperately need the exercise, that massive experiment in typing exhaustion gets old fast.

Using the *-a* flag, you could save yourself typing that path (*open -a "Acrobat Reader 5.0"*—but you're still typing out long program names. A single missing space or ™ symbol will break your command.

One solution is to fashion an alias (hint 15-26) so that you can just type *bbedit* to accomplish the same result. But if you wanted to create an alias for *every* program you run, you'd have to take off three days of work to do it.

Variables

The aliases in hint 16-26 work thanks to the *cd* command's flexibility. If you type *cd gristle*, the program first checks to see if *gristle* is a directory. If it is, then *cd* switches into it. If it's not a directory, *cd* then checks to see if it's a *defined variable* (a container for another value—in this case, a path) in *.dirs*. If it is, *cd* inserts the associated path and attempts to switch to that directory.

You can use variables in other operations, too, like *cp*, the copy command. When you use variables in other commands, however, you must insert the *tcsh* variable indicator, a *$*, like this:

```
cp ~/Desktop/news.html $webstuff
```

This command copies the news.html file from your desktop into the directory associated with *webstuff*.

Instead, you can change some of your shell startup files to create and maintain aliases for every program on your machine—automatically. Here's how.

1. **Type cd ~/Library/init/tcsh.**

   You've just switched to your *tcsh* setup directory.

2. **Open aliases.mine (or create it if you don't already have it; see the box on page 351), and then add the following lines, anywhere in the file:**

   ```
   foreach f ( $ALIASDIR/* )
     source $f
   end
   ```

   These lines will read in the contents of a directory of files that you'll create in the next step.

3. **Save the file.**

   Before proceeding, create an rc.mine file—or, if it already exists, open it. All of this is described in the box on page 351.

4. **Type the following script into the rc.mine file:**

   ```
   set OSXDIRLIST="/Applications"
   ```

   You're showing Terminal where you keep your programs. And if you keep your programs in *more* than one folder, you can specify more than one path to them, as long as you separate each with a space. Here's how you'd list *three* folders full of programs—your Applications folder, your Developer→Applications folder, and a Home→Programs folder (pretend your name is *chris*):

   ```
   set OSXDIRLIST="/Applications /Developer/Applications
   /Users/chris/Programs"
   ```

5. **Continue the script like this:**

   ```
   set ALIASDIR="~/.osxaliases"
   if ( ! -e $ALIASDIR ) then
    mkdir $ALIASDIR
   endif
    foreach dir ( $OSXDIRLIST )
      set file=`echo $dir | sed -e 'y#/#_#'`
      if ( -M $dir > -M $ALIASDIR/$file ) then
      echo "Updating $dir aliases..."
      find $dir -name '*.app' -prune -or -name '*.dock' -prune |
   awk\
      '{\
      count = split($0,path,/\/|\.app|\.dock/);\
      name = path[count-1];\
      name = tolower(name);\
      gsub(/ |\(|\)/, "", name);\
   ```

```
      print "alias", name, "'\''open -a \"" $0 "\" \\\\!* &'\''";\
   }' >> $ALIASDIR/$file
endif
end
```

This script reads through each directory you specified in step 3 and scans it for applications. For each program it finds, it creates a shortcut in the $ALIASDIR directory. The three lines in step 2 read in these files.

6. **Save the file and quit the editor. In Terminal, activate your changes by typing:**

```
source ~/Library/init/tcsh/rc.mine
source ~/Library/init/tcsh/aliases.mine
```

If everything worked correctly, you now see something like:

```
Welcome to Darwin!
Updating /Applications aliases...
Updating /Developer/Applications aliases...
Updating /Users/username/Applications aliases...
[machine_name:~] username%
```

You see this message only the first time you launch Terminal, or when you've added new programs to any of the directories you included in step 5.

7. **To see the aliases that the script created, type *alias*.**

Figure 16-5 summarizes the magic of what you've just done.

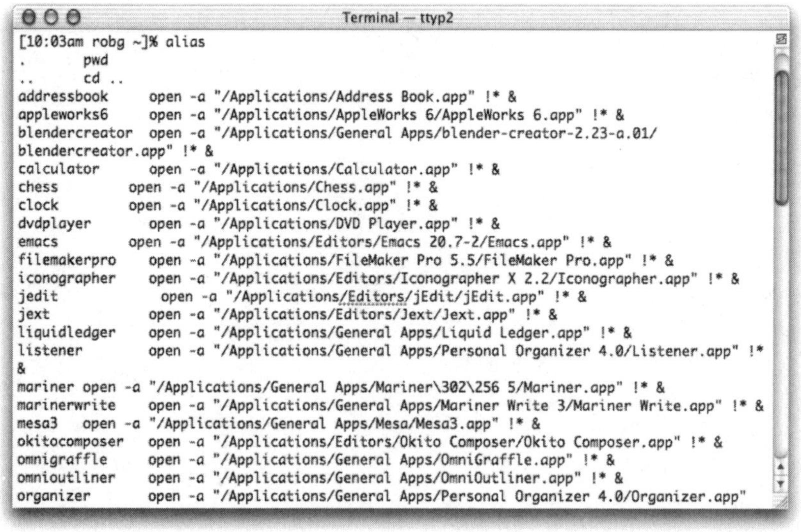

Figure 16-5:
You've just saved yourself a heck of a lot of typing. From now on, you can open any program shown at the right side of this list by typing the abbreviation on the left. For example, dvdplayer *instead of* /Applications/DVD Player.app" !* &.

If you're ever inclined to undo your work, comment out the added code from both aliases.mine and rc.mine, and then *source* the files again. (Thanks to Michael Heinz for these tweaks.)

16-27   Enhanced Unix File Utilities

Mac OS X includes a number of standard tools for dealing with files, including *ls* (file lists), *du* (disk usage), *df* (disk free space), *chmod* (change a file's permissions), and many others. They're OK, but they're not the top of the line. You may sometimes want more features or detail.

For example, the built-in *df* command generates a free-disk-space report something like this (the -*k* option reports the results in 1 KB blocks):

```
df -k
Filesystem  1K-blocks Used Avail Capacity Mounted on
/dev/disk0s5  9819200 3185564 6535444 32% /
devfs    90 90 0 100% /dev
fdesc    1 1 0 100% /dev
<volfs>   512 512 0 100% /.vol
automount -fstab [318]  0 0 0 100% /Network/Servers
automount -static [318]  0 0 0 100% /automount
```

The second line shows how much free space is available on the boot disk, but it's not exactly easy to read. It lacks commas, and it would be much more meaningful if it reported the space in megabytes or gigabytes.

The GNU Project, *www.gnu.org,* has created a set of replacement file utilities that add features to many of Unix's file-manipulation programs. This package is known as the GNU fileutils, and it includes new or enhanced versions of *chgrp, chmod, chown, cp, dd, df, dir, dircolors, du, ln, ls, mkdir, mkfifo, mknod, mv, rm, rmdir, shred, sync, touch,* and *vdir.*

Consider the *df* example again. After installing GNU fileutils, you can use the -*h* (human readable) option to get this output:

```
df -h
Filesystem  Size Used Avail Use% Mounted on
/dev/disk0s5  9.4G 3.1G 6.2G 33% /
devfs    1.0k 1.0k 0 100% /dev
fdesc    1.0k 1.0k 0 100% /dev
<volfs>   512k 512k 0 100% /.vol
```

Now you can easily see that your hard drive is 9.4 GB and has 6.2 GB still available.

All of the new programs go into your */usr/local/bin* directory, and they don't overwrite the standard Mac OS X versions. It's also relatively easy to remove some (or all) of the commands if you later decide you prefer the original version. Here's how to install the package.

1. **Visit the GNU Project's Web site and download the latest version of fileutils.**

   The home page for the package is *www.gnu.org/software/fileutils/*. Follow the links in the Downloading section. After downloading, use StuffIt Expander (or Terminal if you prefer) to expand the package.

2. **Open a Terminal window and type** *cd ~/Desktop/fileutils-4.1.*

   If you didn't save the downloaded stuff to your desktop, substitute the path and name of the folder on your particular machine.

   To install fileutils, use the same basic four commands you'd use to install the *links* Web browser (see hint 16-31 for more detail on each command), which are:

   ```
   ./configure—mandir=/usr/local/share/man
   make
   sudo make install
   rehash
   ```

   Depending on the speed of your machine and what else it may be doing while compiling, these steps could take 10 minutes or more.

3. **Once the process is finished, you can use any of the new commands by typing its name.**

   If you set up your *tcsh* environment as described in the box on page 350, the new program executes instead of the old because the */usr/local/bin* directory (which contains the new programs) is listed earlier in your path than the standard Mac OS X binary directories.

Use the *man* command on any of the installed utilities for additional information on how they work. In addition to its manual pages, fileutils has an extensive online manual, which you can find at *www.gnu.org/manual/fileutils-4.1/fileutils.html*.

One of the most visible demonstrations of fileutils is the new *ls* command. Type *ls --color* for a whole new way of looking at your files and folders: your directory listings are now in living, breathing color!

Tip: If you'd like to learn more about how to customize the colors, type *man dircolors*.

If, after using these commands for a while, you find that you'd prefer to use the original Mac OS X version of one or more, you can switch back relatively easily. In Terminal, type *cd /usr/local/bin*, and then use the *mv* command to rename the program you no longer wish to use, like this:

```
sudo mv chmod chmod.bak
```

You need to do the same thing with the program's manual pages, which live in */usr/local/share/man/man1*:

```
cd /usr/local/share/man/man1
sudo mv chmod.1 chmod.bak
```

By moving these files instead of deleting them, you can put them back to use later by reversing the name change.

Note: If the file you wish to turn off is, for example, the *mv* (move) command itself, you should do so using the Mac OS X installed *mv* command: *sudo /bin/mv mv mv.bak.*

16-28   A *bin* Directory for Personal Scripts

If you work with shell scripts, you should create a *bin directory* (a directory in which to store your executable files) in your Home folder. If you've followed the advice in the box on page 350, then the preset *$PATH* variable already includes this *bin* directory, and the scripts you've created are available from anywhere within the shell.

Apache and Web Hints

One of Mac OS X's greatest perks is its inclusion of *apache,* an industrial-strength Web server that's used on thousands of "real" Web sites every day. While you probably won't want to use your everyday Mac to serve up a site that thousands of people hit every day, having a local Web server makes it a breeze to test your own site designs before they go public, or to even serve up a small site directly from the machine for family and friends (assuming your Internet service provider allows such things).

16-29   The Apache Web Server Manual

The Apache manual is very detailed, and includes both definitions and examples of various configuration variables. You can find it online in the Documentation section of the Apache Web site, *httpd.apache.org/docs-project/.*

But if you've turned on Personal Web Sharing (in System Preference→Sharing), you can read the whole enchilada right from your hard drive. This is handy when you need info about working on Apache but happen to be somewhere without an Internet connection, like 35,000 feet over Denver.

In your browser, load your account's home page by typing *http://127.0.0.1/~chris* (or whatever your account name is). Click the Manual link; now you're browsing the Apache manual from your own hard drive.

16-30   Port Scans from Terminal

Mac OS X's Network Utility (in your Applications→Utilities folder) lets you run a *port scan* (a way to identify security holes) on any machine on your network. But if you're connected to a computer remotely via Terminal, Network Utility won't work. Worse, Unix has no built-in port-scanning tools.

But there's a secret loophole: You can use the same port-scanning program that Network Utility uses, right in Terminal. All you have to do is link to an application buried within the Network Utility program bundle.

First, check to make sure you have a */usr/local/bin* directory. If you don't, create it with this command: *sudo mkdir /usr/local/bin*.

Next, type this command, all on one line, no space after *Utility.app/*:

```
sudo ln -s "/Applications/Utilities/Network Utility.app/
Contents/Resources/stroke" /usr/local/bin/portscan
```

This command creates a *symbolic link* (something like a Mac OS X alias) to the *stroke* program, which Network Utility uses; names it *portscan;* and stores it in your */usr/local/bin* directory.

Now type *rehash* and press Enter to force the shell to find the new program. From now on, you can run your port scans directly from the Terminal by using the new *portscan* command. For example, type this:

```
portscan 192.168.1.150 0 1024
```

where *192.168.1.150* is the host to scan, *0* is the starting port number, and *1024* is the ending port number.

16-31   Installing a Command Line Web Browser

The very idea of a Web browser—something that surfs the Internet using links and graphic information—may strike you as unworkable in Terminal's text-based screen. Yet a Terminal browser can be interesting and useful, particularly if you ever need to browse the Web while connected remotely to your Mac.

Among command line Web browsers, *links* is a good choice. (It's not the same thing as *lynx,* a similar program that's not as good.) Installing the program is not overly complicated, but it does require the Developer Tools (see page 6).

1. Head to the *links* home page, *http://links.sourceforge.net.* Click "links Download," choose a site in your area, and then download the latest source files.

   Source files, of course, are the raw code that's required to build an application.

2. In the Finder, expand the archive with StuffIt Expander.

   You're left with a folder named *links-version_number.*

3. Switch to Terminal, and change into the new *links* folder by typing *cd /path/to/ links-version_number.* Then set up *links.*

   To do that, type the following four commands:

   ```
   ./configure—mandir=/usr/local/share/man
   make
   sudo make install
   rehash
   ```

   The first command automatically configures all the compilation options (the settings for compiling the source code) and specifies that the *man* pages should be stored in the usual Mac OS X location for such things: */usr/local/share/man.* The *make* command compiles (converts) the source code into an actual program, which can take a few minutes.

The third command installs *links,* and the fourth forces Unix to look for new programs—including *links.*

4. **Type** *cd /usr/local/bin* **to tell Terminal where to find** *links,* **and then type** *links* **to fire it up.**

Follow the onscreen directions for using the program. Or type *man links* for more info.

16-32 For Web Designers Only: An Advanced Development Trick

If you're used to working with Unix-hosted Web sites by making edits locally and then using an FTP program to upload them to the server, you may delight in Mac OS X's Apache Web server. Not only is Apache one of the most rugged and respected Web servers on earth, but it's loaded with useful features—including the ability to test your Web sites locally before uploading them to the remote host.

Working on more than one site at a time, though, can be a real hassle, because to switch from one to the other, you have to type *http://127.0.0.1/~username/site_name* or *http://127.0.0.1/site_name* (depending on where you store your development pages).

Fortunately, Apache has a feature called *name-based virtual hosts,* which lets you serve an infinite number of sites from one IP address while providing each site with a unique URL. Even if you don't know the first thing about domain name servers (DNS), and you don't have a customized domain of your own, you can put the power of name-based virtual hosts to work. The feature lets you store a client's work anywhere on your hard drive, yet reach each site with a unique name. Instead of having to type out that complex URL to open the site, you can just load *www.client1.site,* for instance.

Suppose you're building one site for each of two major clients (client1 and client2), and you store their sites' HTML files in directories called *~/Documents/client1* and *~/Documents/client2.* During your testing period, you want to be able to load each client's pages with a unique URL that's inaccessible beyond your own machine.

1. **Switch into the** */etc* **directory by typing** *cd /etc,* **and then edit the** *hosts* **file by typing** *sudo vi hosts.*

The file has a few lines of comments followed by these three lines:

```
127.0.0.1 localhost
255.255.255.255 broadcasthost
::1  localhost
```

2. **Insert two new rows after the 127.0.0.1 line, and then type:**

   ```
   127.0.0.1 www.client1.site
   127.0.0.1 www.client2.site
   ```

   Don't include the *http://* prefix, and stay away from .com, .biz, .edu, .net, and any other real-world domain. Use a fictitious name that's easy to type and remember. You could even use your account name (*www.client1.chris,* or whatever).

3. **Save the file and quit the editor.**

   Next, you'll edit the Apache configuration file to allow name-based virtual hosts.

4. **Type *cd httpd* to switch to the Apache configuration directory within */etc.***

   The file you want to edit is named httpd.conf. Create a backup copy before you do anything else (type *sudo cp httpd.conf httpd.conf.bak*).

5. **Type *sudo vi httpd.conf,* and then enter your administrator's password when prompted.**

   Of course, you can substitute any editor you like. Oh, and see hint 358 for more on *sudo.*

6. **Search for the string *### Section 3.***

   In *vi,* you search by typing a forward slash followed by the search string, and then pressing Enter.

   A few lines below *### Section 3,* you'll find this line:

   ```
   #NameVirtualHost *
   ```

7. **Change the #NameVirtualHost line to this:**

   ```
   NameVirtualHost 127.0.0.1
   ```

   You've removed the comment marker, making this line active, and you've pointed the NameVirtualHost function at your local machine.

   Next, you'll add an entry to ensure that the normal *http://localhost* continues to work as expected.

8. **Leave the existing "<VirtualHost *>" example alone (it's already commented out). Insert the following lines below that existing example:**

   ```
   # Enable http://localhost
   <VirtualHost 127.0.0.1>
   DocumentRoot /Library/WebServer/Documents
   ServerName localhost
   </VirtualHost>
   ```

   This section ensures that the existing behavior will work after you turn on name-based virtual hosts.

9. **Add entries for the two client Web sites just below the new entry you created.**

   The entries should look like this (replace *www.client1.site* and *www.client2.site* with the names you chose):

   ```
   # Client Website #1
   <VirtualHost 127.0.0.1>
   DocumentRoot /Users/username/Documents/client1
   ServerName www.client1.site
   </VirtualHost>
   # Client Website #2
   <VirtualHost 127.0.0.1>
   DocumentRoot /Users/username/Documents/client2
   ServerName www.client2.site
   </VirtualHost>
   ```

10. **Save the changes, quit the editor, and restart the Web server.**

    You can restart the Web server in System Preferences→Sharing (turn the Personal Web Sharing checkbox off and on). Or you can do it in Terminal by typing *sudo apachectl graceful*.

    Once the Web server has restarted, you should be able to access each client's Web site by typing *http://www.client1.site* or *http://www.client2.site* into your favorite Web browser.

POWER USERS' CLINIC

An Apache CGI Test

Testing Apache's CGI feature can teach you quite a bit about how it works and how it can build Web pages for you automatically. To take a couple scripts for a trial run, try this:

Turn on Web sharing in System Preference→Sharing.

Apache includes two test CGI test scripts that don't come set with *execute permissions*. This weirdness means the scripts don't run when the Web server calls them. To solve this problem, open Terminal and type:

```
cd /Library/WebServer/CGI-
   Executables
sudo chmod 755 printenv
sudo chmod 755 test-cgi
```

(Note: Disk Utility's Repair Privileges feature removes the

execute permission from these two scripts. If you use it, you'll have to remember to reset them yourself after repairing the privileges.)

Now, in your Web browser, try these two URLs:

http://127.0.0.1/cgi-bin/printenv
http://127.0.0.1/cgi-bin/test-cgi

Both CGI scripts give you general information about your server and client environment. You'll know they're working if you get a page loaded with text.

You can learn a lot about CGI scripting by looking at the source for these two scripts, especially the *printenv* script that builds an actual HTML page.

Note: When you add more clients in the future, repeat these basic steps: Add another entry to the /etc/hosts file; edit the httpd.conf file and add another VirtualHost entry; and then restart the Web server.

16-33 Jazzing Up Your Site: *Server-Side Includes*

Suppose you've created a basic Web site, which you host on your Mac. It's nothing fancy, but it lets you keep your family and friends up to date on what's going on in your neck of the asphalt. You would, however, like to include some *dynamic data* at the top of each page (data that changes automatically, like a visitor count).

Apache uses *CGI scripts* to handle placing dynamic data on Web pages. CGI stands for Common Gateway Interface, a system that allows you to run an external program (like a Perl script) from within your Web server.

Most of the time you simply want to embed a CGI script's output in an existing page. For example, maybe you want today's date to appear at the top of that family home page.

Apache lets you embed CGI scripts through something known as *Server-side Includes,* which are instructions to the server on how to modify a page before sending it to the browser. Once you've turned on this feature, inserting the date at the top of your Web page becomes as easy as adding this line to your HTML file:

```
<-#echo var="DATE_LOCAL"->
```

In order to turn on Server-side Includes, you must edit the Apache configuration file. While not massively complex, this process does require editing a file with root privileges, and using a command line editor like *vi, pico,* or *emacs.*

The configuration file is named httpd.conf, and it lives in */etc/httpd.* Before you begin, make a backup copy of it in case you make a mistake somewhere along the line. To do so, type:

```
cd /etc/httpd

sudo cp httpd.conf http.mybackup
```

Later, you'll be able to revert to the original files by typing *sudo cp httpd.mybackup httpd.conf,* which copies your backup over the dysfunctional edited version.

All right, you're backed up and ready to go. It's time to open the configuration file and get it ready to edit with root privileges.

1. **If you use *pico* as your editor, type:**

   ```
   sudo pico httpd.conf
   ```

   If you don't use *pico,* type the same command but swap in the name of your editor.

2. **Once you've opened the httpd.conf file, search for *ExecCGI*.**

   (In *pico,* press Control-W to bring up the search mode.)

The search takes you to a line that looks like this:

```
# "Includes", "FollowSymLinks", "ExecCGI", or "MultiViews".
```

The line you need to edit is five rows below that:

```
Options Indexes FollowSymLinks MultiViews
```

3. **Add *ExecCGI +Includes* at the end, with a space between each term, like this:**

```
Options Indexes FollowSymLinks MultiViews ExecCGI +Includes
```

Now you need to tell Apache that files with a different extension (.shtml instead of .html) are also valid index files (the startup or welcome pages that load when someone types your site's URL). If you skip this step, your index.shtml home page won't load if someone just enters your URL.

4. **Bring up a search again, type *DirectoryIndex,* and press Enter.**

The editor jumps to this line:

```
# DirectoryIndex: Name of the file or files to use as a pre...
```

Four lines below that is the line that sets the valid index types:

```
DirectoryIndex index.html
```

5. **Add a space after *index.html,* and then type *index.shtml* at the end of the line.**

The result should look like this:

```
DirectoryIndex index.html index.shtml
```

6. **Start another search, and type *server-parsed.***

You jump to this line:

```
# To use server-parsed HTML files
```

Two lines down are two lines that start *AddType* and *AddHandler.* Both begin with a #, which indicates that they're comments rather than commands.

7. **Remove the comment (#) symbols, but don't change anything else. Save your changes (in *pico,* press Control-O), and then press Enter to accept the given file name. Quit the editor (Control-X in *pico*).**

The edits you made turned on Server-side Includes for any Web sites that you run from your Library→WebServer→Documents folder. (You can find out if you store pages there by entering *http://127.0.0.1* into a Web browser and seeing what you get.) But if you store pages in your account's Home→Sites folder (which you can test by pointing a browser to *http://127.0.0.1 ~/user_name*), you need to make one more edit.

8. **Type *sudo pico users/chris.conf.***

Type your own account name instead of *chris,* of course.

This file is just a much smaller version of the main configuration file you just edited.

9. **Edit the second line so that it matches the Options line you created in the main configuration file, like this:**

```
Options Indexes FollowSymLinks MultiViews ExecCGI +Includes
```

10. **Save the changes.**

You must repeat this edit for each account that's permitted to use Server-side Includes on their pages. Using *ls*, list the contents of the *httpd* directory to see all the accounts on your machine.

11. **Once you've made and saved all the changes, quit the editor.**

You've now done all the editing. But in order for your changes to take effect, you need to stop and restart the Apache Web server.

12. **Open System Preferences→Sharing, and then turn the Personal Web Sharing checkbox off and then on again.**

You can also perform this operation by opening a new Terminal window and typing *sudo apachectl graceful.*

If everything goes well, you should see a message that reads "/usr/sbin/apachectl graceful: httpd gracefully restarted." (If things don't go well, you might want to use *sudo apachectl configtest* to see where the problems lie.)

13. **To test the Server-side Includes, create the following test.shtml file in any text editor:**

```
<HTML>
<HEAD>
<TITLE>
My SSI Test Page
</TITLE>
</HEAD>
<BODY>
<b>Today is:</b><br>
<!-#echo var="DATE_LOCAL"->
</BODY>
</HTML>
```

Save the file in your Home→Site's folder, and then type *http://127.0.0.1/~user_name/test.shtml* in your browser (see Figure 16-6).

This hint is just the tip of what you can do with Server-side Includes. Spend some time reading the Apache manual for examples of some of the other tricks.

And if you catch the CGI bug, try installing some of the hundreds of shareware, freeware, and commercial CGI scripts available. A good place to start is the CGI Resource Index, *www.cgiresourceindex.com*.

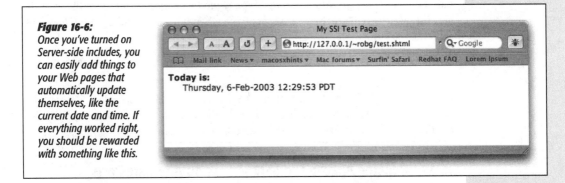

Figure 16-6:
Once you've turned on Server-side includes, you can easily add things to your Web pages that automatically update themselves, like the current date and time. If everything worked right, you should be rewarded with something like this.

16-34 Parsing Regular HTML Pages for CGI Scripts

If you use CGI scripts on your Web pages, then you've turned on SHTML processing in your *httpd.conf* file (see the previous hint). But when you want to stick a CGI counter on a plain old HTML page, you have to rename the file with a *.shtml* extension so Apache will understand it.

But if you rename your files, you'll break all the links to them from the other pages on your site. Is it really worth doing that for a simple counter?

Happily, you can use the *XBitHack* flag (a special Apache variable), which tells Apache that files with the *user-execute bit* set should be treated like HTML files. (The user-execute bit is a little flag that identifies a file that Terminal can run. It includes programs like *ls, cd,* and any shell scripts that you've written.)

Here's how you go about it. Open the httpd.conf file in a text editor, exactly as described in the previous hint. For example, type:

```
cd /etc/httpd
sudo pico httpd.conf
```

Search for " ### Section 2: 'Main' server configuration." Add the following line anywhere in Section 2:

```
XBitHack on
```

(You can also add this line within a VirtualHosts section, if you prefer to set it on a host-by-host basis.)

Save your changes, and quit the editor. To make your changes take effect, stop and restart the server using *sudo apachectl graceful*, as described in the previous hint.

From now on, you can turn any "normal" HTML page into a page that will be parsed (checked) for CGI code, just by changing the file's mode to user executable. (To do that in Terminal, type *chmod u+x filename.html*, where *filename.html* is the name of the HTML page with the included CGI code.)

For example, instead of renaming your index.html to index.shtml to get a CGI-based date to show up, you could just type *chmod u+x index.html* to set the executable bit. Apache will see this file is executable when it loads it, and the *XbitHack* will send the page through the CGI parser.

To turn this feature off, delete the row from your *httpd.conf* file (or change *on* to *off*).

Note: You might think it would be simpler to just add .html to the AddType and AddHandler lines you turned on in hint 16-33. No dice. If you were to do so, Apache would have to parse every single HTML file for CGI code, which would slow down the Web server like nobody's business.

16-35 Running Apache and SSH Servers on Alternate Ports

It's very cool that Apache lets your Mac become a first-class Web site on the information highway. It's not so cool that your DSL or cable-modem company might deliberately block the port (networking channel) that would let you do just that. These companies assume that you're just a humble individual, not the next Amazon.com. They don't want you to found a thriving commercial Web site out of your home, which could put a serious drag on the ISP's bandwidth.

ISPs often block the ports you need for *ssh,* too (hint 6-9). For example, SSH runs on port 22, Apache on port 80. Most providers block these servers simply by turning off all ports below 1024.

If Unix geeks know one thing, it's that you can fight software with software. This hint shows how to reassign your Apache and *ssh* servers to ports within your ISP's valid range. Each server requires a slightly different technique, ranging from the simple to the moderately complex.

The Apache Server

You can run Apache on an alternate port by editing one line in the httpd.conf file (which is in */etc/httpd*). Type this to open it:

```
sudo vi httpd.conf
```

(Or substitute your favorite editor for *vi*.)

Near the top of the document, look for this section:

```
# Port: The port to which the standalone server listens. For
# ports < 1023, you will need httpd to be run as root ini-
tially.
#
Port 80
```

To use an alternate port with Apache, change *80* to a number that's outside the blocked range. One easy solution is to just add 5,000 to the port number, like this:

```
Port 5080
```

Save the file, quit the editor, and then restart the Web server either in System Preferences→Sharing, or in Terminal by typing *sudo apachectl restart.*

From now on, you can serve Web pages that anyone can reach, but you have to use a modified URL:

```
http://12.34.56.78:5080/index.html
```

Replace *12.34.56.78* with your Mac's IP address, and replace *5080* with the port number you chose. (You can find your IP address in System Preferences –> Network, on the TCP/IP tab.)

Tip: If your pages still don't load, it's possible that you haven't found an open port. Pick another number and try these same steps again.

The SSH server

The SSH server, *sshd,* is similary easy to edit. Its configuration file is called *sshd_config* and it lives in the */etc* directory. Once again, you need to edit the program using root privileges with *sudo.*

Once the file is open, look for the line near the top that reads:

```
#Port 22
```

Remove the comment marker (#), and then change the port number to a number above the restricted range (*5022,* for example). Save the file, head to System Preferences→Sharing, and restart Remote Login.

You can now remotely connect on the new port like this:

```
ssh -l username -p 5022 12.34.56.78
```

Replace *5022* with the port number you chose, and replace *12.34.56.78* with your machine's IP address.

16-36   A Windows-Sharing Management Tool: *SWAT*

Mac OS X 10.2 and later includes an easy method for sharing files with Windows machines (via System Preferences –> Sharing, on the Services tab). But the system doesn't let you set any preferences for this service—which folders to share, what rights to give them, and so on.

No problemo. Samba, the Windows-sharing protocol in Mac OS X, includes a management feature known as SWAT (Samba Web Administration Tool), which gives you complete control over Windows sharing.

1. To turn on SWAT, create a file in */etc/xinetd.d* named *swat,* like this:

```
cd /etc/xinetd.d
sudo vi swat
```

xinetd is a process that controls other processes that deal with Internet services. Instead of launching individual services at startup, the server launches *xinetd* and then hangs around waiting for somebody to request a service that it knows about. When it gets word that one is needed, it fires up the appropriate server. Services like *xinetd* are called *super servers,* because they have the power to start other servers.

2. Once in the editor, create the service by entering these lines:

```
service swat
{
 port = 901
 socket_type = stream
 wait = no
 only_from = localhost
 groups = yes
 user = root
 server = /usr/sbin/swat
 log_on_failure += USERID
 disable = No
}
```

SWAT is actually a small Web server (like Apache), and it needs a port on which to run; the standard SWAT port is 901, which you just typed in the *port* line.

The *only_from* variable is a security measure that restricts SWAT connections to the same machine that's running the Samba server (so evildoers from the Net won't be able to hack in).

The *user* option is set to *root,* which forces the SWAT server to ask for root-level authorization before granting access. The remainder of the file contains standard settings that you shouldn't modify.

3. Save the *swat* file and quit the editor.

Next, you'll add your new service to Mac OS X's list of existing services. This list is cleverly called *services,* and it lives in the */etc/services* directory. You're already in the *etc/* directory, so just type *sudo vi services* to edit it.

4. In *services,* type */telnets* to search for the word "telnets."

The cursor jumps to the beginning of this line:

```
telnets  992/tcp
```

5. Immediately above this line, insert a new line for the SWAT service you just created on port 901, like this:

```
swat    901/tcp
```

Although the services don't have to be listed in numeric order, it's much easier to find them in the future if you store them sequentially.

6. **Save the file and quit the editor. Back at the command line, force *xinetd* to re-read its configuration file.**

For this operation, you'll send something called a *HUP signal* to *xinetd*. A HUP signal is the "Hang up" signal, which tells a process how to exit properly. Confusingly, it has an entirely different function when sent to certain programs, including *xinted*. When *xinetd* receives a HUP signal, it reloads its own configuration file and restarts all the services. Here's the command:

```
sudo kill -HUP 'cat /var/run/xinetd.pid'
```

The section between the backticks (') looks tricky, but it's only a shortcut to get *xinetd's* process ID (PID).

Mac OS X keeps track of the certain PID numbers in the */var/run* directory; within that, each process has its own file that contains nothing more than the PID number. The *cat* command shows the directory's contents, and the backticks send that output to the *kill* command. In other words, everything between the backticks is replaced by the PID number of *xinetd*, which is then used in the *kill* command.

You could do the same thing on two lines by first running *ps -ax | grep xinetd* and then taking the PID number (the number in the first column) and using it as the argument for the *kill* command.

Once you have everything installed and running, you can load SWAT by pointing your browser at *http://127.0.0.1:901*. You'd need another entire book or two to lead you through the whole story of configuring Samba shares via SWAT, but the page you'll see in your browser offers a prominent link to Samba's documentation.

16-37 Apache's Server Statistics

You've created a modest Web site for your family and friends to keep track of your African violets' growth. Lately, however, you've noticed that your Internet connection seems slower than usual, and you suspect that your little site has become more popular than you had planned. How to tell if you're right? And if you are, where is all that traffic is coming from?

To answer these questions, use your log files, the documents where Apache nicely records all access and error information. Both *access_log* and *error_log* live in your */private/var/log/httpd* directory.

The error log is usually relatively small; you can browse around it to find bad links, missing images, and glitches on your Web pages. On the other hand, the access log—which has goodies like the volume of traffic on your pages, where your visitors come from, and which files they most often open—is a large file and hard to work with.

Luckily, the world is crawling with free log-analysis programs. A good one is The
Webalizer. Figure 16-7 gives you a taste of the information the program can generate and why its onerous installation process is worthwhile in the end.

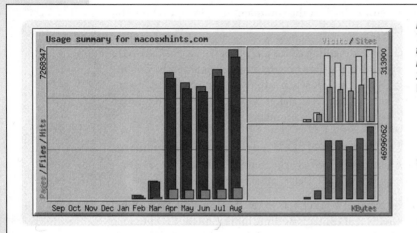

Figure 16-7:
*The Webalizer reveals
that when Jaguar was
released (in August
2002), traffic to this
Web site jumped.*

1. **Download the program from** *www.webalizer.com/download.html.*

   If it didn't expand automatically, double-click the Webalizer icon on your desktop.

   You now have a Webalizer folder sitting on your desktop, ready for action.

2. **If you've never installed Unix programs before, type the following in Terminal:**

   ```
   sudo mkdir -p /usr/local/bin
   sudo mkdir -p /usr/local/share/man/man1
   ```

   These commands ensure that the necessary directory trees exist. (The *-p* flag tells
   mkdir to create any and all of the structure needed to create the final directory.)
   Skip this step if you've installed Unix programs before.

3. **In Terminal, type** *cd,* **press the Space bar, and the drag the Webalizer folder into
   Terminal.**

   When Terminal completes the path, press Enter.

4. **Now type:**

   ```
   sudo cp webalizer /usr/local/bin/webalizer
   sudo chmod 755 /usr/local/bin/webalizer
   sudo cp webalizer.1 /usr/local/share/man/man1/webalizer.1
   rehash
   ```

   These four lines move the program into the directory where it will run; change
   the program from useless code into an executable application; install the manual

pages so that you can get help by typing *man Webalizer*; and tell the shell to re-examine the paths to find new executable code.

You're now ready to analyze your Web log.

Unless you want the analysis to wind up in the current directory, create a new folder called, say, WebAnalysis, and then type *cd WebAnalysis* before running the program.

5. **Type *Webalizer /var/log/httpd/access_log* to run the analysis.**

   The Webalizer creates *index.html* and a number of support files in the new folder. Open *index.html* in your browser and follow the links to get the details on who's visiting your site and what they're doing while they're there.

Tip: The Webalizer is a very sophisticated program and it has a number of options that you can invoke from the command line or via a configuration file. Spend some time with the manual pages or on the program's Web site to get the most out of it.

16-38   PHP Scripting on the Apache Web Server

Hint 16-33 covers dynamic *data*, but whole Web sites can be dynamic, too. A dynamic site is one that creates a page not just from some HTML files you have stuck in a folder, but uses programming code to generate different pages depending on who is viewing them and what they're looking for. (Ever been to Amazon.com?)

Mac OS X even offers this feature at no additional cost. It includes *PHP*, a powerful scripting language for creating dynamic Web sites.

PHP is most often used with the popular (among Web programmers) MySQL database package, which is covered in hint 16-39. Once you've activated the language and installed MySQL, you can download a variety of *PHP*-based packages that run goodies like chat rooms, forum boards, and mailing lists. (Visit the *PHP* Resource Index at *www.phpresourceindex.com* for a great collection of *PHP* scripts.)

Turning on *PHP* requires editing the same configuration file you mucked around in hint 16-32: *httpd.conf,* which lives in */etc/httpd.*

1. **If you haven't already done so, make a backup copy of *httpd.conf.***

   Type these lines:

   ```
   cd /etc/httpd
   sudo cp httpd.conf http.mybackup
   ```

   If you make a mistake, you'll be able to revert to the original by typing *sudo cp httpd.mybackup httpd.conf,* which copies your backup over the dysfunctional edited version.

2. **Open the configuration file.**

   If you use *pico* as your editor, type:

```
sudo pico httpd.conf
```

If you don't use *pico,* swap in the name of your editor.

3. Once the editor has started, bring up the search function (in *pico,* press Control-W), type *php4_module,* and then press Enter.

The screen should jump to this line:

```
#LoadModule php4_module libexec/httpd/libphp4.so
```

4. **Remove the # sign, then search for *mod_php4.***

The screen should jump the screen to this line:

```
#AddModule mod_php4.c
```

5. **Again, remove the # sign. Then search for *index.html,* which should take you to this line:**

```
DirectoryIndex index.html index.shtml
```

(That last part—index.shtml—is there only if you've turned on Server-side Includes, as described in hint 16-33.)

6. **Add a space at the end of the line, and then type *index.php.***

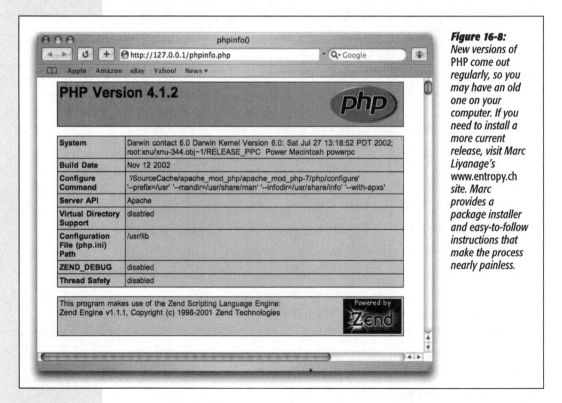

Figure 16-8:
New versions of PHP come out regularly, so you may have an old one on your computer. If you need to install a more current release, visit Marc Liyanage's www.entropy.ch site. Marc provides a package installer and easy-to-follow instructions that make the process nearly painless.

This change allows Apache to load your Web page whenever somebody types in the URL. (Otherwise, visitors would have to attach "index.php" to the end.)

7. **Search for *x-tar*.**

The screen should jump to this line:

```
AddType application/x-tar .tgz
```

8. **Leave this line alone, but immediately below it, insert these two lines:**

```
AddType application/x-httpd-php .php
AddType application/x-httpd-php-source .phps
```

9. **Save the file, quit the editor, and then restart the Web server.**

You can do that either in System Preferences→Sharing, or in Terminal by typing *sudo apachectl restart*.

That's it! You've turned on *PHP*.

To test PHP, create the following file in any text editor:

```
<? phpinfo() ?>
```

Name it "test.php," and save it in your Home→Sites folder.

In your Web browser, load *http://127.0.0.1/~username/test.php*. You should be greeted with a page of information about the *PHP* environment, as shown in Figure 16-8.

16-39 The MySQL Database Server Package

MySQL is a free, open-source relational database server that can run in a number of operating systems, including Mac OS X. (A relational database keeps data in tables that are all interrelated and easily accessed.)

MySQL excels in providing data to Web-enabled programming languages like PHP. In fact, PHP and MySQL combine to make a nearly perfect tool for creating dynamic Web sites. For example, the entire *www.macosxhints.com* site (both the hints site and the forum site) are driven exclusively by PHP and MySQL.

MySQL isn't included with regular copies of Mac OS X (it does come with Mac OS X Server), but it's a free download.

Point your browser to the official MySQL site, *www.mysql.com,* and then head over to the downloads page, *www.mysql.com/downloads/mysql-4.0.html.* (At this writing, MySQL 4.0 is the official production version of MySQL.) On that page, you want the "Standard" download in the Mac OS X Package Installer downloads section (*not* the Mac OS X Downloads section). If it doesn't automatically expand, double-click the downloaded archive, and then mount the disk image.

On the disk image is a ReadMe.txt file, which is worth reading. To install the database server, double-click the *mysql-standard* package file on the disk image, and follow the instructions. When the installer is done, you'll have a full-fledged database server sitting in the */usr/local/mysql* directory.

Although installed, the server is not yet running. To launch the MySQL server, type the following in the Terminal:

```
cd /usr/local/mysql
sudo ./bin/mysqled_safe
Control-Z
bg
```

These commands switch to the *mysql* directory, launch the server, and then interrupt the job (the Control-Z returns control of the Terminal to you). The *bg* (background) command moves the job into the background, where it will run silently. The ReadMe file contains additional information on running the server.

As explained in the ReadMe file, the very first thing to do after the server starts is assign a password to the MySQL root user (which is different from the Mac OS X root user). You assign the root user's password with these two commands (enter the second command on one line with a space after *password*):

```
/usr/local/mysql/bin/mysqladmin -u root password 'new_password'
/usr/local/mysql/bin/mysqladmin -u root -h $hostname password
'new_password'
```

Replace *new_password* with the password you'd like to use. Once you've assigned the password, you can launch the MySQL command line interface by typing */usr/local/mysql/bin/mysql -u root -p*. Make sure to put a space between *-u* and *root*, and enter the newly assigned *new_password* when prompted after hitting Enter.

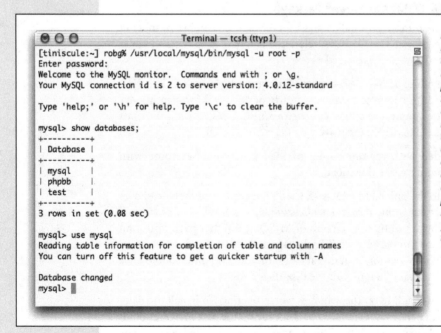

```
[tiniscule:~] robg% /usr/local/mysql/bin/mysql -u root -p
Enter password:
Welcome to the MySQL monitor.  Commands end with ; or \g.
Your MySQL connection id is 2 to server version: 4.0.12-standard

Type 'help;' or '\h' for help. Type '\c' to clear the buffer.

mysql> show databases;
+----------+
| Database |
+----------+
| mysql    |
| phpbb    |
| test     |
+----------+
3 rows in set (0.08 sec)

mysql> use mysql
Reading table information for completion of table and column names
You can turn off this feature to get a quicker startup with -A

Database changed
mysql>
```

Figure 16-9:
It's not pretty, but this is the public face of the powerful (and free) MySQL database server. Here you can see the two sample databases (test and mysql), as well as the phpBB database for the phpBB Forum Software (which you can install in the next hint).

As seen in Figure 16-9, the MySQL interface isn't much to look at, but running the program and accessing a database proves the server is running.

Before you try to put MySQL to work for you in a PHP script or some other Web-enabled program, spend some time learning about account security in MySQL. The MySQL Web site has excellent information on this subject; study section 4.3 of the online manual thoroughly.

While you're on the site, also check out the Mac OS X installation instructions page at *www.mysql.com/doc/en/Mac_OS_X_installation.html*. In addition to more detail on the steps provided here, the online instructions tell you how to create a startup item that will launch the MySQL server automatically when you start up the Mac.

Just installing PHP and MySQL won't do much for you unless you're a full-fledged PHP and MySQL developer. Now you'll want something to show off all that power that doesn't require you to learn a ton about programming or database design—like the next hint.

16-40   A *phpBB* Forum on Your Web Site

The following tutorial pulls it all together; many of the tips and tutorials in this chapter and the last have been leading up to this. The instructions assume that you're comfortable in Terminal, and that you're running the Apache Web server with PHP enabled and the MySQL database package installed.

Note: Open-source software versions change rapidly. These instructions aren't guaranteed to work for versions of phpBB newer than 2.0.4.

Forum software is very popular on the Web, because it provides a venue for people to exchange ideas and carry on conversation. Plenty of forum software packages are available, ranging in price from free to several thousands of dollars. This tutorial will help you install the popular free forum software, phpBB, on your Mac.

The first step is to download the software from *www.phpbb.com*. Click the Downloads button on the site, and download the full version of the "Latest Release" to your desktop. Use StuffIt Expander to expand the package. You wind up with a phpBB2 folder on the desktop.

In the Finder, use Go→Go to Folder. Type */L /W /D,* pressing Tab after each letter, into the Go to Folder dialog box, and then press Enter. You'll see that Mac OS X expands that abbreviation to the /Library/WebServer/Documents folder. Drag the phpBB2 folder from the desktop into this Documents folder.

Before installing the forum software, you'll need to create a database for it to use. Open a Terminal window and start MySQL with a user account that has rights to create a new database, like this:

```
mysql -u phpbb_user -p
```

Enter your MySQL user's password when prompted, and then create the database by typing *create database phpbb;*. You can name it whatever you wish, but you'll find it much easier later on if the database name is somewhat related to what it does. You can quit MySQL at this point and then switch over to the phpBB2 directory:

```
cd /Library/WebServer/Documents/phpBB2
```

In order to run the Web-based configuration program, you need to tweak the permissions on the config.php script so that any account holder can make changes to it. To do that, type *chmod 777 config.php*.

Now, in your Web browser, go to *http://127.0.0.1/phpBB2/install/install.php.* You should see a "Welcome to phpBB2 Installation" message and a screen full of questions. This table shows you how to fill in the blanks:

Default board language	Pick the most applicable language
Database Type	Select either *MySQL 3.x* or *MySQL 4.x* based on which version you installed. (If you've followed the steps in hint 16-39, that would be 4.x.)
Choose your installation method	Leave unchanged as *Install*
Database Server Hostname / DSN	*Localhost*
Your Database Name	*phpbb* or the name you used instead
Database Username	*phpbb_user* or as defined in MySQL
Database Password	*some_password* or as defined in MySQL
Prefix for tables in database	Delete the prefix. It's not necessary if you're not sharing one database with more than one package.
Admin Email Address	Your email address
Domain Name	*127.0.0.1*
Server Port	*80* unless you've changed it to another port
Script path	Leave unchanged as */phpBB2/*
Administrator Username	A user name you'd like to use
Administrator Password	A password you'd like to use
Administrator Password [confirm]	The same password again

After you've completed the form, click the Start Install button. If all goes well, you'll be greeted with another screen that lets you know the *admin* user has been created; click the Finish Installation button.

That button, though, is a bit of a tease. Instead of finishing the installation, you'll be led to yet another screen. It contains some very important instructions—to delete the *install* and *contrib* directories. (If you skip this step, phpBB will not work correctly.) To make that deletion, switch into Terminal and use these commands:

```
rm -r /Library/WebServer/Documents/phpBB/install/
rm -r /Library/WebServer/Documents/phpBB/contrib/
```

Then click the Go to Administration Panel button at the bottom of the same screen. You arrive at the *really* final screen, which simply asks for the admin user name and password you supplied during installation. Enter those values and click Log In. If you've stuck with the program this far, you'll be rewarded by the phpBB administration screen, shown in Figure 16-10.

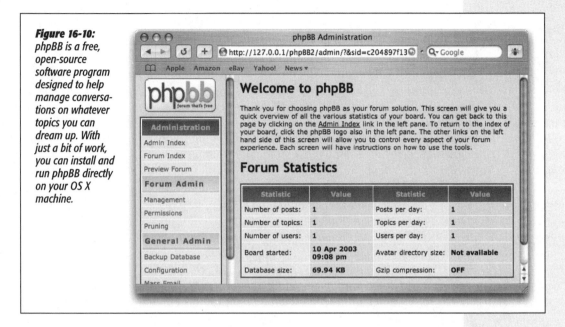

Figure 16-10:
phpBB is a free, open-source software program designed to help manage conversations on whatever topics you can dream up. With just a bit of work, you can install and run phpBB directly on your OS X machine.

Before you spend a bunch of time figuring out exactly how to configure and use your new forum software, take a couple seconds to close a post-install security hole by switching to the Terminal and typing:

```
chmod go-rwx config.php
```

This command resets the permissions on the *config* file so that other account holders can no longer read its values.

To get the most out of phpBB, read the instruction manual in your browser by opening the file at *http://127.0.0.1/phpBB2/docs/README.html*. This document contains information on configuration, security, and so on.

Congratulations: You're now running an open-source, free forum site (phpBB) driven by a combination of free and open source database (MySQL), scripting (PHP), and Web serving (Apache) software!

Index

312–313
Stickies and, 251–252

Quit menu
Dock Finder icon, 75–76
Finder, 40–41

R

radio stations, 195
red dotted line under words,
109
refreshing Web pages, 260
regular expressions, 370
remote access, Terminal
restarting services, 399
sleeping Mac wakeup, 398–
399
Remote Apple Events, 23
remote connections,
networks
file sharing, 157–159
location files, 152–154
passwords, 160–161
ssh (secure shell), 159–160
Remote Login, 23
renaming
batch files, Terminal, 375
files, 56
A Better Finder
Rename, 329
folders, system folders, 59–
60
Trash, Terminal, 389–390
resizing. *See* **sizing**
resolution, 17
resource forks, Terminal,
370–371
Restart, 14
Restart/Sleep/Shut Down
dialog box, 15
restarting, Dock, 84
rewritable disks, erasing, 240
root
login as, 12
SWAT, 436
Rotate icon, iPhoto, 202

S

Safari
addresses, highlighting,
267–268
appearance, 276–277
bookmarks
folders, 269, 270–271
keyboard shortcuts, 270
Debug menu, 275–276

favicon.ico files, clearing,
272–273
fonts, 274–275
Google searches, 269
history, 268
deleting entries, 272
keyboard shortcuts, 267
status bar, 271–272
title bar, 268
URLs, emailing, 273–274
window position, 267
window size, 267
Samba, SWAT (Samba Web
Administration Tool),
433–435
Save dialog box, 91–92
Default Folder X and, 328–
329
shortcuts, 92–93
save sheets, keystrokes, 93
saving
documents, 94
files, Pico, 22
scanners, VueScan, 320–321
screen saver (Screen Effects)
as desktop background, 63–
64
Dock, activating, 82–83
as Finder background, 67
iPhoto, 143
slide show, folders, 143–144
screenshots
capturing, 100–102
DVDs, VideoLAN Client,
335–336
Snapz Pro X, 311–312
Terminal, 371
Script menu
AppleScript
Internet Services, 97
Mail scripts, 98
Sherlock scripts, 98–99
AppleScripts, 96–97
Finder scripts, 97
Info scripts, 97
scripts, folder actions, 57–58
scroll bars, 19
arrows, 19–20
BBEdit, 302
Cocoa programs, 19
diagonal scrolling, Finder,
44
Internet Explorer, 260–261
scrolling

BBEdit and, 302
Internet Explorer, 260–261
mouse, 44
OmniWeb, 277–278
Word, 307–308
Search button, Finder
toolbar, 47
searches
bookmarks, Safari, 270
Finder, results, 29
Google, Web pages, 259–
260
history, Safari, 270
iTunes, clearing, 188
Mail, 169–170
Sherlock scripts, 98–99
TextEdit, 254
Searchling, 328
security
passwords, 160–161
public key cryptography,
160
secure login, 12
sed **command,** 341
serial numbers, 124
servers
deleting, 151–152
icons, permanence of, 50–
51
SetInfo **command,** 367
setup
Help, 24–25
memory, saving, 23
Printer Sharing, 23–24
system maintenance, 24
SharePoints, 164–165, 320
shareware, 315
sharing
fonts, iDVD, 228–229
printers (*See* Printer
Sharing)
Sharing icon, Printer
Sharing, 23–24
shell
prompt, customizing, 410–
413
Terminal, selecting, 416–
417
Unix, 343
shell scripts
bin directory, 423
Finder, 404
shells file, Terminal, 404
Sherlock scripts, 98–99
shortcuts. *See also* **keyboard**

Colophon

This book was written and edited on various Macs around the country using Word X and its indispensable revision-tracking features, with iTunes occasionally providing background entertainment.

The screenshots were captured with Ambrosia Software's Snapz Pro X *(www.ambrosiasw.com)*, and Adobe Photoshop Elements *(www.adobe.com)* was called in as required for touching them up.

The book was designed and laid out in Adobe PageMaker 6.5 on a PowerBook G3 and Power Mac G4. The fonts used include Formata (as the sans-serif family) and Minion (as the serif body face). To provide the and ⌘ symbols, a custom font was created using Macromedia Fontographer.

The book was generated as an Adobe Acrobat PDF file for proofreading and indexing, and finally transmitted to the printing plant in the form of PostScript files.

Other Titles Available from O'Reilly

The Missing Manuals

Mac OS X: The Missing Manual, 2nd Edition

By David Pogue
2nd Edition October 2002
728 pages, ISBN 0-596-00450-8

David Pogue applies his scrupulous objectivity to this exciting new operating system, revealing which new features work well and which do not. This second edition offers a wealth of detail on the myriad changes in OS X 10.2. With new chapters on iChat (Apple's new instant-messaging software), Sherlock 3 (the Web search tool that pulls Web information directly onto the desktop), and the new Finder (which reintroduces spring-loaded folders).

Mac OS X Hints

By Rob Griffiths
1st Edition April 2003 (est.)
400 pages (est.), ISBN 0-596-00451-6

With this handy reference, intermediate to advanced Mac OS X users can adjust the desktop, tweak applications, reconfigure the system, and even fine-tune the software in Mac OS X's Unix-based core. It's full of tips for the iApps, showing how to reshuffle the iTune song order or resynchronize IMAP mailboxes in Mail.app. For the more technically inclined, it shows how to handle system administration tasks, such as backing up Apache log files or creating NFS exports from the command line.

iPhoto 2: The Missing Manual

By David Pogue, Joseph Schorr & Derrick Story
2nd Edition May 2003 (est.)
304 pages (est.), ISBN 0-596-00506-7

With this guide, Macintosh fans can take their digital photos to the screen, to the Web, to printouts, to hardbound photo books, and even to DVDs, CDs, and iMovies. And they'll learn how to take iPhoto far beyond its deceptively simple list of features. *iPhoto 2: The Missing Manual* also tells readers how to choose and master a digital camera, offers basic photographic techniques, and includes tips for shooting special subjects like kids, sports, nighttime shots, portraits, and more.

iMovie 3 & iDVD: The Missing Manual

By David Pogue
3rd Edition May 2003 (est.)
456 pages (est.), ISBN 0-596-00507-5

This entertaining guide covers every step of iMovie video production, from choosing and using a digital camcorder to burning the finished work onto DVDs. This new edition also explores how iMovie 3 functions with Apple's other iLife applications—iPhoto 2, iTunes 3, and iDVD—and shows you how to bring in and send out digital media content directly from one to another.

Office X for Macintosh: The Missing Manual

By Nan Barber, Tonya Engst & David Reynolds
1st Edition July 2002
728 pages, ISBN 0-596-00332-3

This book applies the urbane and readable Missing Manuals touch to a winning topic: Microsoft Office X for Apple's stunning new operating system, Mac OS X. In typical Missing Manual style, targeted sidebars ensure that the book's three sections impart business-level details on Word, Excel, and the Palm-syncable Entourage, without leaving beginners behind. Indispensable reference for a growing user base.

AppleWorks 6: The Missing Manual

By Jim Elferdink & David Reynolds
1st First Edition May 2000
450 pages, ISBN 1-56592-858-X

AppleWorks, the integrated application that arrives in 4 million homes, schools, and offices a year, includes everything—except a printed manual. In *AppleWorks 6: The Missing Manual*, authors Jim Elferdink and David Reynolds guide the reader through both the basics and the hidden talents of the new AppleWorks, placing special emphasis on version 6's enhanced word processing, Internet, and presentation features. As a Missing Manual title, the book is friendly, authoritative, and complete, rich with clever workarounds, examples, and step-by-step tutorials.

POGUE PRESS™

To order: *800-998-9938* • *order@oreilly.com* • *www.oreilly.com*
Online editions of most O'Reilly titles are available by subscription at *safari.oreilly.com*
Also available at most retail and online bookstores.